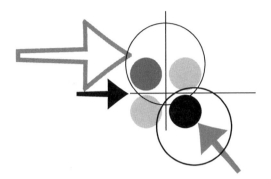

# Understanding Policy Change

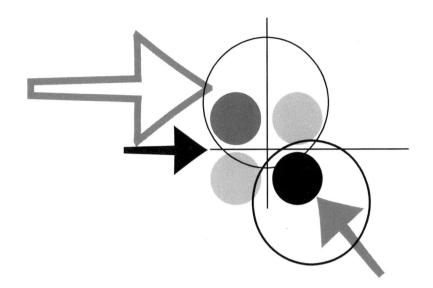

# Understanding Policy Change

How to Apply Political Economy
Concepts in Practice

Cristina Corduneanu-Huci
Alexander Hamilton
Issel Masses Ferrer

**THE WORLD BANK**
Washington, D.C.

*Cover design:* Debra Naylor, Naylor Design, Inc.

**Library of Congress Cataloging-in-Publication Data**

Corduneanu-Huci, Cristina, 1976–
  Understanding policy change : how to apply political economy concepts in practice / by Cristina Corduneanu-Huci, Alexander Hamilton, Issel Masses Ferrer.
    p. cm.
  Includes bibliographical references.
  ISBN 978-0-8213-9538-7 — ISBN 978-0-8213-9539-4 (electronic)
  1. Policy sciences.  2. Economics.  I. Hamilton, Alexander, 1984–  II. Ferrer, Issel Masses, 1987–  III. Title.
  H97.C668 2012
  320.6—dc23
                                                                                    2012011964

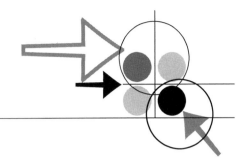

# CONTENTS

**Box**

**Concepts in Practice**

## Figures

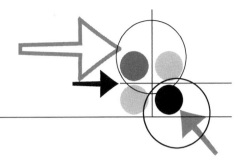

# FOREWORD

This book is the outcome of a rather unique conjunction of circumstances that prevailed at the World Bank Institute in Washington, DC, in the years from 2008 to 2012. There and then, a talented group of young staff in the Governance and Leadership Unit, working in the atmosphere of creativity and the supportive authorizing environment provided by the renewal the World Bank Institute was undergoing, began putting their minds together to explore a number of questions few others at the World Bank had addressed.

What are the types of constraints that conspire to derail otherwise sensible policies? When can these constraints prevent a reform process or a project from achieving its declared objectives? How can these constraints to change be unlocked? Under what conditions do individuals and organizations engage in collective action, and when does this lead to the sort of lasting institutional change that is conducive to sustainable development? These were the sorts of questions the team probed tirelessly over three years.

In line with the World Bank Institute's global learning and training mandate, this book was initially conceived as an instructor's guide, with games and exercises, and addressed to those charged with equiping practitioners with the analytical tools and practical exercises to navigate the treacherous and often murky waters of policy reform. Upon closer scrutiny, it dawned upon the team that few books explain these tools to lay readers, and even fewer had ventured to jump the fence and reach out to practitioners. It is to attempt to address these gaps that the idea of this book in its present form first emerged.

Policy making does not occur in a vacuum; rather, it takes place amidst complex political and social environments in which different stakeholders, operating within a changing institutional context, interact strategically as they pursue conflicting agendas. Here, political economy analysis (PEA) provides a set of powerful tools to diagnose and analyze these factors and evaluate the feasible space for policy change when designing projects for an optimal chance of success. Therefore, by providing a systematic way of incorporating the impact of such factors into a project's benefit–cost analysis, PEA enables a more realistic appraisal of what reformers can hope to achieve in practice.

This volume is intended to provide policy makers, civil society activists, students, and bureaucrats alike with a comprehensive introduction to the core PEA concepts and building blocks, including collective action, institutional analysis, agenda setting, information asymmetries, principal-agent dynamics, credible commitment, leadership, and coalition building. By using real world examples and case studies, as well as a basic game theoretic exposition of key concepts, it builds for readers a step-by-step understanding of how political and social factors may work to shape incentives and facilitate or impede collective action. In addition, several chapters provide a practical guide on how to use the portable tools of PEA in specific policy contexts. This book aims to develop a basis for more successful project identification, feasibility assessment, and realization. We hope it has achieved its objectives.

J. Edgardo Campos
Practice Manager
World Bank Institute

Edouard Al-Dahdah
Senior Economist
World Bank Institute

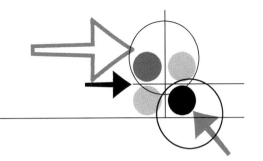

# ACKNOWLEDGMENTS

This book is a product of the World Bank Institute's Governance and Leadership Unit, headed by J. Edgardo Campos. The project was housed with the Political Economy Team under the supervision of Edouard Al-Dahdah.

The main authors of the book are Cristina Corduneanu-Huci, Alexander Hamilton, and Issel Masses Ferrer.[1] The manuscript benefited greatly from the immensely helpful input provided by its formal reviewers, Philip Keefer, Margaret Levi, and Nimah Mazaheri.

Skillful editorial support was provided by Hilary Hendricks and Dana Lane. Yianna Vovides provided critical guidance for the pedagogical elements of this book. Stephen McGroarty, Rick Ludwick, and Andres Meneses ushered the project to completion.

Furthermore, the book benefited from the work of Audrey Sacks who drafted an early outline of this project, as well as from the helpful feedback of Antonio Lambino. Participants at a training event organized by World Bank Institute and the Ghana Institute of Management and Public Administration (GIMPA), held in Accra in January 2012, offered useful comments on the theoretical and pedagogical approaches of this project. We are also grateful for the support provided by Brett Beasley, Monali Chowdhurie-Aziz, Craig Hammer, Hirut McLeod, Jeesun Lee, Ceren Ozer, Ajay Tejasvi, and Kay Winning.

Finally, we would like to thank Ray Duch, Keith Poole, Cambridge University Press, The University of Chicago Press, Oxford University Press, and Princeton University Press for their kind permission to reproduce citations and/or diagrams.

[1]The authors can be contacted at: cc97@duke.edu, a.hamilton@oxon.org, im3050a@american.edu.

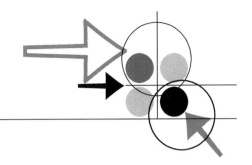

# ABBREVIATIONS

| | |
|---|---|
| ANC | African National Congress |
| CDF | Constituency Development Fund |
| DRC | Democratic Republic of Congo |
| GDP | gross domestic product |
| LCA | logic of collective action |
| MP | member of parliament |
| NGO | nongovernmental organization |
| NPM | new public management |
| PEA | political-economic analysis |
| PAC | public account committee |
| PD | the prisoner's dilemma |
| PR | proportional representation |
| PRI | the Institutional Revolutionary Party of Mexico |
| RTC | regional transport committee |
| TC | the tragedy of the commons |

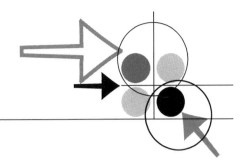

# Introduction

The introductory chapter sets the stage and outlines the logic of the rest of the handbook. First, we present the main learning objectives; second, we introduce the pedagogical approach, methodology, and structure of the book.

This handbook is intended to introduce the concepts of *political economy* to a wide audience of development practitioners, including civil society activists, journalists, students, and bureaucrats. Since the target readers vary widely in their previous exposure to the subject matter, the book summarizes a vast academic field and presents a comprehensive repertoire of concepts, theories, and empirical examples. Rather than offering a "do-it-yourself" framework, we opted for developing a step-by-step analytical puzzle. First, we introduce the core mechanisms of political economy and their inner logic, and, subsequently, we help our readers learn how to recognize these mechanisms in their daily development-related work. By the end of the book, we hope that readers will be able to:

- Recognize core development problems stemming from the political-economic environment
- Link theoretical concepts to real-life situations
- Diagnose the symptoms and the root causes of malfunctions
- Understand the short-term and long-term consequences of poor governance and low institutional equilibria

- Grasp the intersections of collective action, types of political institutions, the incentives they generate, and development outcomes
- Recommend possible solutions for pro-development collective action and reform.

In addition, readers will explore why political-economy analysis is a valuable tool for assessing the underlying causes of poor governance in a more nuanced way and learn what it actually entails, as well as its many virtues and pitfalls.

This handbook is also designed to provide trainers with some of the pedagogical materials they need to develop an introductory course on political-economy analysis for policy practitioners. The content focuses on the *what*, the *why*, and the *how to* of policy change. The readers or trainees will encounter key theories and concepts and learn how to apply the analysis to an understanding of their own policy-making environment.

Pedagogically, the handbook uses interactive classroom exercises and the case study method to reinforce learning objectives and to capture the concepts, methods, experiences, and challenges relevant for practitioners. Structured learning activities at the end of most chapters and a comprehensive group exercise in appendix D will also give readers and trainers the opportunity to apply the knowledge and tools of political economy to simulated or specific development puzzles.


## What Is This Handbook About?

This book explains and illustrates how incentives shape the decisions of policy makers. These decisions determine (intentionally or unintentionally) who gets what, when, and how. Therefore, being able to identify the sources and intensity of such incentives can help explain development policy outcomes. Here are some questions that political economy can help us answer:

- Why do some states promptly initiate and implement relatively healthy economic reforms, while others opt for policies that are blatantly inefficient from the point of view of development?
- What factors explain policy and institutional change and continuity?
- How do institutions shape the content, feasibility, timing, and pace of necessary economic reforms?
- Why is economic development stalled in many contexts?
- How can large shares of non-tax revenue derived from natural resources or foreign aid be harnessed to promote development instead of hampering it?

- Why is tax revenue in many developing countries so low?
- What explains the divergent paths of states at similar stages of development with respect to their ability to reduce poverty?
- What role do collective action and leadership play in development?
- How do incentives at work in different political systems shape government responsiveness to natural calamities such as famines, floods, or earthquakes?
- Why do bad or wasteful policies persist even though it is technically feasible to adopt a better modus operandi?
- Do bad policies endure because of voter ignorance or because of the power of entrenched interest groups?
- What are the opportunities for effective pro-development collective action?
- Will providing a development loan to country $x$ facilitate development because policy makers have strong incentives to better the lives of marginalized groups, or will the loan be diverted to the bank accounts of the politically connected?

Identifying how the incentives of politicians and bureaucrats emerge, evolve, and differ across policy-making contexts and time requires an understanding of some basic tools and concepts. These heuristic devices can help practitioners break down a complex environment into manageable analytical components and think with greater nuance about the development issues they encounter in their daily work.

Beyond standard diagnostics, conventional Western-centric primers and textbooks on political economy often fail to capture many context-specific innovations. We attempted to remedy or bypass this problem by incorporating numerous examples of problems and solutions from around the world. Readers or trainees can also contribute to enriching the analytical repertoire of solutions to basic political-economic problems and dilemmas encountered in their specific contexts.

## A Guide for Reformers, Journalists, and Civil Society Activists

Despite their inherent limitations and pitfalls, political-economy diagnostics are recognized as useful for answering the *what* and the *why* of development (that is, What are the central development problems? Why do they persist?) and for guiding the *how* to change. In a landscape of challenges and obstacles, a map of all possible routes is the first piece of navigational equipment needed.

Our approach to political economy attempts to be pragmatic and aims to allow enough flexibility for readers to fill in the blanks of the conceptual building blocks with their own development work experience or to use the analytical tools for concrete problems and contexts.

To achieve this goal, we survey many theories and empirical findings in the fields of political science and development economics. In doing so, we hope to avoid the really big questions and big answers as much as we can and yet still capture the logic of quite abstract concepts such as *collective action* and *institutions*. The examples are quite heterogeneous, gathered from a variety of studies dealing with development and reform.

The approach is more didactic than meta-theoretical and seeks to accomplish four things:

- First, we introduce a vast theoretical and empirical literature for readers who have had little or no previous exposure to political economy. Therefore, the text errs on the side of comprehensiveness and provides a "one-stop shop" for relevant concepts and tools. Needless to say, like any survey book, it cannot cover individual components in depth. In an attempt to compensate for this shortcoming, the reference list at the end of each chapter offers in-depth readings on the specific topics covered.

- Second, we present analytical devices that practitioners can use in addressing their own questions related to development issues. These concepts are also accompanied by blank do-it-yourself templates designed to help readers think analytically and systematically about the actors, institutions, and constraints with which they deal.

  Games and class activities at the end of most chapters are meant to illustrate the concepts, to entertain, and to make analytical thinking in general more fun and interactive.

- Third, the case study we use in appendix C gets into the specifics of the "how-to" of reform, once the analysis is done and the problem clear. Most handbooks on political economy address big questions, and their answers focus on the *what* and the *why*. Why does the problem persist? What works? We try to go beyond the *why* and the *what* into the everyday details of the *how* to navigate the tricky terrain of policy change. Readers will be guided through the story of the 2002 public procurement reform in the Philippines.

- Finally, appendix D provides the materials necessary for a group activity designed to give readers or trainees the feel of a real diagnostic produced through team work.

## The Main Theoretical Narrative and the Guiding Principle of the Handbook

To what extent do political incentives interact with, undermine, or bolster the economic and administrative targets of policy reforms? The main culprits—corruption, poor governance, and pervasive patron-client networks—hamper and derail development in many parts of the world. Sometimes, these pathologies are simply a "second best," either because they are deeply embedded in complex systems of social relations or because attempts to dismantle them might cause more harm and disruption than correction. In contrast, good governance entails political accountability, the capacity of the government to design and implement development policies demanded by the citizens, and the commitment of key political actors to the rules of the game.[1] The first two chapters will ponder the various manifestations of development failure, or the *what*, in greater detail.

From the *what*, we will then move to the *why* and the *how* of change. Why do development failures persist? Our anchoring stories will suggest a list of potential explanations. Without mechanisms of accountability that align good policies with good politics, bureaucrats and politicians have incentives to satisfy only narrow segments of the electorate, to build patronage machines, and to divert public spending to further their own careers instead of boosting literacy and saving lives. Why do reforms often fail? How can change occur? Is there a repertoire of solutions for diagnosed problems? Last but not least, we address a perennial question, What kinds of incentives can align good policies with good politics? We will isolate theoretical mechanisms and walk through their logic with the help of game theory, a methodological toolkit developed at the intersection of economics and decision sciences.

From diagnostics, the handbook will break down real-world examples into analytical pieces, generalize and abstract from their specific context, and try to guide readers to the bare-bones theoretical mechanisms of causation. This process entails distilling the core political-economic logic from the thick description of numerous details surrounding specific cases (Teune and Przeworski 1970). Accordingly, from concrete examples of electoral rules that give incentives to Honduran or Brazilian politicians to obey party discipline, we will move up a level of abstraction to institutions, or the rules of the game, and explore what they are, what they do to behavior, why they persist, and when they change.

The independent supreme audit institutions and central banks from our vignettes are just outward manifestations of and labels for broader *credible-commitment* mechanisms through which politicians signal to voters that they mean business and take their mandate seriously. Politics, by definition, implies delegation of mandates. Voters delegate decision making to their political representatives, and these, in turn, delegate policy implementation tasks to bureaucracies. In decentralization reforms, central states give away power and resources to lower-tier governments. We will take this whole process apart, call it a *principal-agent relationship,* and deconstruct it into analytical pieces.

A major obstacle to pro-development change is the large discrepancy in information among voters, politicians, and bureaucracies. This information gap is an intrinsic part of a principal-agent mechanism. Voters are often uninformed about elections, policies, institutions, or the existence of other voters, just like them, who share exactly the same policy concerns. Legislatures are often left in the dark when the annual budget proposal coming from the powerful offices of the executive has only 10 pages or excludes half the actual spending. We will call these discrepancies *information asymmetries.* If they are large enough, they give rise to moral hazard problems: the executive who conceals information has incentives to go against voters' preferences.

Finally, we will look at how acting together and mobilizing effectively for better development outcomes can make change happen. Participating in city budgeting in Porto Allegre, Brazil; increasing electricity access in Uttar Pradesh, India; reforming corrupt public procurement in the Philippines; or building successful irrigation systems at the grass roots in Nepal are all cases of costly efforts to change the rules of the game. We will call this process *collective action* and explore the theoretical obstacles against it and some of the conditions under which it can happen against all odds of success.

## Collective Action: The *How To* Change Solution

Collective action is the organizing principle of this narrative and our answer to the *how* question. To paraphrase Nobel Prize winner Elinor Ostrom, collective action is the very heart of development.

Pro-development reforms entail moving from a "bad" to a "good" equilibrium, or changing the rules of the game if they generate suboptimal outcomes. This path is not really controversial, as the importance of institutions has long been recognized. Changing institutions that produce the wrong kind of incentives requires the concerted action and cooperation of dedicated individuals and organizations. In this sense, understanding when and under what conditions collective action occurs—despite seemingly insurmountable challenges—gives us the magic key to the *how* of change.

There are many modes of collective action or ways in which citizens come together to influence public policies:

- *Political parties* aggregate preferences of voters and aim to participate in decision making.
- *Interest groups* represent industries and causes, raise funds, and lobby politicians to obtain favorable policy outcomes for their constituencies.
- *Social movements* amass large numbers of citizens to protest policies perceived as detrimental to their welfare.
- *Reform teams* like the one featured in the Philippines case study build networks of organizations and influential politicians to push institutional change.
- *Collective arrangements* (cooperatives, irrigation systems, and the like) at the grass roots fill the role of a missing or malfunctioning state and deliver public services.

Some of these groups join forces in networks, platforms, and coalitions that increase their power and influence vis-à-vis the opposed vested interests. Many political parties have to participate in coalition governments or form broad electoral coalitions. Citizens and civil society organizations often build platforms for social accountability. Others either work alone or are unable to sustain fragile coalitions within which many divergent policy directions cannot be reconciled.

As the sequence of events in the Philippines case study will show (see appendix C), reform also goes through many stages over its life cycle. Between initiation and consolidation, the main protagonists and the ties among them might even change considerably. More certain is the fact that *consolidation* of policy gains requires higher standards of commitment from stakeholders than *initiation* (Haggard and Kaufman 1995, 9–11). If, under certain conditions, a single organization or individual can spark change, reform consolidation requires coalition building, as well as the cooptation or—more challenging—the re-creation of various societal interests in the process. To reach this point, successful reformers must solve several problems simultaneously: sustaining collective action, mediating distributional conflicts, and building political credibility (Haggard 1990; Waterbury 1989; Haggard and Kaufman 1995; Crisp 2000). Juggling so many challenges is an art that requires rare leadership skills.

When we think of collective action, probably because of the emphasis on *action*, we tend to associate it with change, reform, and institutional shifts. Several chapters will argue that these are only one part of the story. Routine collective action capabilities also ensure that the "good" institutions that align good politics with good policies work as they are supposed to. For example, in democracies, elections do less to discipline political leaders if voters cannot act collectively and effectively to punish them because of lack of information, skewed electoral laws, malapportionment, gerrymandering, or ethnic fractionalization. Politicians do not have incentives to make credible commitments not to overspend before elections if groups of citizens cannot monitor and collectively sanction such behavior.

Normatively, for pro-development policy, not all forms of successful collective action are benign. In fact, more often than not, necessary reforms are blocked by groups that have the resources and power to coalesce, whereas the interests and preferences of the majority (that is, the poor) remain latent and are never articulated. In public procurement processes, as we will see, influential private sector companies can either lobby government agencies effectively or bribe bureaucrats. As a result, under tight budgets and a poor regulatory environment, the favorable contracts they obtain come at the expense of basic public services. Political and administrative networks of corruption and patronage are also forms of very well solved collective action problems that often block change and severely stall development. They are hard or impossible to dismantle, even when domestic reformers and international donors have considerable organizational capacity and are able to mount concerted action. Needless to say, political parties and social movements are not always benign either. Sometimes, their leaders rally support on radical political platforms, fuel ethnic tensions, or initiate conflicts to divert attention away from their own inability to boost development and alleviate poverty. With these caveats in mind, the handbook will deal primarily with those types or modes of collective action that relate to economic development policies.

## Collective Action and Institutions: Coming Full Circle

The rules of the political game generate incentives that often undermine the technical targets of reforms. Unfortunately from a theoretical perspective, the same rules or institutions that lock in the wrong incentives for development policies are also often responsible for obstructing pro-reform collective action, that is, the ability of groups and individuals with shared agendas to work together.

Political institutions are about collective choice and preference aggregation. They add up, combine, and filter the ideal policy goals of voters or stakeholders to produce concrete outcomes. They come into existence to solve collective action problems in the first place. By definition, then, they arbitrate power relations among different groups in society. However, by solving the motivational and informational problems that undermine cooperation between individuals and groups, they also create the incentives that facilitate certain types of collective action but not others. These might or might not always be favorable for development.

In some autocratic states, the poor are completely eliminated from policy making because they lack all channels of collective action and recourse for their complaints. Political parties and trade unions are banned, and protests suppressed. Martial law often legally forbids "public" gatherings of more than five people. To give an extreme example, in 1979, in Bangui in the Central African Empire, food riots were severely repressed, and the head of state participated directly in the beating deaths of some protesters. Several months later, around 100 schoolchildren protested against a mandate to buy expensive school uniforms from the government, featuring the picture of no other than Jean Badel Bokassa, emperor of the country. Many of the students were tortured, killed, and, allegedly, eaten.[2] During his public trial later that year, Bokassa faced allegations of cannibalism.

In contrast, democracies allow political parties, labor unions, and popular protests against unpopular government policies. However, these rights do not guarantee that the poor can collectively and effectively mobilize and pursue policies that alleviate poverty. None of the political parties might put forward pro-poor platforms, the electoral rules might be unfavorable to the geographical representation of the poor, the parties in government might need to make policy concessions to their coalition partners, or the legislature might not even be politically relevant in the presence of a powerful executive. By the same token, sometimes, in very unfavorable environments, grassroots communities find internal solutions to their collective action problems and organize successful governance arrangements for dealing with scarce resources. Information, monitoring and sanctioning, commitment, leadership, and clear rules of engagement all interact with the overall institution (say, democracy or federalism) to lead to collective action—or not.

Thus, institutions or rules of interaction, on the one hand, arise to solve collective action problems and induce people to cooperate. On the other hand, sustained joint action of citizens and groups can sometimes lead to major pro-development changes in such rules and dismantle forms of cooperation that blocked them in the past from joining forces. This circular relationship between the rules of the game and collective action is also the source of a major theoretical challenge. If institutions structure a certain type of actor interaction and political incentives to pursue development or not but are also simultaneously responsible for collective action opportunities, the amount of information, the resource endowments of actors, or the technologies of political commitment that politicians have, how can change happen at all? There are no easy answers.

Sometimes, as we will see in chapter 4, institutional change and major equilibrium shifts occur in the total absence of collective action (that is, in the aftermath of major economic or political shocks such as war, natural calamities, or dramatic changes in world prices of goods and services). At other times, internally sparked collective action drives change and overhauls long-established institutions whose stability has been taken for granted. The 1989 post-Communist transitions and the Arab Spring are powerful and inspirational examples of this type of change.

Uppercase *INSTITUTIONS* and lowercase *institutions,* a distinction recently made by Abhijit Banerjee and Esther Duflo (2011, 243), might have different susceptibilities to change through collective action. The former refer to the fundamental rules of society (democracy, federalism, types of checks and balances), whereas the latter are more granular manifestations of institutions (local norms of interaction, specific electoral rules, and so on). Even if the former rarely change except in unusual conditions, the latter are sometimes much easier to dismantle or replace. Development reforms, or positive policy steps, can happen in surprising circumstances. For example, despite the fact that the Saudi Arabian *Majlis* (legislature) lacks both authority over the expenditure side of the annual budget and institutional power, it can veto tax bills. When the government wanted to impose an income tax on foreign workers, the members of parliament (MPs) and the businesses reliant on foreign labor mobilized and successfully blocked the reform.

In some cases, the mere availability of information, or the correction of information asymmetries, has sparked popular collective action and changed overnight the INSTITUTIONS that skewed development outcomes. In Peru, it took only one "bribe-free" television station to show a video of Vladimir Montesinos—the powerful head of the Peruvian secret police and right hand of President Fujimori—bribing an opposition MP to switch to Fujimori's party, to bring people to the streets and take down a very corrupt regime.

For pro-development reform, collective action is often the engine as well as the source of hope. Even if *INSTITUTIONS* and the power relations that underpin them rarely change, if the *institutions* at least can be transformed to align good politics with some good policies, reformers will have achieved their goals.

Chapter 4 will continue the conversation about the relationship between collective action and institutions, the two major theoretical pillars of this handbook.

Besides this general debate, individual chapters will go more deeply into the specific constraints of the institutional environment that shape the possibilities, as well as the aspirations, of participants in collective action. Without information, reformers cannot come together (the problem of information asymmetries). When communities cannot monitor their members to prevent lack of cooperation or overconsumption of a public good or when politicians go against the wishes of the voters (principal-agent problems), collective action is not effective. If political leaders lack technologies of commitment through which they can signal to voters and citizens that they will respect their preelectoral promises or if those leaders are weak, uncertainty about the policy environment persists, and underinvestment is the result, unless collective action redresses the problem. On a different scale, leaders of organizations such as political parties and nongovernmental organizations facilitate joint efforts when they manage to signal to their rank and file that they will not break their promises. Often, pro-development collective action is either hampered or facilitated by institutional manipulation or agenda setting. In the Philippines procurement case, for example, the reform team greatly benefited from the actions of an influential agenda-setting MP, who managed to pass an important bill in the legislature on the day when many opposition MPs were absent. Agenda setting, which by definition solves problems of preference aggregation, also raises concerns. In certain circumstances, even if the poor are able to act collectively (through, say, an effective pro-poor party represented in the legislature), institutional manipulation can make their collective action irrelevant and instead push legislation that avoids sensitive development issues altogether. The chapters of the handbook will follow the conceptual map illustrated by figure 0.1, and explore how these four institutional constraints facilitate or inhibit joint efforts for policy change.

Most of the theoretical mechanisms will be illustrated with the help of game theory, a methodological field developed at the intersection of economics and decision sciences that captures best the strategic interaction of actors or stakeholders.

## Game Theory and the Dynamics of Political Economy

By its very nature, decision making is usually not just about what policy makers think and want but also about how they expect other stakeholders (or actors) to react to their choices. Because of the inherently strategic nature of policy making, it is useful to include some of the basic tools of game theory to make sense of the strategic environment. Without being overly formal, most chapters of the book conclude with a discussion of how the key tools

**FIGURE O.1 Institutional Constraints That Affect Collective Action**

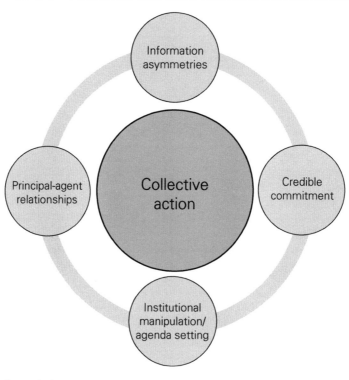

*Source:* Authors.

and concepts of political economy work in situations of strategic interaction. Therefore, by illustrating them intuitively, we hope that the reader will identify real-world situations in which a similar logic applies.

In order to understand social and political dynamics in terms of a game, we need to learn to use a few simple tools and concepts that will be further expanded and refined as the chapters progress. Appendix A is an essential starting kit, and readers should get acquainted with its basic concepts in order to follow the games and interactive exercises presented in subsequent chapters. Appendix B introduces the more technical definitions and solution concepts of game theory.

Besides interactive exercises, our case study, detailed in appendix C but referred to throughout the handbook, will give the reader the feel of a real reform that demonstrates the power of collective action for reaching better development outcomes.

## Procurement Reforms in the Philippines: A Case Study in the Political Economy of Change

The processes through which government agencies purchase goods and services from the private sector are plagued by severe corruption in many countries. It is estimated that globally some US$400 billion is lost in bribery every year, at the expense of about 20–25 percent of all costs incurred by governments (Ware et al. 2007, 295–96). Because public procurement lies at the interface of politics, bureaucracies, and private companies and involves high financial stakes, attempts to reform the system are daunting, if not often futile. Government contracts (especially for large infrastructure projects) are a lucrative source of commissions, bribes, illegal transactions, and collusion among various stakeholders. Often, these funds supplement the regular income of bureaucrats, are used for political campaigns, and fuel patronage machines. Despite being imperative for better development outcomes, changing the rules of the game through new regulations and better implementation is rarely successful. Powerful vested interests opposing reform are likely to be responsible for a vast cemetery of aborted attempts.

The Philippines case gives us a unique chronological log, or a reform diary, of many events, institutions, incentives, and individuals involved in the attempt to reform procurement. The aim of this convoluted journey was to overhaul a system that lost about US$48 billion to corruption over a 20-year period. The case is particularly fascinating for two reasons. First, it is a mini-laboratory of political-economy analysis, narrating the stories of two reform attempts, one of which was prematurely halted and the other successful. Comparing the configurations of actors, institutions, time sequencing, and pacing of the two episodes clarifies the factors that made or broke these efforts. Second, the case study was codeveloped by one of the reformers, making it a primary source of firsthand information from a participant-observer.

***Setting Up the Case Study.*** The text discusses the analytical components that facilitate or hinder collective action for change. Appendix C summarizes the main events and provides a detailed chronology. We hope that the broad outlines of the story will set the stage for analysis. What institutions were relevant for reformers? Who were the key actors? Did agenda setting push the reform bill through the legislature?

As with all case studies, reality is complex and multidimensional, never quite fitting nicely into our constricted analytical models. The danger of breaking the story piecemeal into components is that our understanding of the final outcome is overdetermined. Simply put, there are too many factors at too many points in time responsible for the initial failure and later success of the procurement reform. How do we know which one was crucial? Were the politicians' incentives to stop the bill before an upcoming election more important than agenda setting in legislative committees? Did the electoral rule according to which representatives were elected skew incentives more than interest group politics?

To clarify, we are not presenting a theoretical explanation but are rather taking the reader along on a journey through a complex world, with adaptive processes in which every potential analytical mechanism contributed something, no matter how marginally, to the final reform outcomes. In this sense, our take on the case study approaches the "analytical narrative" method used in social science research to combine the factual richness of the case with a rigorous understanding of the analytics underpinning it and the use of game theory (Bates et al. 1998).

## The Rest of This Book

The structure of this book is designed so that readers are walked through the different tools and concepts of political economy that can be used to explain policy outcomes. Chapter 2 examines how accountability (and the lack thereof) and general governance issues may help explain variations in the degree of corruption, political clientelism, and waste in policy making. This is the *what* question of development, as it reveals pathologies and symptoms of failure and malfunctions. Chapter 3 introduces readers to collective action problems. As we have argued, the existence of coordination and joint efforts or their absence is absolutely central to understanding and enacting change. The ability of stakeholders to turn their aspirations into actual policy means that collective action problems have to be solved.

Of course, to identify which stakeholders are more likely to be effective in incentivizing policy makers in a specific time or place, we must be able to map the institutional context; that is the objective of chapter 4. Because institutions determine the rules of the game, they are critical to knowing which stakeholders enjoy more or less power than they would in a different institutional setting. Thus, chapters 3 and 4 explore the *why*. Then we move into the *how*, which is the conceptual territory of change.

After the consequences of collective action problems have been identified and how to map the institutional context has been explained, chapter 5 brings the two together by demonstrating how the (institutional) power of agenda setting can enable some stakeholders to exercise disproportionate policy-making power. This discussion leads naturally into chapter 6, which introduces the principal-agent framework as a useful tool for analyzing how information asymmetries, monitoring, sanctioning, and other delegation dilemmas may work to amplify or check power and hence create the effective incentives that different policy makers face.

Chapter 7 is more generally concerned with exploring the existence of political-economic market imperfections and how these can enable some stakeholders or policy makers to exercise more influence than others. The role of information in the policy process is central.

Chapter 8 then introduces *credible commitment* and how this concept can be used to understand the conditions under which it might be possible for principals (voters, elected officials, and so forth) to incentivize agents (elected officials, bureaucrats) to comply with their agenda rather than engage in blatant corruption or rent extraction. The conceptual section of the book ends with chapter 9, which comes full circle and provides a comprehensive introduction to solutions to collective action problems and how these can be realized more or less effectively in different institutional contexts.

The second major section of the book, chapters 10 and 11, is concerned with providing readers with the practical ability to use these problem-solving tools in their own projects. Through a generic political-economy checklist, the chapters show how stakeholder preferences and power (determined by their potential for collective action) and institutional constraints (agenda-setting power, delegation issues, information discrepancies, and credible commitment) can enable reformers to map the policy-making process.

To help make the material in the book more accessible, each chapter begins with an introductory section that includes a discussion of how and why the analytical concept highlighted in the chapter affects development outcomes. A game theory section at the end of each chapter provides readers with the tools and exercises for rigorous analysis.

## Summary

The diagnostics and tools of political economy help focus analyses on the actors, their potential for collective action, the costs and benefits of reform, and the relevant institutions and incentives. They also provide a navigational compass for reformers. Political-economy analysis helps explain why suboptimal development outcomes occur.

## Note

1. See Kaufman, Kraay, and Zoido-Lobatón (1999).
2. According to Amnesty International's investigations of this episode, it seems that the public rumors and allegations were more extreme than what actually happened. It is beyond doubt, though, that most of the students died by either beating or suffocation (Borgenicht and Regan 2008).

## References

Banerjee, Abhijit, and Esther Duflo. 2011. *Poor Economics: A Radical Rethinking of the Way to Fight Global Poverty*. New York: Public Affairs.

Bates, R., A. Greif, M. Levi, J. L. Rosenthal, and B. Weingast. 1998. *Analytic Narratives*. Princeton, NJ: Princeton University Press.

Borgenicht, D., and T. Regan. 2008. *Worst-Case Scenario Almanac Politics*. San Francisco: Chronicle Books Llc.

Crisp, Brian F. 2000. *Democratic Institutional Design: The Powers and Incentives of Venezuelan Politicians and Interest Groups*. Palo Alto, CA: Stanford University Press.

Haggard, Stephen. 1990. *Pathways from the Periphery: The Politics of Growth in the Newly Industrializing Countries*. Ithaca, NY: Cornell University Press.

Haggard, Stephen, and Robert Kaufman. 1995. *The Political Economy of Democratic Transitions*. Princeton, NJ: Princeton University Press.

Kaufmann, D., A. Kraay, and P. Zoido-Lobatón. 1999. "Governance Matters." Policy Research Working Paper 2196. Washington, DC: World Bank.

Teune, Henry, and Adam Przeworski. 1970. *The Logic of Comparative Social Inquiry*. New York: John Wiley & Sons.

Ware, Glenn, Shaun Moss, Ed Campos, and Gregory Noone. 2007. "Corruption in Public Procurement: A Perennial Challenge." In *The Many Faces of Corruption: Tracking Vulnerabilities at the Sector Level*, ed. J. Edgar Campos and Sanjay Pradhan, 295–334. Washington, DC: World Bank.

Waterbury, John. 1989. "The Political Management of Economic Adjustment and Reform." In *Fragile Coalitions: The Politics of Economic Adjustment*, ed. Joan Nelson, 39–56. New Brunswick, NJ: Transaction Books.

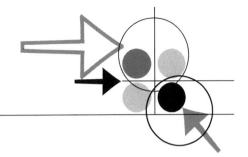

**CHAPTER 1**

# Political Economy: What It Is and What It Is Not

In this chapter, we begin to define *political economy* and look at how it seeks to explain development outcomes by identifying the incentives of the actors and the context in which they make decisions and interact strategically.

## Objectives of Chapter 1

By the end of this chapter, readers should have a clear map or guide to the main concepts, mechanisms, and theories related to political economy that will be covered in this handbook. They should be able to do the following:

- Define *political economy* and recognize its products
- Understand the value that political economy can add to the design and implementation of reforms
- Clarify what political-economy analysis entails and what it does not
- Be aware of the main virtues and shortcomings of the approach
- Critically evaluate analytical and practical alternatives.

# Political-Economy Analysis, Diagnostics, and Tools

The powerful role that governance and political factors play in a country's development path is increasingly recognized. Policies in sectors as diverse as natural resource management, transportation, procurement, and urban planning, to name just a few, are continuously shaped by the interaction among governments, civil society actors, the private sector, and organized citizens. An analytical approach to governance and the political-economic environment that accounts for these complex interactions is essential to understanding root problems, why they persist, and how they can be changed. Uncovering development traps requires knowing the policy landscape well and identifying the obstacles to reform before navigating it.

## Political Economy: The Meeting of Good Politics and Good Policies

*Political economy* is an established academic field that studies the intersection (or the relationship) between *politics* and *economics*. Its first parent, politics, is in no need of introduction. We all recognize it in our everyday lives. It affects us, we love it, we hate it, and we participate directly or indirectly in its course.

To quote a famous definition, politics is about who gets what, when, and how (Lasswell 1936). Collective decision-making processes generate the answers to these three fundamental questions. The way in which societies select leaders enshrines power relations; the way they deal with conflicts over the allocation of scarce resources determines policies and ultimately outcomes. The nature of political regimes, the electoral laws, the transparency of elections, the access of interest groups to the decision-making arena, the quality of the judiciary, and the degree of political stability determine the laws of the land and their implementation.

The second parent, *economics*, deals with the production, consumption, and allocation of goods and services. Supply, demand, and market equilibria are more or less household concepts. Governments regulate markets and the behavior of economic agents, collect taxes, and reallocate resources.

In relation to specific development issues and reforms, political economy brings the two fields of inquiry together to identify problems and look for solutions. Why are health services or education underprovided to the poor or available in certain regions only? Why are bridges and highway projects started but never finished in many locations? Why does widespread poverty persist in some areas despite foreign aid, institutional reforms, or entire batteries of policies meant to address it?

Economics would answer *market failure*. Significant information discrepancies among parties in a transaction, monopoly powers, and negative externalities lead to underinvestment and inefficiencies. Therefore, either markets or governments fail to provide crucial goods and services to the poor. Politics focus less on efficiency and more on the distributional impact of choices. Its answer to the question of high poverty rates would be *collective action problems* or the difficulty of some groups—say, the poor—in joining forces and demanding that governments enact policies favorable to them.

Political economy combines the two approaches and asks bidirectional questions:

- *How do political factors and institutions affect development outcomes?* For example, are democracies providing more public goods than autocracies? Do federal systems lead to higher fiscal deficits than unitary modes of government? Does political clientelism undermine the ability of governments to provide education and health services to the majority of the population? Do certain political parties provide more electricity, water, or better services to the poor? Does the lack of political mobilization of certain groups in society hamper policy change?
- *How do economic factors and institutions related to development affect political outcomes?* Does socioeconomic inequality make transitions from autocracy to democracy more likely? Does democracy survive longer in countries that have already reached a certain level of development? Do regional patterns of economic production and resource endowments lead to the choice of decentralized as opposed to centralized systems of government? What tax and spending policies extend the political tenure of leaders (for example, presidents or prime ministers)?

The tools and diagnostics of political economy comprise a range of thematically diverse streams of research: the politics of regulation, campaign finance, trade policies, municipal service delivery, legislative institutions, budgetary processes, poverty reduction, and decentralization, among many others. Methodologically, political economy uses economic tools to understand development problems and guide reform (Gerber 2003). For readers exposed in any way to economics, some of the chapters of this textbook will sound familiar. Major analytical blocks—principal-agent relationships, information asymmetries, and credible commitment—are the bread and butter of economic analysis. To this mix, political economy adds political parties, bureaucracies, interest groups, and civil society organizations as key actors

**FIGURE 1.1 Political Economy: The Intersection of Politics and Economics**

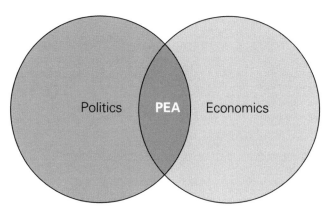

Politics    PEA    Economics

*Source:* Authors.

and policy ingredients and looks at how states and markets interact. All the exercises and interactive activities in this text build on game theory, another family of key tools closely related to economics and decision sciences.

Simply put, political economy is the politics of economics (see figure 1.1). The field is built around a simple but powerful intuition: good policy is not always good politics (Bueno De Mesquita et al. 2003; Guriev 2012). If politicians face a clear trade-off between promoting policies beneficial to society and staying in power, they are likely to choose the latter. This choice, caused by incentives generated by the rules of the political game, often derails development and stalls reforms. We also know that institutions are not all the same: they generate different incentives that lead to degrees of match or mismatch between "good policy" and "good politics." If political leaders are elected, monitored, and kept accountable for their campaign promises, their reelection incentives often align with policies demanded by voters. If, however, the political survival of politicians depends in reality only on a handful of powerful local elites or on vote buying, or if their performance in office is not monitored, they lack incentives to allocate resources to health and education. For them, it pays off politically to keep their small circle of cronies happy through favorable government contracts, subsidies, and tax loopholes and to build patronage machines or invest in a repressive apparatus to deal with public discontent in case it arises. This (mis)alignment between politicians' incentives to pursue good policies and good politics is central to political economy.

## What Is—and What Is Not—Political-Economy Analysis?

Some rules of thumb can help explain what political-economy analysis (PEA) is and is not (Gerber 2003, 4). Not all analyses of political economy pertain to the study of the economy per se: many PEA products model political actors as strategic utility maximizers[1] operating in different institutional contexts and use important insights from this assumption. The study of legislatures is an example of political-economy work that has only indirect implications for economic development policy or reform.

At the other end of the spectrum, while some research agendas use the tools, methods, and language of modern economics to study politics, they do not capture the intrinsically political mechanisms at work in their studies of a particular problem. For example, classic public finance scholars simply assumed that the public sector would have an incentive to increase transparency, provide information, and prevent fiscal deficits without considering whether the political incentive structure would be conducive to that objective.

This being said, political economy covers a vast territory of concepts, problems, methods of research, and standards of evidence. Rather than dwelling on meta-theoretical or methodological issues, we focus simply on raising awareness about the conditions under which various configurations of political actors and institutions can skew incentives and, as a result, hinder or advance a reform agenda. To be fair, politics is not always the culprit. Sometimes it corrects the incentives of markets, it regulates, it redistributes, or it internalizes externalities generated by markets.

We operate under the assumption that there is no silver bullet. Otherwise, the world would be a better place by now. That point aside, a critical way of thinking about policy reform is necessary in order to gain at least a glimpse of what is behind organizational mantras, fads in the international community, or whatever constitutes the latest spin, if nothing else. This handbook tries to survey a vast field and to organize information that development practitioners can then transfer to their own specific questions and contexts.

It is also important to note what political-economy analysis is *not* about. Even if the discipline of study and the set of diagnostics and tools it provides contain the word *political*, it is not prescriptive or normative, and it does not intend to provide endorsements or recommendations to readers of any specific political institution or arrangement. Its only aim is to point out core concepts and mechanisms of causation that shed light on the allocation of scarce resources and apply to a wide variety of cultural contexts, organizations, and institutions. In fact, the core logic of political economy has been used to explain dynamics and outcomes generated by entities as different as family units, religious organizations, business associations, social networks, prison gangs or other forms of organized crime, and state bureaucracies. In this sense, this handbook showcases the analytical tools that can help practitioners and researchers diagnose problems, navigate around obstacles, generate alternative scenarios of action, and come up with feasible and creative solutions.

Moreover, the content discussed throughout this book evolves constantly, and our hope is to encourage readers to develop the analytical thinking that can create less conventional models of problem solving in development. Various cultural contexts and communities around the world generate innovative ways to solve collective problems and take full advantage of technology, preexisting social networks, and windows of opportunity for action. Despite the fact that good policies and good politics are rarely in sync, leadership and local solutions to such misalignments identified throughout the handbook are emerging every day and generate good policies even under conditions of bad politics. In many cases, self-help groups and cooperatives organize around the mistrust of corrupt state institutions. Hometown associations in Nigeria, for example, fulfill the de facto role of a missing (or malfunctioning) local government. Lineages, elders, faith-based communities, women's credit groups, and self-help associations have played a similar role in Tanzania and Uganda. Communities of farmers in Nepal, despite employing less sophisticated irrigation techniques than the ones provided by the government, have managed to grow more crops than ever before because of clear community rules about contributions and sanctions.

## Reform Stories: Seeing the World through the Lens of Political Economy

The following examples briefly sketch the stories of several reforms that seem, at a first glance, dry and technical. The problems appear to be clearly identifiable and the solutions seem to reside in either standard economics textbooks or mainstream public administration manuals. Yet, despite this first impression, without accounting for political (or "nontechnical") explanations, we cannot fully understand their course.

### Public Procurement Reform

Perhaps very few policy areas are as prone to corruption, bribery, graft, and bad governance as public procurement, a sector that lies at the dangerous intersection between powerful private and public interests (see Ware et al. 2007; Frøystad, Heggstad, and Fjeldstad 2010). It is estimated that at least US$400 billion annually is lost to corruption in procurement worldwide. Because corruption raises the costs incurred by governments and distorts budget allocations for universal public services (such as education and health), dubious procurement practices lead to inferior development outcomes. Procurement brings together politicians, bureaucrats, and firms that want to win lucrative contracts and that have incentives to collude. Members of the legislature often provide "pork-barrel" spending to their constituency to be reelected. Civil servants, sometimes closely connected to the politician, have enough discretion to award the contract to private companies. The chain of political influence and the large sums of money involved render reforms in this area extremely difficult even in developed countries, not to mention in contexts with weaker regulatory frameworks and rule of law.

The package of technical solutions contains a variety of demand- and supply-side interventions that have worked in some contexts: the use of technology for e-procurement systems, mechanisms of forensic auditing, voluntary disclosure programs, engagement of civil society organizations for better monitoring, and information-sharing platforms, among others. Nevertheless, the technical correctives of incentives are by far overshadowed by the larger political-economic environment in which reform occurs. Even in cases in which some level of technical reform has been achieved, implementation still remains an unresolved issue. Despite the fact that many local companies active in the road construction sector in Uganda, for example, prefer and support a proper tender-based system for contracting, fears of political retaliation or blacklisting in case they challenge the winners still persist (Frøystad, Heggstad, and Fjeldstad 2010, 23). This reality is recurrent in many countries where even the anticipation of weak incentives for implementation and the fear of political retaliation push potential reform supporters to refrain from actively seeking justice and promoting change.

## The Setting of Interest Rates

The cost of borrowing (that is, interest rates) affects the willingness of businesses and consumers to spend money: lower interest rates stimulate demand, and higher interest rates increase savings (Fischer 1995). Interest rates that are too low can precipitate too much short-term borrowing and result in a boom that ends when unsustainable debt levels force consumers and businesses to cut back on spending. Therefore, the interest rate has to be set so that the level of spending is not unsustainable. This is a classic example of a technical element in financial policy making.

However, elected politicians are a crucial part of the story. Governments may wish to overspend just before elections to make certain categories of voters feel better off. If government can control the setting of interest rates, the result may be what is usually called "a political business cycle" in which rates are driven by the career concerns of the incumbent policy makers rather than by the fundamentals of economics. An approach based entirely on the standard economic prescriptions would not explain what really happens in most of the world.

This political-economy dynamic has been one of the reasons why after World War II many countries have sought, with varying degrees of success, to make the central banks that set interest rates independent of political pressure. This institutional reform is the product of an explicit recognition that "nontechnical" or political factors can often skew incentives and derail the outcomes predicted by textbook best-practice types of policy.

## Civil Service Reforms

Making bureaucracies function well has been at the forefront of development work for quite a long time. The recognition that governance matters and that administrative corruption thwarts development outcomes has led donors and governments to make concerted efforts to improve the quality and the probity of the civil service. In an initial wave of reforms, the problem was approached from a fiscal-administrative angle and focused on employment reduction in the public sector. The subsequent shift to governance concerns brought in a combination of managerial solutions to boosting performance but also the realization that politics is a crucial part of the story. Even if the right financial and professional incentives are in place, even if the salaries of public servants are high enough, and even if there are established rules of meritocratic recruitment on paper, bureaucracies are, more often than not, colonized by the political supporters of the leaders. In the absence of institutions that stand in the way, the incumbent political parties have incentives to politicize bureaucratic agencies (Grzymala-Busse 2007; O'Dwyer 2006; Shefter 1994).

Just as in the previous example, civil service reform is a typical policy domain that was initially thought to have purely fiscal and administrative characteristics, only to end up explicitly incorporating prescriptions aimed at depoliticization. Nevertheless, that realization by itself, without a context-specific understanding of political incentives, has led, in the best-case scenarios, to only marginal improvements. An evaluation of 124 World Bank lending projects designed to address civil service reform between 1980 and

1997 found a poor level of outcomes (Shepherd 2003). Civil service commissions established overnight—or tenure and pension provisions supposed to detach bureaucrats from political influence—could not do much in the absence of robust party competition that could effectively keep in check the incumbent's incentives to staff the bureaucracy with supporters. In some cases, the timing and sequencing of democratization, state building, and party building have shaped the degree of bureaucratic autonomy, as well as the nature of the political coalitions protecting it (Shefter 1994).

## Decentralization

Economic theories of fiscal federalism, seconded by a search for pragmatic ways to bring decision making closer to citizens, have generated a worldwide wave of reforms aiming to devolve power and resources to lower tiers of government. Decentralization was expected to correct democratic deficits, improve public service delivery, make local governments more likely to foster a better investment climate for attracting businesses, and reduce incentives for corruption. In many cases, these expectations never materialized or went in the opposite direction. In some contexts, like Argentina and Brazil, the economic performance deteriorated as a result of the reforms. In others, like Nigeria, it exacerbated ethnic tensions (Wibbels 2006).

What went wrong? It turns out that the normative assumptions that underpinned initial models were highly problematic (see Wibbels 2006, 168; Remmer and Wibbels 2000; Rodden 2002; Gelineau and Remmer 2006; Eaton, Kaiser, and Smoke 2010). Often, local governments either were more corrupt than the center or, for political or bureaucratic reasons, were deprived of capacity and resources. On the demand side, the aspirations to correct democratic deficits also often fell short of expectations. Voters lacked information on who should provide services and therefore became more confused and were unable to keep politicians accountable. Businesses and citizens were not as mobile across subnational units as initially thought. The very origins of decentralization often concealed political incentives that distorted development outcomes. The pace and scope of reforms, in many cases, were dependent on electoral calculations of the incumbent political party and on the regional and local power of the opposition. These frictions resulted in lack of coordination among tiers of government, overtaxation of citizens, overspending by local units, and widespread misunderstanding over which level of government was responsible for providing public goods. Overall, these side effects greatly diminished the intended benefits of the reforms.

## Reforms of Public Financial Management

Finally, budgets are the true battleground for distributive decisions (see Dorotinsky and Pradhan 2007). In many ways, annual budgets are the official script of the social contract between rulers and citizens. Budget proposals go to legislatures, are debated, are voted on, and decide the amount and structure of revenue to be collected and public expenditure to be allocated in the coming fiscal year. Afterward, they are usually submitted to an audit institution that makes sure that commitments were adequately fulfilled. During the full budget cycle, the draft involves almost every political institution, from the presidency to the line ministries all the way to parliaments and specialized public accounts committees. Therefore, it is widely recognized that reforms entail building the mechanisms of accountability within and outside the government as much as they entail dealing with the technical issues related to resource management.

Corruption and political clientelism (the usual suspects by now) go hand in hand with budget systems that lack capacity, internal controls, external accountability, and transparency. Beyond informal networks of patronage, the formal rules of the political systems create a whole world of incentives that shape the fiscal deficit levels, revenue shares, and expenditure allocations for certain constituencies. Presidential and parliamentary systems assign different powers to the legislature during the budget formulation and approval process. If a powerful executive is unchecked because the parliament receives the budget late for review—and is therefore deprived of key information on tax and spending—or because the legislature lacks the power to amend the budget draft, the accountability of the system is weak. Even the number of pages of budget proposals varies dramatically around the world, from one or two pages to thousands. The percentage of off-budget accounts in total spending also ranges from zero to over 60 percent. In many contexts, these accounts do not go through the legislative process, remaining entirely at the discretion of the executive. Without supreme audit institutions to trace budget implementation and ask for explanations in case of discrepancies, the government can engage in corrupt or clientelistic practices at will.

Even when legislatures have a significant say in the budget process, electoral rules, the strength of political parties, and coalitional requirements create different incentives for members of parliament (MPs). For example, parliamentary regimes seem to lead to a larger government than presidential regimes do, as politicians have incentives to claim higher individual shares from a common-pool resource.[2] Other political institutions such as federalism have been found to interact with fiscal policy outcomes in general, and expenditures in particular, in both developed and developing countries (see

Beramendi 2007; Remmer and Wibbels 2000; Rodden 2002; Wibbels 2005; Haggard and Kaufman 1995; Niskanen 2003). In federal arrangements, for example, subnational units do not bear the costs of tax collection but can overspend in anticipation of bailouts from the center. These incentives create the so-called "tragedy of the commons" discussed at length.

Even the electoral rules of candidate selection affect budgets. In some Latin American countries, for example, regional governors have more weight in the selection of political candidates than party leaders. This arrangement often leads to fragmented party organizations, and to incentives of individual politicians to secure funds for their own geographical districts as opposed to more universalistic expenditure programs (Mainwaring and Shugart 1997, 83).

This list of political incentives at play in public financial management is not exhaustive, but it aims to show that any reform has to take into account first the political-economic dynamics and mechanisms of accountability.

These examples of reforms showcased some of the political or "non-technical" factors that skewed incentives, intersected with the initial policy targets, and changed final outcomes. How can development practitioners identify the specific sets of incentives that are likely to travel this long path of causation to affect their own outcome of interest? What kinds of constraints and opportunities inherent in the political-economic environment are they likely to face when funding or managing concrete development projects as diverse as bridge building, financial management information systems, or public health care policies? Why, despite a continuous stream of financial resources allocated to these projects, are the results lagging? Why do other operational contexts achieve surprising results with much lower budgets?

To help readers think systematically through the list of factors that might help or hamper their own project path, we designed a hypothetical exercise. Let us imagine that the reformer or practitioner sees only the two ends of the policy process: the initial investment and the tangible change in outcomes following the intervention. How can he or she unpack the black box of the policy process in between? We illustrate the task with a specific development puzzle: why do some countries manage to achieve better primary school enrollment and infant mortality indicators despite lower health and education spending? How do we explain the development failure in some contexts and success of others? First, we will introduce the puzzle. Then, we will build an inventory of economic, administrative, and political constraints that could be responsible for outcome divergence. Let's try to organize and analyze the individual pieces.

## Deconstructing and Understanding Poverty Reduction Reform: An Empirical Puzzle

One of the major debates on what really matters for poverty reduction features at least four key positions:

- The first argues that underdevelopment persists because the objective conditions that some countries face are abysmal: difficult weather, unfavorable geographical locations (landlocked or arid areas), exposure to pandemics, and sheer lack of resources. According to this argument, it is hard for people to escape the so-called poverty trap without major upfront investments that lead to higher incomes. Foreign aid, in this version of the story, is crucial. If rich countries committed more funds to poverty reduction, not only could ambitious goals be achieved but also global poverty could be eliminated as early as 2025 (Sachs 2005).
- The second version of the story pays more attention to the institutions, corruption, and bad governance that filter aid funds in the recipient countries and transform them into development outcomes (World Bank 1997).
- The third version is less keen on aid interventions from donors and more focused on building the right incentives for domestic actors to promote growth through their own participation in markets and self-reliance (Easterly 2002).
- Finally, the fourth approach is the most pragmatic (Banerjee and Duflo 2011). Instead of asking big and sweeping questions about the relationship between more spending and outcomes, it concentrates on very specific questions: What kinds of aid programs work well and in what kinds of institutional settings in country $x$ or $y$? Why?

Without getting into the theoretical details of this debate, we will now explore how political economy can weave into these stories (see Banerjee and Duflo 2011, 9–11 for a concrete application of the development polemic). Figure 1.2, which appeared in the 2004 *World Development Report Making Services Work for the Poor*, captures variations in implementation gaps between public spending on health and education and the tangible outcomes (reducing infant mortality and achieving a high primary school completion rate). What explains divergent results achieved with similar spending or similar results generated by dramatically different expenditure allocations?

If the problem were more or less technical (that is, lack of development funds as one of the positions in the development debate suggests), then we would expect that increased allocations for health and education would lead to better results for infant mortality and primary school enrollment. This is

**FIGURE 1.2 Implementation Gaps—Spending versus Outcomes in Selected Countries, 1980s and 1990s**

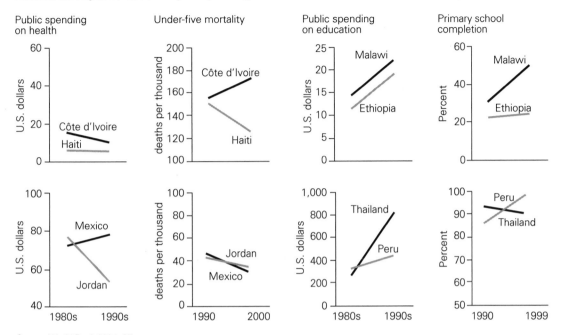

*Source:* World Bank 2004, 37.

*Note:* Spending is measured as total annual public spending for education on each primary-school-age child, in 1995 U.S. dollars, averaged for two decades: the 1980s and the 1990s. For the health graphs, the data show total annual per capita public spending on health, in 1995 U.S. dollars, averaged for two decades: the 1980s and the 1990s.

not the case. What could account for this wide gap between spending on education and health, on the one hand, and outcomes, on the other hand? We know by now that development failure can have many manifestations: severe corruption, rent seeking, political patronage, poor service quality, low capacity, and lack of financial resources. What, then, are the incentives that lead to better outcomes?

Often, this question simply lacks a satisfactory answer. Too many factors filter the amount of spending and decouple it from real results on the ground. For the purpose of this handbook, however, it is still worth thinking systematically about these intermediary steps, because they introduce the core analytical blocks that the chapters later explore in greater depth.

A discussion of the economic, administrative, and political factors or constraints that could, at least in theory, account for this stunning divergence between spending and outcome follows. Readers should feel free to add potential explanations based on their own research and development work experience.

## Examples of Economic Constraints

Governments offer *different policy incentives* to increase demand for education or health care services. Some use direct cash transfers to households to stimulate school enrollment and regular visits to clinics, while others, for an equivalent budget allocation, focus more on the supply side (delegation of service delivery to localities, for example).

The choice to *contract out or to provide services* is another difference. In health care, some governments choose to delegate selected services to nongovernmental organizations (NGOs) or private sector providers. In some cases, studies suggest that similar levels of spending can result in significant differences in the efficiency of service delivery.

*Economic crises* (debt, currency, financial, and so forth) can trigger sudden country- or region-specific effects on infant mortality and educational enrollment. In the wake of crises, increased unemployment, poor nutrition, low caloric intake, and program cuts in prenatal care have been found to lead to increases in neonatal mortality. A study looking at the effects of the 1997 Asian currency crisis on child health in Indonesia, for example, found a drastic hike in neonatal mortality, despite foreign aid flows meant to supplement declines in spending. In 1998, the food prices skyrocketed by 250 percent. In a country in which food accounted for about 50 percent of household expenditures, and in which public hospitals had scarce supplies at the peak of the crisis, the visits to health clinics declined, and the infant mortality rate increased 3.2 percent in both rural and urban areas (Rukumnuaykit 2003).[3]

Countries also adopt policies at different *development baselines*. Reducing infant mortality or improving the primary school completion rate depends on a complex web of institutions and services, not on budgetary allocations to line ministries alone. Without electricity and clean water to improve sanitation and prevent infant death and without proper infrastructure and transportation to allow children to go to school, positive development outcomes are harder to achieve. It is thus important to take into account the level of development, since it has an obvious impact on the complex ecology of the complementary institutions needed for achieving real infant mortality and literacy targets.

The gap between spending and outcomes also depends on *preexisting social and economic inequalities*. Access to basic services in health and education disproportionately affects the poorest segments of the population. In Cambodia, for example, the poorest fifth have up to three times higher infant mortality rates than the richest fifth (World Bank 2004, 3). High differences between the rich and the poor increase the magnitude of the problem and make targets harder to achieve.

*Macroeconomic factors,* like currency fluctuation and inflation, have an impact. Under conditions of high inflation, the real budget allocations to health and education can plummet dramatically very quickly and become insignificant. Thus, they never translate into the outcomes planned in the beginning of the budget year.

The *structure of public spending* matters: higher allocations for infrastructure investments or wages and salaries of health and education staff, for example, as opposed to spending on actual services in health or education, might not translate into outcomes at all. Moreover, schools without teachers or health clinics without qualified health care professionals but with a high number of "ghost" workers on the payroll, do not do much for lowering infant mortality and increasing school enrollment. Another spending typology relevant for achieving outcomes breaks down budgets into primary, secondary, and tertiary allocations, depending on the level of health and education services provided. Just as in the case of socioeconomic inequalities, this classification has profound distributive implications. The middle class and the richest quintile of the population are more likely to benefit from university education than the poor. In Nepal, for example, 46 percent of total education spending accrues to the richest fifth, while the poorest quintile receives only 11 percent (World Bank 2004, 3).

## Examples of Administrative or Bureaucratic Constraints

*Low salaries for public health professionals and schoolteachers* might lead to corruption. Having to pay bribes for health care and education services acts as a regressive tax and affects the poor disproportionately. In many post-Communist countries, between 70 and 90 percent of patients were found to have paid bribes to medical personnel. In contexts where the wages are very low for health and education workers, or where they are paid with large delays, these workers have no incentive to show up to work or to enter the profession in the first place.

Bureaucracies often have *low implementation capacity.* In some countries, the qualifications and number of civil servants involved in the health and education sectors are greater than in others, despite similar budget allocations. Following decolonization in Africa, for example, many new states lacked qualified civil servants in general. The Belgian Congo had only 6 college graduates, and Zambia had only 76 university graduates in spite of being one of the relatively modernized societies. In the 1970s, fewer than 7,000 Africans in Sub-Saharan Africa were pursuing college degrees. Paradoxically, this shortage of qualified bureaucrats was remedied fast, but many countries witnessed "dramatic improvements of individual capacity accompanied by an equally dramatic decline in institutional capacity" (Van de Walle 2001, 133).

Another example illustrates the challenge of staffing in health and education. In Papua New Guinea in the 1990s, many newly built schools had to close because of the insufficient number of teachers with credentials to fill the positions (World Bank 2004, 22). In contrast, many Eastern European and Central Asian countries have a reasonable ratio of staff to patients or teachers to students. In addition to the low number of teachers and doctors, inadequate qualifications have also been identified as a key determinant of soaring inefficiencies in many countries. A cross-national study conducted in the mid-1990s found that a very low number of cases of diarrhea in children under the age of five had been properly diagnosed or treated (for example, in Zambia 30 percent of all cases were accurately diagnosed and only 19 percent adequately treated) (World Bank 2004, 25). The low quality of health care services induced by lack of trained and properly equipped medical personnel led to poor diagnostics and treatment of patients.

Data on outcomes (infant mortality and primary school completion included) are sometimes not reliable. The *data collection process* itself depends on the quality of the bureaucracy and on political incentives to trace and disclose outcomes accurately. For a number of countries in Eastern Europe and Central Asia, studies that compared data on infant mortality reported by national bureaucracies to international databases with survey data collected in the field have found important discrepancies (Aleshina and Redmond 2003). Similarly, for electricity—a service essential to better health and educational outcomes—satellite-reported data on nighttime energy consumption do not always match the data reported by state agencies in charge of delivering electricity (Min 2010).

Many governments simply lack the *capacity, the tools, and the mechanisms to monitor policy implementation*. An often-quoted study in the development community attempted to trace capitation grants awarded to schools for non-wage primary education expenses in Uganda between 1991 and 1995. The findings were puzzling: only 13 percent reached the beneficiaries. Moreover, richer communities managed to claim these funds, whereas in poor areas, most schools received nothing (Reinikka and Svensson 2004). In many contexts, qualified medical personnel do not want to work in remote rural areas. In some cases, even when they are assigned to clinics in these locations, the lack of monitoring mechanisms and of professional punishment leads to high absenteeism and underprovision of services. A survey in Bangladesh found that the absentee rate among doctors was 74 percent (World Bank 2004, 4).

*Lack of bureaucratic coordination* between governmental agencies is another issue. The long and twisted path linking budget allocations with actual outcomes brings together many corners of the bureaucracy: the ministry of finance, different tiers of government (central, local, municipal, and so forth), line ministries (education, health), and the like. In some cases, task duplication creates unnecessary inefficiencies. In other cases, the lack of communication between various agencies blocks important information transfers.

Now, after exploring some of the potential economic and bureaucratic constraints of the development puzzle, we will see what politics adds to the mix.

## Examples of Political Constraints

Just like corruption, *clientelism,* the exchange of concrete benefits for a citizen's vote, is often a conspicuous manifestation of malfunctioning development institutions because it concentrates public services in certain constituencies at the expense of universal provision of health and education services that would benefit all citizens. Patronage networks connecting political parties, bureaucrats, governments, and voters often provide disincentives for development reforms because they lock in complex exchanges of access to public services and political support between citizens and politicians.

In 1989, for example, the Mexican government introduced PRONASOL (the National Solidarity Program), a large-scale poverty alleviation campaign providing school construction, water, electricity, and nutrition to the poorest segments of the population. Despite a large budget allocation of approximately 1.2 percent of GDP, the results were quite insignificant (a reported 3 percent rate of poverty reduction compared to an initial target of close to 64 percent). Why this large gap? According to several studies that analyzed spending in states and municipalities, the political affiliation of the beneficiaries was a major factor in program targeting. Communities that supported the PRI (the Institutional Revolutionary Party), the political incumbent, received significantly higher PRONASOL funds per capita than localities that voted for other parties (Diaz-Cayeros, Estévez, and Magaloni 2002; Magaloni 2006).

*The system of political representation* can create obstacles or opportunities for the access of certain groups to policy making. In autocracies, opposition parties, trade unions, and many other channels of political participation are officially blocked. In democracies, the poor often make up the large majority of the population. At least theoretically, then, their votes should be important to politicians, and policies such as those touching on health and education should closely reflect their preferences. Paradoxically, this electoral power is the exception rather than the rule. Why? Political institutions intermediate both the way in which the poor are represented in the legislature and the incentives of legislators to enact and implement policies favorable to their constituencies. Therefore, even if the majority of voters prefer policies that would increase literacy rates in the rural areas, this preference might not always translate into actual outcomes. Strong executives and irrelevant legislatures skew the political process toward the policy preferences of the executive. In some circumstances, these might closely match the policy preferred by voters. In others, they could not be further apart.

Keeping other factors constant, *formal electoral rules* governing the democratic process can provide their own incentives for legislators to be accountable or not to voters. The design of electoral districts—that is, gerrymandering—might prevent higher representation of the poor in the parliament. The processes of candidate nominations by political parties and the rules by which they are elected to parliaments shape different patterns of interaction and accountability between voters and politicians. In systems of proportional representation, where citizens vote party lists, for example, the control that the party leaders have over candidate selection determines the type of bond that the candidate wants to cultivate. Closed lists in which party leaders exert most control are less likely than open-list systems (in which voters have a say in the candidate order on the ballot) to build a symbiotic link between individual politicians and voters. District size also matters, because in small districts the competition for a limited number of positions gives incentives to politicians to cultivate personalistic votes. A study of electoral politics in Honduras, for example, shows how clientelism interacts with formal electoral rules to produce outcomes. On the one hand, political *caudillos,* all the way from the president to local politicians, are expected to award personal favors, jobs, and tangible benefits to supporters and not to make or implement nationwide pro-development policy. On the other hand, a closed-list proportional representation rule gives no incentives to politicians to cater to local constituencies but, instead, to acquiesce to the party leaders. As a result, the majority of MPs never initiate any bills in the legislature. The ones who do, however, are more concerned with locally targeted bills that would keep their rural constituencies satisfied, rather than national legislation that would improve education and health (Taylor-Robinson 2006, 2010).

*Delegation of authority* can also generate political incentives and affect development. The gap between policies and outcomes is sometimes related to the capacity of the particular tier of government responsible for implementation. For instance, many countries have decentralized education and health policies. Strong political incentives to decentralize or not in the first place are often responsible for the lack of coordination and capacity mismatches between different tiers of governments. In other cases, decentralization occurs on paper at the insistence of donors, without the actual resources that would enable local governments to execute policies.

The *timing of elections* and the assessment of the probability of winning or losing them create strong incentives for politicians to deliver visible results or push reforms consequential for health and education outcomes. Reforms such as decentralization that affect the gap between expenditures and outcomes are sometimes initiated and implemented when the incumbent party estimates that it will lose national elections, in an attempt to preserve at least some power in the regions.

An approaching election makes political representatives want to avoid sensitive or difficult-to-solve development issues. After all, difficult reforms are commonly initiated in the "honeymoon" period or at the beginning of the term in office because the potential political unpopularity would have enough time to dissipate by the time of the next election.

In other cases, election time also provides good opportunities for credit taking. The Constituency Development Fund (CDF) in Kenya, for example, allocates US$1 million to each member of the Parliament for projects in his or her own district. In the absence of a formal accountability mechanism, suspicions of corruption often plague the management of these funds. In 2007, a civil society organization wanted to conduct social audits of these funds and involved community members, but the data on CDF allocations were very hard to obtain. The group approached the representative of the Changamwe district and persuaded him that if he disclosed the accounts, he would be the first MP ever to cooperate with civil society on information release. Understanding that cooperation would boost his public image in an election year, he agreed to share detailed data on 14 projects sponsored by his own district CDF. The strategy paid off for both civil society and the politician. The former discovered and corrected many irregularities at the implementation stage, whereas the MP was reelected in a year in which most sitting MPs lost elections. The representative acknowledged that opening CDF accounts played a big role in his electoral success.[4]

We have already alluded to the resilience of clientelistic politics in many countries around the world. One of the most common reasons for it is the politicians' *lack of credibility in delivering universalistic policies*, such as reducing infant mortality rates or increasing school enrollment. Often, voters do not trust political party platforms since they have not seen genuine results in the past. Therefore, they would rather accept concrete material benefits in exchange for their turnout and vote. To quote an eloquent evaluation of this type of voters' cynicism: "Honduran voters do not understand that a deputy's job is to legislate, and they do not value legislation because you cannot eat a law" (Taylor-Robinson 2006, 111).

In addition to this type of commitment, at the policy implementation stage politicians often lack incentives to build *credible mechanisms* that would guarantee that budget allocations translate into genuine outcomes. Positions in public bureaucracies can be used to reward supporters, and uncontrolled or unaudited budgets can provide campaign funds for the incumbent party. Depoliticizing the ministry of education or creating a politically independent supreme audit institution that would audit health expenditures is a typical example of "good policies" that are not "good politics."

*Lack of information* about policies and outcomes can also limit the extent to which citizens can award or sanction political behavior. Unless citizens and voters are informed about the gap between planned and achieved outcomes or, more generally, about government's performance in providing effective health and education services, they cannot sanction politicians at the ballot box. Media and civil society organizations play a key role in translating the process of policy making and implementation for citizens and in raising awareness about the noncompliance of politicians or bureaucrats with their mandate.

The government of Uganda, for example, launched a universal primary education program with the goal of increasing enrollments and literacy rates. In 10 years, this ambitious effort gave tangible results: it increased primary school enrollment from 2.9 to 6.3 million children. The success itself generated its own challenges, however: a severe shortage of school buildings and classrooms. A school facilities' grant incorporated in the national budget disbursed US$600,000 per district to build new school buildings. The community officials' lack of managerial experience coupled with incentives for graft made monitoring imperative. In 2002, a civil society organization mobilized citizens to obtain information on expenditures from local politicians and bureaucrats and match it with the actual construction sites. Finding large mismatches between spending and the existence or quality of school buildings, the citizens petitioned the Office of the Prime Minister and the Ministry of Education and Sports. As a result, problematic subcontractors were fired. Moreover, the community started to post financial information on community boards, reducing teachers' absenteeism and the corruption incentives of local officials.[5]

*The process through which development priorities are selected* significantly affects development outcomes. Often, the geographical maps designed to allow technical targeting of resources to the areas that are most in need do not overlap with the political maps of development. For many political representatives, rewarding key constituencies pays off more than objectively allocating aid to the poor. Visibility of outcome matters for politicians, since they can take credit for good policy implementation. Lack of visibility also matters: if political representatives or bureaucrats can slip poor performance under the rug or pass the blame to somebody else, they have incentives to do so to avoid electoral defeat. Occasionally, the search for results that voters can easily identify and attribute to the officials or representatives leads to unexpected results. In some cases, national governments invest in and monitor the implementation of innovative education or health policies, mostly in areas with the capacity already in place to implement them, since they are more likely than localities or regions with more questionable capacity to achieve tangible and visible results quickly. In such cases, policy visibility comes at the expense of growing inequalities. Regions that already have resources and capacity are empowered, while areas that lack them in the first place suffer from neglect. In two countries that spend the same share or amount on education and health, such selection effects can nonetheless lead to discrepant outcomes.

Variations in the *capacity of groups to mobilize* will fundamentally shape the result of their efforts to demand services. Low-income groups often lack the resources and organizational capacity to campaign effectively. Furthermore, the lack of information, skewed electoral rules, the ways in which electoral districts are drawn, and the existence and power of pro-poor political parties can all constitute severe obstacles or opportunities for the poor to mobilize and demand bureaucratic or political accountability.

In some cases, the poor are well mobilized and regimented by patronage networks, have a large vote turnout, but fail to select and hold accountable politicians who would credibly commit to provide and implement health and education. The appeal of tangible clientelistic benefits handed out in front of the ballot box is simply higher in some contexts than the noncredible electoral promises of other parties. On the other side of the spectrum, in many cases the capacity for mobilization and collective action has led to significant improvements in policy implementation. The by-now famous case of participatory budgeting in the Brazilian town of Porto Alegre initiated in 1989 by a left-wing mayor committed to large-scale community mobilization and citizens' involvement in city finances led to tangible outcomes: over a 15-year period, the access to water and sewage reached almost 100 percent, and the number of schools quadrupled. In the Indian state of Uttar Pradesh, a low-caste political party managed to increase the electricity coverage of villages (Min 2010).

Despite such inspiring stories, more often than not, the poor fail to mobilize as effectively as other interest groups. This failure skews resource allocation in favor of the most politically vocal and influential. The health sector provides an example. If the public procurement process for medications is plagued by corruption, then a large share of public spending on health goes toward purchasing overpriced drugs from powerful private sector companies rather than toward basic services that would, for example, significantly lower infant mortality rates among the poor. In the late 1990s, Albania spent a large share of its health care budget on the problematic procurement of drugs through direct purchase and leakage of confidential information to pharmaceutical companies, as opposed to competitive bidding and a transparent process (Cohen, Mrazek, and Hawkins 2007, 32).

*Mechanisms of accountability* are key to providing politicians with incentives for implementing good policies. Some cross-national studies have found that poor democracies have higher primary school enrollment than authoritarian equivalents, since electoral pressures make politicians more responsive and accountable to the educational needs of voters (Brown 1999). In the same vein of argument, a study of education spending in Brazil found that the periods of democratic rule, as opposed to autocratic episodes, significantly affected the allocation of primary education funds between state and local governments, as well as the share of primary versus tertiary education spending (Brown 2002). But democracy and elections might not be the only institutions that can generate incentives for public service delivery. As other findings indicate, autocratic forms of government with alternative mechanisms of accountability might outperform democracies in delivering selected basic health and education outcomes. Cuba has better health and literacy indicators than many countries with much higher income, and China has reduced infant mortality to a great extent and achieved almost universal primary school enrollment (World Bank 2004).

An *effective and independent judiciary* can protect citizens against political attempts to promote policies that may hinder their basic rights. Even in the absence of a responsive government, a robust system of checks and balances and separation of powers creates paths other than the ballot box through which citizens can influence outcomes and hold the executive accountable. Especially in the case of health and education policies, many national constitutions inscribe basic services as human rights that states should provide to all citizens. If the courts are free of political interference from the government or the legislature and if citizens have the informational and financial capacity and the ability to mobilize and access the judicial system, then tangible outcomes are more likely to be achieved. The Treatment Action Campaign Case, for example, brought in front of the South African Constitutional Court in 2002 by a civil society organization, claimed that an antiretroviral medication crucial to the prevention of HIV transmission from mother to child at birth should become available in public hospitals. Despite the government's resistance to the dissemination of the drug on financial grounds, the court ultimately awarded the case to the claimants. The case is now considered a major milestone on the long and winding path of HIV/AIDS policy reform in South Africa (Gauri and Brinks 2008).

Last, but certainly not least, *conflict and political instability*—such as wars, civil unrest, or other fragile situations—can significantly affect development outcomes. Several cross-national studies have found that fragile states have, on average, 10 percent higher infant mortality rates than comparable countries, irrespective of the line ministry spending (Gates et al. 2010). By the same token, according to estimates, 38 million out of approximately 230 million children in countries affected by conflict do not attend primary schooling. In fact, 30 percent of all the children in the world who do not complete primary education live in fragile states (Gates et al. 2010, 19).

## Economic, Administrative, and Political Factors: Blurry Areas of Conceptual Overlap

The factors behind development failure and success just discussed are by no means a complete list. Moreover, only problem- and context-specific empirical testing can confirm whether each of these constraints is relevant. The list is hypothetical. It is rather supposed to start a conversation about a broader range of potential causes of development failure, beyond a narrow "technical" (or nonpolitical) core of explanations and solutions.

A good understanding of political economy helps us sort through these constraints and incentives responsible for such a divergence in final outcomes. Sometimes the intersection of distinct political and economic causes is the best explanation. Other times, what may appear to be a purely economic or political factor might hide incentives characteristic of the other two categories. Here are some examples:

- *Economic inefficiencies* in the implementing agency might stem from several causes: lack of basic capacity, lack of adequate coordination among bureaucratic units, and problematic public procurement practices for private contractors, among others. These constraints pertain to the bureaucratic and political domain as well, as they skew incentives across all levels.
- To an equal extent, *seemingly political factors* that decouple health or education outcomes from the spending levels (such as lack of political will to

implement policies effectively, weak rule of law, weak voice and account-ability, and the like) are often problems closely associated with or exacer-bated by resource scarcity, the degree of development, a low level of urbanization and modernization, or sheer poverty.

- *Bureaucracies malfunction* for many reasons. On the one hand, malfunc-tions might be the product of insufficient economic development or the lack of basic state capacity to establish a critical mass of competent bu-reaucrats. On the other hand, in the absence of mechanisms that prevent politicization, bureaucracies are often at the mercy of the political incum-bent. The winning party can staff the state with party supporters and use regulatory agencies to retaliate or persecute opponents.

- Even *data on budgets and outcomes*—which we usually take for granted—are not "politics" free. Sometimes key budgetary indicators are not re-leased at all or are distorted precisely because politicians try to prevent being sanctioned electorally if such data reveal underperformance.

The rest of this handbook will deal mainly with the third category, politi-cal constraints, and explore how they derail or promote development out-comes and reform attempts.

## The Limits, Perils, and Promises of Political-Economy Analysis

Before we move forward, we present some of the main arguments for and against political economy that the development community has raised.

The arguments in favor of this approach claim that it provides the ana-lytical tools, methods, and diagnostics that allow us to understand and map the policy context. Without explicitly incorporating political institutions, actors, and their interaction into our analyses of the policy-making environ-ment, we leave out at least half the story and fail to properly account for context specificity. The arguments opposed to it say that political economy focuses on large-scale institutions and processes that rarely change but neglects or ignores the marginal improvements feasible even in bleak envi-ronments. In addition, political economy is less practical in addressing how reform should proceed and is often overly pessimistic, given that the con-straints in many developing countries are severe and the feasibility of policy change is low. According to its critics, political economy is also not sensitive enough to context because of its rational choice underpinnings that over-simplify incentives, payoffs, and the nature of information flows between actors.

In the following section, we briefly introduce some arguments and alternatives that aim to respond to these issues. Then we will clarify how this handbook plans to address (or bypass) at least some of the criticisms.

## Insurmountable Problems, Policy Resignation

One of the critiques of applying the approach of political economy to development comes from its fatalistic flavor. The analytical focus generally falls on *institutions*, the *incentives* they generate, and the effects these incentives have on *development outcomes*. The implication is that if a reformer wants to shift the development equilibrium and reverse the path—which means changing outcomes, which means changing incentives, and which means altering or creating institutions—the set of potential solutions is usually overly challenging to tackle. Voter-politician accountability relations, decentralized government, or anticorruption agencies cannot be transformed overnight to suddenly become functional without the necessary buy-in from key actors.

Especially if the fundamental institutions (that is, democracy, federalism, and the like) are a reflection of underlying conditions and power configurations in the society, institutional change requires a fundamental overhaul of social relations and background conditions and might not be feasible or even desirable. This view is often quite cynical with respect to the idea of "true" institutional change often showcased by international donors. Provocatively, one observer argued that even the editorial template chosen for the presentation of reform outcomes in the policy reports of international organizations often signals the uniqueness of such success stories. In-text boxes usually highlight the rarity of institutionally induced change, possible only when the underlying conditions are ripe for success. Otherwise, if institutions were the true drivers of results on the ground, irrespective of deeper structural factors, the readers would expect to see tables or graphs that would record empirical patterns more systematically (Przeworski 2004, 530).

In practice, this is the "go home and cry" scenario. If, say, we know that democratic accountability through elections gives the "right" incentives to politicians to perform and that as a result, it leads to the prevention of large-scale famines, we might understand the problem analytically while being further than ever from a feasible solution. Promoting clean elections and developing accountability in a poor country over a short period of time in order to apply an institutional solution to food crises are as challenging as reducing inequality or promoting economic growth overnight. We argue, however, that practitioners and reformers should be aware of the limits and perils of change, even if in the end of their analysis they discover that there is nothing to be done. Otherwise, they run the risk of institutional engineering with limited or missing domestic ownership and possibly detrimental consequences for development.

## "The Quiet Revolution of Small Successes" versus "Big Questions and Big Answers"

In a recent influential book in development economics, the authors Abhijit Banerjee and Esther Duflo make a useful theoretical distinction between uppercase *INSTITUTIONS* and lowercase *institutions*. Whereas the former are the broad fundamental rules in a society (democracy, federal arrangements, or parliamentary or presidential regimes), the latter include more granular and localized forms of interaction between actors. A second related critique argues that political economy is overly focused on political INSTITUTIONS: democracy and autocracy, federal versus unitary systems, or any other broad set of core rules that keep the machinery running (Banerjee and Duflo 2011, 238–42). Reform in this view, again, is hard or impossible because the approach is simply too ambitious and too pessimistic. While key rules might explain why things do not work well, they are often hard or impossible to change precisely because they lie at the core of the beast. An alternative approach has furthered our understand-ing of how development works on the ground and has infused some optimism in the debate between academia and practice. Its proponents adopt instead a more pragmatic plan of action, leaving aside the big questions such as why democracies foster growth and development and focusing instead on manageable marginal successes based on the concrete institutional arrangements on the ground rather than on the big INSTITUTIONS themselves.

Here are examples of questions that this approach answers: Are the specifics of democratic institutions—characteristics of elections, checks and balances, patterns of popular participation, the nature of the legislative process—in country $x$ conducive to less corruption, better public procurement systems, more budget transparency? How are various leadership structures and forms of authority affecting the production of public goods and collective action at the village level? Why are there fewer malaria cases in region $x$ than in region $y$, despite similar environmental conditions? From this perspective, the view from below, based on the realities on the ground and not on meta-theoretical questions, is more likely to be better equipped to inform policy choices. Even changes in small rules can adjust incentives and ultimately lead to better outcomes.

This approach is complementary to our view of political economy in practice as it restores hope in the feasibility of change. We argue for empirically grounded analysis built around a concrete problem that uses a variety of methodological tools and conceptual building blocks. However, big questions and big answers related to INSTITUTIONS often bring theoretical and empirical insights that inductive, narrow, or localized findings do not always provide. A mixture of both forms of inquiry into why development problems persist can paint a complete feasibility map for policy navigation. It can also build an active repository of cumulative analytical findings and policy solutions to overcome external validity issues stemming from exclusive reliance on context-specific findings.

## Actionable Political Economy Analysis as Opposed to Static Research Outputs

Another prevalent criticism of the political-economy approach persistent in the development community comes from the "so what?" problem. Once we have conducted an analysis and understand the policy dynamics taking place, what do we do next? Most studies or reports are valuable in drawing the landscape and the obstacles surrounding reform but are less useful in guiding us through that landscape. One of the responses to this shortcoming is the "actionable" component (Pradhan 2010). Accordingly, political economy has to go beyond analysis and directly fuel a process of knowledge-driven change by translating analysis into actual reform. The type of dynamic knowledge that has local legitimacy and ownership would not only identify the actual actors and their obstacles but also actively catalyze and nurture their collective capacity for action.

This view aspires to organically connect the knowledge production process with action. Successful and sustainable operationalization, therefore, requires a paradigm shift along three dimensions: analysis *for whom, by whom,* and *how?* The answers require the redefinition of roles, as follows: (1) *the client*—the final beneficiary of the analysis—should be the change agent on the ground and not the donor agencies; (2) *the producer*—the local teams—should undertake political-economy analysis to develop understanding and trigger ownership of reform; and (3) *the process*—instead of generating a passive research output—should result in analyses commissioned and produced locally for the change agents and organically integrated into the process that they are about to initiate. As a one-stop source of basic information, interactive activities, and case studies, this handbook is designed to encourage and serve this precise purpose.

### Incorporation of Political-Economy Analysis in Donor Operations

Last but not least, the World Bank, the United Nations Development Programme, and the U.K. Department for International Development, as well as many other development agencies and think tanks, have generated a plethora of studies, frameworks, guidelines, and manuals to help their staff better understand the operational environments and think in a more nuanced way about policies. Pockets of reluctance still persist, however, because factoring in the political process occasionally seems to be at odds with the technocratic mandate of these organizations. Nonetheless, we argue that mainstream recognition of the fact that politics matters is long overdue. Donor organizations have always been an integral part of the political-economic environment, given their own incentives and interactions with local actors. A deep understanding of the underlying politics of reform, as well as one's own role in it, is crucial for successful policy design and implementation.

## Summary

As the opening vignettes suggested, the rules of the political game generate incentives that often undermine the technical targets of reforms. Despite all their limitations, political-economy diagnostics are recognized as useful for answering the *what* and the *why* of development and for guiding the *how* to change. In a landscape of nontechnical challenges and obstacles, a map of all possible routes is the first piece of navigational equipment needed.

### Notes

1. *Rational utility maximization* is a key assumption of economics; simply put, it means that, when making a decision, the individual (as a consumer, voter, or the like) settles for the greatest "value" possible derived from the choice, for the lowest cost (or investment).
2. According to some studies, public spending is, on average, 10 percent of gross domestic product (GDP) lower in presidential than in parliamentary regimes (Persson and Tabellini 2003).
3. See http://pdf.usaid.gov/pdf_docs/PNACT315.pdf.
4. International Budget Partnership (IBP), "Social Audits in Kenya: Budget Transparency and Accountability," http://internationalbudget.org/wp-content/uploads/Impact-Story-Kenya-English.pdf.
5. IBP, "School Building Fund Provides Lessons on Community Mobilization in Uganda," http://internationalbudget.org/wp-content/uploads/UgandaStory English.pdf.

# References

Aleshina, Nadejda and Gerry Redmond. 2003. "How High is Infant Mortality In Central and Eastern Europe and the CIS?" *UNICEF Innocenti Research Center,* Florence: Innocenti Working Papers No. 95.

Banerjee, Abhijit V., and Esther Duflo. 2011. *Poor Economics: A Radical Rethinking of the Way to Fight Global Poverty.* New York, NY: Public Affairs, a Member of the Perseus Books Group.

Beramendi, Pablo. 2007. "Inequality and the Territorial Fragmentation of Solidarity." *International Organization* 61 (4): 783–820.

Brown, David S. 1999. "Reading, Writing, and Regime Type: Democracy's Impact on Primary School Enrollment." *Political Research Quarterly* 52 (4): 681–707.

———. 2002. "Democracy, Authoritarianism and Education Finance in Brazil." *Journal of Latin American Studies* 34 (1): 115–41.

Bueno De Mesquita, Bruce, Alastair Smith, Randolph M. Siverson, and James D. Morrow. 2003. *The Logic of Political Survival.* Cambridge, MA: MIT Press.

Cohen, Jillian C., Monique F. Mrazek, and Loraine Hawkins. 2007. "Corruption and Pharmaceuticals: Strengthening Good Governance to Improve Access." In *The Many Faces of Corruption: Tracking Vulnerabilities at the Sector Level,* ed. J. Edgar Campos and Sanjay Pradhan, 29–62. Washington, DC: World Bank.

Diaz-Cayeros, Alberto, Federico Estévez, and Beatriz Magaloni. 2002. "The Erosion of One-Party Rule: Clientelism, Portfolio Diversification and Electoral Strategy." Paper presented at the American Political Science Association Annual Meeting, Boston, MA, August 29–September 1.

Dorotinsky, William, and Shilpa Pradhan. 2007. "Exploring Corruption in Public Financial Management." In *The Many Faces of Corruption: Tracking Vulnerabilities at the Sector Level,* ed. Jose Edgar Campos and Sanjay Pradhan, 267–94. Washington, DC: World Bank.

Easterly, William. 2002. *The Elusive Quest for Growth: Economists' Adventures and Misadventures in the Tropics.* Cambridge, MA: MIT Press.

Eaton, Kent, Kai Kaiser, and Paul Smoke. 2010. "The Political Economy of Decentralization Reforms: Implications for Aid Effectiveness." Washington, DC: World Bank.

Egel, Daniel. 2009. "Tribal Diversity, Political Patronage and the Yemeni Decentralization Experiment." Unpublished manuscript, University of California, Berkeley.

Fischer, Stanley. 1995. "Central-Bank Independence Revisited." *American Economic Review* 85 (2): 201–06.

Frøystad, Mona, Kari Heggstad, and Odd-Helge Fjeldstad. 2010. "Linking Procurement and Political Economy." Chr. Michelsen Institute Report commissioned by U.K. Department for International Development and World Bank Institute, http://www.cmi.no/publications/file/3955-linking-procurement-and-political-economy-a-gui.pdf.

Gates, Scott, Håvard Hegre, Håvard M. Nygård, and Håvard Strand. 2010. "Consequences of Civil Conflict." Background paper for the *World Development Report*

*2011*, World Bank, Washington, DC, http://wdr2011.worldbank.org/sites/default/files/pdfs/WDR%20Background%20Paper_PRIO.pdf.

Gauri, Varun, and Daniel M. Brinks, eds. 2008. *Courting Social Justice: Judicial Enforcement of Social and Economic Rights in the Developing World.* Cambridge: Cambridge University Press.

Gelineau, François, and Karen L. Remmer. 2006. "Political Decentralization and Electoral Accountability: The Argentine Experience, 1983–2001." *British Journal of Political Science* 36 (1): 133–57.

Gerber, Elisabeth. 2003. "What Is Political Economy?" *Political Economist* 11 (2):1–3.

Grzymala-Busse, Anna. 2007. *Rebuilding Leviathan: Party Competition and State Exploitation in Post-Communist Democracies.* New York: Cambridge University Press.

Guriev, Sergei. 2012. "Why Good Policy Is Not Good Politics." In *Policymic. Next Generation News and Politics. Office Hours,* http://www.policymic.com/group/showCompetition/id/1973.

Haggard, Stephan, and Robert R. Kaufman. 1995. *The Political Economy of Democratic Transitions.* Princeton, NJ: Princeton University Press.

Lasswell, Harold. 1936. *Politics: Who Gets What, When, and How.* New York: McGraw-Hill.

Magaloni, Beatriz. 2006. *Voting for Autocracy: Hegemonic Party Survival and Its Demise in Mexico.* Cambridge Studies in Comparative Politics. New York: Cambridge University Press.

Mainwaring, Scott, and Matthew Soberg Shugart. 1997. *Presidentialism and Democracy in Latin America.* Cambridge Studies in Comparative Politics. New York: Cambridge University Press.

Min, Brian. 2010. "Distributing Power: Public Service Provision to the Poor in India." Unpublished manuscript. Ann Arbor, MI: University of Michigan.

Niskanen, William A. 2003. *Autocratic, Democratic, and Optimal Government: Fiscal Choices and Economic Outcomes.* Northhampton, MA: Edward Elgar Publishing, Inc.

O'Dwyer, Conor. 2006. *Runaway State-Building: Patronage Politics and Democratic Development.* Baltimore, MD: Johns Hopkins University Press.

Persson, Torsten, and Guido Tabellini. 2003. *The Economic Effects of Constitutions.* Cambridge, MA: MIT Press.

Pradhan, Sanjay. 2010. Keynote address at the World Bank Institute and CommGap, "Political Economy Analysis to Action, a Global Learning Event." June 21–22, Washington, DC., http://siteresources.worldbank.org/EXTGOVACC/Resources/PoliticalEconomyAnalysistoActionFinalReport.pdf.

Przeworski, Adam. 2004. "Institutions Matter?" *Government and Opposition* 39 (4): 527–40.

Reinikka, Ritva, and Jakob Svensson. 2004. "Local Capture: Evidence from a Central Government Transfer Program in Uganda." *Quarterly Journal of Economics* 119 (2): 679–705.

Remmer, Karen L., and Erik Wibbels. 2000. "The Subnational Politics of Economic Adjustment." *Comparative Political Studies* 33 (4): 419–51.

Rodden, Jonathan. 2002. "The Dilemma of Fiscal Federalism: Grants and Fiscal Performance around the World." *American Journal of Political Science* 46 (3): 670–87.

Rukumnuaykit, Pungpond. 2003. "Crises and Child Health Outcomes: The Impacts of Economic and Drought/Smoke Crises on Infant Mortality and Birthweight in Indonesia." Unpublished manuscript, Department of Economics, Michigan State University, http://pdf.usaid.gov/pdf_docs/Pnact315.pdf.

Sachs, Jeffrey. 2005. *The End of Poverty: Economic Possibilities for Our Time.* New York: Penguin Press.

Shefter, Martin. 1994. *Political Parties and the State: The American Historical Experience.* New York: Cambridge University Press.

Shepherd, Geoffrey. 2003. "Civil Service Reform in Developing Countries: Why Is It Going Badly?" Paper presented at the 11th International Anti-Corruption Conference, May 25–28, Seoul, Republic of Korea.

Taylor-Robinson, Michelle. 2006. "The Difficult Road from Caudilliismo to Democracy." In *Informal Institutions and Democracy: Lessons from Latin America,* ed. Gretchen Helmke and Steven Levitsky, 106–24. Baltimore, MD: Johns Hopkins University Press.

———. 2010. *Do the Poor Count? Democratic Institutions and Accountability in a Context of Poverty.* University Park, PA: Pennsylvania State University Press.

van de Walle, Nicolas. 2001. *African Economies and the Politics of Permanent Crisis, 1979–1999.* Cambridge: Cambridge University Press.

Ware, Glenn, Shaun Moss, Ed Campos, and Gregory Noone. 2007. "Corruption in Public Procurement: A Perennial Challenge." In *The Many Faces of Corruption: Tracking Vulnerabilities at the Sector Level,* ed. J. Edgar Campos and Sanjay Pradhan, 295–334. Washington, DC: World Bank.

Wibbels, Erik. 2005. *Federalism and the Market: Intergovernmental Conflict and Economic Reform in the Developing World.* New York: Cambridge University Press.

———. 2006. "Madison in Baghdad? Decentralization and Federalism in Comparative Politics." *Annual Review of Political Science* 9: 165–88.

World Bank. 1997. *The State in a Changing World.* Washington, DC: World Bank.

World Bank. 2004. *World Development Report: Making Services Work for Poor People.* Washington, DC: World Bank.

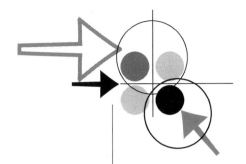

# PART I

The first several chapters of this book describe the major mechanisms and diagnostic tools of political-economy analysis. Public policy making is a complex process, often characterized by the strategic interaction of stakeholders in continuously evolving contexts. To navigate reform successfully, practitioners need to identify the theoretical logic behind development problems, as well as the political-economy tools that will allow the analysis of their causes and the identification of potential solutions. Thinking in a nuanced fashion about the way in which political incentives can promote or hinder development can lead to feasible and desirable agendas for change.

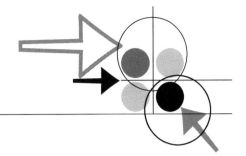

# CHAPTER 2

# Accountability and Corruption: The *What* Question

Let us start with the first essential questions any analysis should ask: *What* is the development problem to be addressed? *What* are its main manifestations? We begin the chapter with some generic answers to these "what" questions and introduce the reader to a preliminary diagnosis of the symptoms. Corruption, pervasive political clientelism, and endemic rent-seeking behavior are signs of development failure. They are highly visible marks of "bad" equilibria, and it is likely that they affect the poor disproportionately. What are their immediate or proximate causes? Corruption, patronage, and other outcome-distorting phenomena imply that somewhere, somehow, in the institutional chain of task delegation and political representation, something is not working well.

These malfunctions are generated by a broken or weak relationship of responsibility or accountability. In some cases, politicians are not doing their job, and the electorate lacks the capacity to sanction them through collective action. In other cases, bureaucrats shirk their duties and fail to implement accurately the mandates conferred on them by politicians. Even if the locus and depth of the problem differ across policies, sectors, and countries, the generic diagnostic of problematic accountability mechanisms applies widely.

**FIGURE 2.1 Conceptual Map of Accountability, Corruption, and Related Governance Problems**

| Accountability | Types of accountability | Corruption | Addressing accountability |
|---|---|---|---|
| • What does it mean?<br>• How is it relevant to development?<br>• Consequences of accountability | • Accountability in democratic regimes<br>• Accountability in single-party regimes<br>• Accountability in authoritarian regimes | • What is corruption?<br>• How is it relevant to governance and accountability?<br>• Types of corruption | • Mechanisms to address accountability and governance<br>• Unintended consequences of such mechanisms |

*Source:* Authors.

Therefore, this chapter focuses on accountability and the varieties of governance problems as key areas of interest for any development practitioner. Among the entire universe of governance problems, we focus mostly on corruption and political clientelism (or patronage) as prime suspects for derailing development in many parts of the world. Figure 2.1 introduces the conceptual map of the chapter.

## Objectives of Chapter 2

By the end of this chapter, readers should be able to do the following:

- Understand the varieties of accountability.
- Recognize the different types and manifestations of poor governance, corruption, and patronage.
- Go beyond normative connotations of *accountability, clientelism,* and *corruption.*
- Link general concepts of accountability, corruption, and clientelism to real-life situations.

## What Is Accountability?

The concept of accountability is closely related to other notions such as *political representation, responsiveness, reliability, responsibility, mandate responsiveness,* and *governance* (based on Przeworski, Stokes, and Manin 1999, 8–10).[1] In a general sense, accountability refers to the normative assumption that governments act in the best interest of the people or their citizens.[2] Accountability implies a relationship between citizens (as "principals") and politicians (as "agents"), through which the agents are routinely monitored and sanctioned to ensure effective delivery of benefits to their constituencies (Kitschelt et al. 2009, 742).

However, given the diversity of individual preferences in society, how can citizens make sure that the aggregated opinions of the majority lead to policy outcomes that reflect the will of the people? More precisely, in what forms of political representation do government actions and outcomes most closely align with citizen mandates for politicians?

Nobel Prize winner Amartya Sen endorsed multiparty democracy as the best vehicle for accountability by positing that no famine has ever occurred under that type of rule:

> It is not surprising that no famine has ever taken place in the history of the world in a functioning democracy—be it economically rich (as in contemporary Western Europe or North America) or relatively poor (as in postindependence India, or Botswana, or Zimbabwe). Famines have tended to occur in colonial territories governed by rulers from elsewhere (as in British India or as in an Ireland administered by alienated English rulers), or in one-party states (as in the Ukraine in the 1930s, or as in China during 1958–1961, or Cambodia in the 1970s. (Page 16 in Sen, Amartya ©. 1999. *Development as Freedom*. By permission of Oxford University Press, www.oup.com)

Elected officials, according to the argument, do not want to be voted out of office for failing to prevent a famine. The explanation implies that at the opposite end of the spectrum, authoritarian governments do not have incentives to respond promptly to food crises since the public cannot hold them accountable (see Concepts in Practice 2.1).

Complicating Sen's observation is the fact that both representation and accountability come in many shapes and forms. In fact, there is no single path linking political representation to any uniquely robust type of accountability. Democracies rely on regular elections, through which voters can sanction nonperforming politicians. Despite the fact that this possibility of penalizing representatives is a crucial component of mandate responsiveness, it does not automatically translate into accountability and good governance. If elections are not free and fair, or if the poor lack the capacity for collective action, voters fail to punish corrupt representatives. In contrast, autocracies either dilute or completely lack direct electoral accountability. In some cases, however, they feature sophisticated systems of institutional checks and balances that ensure effective sanctioning of politicians and bureaucrats who shirked their mandates. The following sec-

## Democratic Institutions, Famines, and Food Shortages

What is the logic that brings together famine occurrence and democratic elections in developing countries? If politicians fail to prevent catastrophic deaths as a result of widespread famines, they are penalized by the voting public and lose elections. Therefore, the political incentives generated by elections in democracies drive food policy to a better outcome than could be achieved otherwise, in the absence of the mechanisms of accountability.

Before Amartya Sen brought to the fore the role of democratic institutions and accountability, the dominant theory on the cause of famines focused on severe food shortages brought about by natural causes (drought, floods, unfavorable weather, and the like). The author analyzed the great famine of Bengal, which occurred in 1943 and caused around 3 million deaths, and concluded that food decline was not the major cause of the catastrophe. The problem, instead, resided in the declining real wages of the rural workers and farmers, combined with increasing prices for food. Since these factors pertain to the political-economic domain, the argument suggested that the solution might lie in the institutional capacity of the public to sanction politicians and bureaucrats who fail to enact preventive policies.

After 1947, India has experienced many episodes of severe hunger, but the death toll has rarely reached the threshold that qualifies food scarcity as famine (a possible exception is the Bihar famine of 1966–67). In contrast, China lost tens of millions of lives in the aftermath of the severe famine of 1958–61. Not only did the government fail to prevent this devastation, but the real damage was carefully hidden from the public eye. The data on the number of starvation deaths were publicized only after Mao's death. In the absence of an alert media or any form of political opposition and accountability, the autocratic government failed to respond to the crisis, with dramatic consequences.

Despite the fact that the argument has been criticized for not explaining the occurrence of famines in some democratic countries (like Ethiopia) or numerous starvation deaths in many Indian states since independence, it still sets the standard for the debate on "nontechnical" solutions to development problems. Indeed, bringing in political institutions, incentives, collective action, and broad questions of the accountability of politicians to voters has enhanced our understanding of the variation in policy responses to food crises around the world.

*Source:* Sen 1999, http://www.nytimes.com/2003/03/01/arts/does-democracy-avert-famine.html?pagewanted=all&src=pm. See also Brass 1986.

tions examine accountability mechanisms in democratic and nondemocratic settings.

This chapter next discusses different forms of political representation and the variety of accountability relations they trigger. For now, let us start with democracies.

## Government Accountability in Democratic Settings

To illustrate accountability pathways in democracies, let us imagine that in democratic Country X, where the infant mortality rate is among the highest in the world, the public demands a reform of the health care system that addresses the issue promptly and effectively. Subsequently, the majority preference for health policy is transmitted to politicians through a number of channels: voting for the party or candidate that runs on a health care platform in elections, writing letters to the elected district officials, and conducting national opinion polls confirming the popular will. Once politicians who ran on an electoral platform to address health care reform are in office, voters can check government responsiveness by comparing campaign promises with actual policies. Has the government promptly initiated a health care bill? Did Party A, which won a majority in the legislature, maintain the political position on health care reform advertised during the campaign? If the answers to these questions are positive, based on the best abilities of voters to evaluate the match between campaign promises and actual policies, then the government is responsive to the preferences of the electorate. Achieving robust accountability, however, requires two extra steps:

- An *evaluation of the implementation* of the health care reform voted on in the parliament, approved by the president, and actually carried out on the ground must be conducted. Has the infant mortality rate, for example, improved at a reasonable pace following the new law or reform?
- Contingent on the answer to that question, the voters must be able to *punish* or *reward* the government for the concrete results achieved. For example, if the outcome satisfied or did not satisfy the majority of citizens, then the political party in office could win or lose the next election.[3]

Figure 2.2 shows the causal path between the heterogeneous preferences of citizens and final policy outcomes. The institutionalization of such a sanctioning mechanism through which citizens can punish or reward politicians based on their policy performance is key to the concept of government accountability. Democracy is the only such institutional arrangement, or "rule of the game," that formalizes a *direct* relationship of responsibility between citizens (as principals) and politicians (as agents) through three mechanisms:

- Regular free and fair elections
- Guaranteed political rights and civil liberties
- Institutional checks and balances.

A necessary, if not sufficient, component of democracy and the main ingredient for an accountable democratic government, periodic free and fair elec-

**FIGURE 2.2 The Path between Citizen Preferences and Policy Outcomes**

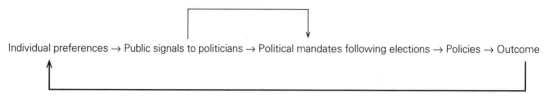

Individual preferences → Public signals to politicians → Political mandates following elections → Policies → Outcome

*Source:* Adapted from Przeworski, Stokes, and Manin (1999, 9). Copyright © 1999 Adam Przeworski, Susan C. Stokes, and Bernard Manin. Eds. *Democracy, Accountability, and Representation.* Vol. 2. Reprinted with the permission of Cambridge University Press

tions ensure that voters have unconstrained access to the political process and that each vote has equal weight in determining the electoral outcome.

***What Are the Inner Mechanics and Modes of Democratic Accountability Relations?*** Politicians use campaigns to identify themselves with the policies preferred by the majority of voters. Ideally, regularly held, free and fair elections guarantee a certain consistency between campaign promises and policies, if the voters have the capacity to act collectively; that is, voters must be informed, be able to adequately monitor politicians and bureaucracies, and be able to elicit credible promises from politicians.

However, accountability can manifest itself in many ways and depends on *the timing of events* (when can voters monitor the delivery of goods—before or after election day?) as well as on *the nature of the promises* (tangible private goods such as cash or consumer appliances, or public goods such as health or education?). Not all relationships of accountability are ideal or desirable. Some, such as the clientelistic exchanges in table 2.1, might be the second-best alternatives, when politicians cannot promise anything else, or might even be detrimental to development.

***Types of Political Accountability in Democratic Politics.*** Table 2.1 summarizes various types of links between citizens and politicians, with implications for the relationship between the two sets of actors.[4] Of the main modes

**TABLE 2.1 Modes of Accountability and Time Horizon for Performance Evaluation**

| Time horizon for evaluation of agent's performance | Mode of accountability | |
|---|---|---|
| | Indirect (programmatic) | Direct (clientelistic) |
| Past performance | Retrospective evaluation of *public* good delivery | Retrospective evaluation of *private* good delivery |
| Future performance | Prospective evaluation of *public* good delivery | Prospective evaluation of *private* good delivery |

*Source:* Authors, building on Kitschelt (2000) and on Kitschelt et al. (2009).

Understanding Policy Change

of political accountability, the "indirect" category—which corresponds to candidate selection based on electoral platforms and the delivery of public goods—often decouples both *timing* and *benefits* of the delegation relationship:

- First, there is a temporal lag between the date of election and the timing of policy evaluation. Usually, pre-electoral policy promises, as opposed to tangible handouts or public sector jobs, take longer to yield fruits. Even more importantly, parties lump many issues together in order to offer policy packages before elections (Kitschelt 2000, 850–851). Improving literacy or reducing infant mortality are only a subset of a much broader political agenda advertised to voters. At the ballot box, citizens vote for labels that often combine their preferences on education and health policy with areas as diverse as gay rights or foreign affairs. This process filters majority will and policy stances over multiple dimensions through concrete forms of political representation. Therefore, the temporal ties of accountability as well as voters' individual policy gains are decoupled and only indirect.
- Second, the benefits and costs of post-election policies, by definition, accrue to all voters, not only to the supporters of the electoral winners (Kitschelt 2000, 845).

The type of relationship that rests on parties offering complex issue packages and on citizens voting the match between their preferences and party platforms is called programmatic linkage between voters and politicians (Kitschelt 2000, 850).

At the other end of the spectrum, political clientelism refers to an exchange of tangible benefits for a citizen's vote. Clientelism (often associated with corruption) reduces the time lag between vote and benefits but has as its main consequence the delivery of private goods targeted to small constituencies rather than to society at large.[5] Monitoring and sanctioning constitute institutional dilemmas for both modes of accountability. In the case of indirect or programmatic ties, they are key devices for disciplining politicians and bureaucrats. For clientelistic ties, they are also tools in the hands of politicians who want make sure that voters comply with their part of the deal (Kitschelt et al. 2009, 744).

Depending on the types of actors involved in a relationship of accountability, we can also distinguish among three accountability types: *political, managerial (internal),* and *social accountability.* This primer will explore all forms of accountability. Some chapters apply more to political or to social accountability. Others, such as chapter 6 on principal-agent theory, are more useful for understanding managerial accountability and dwell less on

**FIGURE 2.3 Varieties of Accountability**

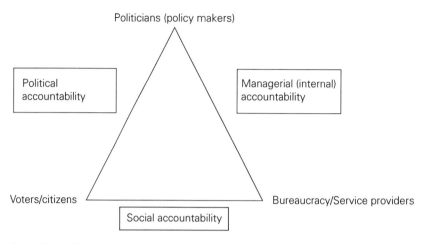

*Source:* Adapted from World Bank (2004), 6–10.

direct relationships between voters and politicians or between citizens and bureaucracies.

Figure 2.3 illustrates the three-way relationship among citizens, politicians, and the bureaucrats charged with implementing policies, along with the types of accountability that are shared by those groups. Governments function best when politicians are accountable to voters, bureaucrats are accountable to both voters and politicians, and individuals and groups are able to act collectively to bring about needed reforms. In reality, sadly, this condition is rare. In diagnostic political-economy analysis, it is worth asking repeatedly, On what leg of the triangle is the problem really located?

## Government Accountability in Nondemocratic Settings

Despite the fact that free and fair elections provide a direct channel for monitoring and sanctioning politicians who did not deliver on their promises, elections might not be the only mechanism of accountability that leads to provision of public services and development. Chapter 1 pointed out that even if, relative to other regimes, competitive elections create incentives for good governance, the theoretical and empirical literature suggests that democratic institutions do not automatically eliminate the potential conflict of interest between voters and (elected) public policy makers. As later chapters will demonstrate, problems of information asymmetries or agenda manipulation mean that elections do not necessarily correct this divergence (see

Barro 1973; Besley 2006; Ferejohn 1990). As long as voters' potential for collective action is severely constrained by informational or institutional problems, democracies cannot do much to improve development outcomes. Elections by themselves are not sufficient for ensuring robust accountability. In fact, studies show an ambiguous empirical relationship between democracies and the redistribution of wealth and income, as well as between democracies and the provision of better public services for the majority of the population. This area of research deserves further attention.

We will now discuss forms of accountability under various types of nondemocratic political regimes, as well as the importance of institutional mechanisms in ensuring government responsiveness. First, a clarification is in order. Both democracy and authoritarianism are umbrella categories for many subtypes of institutions that generate their own incentives and obstacles to collective action. One-party regimes tend to rely heavily on coercion and ban other parties or political challengers. Authoritarianism includes a plethora of institutional arrangements, such as military regimes (which may or may not allow party competition), monarchies, partyless polities, theocracies, and hybrid regimes that combine elements from both democracies and autocracies and, in many cases, allow elections and limited multiparty competition.[6] We explore varieties of accountability in some of these institutions in the section that follows.

***Single-Party Regimes and Accountability.*** As a prominent extreme example of a one-party political arrangement, the classic Communist system adopted in the former Soviet Union and Eastern Europe was characterized by the fusion of the unique party apparatus and the state.[7] The window dressing of formal elections combined with repression or totalitarianism allowed only weak or nonexistent accountability mechanisms. Several factors underlie the lack (or weakness) of government accountability within this type of regime:

- Citizens can make no direct institutionalized appeal to government; the members of the legislature are often selected either directly by the bureaucracy or by citizens participating in elections that are usually neither free nor fair.
- State power is self-legitimized; because the officials are self-declared "permanent repositories of public good," accountability, by definition, is not an issue.[8]
- The majority of policies are designed by a small nucleus of party leaders, are often passed by decree, and relatively few even reach the compliant legislature.

- The principle of duplication of functions applies: a small number of party members execute the same de facto governing functions as the state bureaucracy. Therefore, there are no robust institutional checks and balances.
- The system, in general, lacks processes of routine policy contestation: the factions or party "wings" are usually purged, and the repressive mechanisms keep the civil society under tight control.

These obstacles do not automatically imply that there are no private or public spaces of dissent. In some contexts, local councils or municipal governments become vibrant forums of policy contestation; in others, selected policies are submitted for real debates in the national parliaments. Overall, however, single-party regimes have significantly fewer and weaker pockets of dissent and accountability than their democratic counterparts. Ordinary citizens have little or no recourse to public policies.

***Authoritarianism and Accountability.*** In authoritarian states, in general, because of the lack (or poor quality) of elections that would penalize rulers for reneging on policy promises or provision of public goods, there is little or no direct and institutionalized link of accountability between citizens and the government. Nevertheless, as we have already seen, with respect to certain development indicators, some countries that do not hold free and fair elections perform better than their democratic counterparts. Cuba, as noted, has better health outcomes than Chile or Costa Rica, and China has reached high literacy rates. What explains this pattern? According to political economists seeking to understand the mechanics of autocracies, some alternative modes of political accountability might give incentives to the executive to deliver public services (Ames 1987; Tullock 1987; Wintrobe 1998; Haber, Razo, and Maurer 2003; Bueno de Mesquita et al. 2003; Crystal 1989). These incentives derive from the following features:

- Institutional checks and balances
- Certain rules of selection and succession for the top echelon of political leaders
- Time horizon and survival considerations for the political leader
- Specific mechanisms through which autocratic politicians were able to commit to bureaucratic cadres that they will refrain from expropriation of investments (Gehlbach and Keefer 2011)
- Ruling-party institutionalization (Gehlbach and Keefer 2011)

- Political career incentives (that is, climbing up the hierarchy of the hegemonic political party might require demonstrating competency at the local or regional level)
- High capacity of monitoring and sanctioning bureaucratic behavior (for example, prohibitively high penalties for corruption, noncompliance, and the like).

However, these varieties of alternative accountability differ significantly from their democratic counterparts in both *domain* (accountability along a given dimension) and *scope* (accountability to whom). The spaces of public policy contestation are narrower in nondemocracies, and state repression is a disciplinary tool often used to block potential dissenters from effectively articulating sensitive political claims. Moreover, autocratic leaders face threats and must therefore be "more accountable" to a small subset of society that constitutes their coalition of support, not to the citizenry at large (Bueno de Mesquita et al. 2003; Haber 2006).

Testing this theoretical logic, some empirical studies have found a strong correlation between regime type and the delivery of public goods: accordingly, because political accountability is monitored and sanctioned through elections, democracies perform better overall than autocracies in delivering the policies and goods demanded by the vast majority of society (Bueno de Mesquita et al. 2003; Deacon and Saha 2006; Lake and Baum 2001; Acemoglu and Robinson 2006; Boix 2003; Meltzer and Richards 1981). On the other hand, other strands of research contradict these findings, arguing that dictatorships redistribute more than democracies (Wintrobe 1998), or that there simply is no systematic difference in fiscal or development policies across regime types (Cheibub 1998; Mulligan, Gil, and Sala-I-Martin 2004). Between 1990 and 2004, for example, there was no statistically significant difference between democracies and autocracies in total inflows of foreign direct investment (Gehlbach and Keefer 2011). Beyond the generic debate, increasing evidence indicates that in the nondemocratic regimes that perform well in economic growth and development outcomes, some form of institutional checks and balances has evolved (see Concepts in Practice 2.2 for an example of checks and balances in Iran). Over time, the credibility of commitment to some good policies on the side of the government has reduced graft opportunities and corruption.

In sum, accountability is an essential component of governance, whether a regime is autocratic or democratic. When mechanisms for accountability are missing from political institutions, corruption flourishes and growth and development stall. In the next section, we address the symptoms often present when accountability problems arise and persist.

CONCEPTS IN PRACTICE 2.2

## The Case of Budgetary Decisions in Iran

Iran's post-1979 constitution conferred political power on two different institutions: a directly elected president and the supreme leader who is not directly elected. The president formulates the yearly budget, and the *Majlis-e Shora-ye Islami* (the Islamic Consultative Council, or legislature) approves it. The supreme leader has large constitutional powers, ranging from control of *bonyads* (foundations that own many enterprises and that constitute a significant share of the economy) all the way to the right to guide general economic policies and supervise their implementation. In addition, two other bodies have significant powers in the legislative process. The Expediency Council mediates disputes between the Guardian Council and the Majlis, whereas the Guardian Council ensures the compatibility of proposed legislation with Islamic law and the constitution.

On many occasions, the interaction between these branches has highlighted effective mechanisms of alternative accountability and the existence of institutional checks and balances. In June 2002, for example, the Majlis decided to audit the Iranian broadcasting entity, based on an inquiry into its public procurement practices. The debate was blocked by the Guardian Council, which had invoked the fact that the broadcasting agency was under the direct jurisdiction of the supreme leader and that the Majlis did

not have full authority over it. The speaker of the Majlis pleaded the case in front of the supreme leader, arguing that, in the past, parliamentary commissions had conducted public audits of the broadcasting organization. He also asked for a revision of Article 198 of its Internal Affairs Code so that the Majlis could exercise its full audit authority. In the end, the Expediency Council revised the code and allowed the Majlis to exercise full audit authority on *all* state organizations, including those under the direct supervision of the supreme leader.

Another example relates to annual budget institutions in Iran. Since 1979, no budget had ever been contested. However, the Guardian Council rejected the draft of the 2002–03 budget draft ratified by the Majlis. As a result of the disagreement, the Expediency Council convened a meeting with the representatives of the Majlis, members of the Guardian Council, and members of the Budget Committee in the legislature to mediate the dispute in a timely manner. The Expediency Council ruled in favor of the Majlis with respect to some objections of the Guardian Council. Interestingly, out of the five areas of budget dispute, the one most closely related to economic development and growth (the provision of financial guarantees for foreign investors) was awarded to the legislature.

*Source:* World Bank (2005).

# Common Symptoms of Malfunctioning Institutions: Corruption and Its Relatives

One of the most common and detrimental signs of poor governance and lack of accountability in developing countries is corruption, or "the misuse of public office for private gain." The classic illicit transaction usually involves "(. . .) a bribe by a private citizen to a public official in return for some service that the official should either provide free of charge (. . .) or not provide at all." (Treisman 2007, 211–212).

First, it is important to understand what actions constitute corruption. In the context of a principal-agent relationship, corruption occurs when the agent (implementer) shirks the policy implementation tasks in exchange for a private gain, and the principal (boss) lacks either the will or the capacity to monitor or sanction deviant behavior. Some argue that corruption might also have different meanings in different cultural settings. For example, the density of tight solidarity networks in Africa compared to Europe has been put forward as a potential determinant of the social acceptability of corruption in Sub-Saharan Africa (de Sardan 1999). Beyond different potential meanings, corruption also occurs in various forms. One of its close relatives, political clientelism or patronage, is a prevalent phenomenon in many countries and has often been identified as an essential symptom of market failure and suboptimal development.

## Types of Corruption and Clientelism

Some political economists distinguish between different forms of corruption based on two criteria: (1) the scale on which it occurs; and (2) the content and systemic implications. "Low-level" corruption implies deliberate policy misimplementation for the extraction of private gains when the existing laws should normally sanction such behavior (based on Rose-Ackerman 1978, 1999, 53–54; 2006, xviii–xx). Three examples of low-level corruption follow:

- A public official solicits a bribe to tolerate a certain behavior that would otherwise be at odds with extant laws (for example, no traffic ticket in exchange for a small amount of money).
- The bureaucrat in charge of allocating a scarce public benefit selects the beneficiaries based on their capacity to pay an illegal fee (for example, an official in the ministry of education extracts bribes to award coveted scholarships).
- An official can make a certain public benefit appear scarce and take advantage of this distortion (for example, issuing driver's licenses or business registrations in exchange for a bribe).

"Grand" corruption implies a more systemic machinery of rent extraction involving both low- and top-level bureaucrats and politicians (Rose-

Ackerman 2006, xix–xx). For example, an entire branch of the state bureaucracy (such as the police or the judiciary) cooperates with leaders of organized crime organizations in exchange for generous bribes. Another instance of grand corruption is also reflected in the efforts of high-level politicians to extract rents from firms that want to use their influence to obtain government contracts.

Other typologies of corruption based on the systemic implications of the pathology distinguish among several forms of behavior: *administrative corruption, nepotism, state capture, prebendal predation,* and *kleptocracy.* Each is described below.

*Administrative corruption* consists of illegal payments and gifts to bureaucrats for a laxer policy implementation (Hellman, Jones, and Kaufmann 2000, 2). Commonly employed, this type of corruption is the "looking the other way" behavior of many regulatory agencies around the world in exchange for the favorable interpretations of laws and regulations. It occurs everywhere, but the scope of the problem and its probability of detection vary dramatically. For example, the U.S. Department of the Interior was sued for blocking auditors from pursuing US$30 million worth of oil royalties not paid by large petroleum companies operating in the Gulf of Mexico. Thousands of miles away, in the squatter settlement of Kibera, located in the outskirts of Nairobi, Kenya, small water providers pay significant bribes to the officials of the water utility for timely delivery and reasonable pricing. These bribes translate into higher prices for the customers of the water kiosks. The courts cannot do much to remedy administrative corruption in a squatter settlement that is excluded from the city water utility networks altogether (McPherson and MacSearraigh 2007).

*Bureaucratic nepotism,* another type of common governance problem, refers to favoritism, such as favors granted, contracts awarded, or appointments to office made by those in power, shown to narrowly targeted interests. This preferential treatment might or might not be related to clientelism or political patronage.

Another systemic type of corruption is *state capture,* defined as the influence of powerful economic interests "in the formation of laws, regulations, and policies" through the illegal provision of "private benefits for public officials" (Campos and Pradhan 2007, 3; Hellman, Jones, and Kaufmann 2000, 2). State capture can be conceptualized as "the privatization of public policy" in which large companies manipulate the rules of the game to their own advantage by providing illicit payments to politicians and bureaucrats (Hellman, Jones, and Kaufmann 2000, 2). Post-Communist Russia and Ukraine are classic examples of close ties between business oligarchs and the top echelons of the state.

*Prebendal predation* refers to a special form of state capture generated by state bureaucrats who, empowered by their official position and in the absence of state resources directly allocated to them, abusively extract their own discretionary rents directly from citizens (Englebert 2009; Joseph 1998). The term *prebendal* originated from the system of benefits granted to clergy by the Anglican Church. In a development context, it refers to bureaucratic agencies of failed states and individuals associated with them that extract as much as they can from the population, while never providing any public or private services in return. In many African countries throughout the 1980s and 1990s, despite poststructural adjustment fiscal austerity that significantly reduced the salaries of public officials, public employment steadily increased. Bureaucrats, organized in pyramidal prebends, were able to extract resources from officials occupying a lower hierarchical position. Going down the ladder, the lowest-placed officials abusively extracted bribes and illegal fees directly from citizens. In the 1990s, it is estimated that in Malawi, for example, up to one-third of the total collected revenue was "stolen" by civil servants. Similarly, artisanal gold miners in the Democratic Republic of Congo pay exorbitant random taxes and fees to government workers (see Concepts in Practice 2.3).

CONCEPTS IN PRACTICE 2.3

## Prebendalism and Artisanal Gold Mining in the Democratic Republic of Congo

Taxation or rent extraction through the exercise of sovereign authority, legal or not, is a typical prebendal behavior in many African countries. According to World Bank estimations, the "effective" tax rate that poor artisanal miners have to pay to many tiers of bureaucrats, army, and police approximates 60 percent in the Democratic Republic of Congo. In some of the gold mines of the Orientale Province, studies have identified 30 separate taxes and fees levied on gold miners, traders, and operators. For artisanal miners, these include buying mining permits, paying 20–30 percent of their production to mine operators, being taxed several times by multiple layers of officials, and putting aside a certain amount of money each week for payoffs to the army or police. Failing to pay subjects miners to administrative and police harassment. Similar practices have been documented in other DRC provinces such as Katanga and the Kivus.

*Sources:* Fahey (2008); Pole Institute (2007).

Finally, another type of grand corruption, *kleptocracy*, is known as the most extreme form of state capture, usually associated with highly personalistic rule. It implies that the control of the state is in the hands of a highly discretionary individual ruler or his or her small coalition of supporters, who use their political power to pocket a large part of society's resources (Acemoglu, Robinson, and Verdier 2004). There are many examples of heads of states and their close associates amassing large fortunes while in office. In response to the discovery of Swiss bank accounts in his name, Mobutu Sese Seko, the former president of Zaire, replied: "I would estimate my accounts total less than fifty million dollars. What is that for twenty-two years as head of state in such a big country?" (Borgenicht and Regan 2008, 116). Evidence shows that during the 1970s, around 15–20 percent of the operating state budget went directly to the Mobutu family's numerous bank accounts (Leslie 1987; Acemoglu, Robinson, and Verdier 2004).

In content, the broad concept of corruption is closely associated with related theoretical constructs such as *political clientelism*, or the exchange of material benefits for votes. However, despite the fact that corruption and clientelism overlap significantly, their relationship might be more complicated than initially thought. The conceptual territory, for example, of "noncorrupt" clientelism or "nonclientelistic" corruption is currently under theoretical scrutiny (Piattoni 2001; Keefer 2007; Kitschelt and Wilkinson 2007).

Political patronage or clientelism is a "transaction, or a direct exchange of a citizen's vote in return for concrete payments" (such as cash, consumption goods, food, clothes, or household appliances), "or for continuing access to employment, goods, and services" (such as public sector jobs, access to food or housing subsidies, or educational scholarships)[9] (Kitschelt and Wilkinson 2007, 2). This is one of the most pervasive intersections between skewed political incentives and underprovision of public services around the world.

A growing body of literature looks at the causes, manifestations, and effects of political patronage. What is its effect on voting patterns? Are some groups more susceptible than others to handouts at the expense of services? Is there always a trade-off between programmatic and clientelistic politics? Is clientelism independent of coercion, or do the two travel together? How does clientelism affect the provision of public goods and economic development? How do political parties or individual candidates monitor voters' behavior on election day? Do voters or citizens always correctly attribute the tangible goods received in exchange for their votes to the right party or tier of government? The answers to such questions are consequential for our understanding of the relationship among political patronage, accountability, and, ultimately, development. As previously suggested, in some circumstances, clientelism might just constitute a "second-best" alternative form of

**CONCEPTS IN PRACTICE 2.4**

## Clientelism, Ethnicity, and Gender in Benin

In a unique case set in Benin, the author of a study was able to randomize the messages of electoral candidates to voters during the first round of the March 2001 presidential election. In some villages, candidates running for office communicated to voters a broad public policy platform. They emphasized political issues related to national unity, eradication of corruption, poverty alleviation, and education reform, among many others. In other local communities, politicians used electoral appeals focused more narrowly on patronage jobs or financial support for local fishermen and cotton producers. This field experiment enabled the researcher to compare the effect of the two types of messages— programmatic (public good) messages and clientelistic (narrowly targeted goods) messages—on the electoral behavior of voters. The findings suggested that (1) keeping ethnic affiliation constant, clientelistic appeals were particularly effective when undertaken by incumbents or local politicians and (2) men were more likely than women to respond to clientelistic messages communicated by local candidates for office. The study found strong support for the hypothesis that clientelistic campaign messages affect individual voting behavior.

*Source:* Wantchekon (2003).

accountability and substitute for the void of general policy responsiveness of politicians to voters. In other cases, patronage might act as a de facto form of corruption and undermine robust electoral accountability. Concepts in Practice 2.4 examines clientelism and voting patterns in Benin.

In all their forms, severe clientelism and corruption can have devastating consequences for development and economic well-being. Occasionally, however, positive side effects emerge. Both negative and positive features are discussed below.

## Negative Consequences of Clientelism and Corruption

The most immediate consequences for economic development, social welfare, and government legitimacy are severe misallocation of public resources, budgetary distortions, expanding underground economies, and low state capacity for revenue extraction. Clientelism or patronage implies conditional relations between citizens and politicians. By definition, then, the poor who do not vote or support their patrons do not receive cash, water, electricity, access to public jobs, and the like.

Consider the impact of clientelism on traffic control in Dhaka, Bangladesh, for example. The traffic chaos generated by inefficient transportation scheduling and the poor condition of the 6,700 buses operating in the city have many negative effects: the high number of pedestrian accidents, deaths, general lack of safety, air pollution, delays, and so on. One traffic corridor alone has 50 percent of total buses operating on less than 30 percent of the total number of routes. Despite an extensive regulatory framework and stakeholder involvement, problems have persisted for a long time. The challenge seems technical at first glance: with better scheduling and newer buses, traffic could improve significantly. It turns out, though, that political patronage is a key part of the story. The Regional Transport Committee (RTC) is the public agency that grants route permits to bus owners. Political party leaders dominate bus owner associations, and they are represented in the RTC. Therefore, the RTC is the real hub of patronage distribution and has to allocate many more routes than technically feasible to satisfy multiple clients with political connections. Moreover, bus control is strategically important for political parties whenever they want to provide transportation for supporters to the sites of protests and demonstrations. As a consequence, all bus companies need political contacts even to obtain route allocations and scheduling favors. The result is severe overcrowding, increased pollution, and heightened risk of accidents (World Bank 2009).

In some cases, specific economic sectors or geographic locations are more prone to patron-client relations than others. The following example illustrates the intersection between reconstruction and political patronage in Malawi. In 2008, months before the parliamentary and presidential election, the Ndirande market in Malawi burned to the ground. Many small vendors lost all the booths and merchandise on which their livelihood depended. When similar incidents happened in other markets in the past, the reconstruction was relatively fast and efficient, with joint efforts of vendors and local officials. In contrast, in Ndirande, one year later, the first phase of reconstruction was not yet completed. Why?

The story starts many decades ago, during the nondemocratic period, when the single political party dominated the committee that regulated the market, coordinated vendors, and mediated disputes. At the time, there were no factions in the market-management institution. The advent of multiparty competition politicized the committee and splintered it into three sections, each one backed up by a party. What makes Ndirande special compared to other markets in Malawi is the overlap of ethnicity and political support. Because most vendors are ethnic Yao, Ndirande is the political fiefdom of one of the parties, the UDF, whose leader—a former president—is also Yao. The party leader himself, as well as other politicians, donated money to the market committee for reconstruction efforts. It so happens that during the reconstruction attempts, a competing party, the DPP, won the national elections and replaced the committee leadership. When vendors went to the office in charge of collecting and disbursing money, they were told that the donated amount was much lower than what was needed and that some of it was "borrowed" by an official. Feeling a sense of injustice, vendors went to the DPP office and set it on fire. In retaliation, the incumbent party significantly cut funds for reconstruction and delayed the whole process (Cammack 2011).

Obviously, corruption takes a heavy toll on development. Bribes, extortion, and unpredictability of costs act as a deadweight tax on businesses, NGOs, and other organizations that may generate wealth and the provision of desirable public goods. To the extent that corrupt officials do not use such bribes to pursue progrowth investment, corruption may reduce the rate of economic growth and modernization of a country. Therefore, it can have the effect of making a society worse off.

***Effects of Corruption on Resource Allocation.*** If public policy goals can be easily altered by the payment of bribes to policy makers, some individuals and organizations may devote resources to furthering their own agenda. Because small organized groups (for example, trade unions or business associations) are able to lobby more effectively than larger groups (the general public), corruption and rent seeking opportunities may facilitate the growth of special interest legislation and regulation. Such regulations are likely to impose costs on large groups but generate benefits for only a narrow subset of the population (those who can lobby) (Tullock 1987). For example, protectionist tariffs against foreign competitors may increase the profits of an industrial sector even if, in some circumstances, they condemn the general public and other business sectors to consuming more expensive or inferior domestic goods and services.

In addition, to the extent that corruption is a form of arbitrary decision making by government and bureaucrats, the increased uncertainty of doing business may result in the outflow of money or in less foreign direct investment in a country (Wei 2000).

Even if some countries have simultaneously experienced growth and corruption, they face higher economic risks than contexts in which corruption is not prevalent. Systemic corruption also undermines government legitimacy, efficiency, and equity. Sometimes it can lead to the reversal of the political regime, or it can consolidate forms of predatory nondemocratic rule (Rose-Ackerman 1997).

Finally, as political power is correlated with economic wealth, it may be the case that the existence of corruption further entrenches inequality, as

**FIGURE 2.4  The Link between per Capita Income and Corruption**

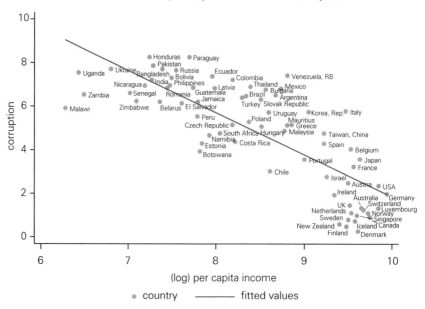

Source: Data from Persson and Tabellini (2003).
Note: Lower score = less corruption. The perceptions of corruption are an average score of Transparency International's Corruption Perceptions Index between 1995 and 2000. The per capita data is from the World Development Indicators (1993–1998).

the rich and politically powerful are able to protect themselves from the government (through bribes or political action), while more marginalized groups are less able to prevent the abuse of public office for private gain (Olson 1982). As seen in figure 2.4, corruption affects—negatively and significantly—the general level of economic development.[10]

## Can Corruption and Clientelism Have Some Positive Consequences?

The earlier literature on the causes and consequences of corruption argued that both low-level and grand corruption may play several political-economic roles in the functioning of developing states. The two types of corruption affect individuals and states in different ways.

*Small-scale corruption* might be a symptom of a state experiencing the inherent tensions of rapid modernization. In some contexts, corruption and clientelism are just the natural expression of social capital; they divert politi-

Understanding Policy Change

cal claims from the class-based Western-centric left-right axis to ethnic and tribal affiliations (Chabal and Daloz 1999; de Sardan 1999).

As for *large-scale corruption,* under some circumstances, its side effects were thought to lead to more resources for private investment, open up access to marginalized segments of the population, and compensate for the low level of tax revenues characteristic of many developing states (Leff 1964, Huntington 1968, Bayley 1966, for a brief review see Szeftel 1998, 227).

In some developing countries, certain forms of corruption might be a necessary compromise between the state and vested interests, guaranteeing opportunities for corruption in some sectors while gradually creating "pockets of efficiency" in others (see Nye 1967 for Asia; see Geddes 1996 for Latin America).

In other contexts characterized by complicated ethnic, clan, regional, and religious loyalties and by factionalism, political clientelism has been hypothesized to help the democratic process. In other words, rather than being the problem or cause of malfunctions, it could allow a second-best equilibrium through which patronage relations and concrete material benefits to selected groups prevent or impede polarization and open conflict (Szeftel 1998).

A more recent and related theoretical contribution (North, Wallis, and Weingast 2009) seeks to explain the relationship between rent seeking and political violence. According to this narrative, in some contexts there is a clear trade-off between a certain level of patronage (or corruption) and conflict, with the implication that suddenly dismantling these rents would have unintended consequences for political stability. In other words, the feasibility of reform is constrained by the probability that violence would erupt if key groups in society stopped receiving the benefits they are used to. In a vicious circle, however, these rents generate a low developmental equilibrium. In contrast, societies that have solved this dilemma allow economic and political competition and are more developed in general.

Nevertheless, the more recent research on the topic overwhelmingly converges toward the negative consequences of corruption: perverse political and economic incentives, lower levels of accountability, and derailed development.

Both analytically and practically, the conceptual angles from which policy makers view corruption and political clientelism have profound repercussions for reform trajectories. With few exceptions, the governance reform agendas focus heavily on the civil service and public financial management as classic areas for dismantling political rents. According to several researchers, however, understanding the root causes of the phenomena might lead to different context-tailored recommendations. For example, efforts to create more job opportunities in the private sector could be an effective alternative to combating corruption and clientelism in job-scarce environments where public sector employment is heavily politicized (Grindle 2007; Khan 2006).

In some sense, political-economy analysis gives the development practitioner both the feasible and the normative answer to such reform questions. "Second-best" solutions, or "good enough" governance, might be more sensible than textbook "first-best solutions" (Grindle 2007; Khan 2006; Rodrik 2008; Fritz, Kaiser, and Levy 2009).

## Why Is Corruption More Prevalent in Some Countries Than in Others?

To date, we have a number of cross-national indicators of corruption that allow researchers to distinguish among possible causes. Although subject to continuous debates in academic and policy circles, several explanations have been proposed for variation in corruption among countries (Shleifer and Vishny 1993; Lambsdorff 2006; Treisman 2000, 2007):

- Large size of government
- Low economic development
- Low openness to trade
- Heavy reliance on fuel exports
- Short or nonexistent history of democracy
- The absence of a vibrant media
- Heavy government regulations
- Federalism
- The type of colonial legacy.

## What Policy Interventions Have Governments Pursued to Reduce Corruption?

Although the menu of policy interventions is diverse and often the effect of specific policies on outcomes is far from clear, a few examples of reforms that governments have pursued to reduce corruption follow:

- Reform of civil servants' wages
- Investments in a free media
- Establishment of an independent judiciary
- Promotion of some degree of market competition through privatization
- Participation in international anticorruption conventions

- Establishment of independent anticorruption committees
- Adoption of effective oversight institutions.

As discussed in Concepts in Practice 2.5, some of these reforms were initiated as part of an approach called "new public management" (NPM) adopted with varying success by many governments around the world (Dunleavy et al. 2011).

## Summary

Accountability and governance are essential ingredients for durable development. This chapter disentangled the analytical mechanisms at work and suggested that different policy contexts may feature alternative forms of accountability. The second part of the chapter went into the details of corruption and political clientelism and patronage and their complex relationship to accountability and development. Finally, the chapter briefly summarized common policy solutions for tackling corruption.

## Notes

1. *Reliability* is used by Downs (1957); *responsibility* by Riker (1993); *representation* by Pitkin (1967); *responsiveness* by Dahl (1971); *mandate responsiveness* by Stokes (2001); *accountability* by Przeworski, Stokes, and Manin (1999); and *governance,* by Kaufmann, Kraay, and Zoido-Lobaton (1999).
2. This classic definition of political representation comes from Hannah Pitkin (1967). These concepts have a long and complicated intellectual history, but for the purposes of this exposition, it suffices to maintain some level of generality.
3. Needless to say, this example assumes a unidimensional (single issue) policy space and oversimplifies the electoral mechanism. It serves here as just an illustration.
4. This classification builds on Kitschelt (2000, 845–846).
5. The definition of *public good* versus *private and club goods* will be elaborated in chapter 3.
6. Typology based on Hadenius and Teorell (2007).
7. This section is based on Kornai (1992, 37–39).
8. Ibid, 56.
9. Adapted from the definition by Kitschelt and Wilkinson (2007, 2).
10. However, the relationship between corruption and economic development is complicated by the direction of causality: which causes which? Some empirical findings contradict the idea that corruption breeds low development and point at potential positive effects on the economy (Rose-Ackerman 2006).

## References

Acemoglu, D., and J. A. Robinson. 2006. *Economic Origins of Dictatorship and Democracy.* Cambridge, MA: Cambridge University Press.

Acemoglu, Daron, James Robinson, and Thierry Verdier. 2004. "Kleptocracy and Divide-and-Rule: A Model of Personal Rule." *Journal of the European Economic Association* 2 (2/3): 162–92.

Ames, Barry. 1987. *Political Survival: Politicians and Public Policy in Latin America.* Berkeley: University of California Press.

Barro, R. J. 1973. "The Control of Politicians: An Economic Model." *Public Choice* 14 (1): 19–42.

Bayley, David H. 1966. "The Effects of Corruption in a Developing Nation." *Western Political Quarterly* 19 (4): 719-32.

Besley, T. 2006. *Principled Agents? The Political Economy of Good Government.* New York: Oxford University Press.

Boix, Carles. 2003. *Democracy and Redistribution.* Cambridge: Cambridge University Press.

Borgenicht, D., and T. Regan. 2008. *Worst-Case Scenario Almanac Politics*. San Francisco: Chronicle Books Llc.

Bueno de Mesquita, Bruce, Alastair Smith, Randolph M. Siverson, and James D. Morrow. 2003. *The Logic of Political Survival*. Cambridge: MIT Press.

Cammack, Diana. 2011. "Local Governance and Public Goods in Malawi." *IDS Bulletin* 42 (2): 43–52.

Campos, Jose E., and Sanjay Pradhan. 2007. *The Many Faces of Corruption: Tracking Vulnerabilities at the Sector Level*. Washington, DC: World Bank.

Chabal, Patrick, and Jean-Pascal Daloz. 1999. *Africa Works: The Political Instrumentalization of Disorder*. Oxford: James Currey; Bloomington: Indiana University Press.

Cheibub, J. A. 1998. "Political Regimes and the Extractive Capacity of Governments: Taxation in Democracies and Dictatorships." *World Politics* 50 (3): 349–76.

Crystal, Jill. 1989. "Coalitions in Oil Monarchies: Kuwait and Qatar." *Comparative Politics* 21 (4): 427–43.

Dahl, Robert A. 1971. *Polyarchy: Participation and Opposition*, vol. 54. New Haven: Yale University Press.

Deacon, R. T., and S. Saha. 2006. "Public Goods Provision under Dictatorship and Democracy: A Survey." In *The Companion in Public Economics: Empirical Public Economics,* ed. A. F. Ott and R. J. Cebula, chap. 6. Northampton, MA: Edward Elgar Publishing.

Downs, Anthony. 1957. *An Economic Theory of Democracy*. New York: Harper.

Dunleavy, P., H. Margetts, S. Bastow, and J. Tinker, 2006. "New Public Management is Dead—Long Live Digital Era Governance." *Journal of Public Administration Research, and Theory* 16 (3): 467–494

Englebert, Pierre. 2009. *Africa: Unity, Sovereignty, and Sorrow*. Boulder, CO: Lynne Rienner Publishers.

Fahey, Dan. 2008. "Le Fleuve D'Or: The Production and Trade of Gold from Mongbwalu, DRC." In *L'Afrique des Grands Lacs, Annuaire 2007–2008*, ed. S. Marysse, F. Reyntens, and S. Vandeginste. Paris: L'Harmattan.

Ferejohn, John A., and James H. Kuklinski. 1990. *Information and Democratic Processes*. Champaign: University of Illinois Press.

Fritz, V., K. Kaiser, and B. Levy. 2009. *Problem-Driven Governance and Political Economy Analysis*. Washington, DC: World Bank.

Geddes, Barbara. 1996. *Politician's Dilemma: Building State Capacity in Latin America*. Berkeley, CA: University of California Press.

Gehlbach, Scott, and Philip Keefer. 2011. "Investment without Democracy: Ruling-Party Institutionalization and Credible Commitment in Autocracies." *Journal of Comparative Economics* 39 (2): 123–39.

Grindle, M. S. 2007. *Going Local: Decentralization, Democratization, and the Promise of Good Governance*. Princeton, NJ: Princeton University Press.

Haber, S. H., A. Razo, and N. Maurer. 2003. *The Politics of Property Rights: Political Instability, Credible Commitments, and Economic Growth in Mexico, 1876–1929*. New York: Cambridge University Press.

Hadenius, A., and J. Teorell. 2007. "Pathways from Authoritarianism." *Journal of Democracy* 18 (1): 143.

Hellman, J. S., G. Jones, and D. Kaufmann. 2000. "Seize the State, Seize the Day: State Capture, Corruption, and Influence in Transition." Policy Research Working Paper 2444, World Bank, Washington, DC.

Huntington, Samuel P. 1968. *Political Order in Changing Societies*. New Haven: Yale University Press.

Joseph, R. 1998. "Africa, 1990–1997: From Abertura to Closure." *Journal of Democracy* 9: 3–17.

Kaufmann, D., A. Kraay, and P. Zoido-Lobatón. 1999. "Aggregating Governance Indicators." Working Paper 2195, World Bank, Washington, DC.

Keefer, Philip. 2007. "Clientelism, Credibility, and the Policy Choices of Young Democracies." *American Journal of Political Science* 51 (4): 804–21.

Khan, Mushtaq. 2006. "Determinants of Corruption in Developing Countries: The Limits of Conventional Economic Analysis." *International Handbook on the Economics of Corruption,* ed. Susan Rose-Ackerman, 216–44. Northampton, MA: Edward Elgar Publisher.

Kitschelt, H. 2000. "Linkages between Citizens and Politicians in Democratic Polities." *Comparative Political Studies* 33 (6/7): 845–79.

Kitschelt, Herbert, Kent Freeze, Kiril Kolev, and Yi-Ting Wang. 2009. "Measuring Democratic Accountability: An Initial Report on an Emerging Data Set." *Revista de Ciencia Política* 29 (3): 741–73.

Kitschelt, H., and S. Wilkinson. 2007. *Patrons, Clients, and Policies: Patterns of Democratic Accountability and Political Competition*. New York: Cambridge University Press.

Knack, S. 2007. "Measuring Corruption: A Critique of Indicators in Eastern Europe and Central Asia." *Journal of Public Policy* 27: 255–291

Kornai, Janos. 1992. *The Socialist System: The Political Economy of Communism*. New York: Oxford University Press.

Lake, D. A., and M. A. Baum. 2001. "The Invisible Hand of Democracy." *Comparative Political Studies* 34 (6): 587.

Lambsdorff, J. G. 2006. "Causes and Consequences of Corruption: What Do We Know from a Cross-Section of Countries?" In *International Handbook on the Economics of Corruption,* ed. Susan Rose-Ackerman, 3–52. Northampton, MA: Edward Elgar Publisher.

Leff, N. H. 1964. "Economic Development through Bureaucratic Corruption." *American Behavioral Scientist* 8 (3): 8.

Leslie, Winsome J. 1987. *The World Bank and Structural Transformation in Developing Countries: The Case of Zaire*. Boulder, CO: L. Rienner Publishers.

Manning, Nick. 2001. "The Legacy of New Public Management in Developing Countries." *International Review of Administrative Sciences* 67 (2): 297–312.

McPherson, Charles, and Stephen MacSearraigh. 2007. "Corruption in the Petroleum Sector." In *The Many Faces of Corruption. Tracking Vulnerabilities at the Sector Level,* ed. Jose E. Campos and Sanjay Pradhan, 191–221. Washington, DC: World Bank.

Meltzer, Allan H., and Scott F. Richards. 1981. "A Rational Theory of the Size of Government." *Journal of Political Economy* 89 (5): 914–27.

Mulligan, C. B., R. Gil, and Xavier Sala-I-Martin. 2004. "Do Democracies Have Different Public Policies Than Nondemocracies?" *Journal of Economic Perspectives* 18 (1): 51–74.

North, Douglass, John Wallis, and Barry Weingast. 2009. *Violence and Social Orders.* New York: Cambridge University Press.

Nye, Joseph. 1967. "Corruption and Political Development: A Cost-Benefit Analysis." *American Political Science Review* 61 (2): 417–27.

Olson, M. 1982. *The Rise and Decline of Nations: Economic Growth, Stagflation, and Social Rigidities.* New Haven: Yale University Press.

Persson, T., G. E. Tabellini, and I. Brocas. 2000. *Political Economics.* Cambridge, MA: MIT Press.

Piattoni, S. 2001. *Clientelism, Interests, and Democratic Representation: The European Experience in Historical and Comparative Perspective.* New York: Cambridge University Press.

Pitkin, Hanna F. 1967. *The Concept of Representation.* Berkeley: University of California Press.

Pole Institute. 2007. *Rules for Sale: Formal and Informal Cross-Border Trade in Eastern DRC.* Goma: Pole Institute.

Przeworski, Adam, Susan C. Stokes, and Bernard Manin, eds. 1999. *Democracy, Accountability, and Representation,* vol. 2. New York: Cambridge University Press.

Riker, William H. 1993. *Agenda Formation.* Ann Arbor: University of Michigan Press.

Rodrik, Dani. 2008. "Second-Best Institutions." NBER Working Paper 14050, National Bureau of Economic Research, Cambridge, MA.

Rose-Ackerman, Susan. 1978. *Corruption: A Study in Political Economy.* New York: Academic Press.

———. 1997. "The Political Economy of Corruption." In *Corruption and the Global Economy,* ed. Kimberly Ann Elliott, chap. 2. Washington, DC: Institute for International Economics.

———. 1999. *Corruption and Government: Causes, Consequences and Reform.* Cambridge: Cambridge University Press.

———. 2006. *International Handbook on the Economics of Corruption.* Northampton, MA: Edward Elgar Publishing.

Sen, Amartya K. 1999. *Development as Freedom.* New York: Oxford University Press.

Shleifer, Andrei, and Robert Vishny. 1993. "Corruption." *Quarterly Journal of Economics* 108 (3): 599–617.

Stokes, Susan. 2001. *Mandates and Democracy. Neoliberalism by Surprise in Latin America.* Cambridge: Cambridge University Press.

———. 2007. "Political Clientelism." In *The Oxford Handbook of Comparative Politics,* ed. Carles Boix and Susan Stokes, 604–27. New York: Oxford University Press.

Szeftel, Morris. 1998. "Misunderstanding African Politics: Corruption and the Governance Agenda." *Review of African Political Economy* 76: 221–40.

Transparency International. 2012. *Corruption Perceptions Index*. http://www.transparency.org/.

Treisman, D. 2000. "The Causes of Corruption: A Cross-National Study." *Journal of Public Economics* 76 (3): 399–458.

———. 2007. "What Have We Learned about the Causes of Corruption from Ten Years of Cross-National Empirical Research?" *Annual Review of Political Science* 10 (1): 211–44.

Tullock, Gordon 1987. "Public Choice." In *The New Palgrave: A Dictionary of Economics* 1040–44, 3 vols. New York: Palgrave MacMillan.

Wantchekon, L. 2003. "Clientelism and Voting Behavior: Evidence from a Field Experiment in Benin." *World Politics* 55 (3): 399–422.

Wei, Shang-Jin. 2000. "How Taxing Is Corruption on International Investors?" *Review of Economics and Statistics* 82 (1): 1–11.

Wintrobe, Ronald. 1998. *The Political Economy of Dictatorship*. Cambridge: Cambridge University Press.

World Bank. 2004. *World Development Report 2004: Making Services Work for Poor People*. Washington, DC: World Bank.

———. 2005. "The Islamic Republic of Iran. Report on Public Financial Management, Procurement, and Expenditure Systems in Iran." Washington, DC: World Bank.

———. 2009. "Operationalizing Political Economy: Urban Bus Operations in Dhaka." *South Asia Political Economy and Governance Notes* 1: 1–8.

———. 2012. *World Development Indicators*. www.worldbank.org.

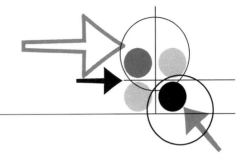

# CHAPTER 3

# The Collective Action Problem in Development: The *Why* Question

Chapter 2 explored the most common manifestations of development failure: corruption, patronage, state capture, and the like. Missing or weak accountability relations among citizens, politicians, and bureaucrats skew incentives, allow abuses of power, and lock in suboptimal outcomes. In this chapter, we start asking *why* accountability fails and poor governance thrives. Why do citizens not act together to challenge their nonperforming representatives? Why are some interest groups effectively shaping policy, while the poor can rarely act collectively to claim public goods? Why do some groups mobilize despite all odds of success, challenge corrupt governments, and take up ambitious pro-development reforms?

Once the practitioner or reformer has diagnosed the specific development problem or the answer to the *what* question discussed in the previous chapter, joint action of various actors is necessary in many cases to correct it. In legislatures, party coalitions are often needed to form governments or to pass reform bills. Broad platforms of civil society organizations are sometimes the solution for reaching a well-functioning social accountability relation between citizens and bureaucrats. Popular protests against corrupt politicians or governments come to life because of individuals and organizations that invest significant resources and efforts in shaping social movements.

In some circumstances, the poor obtain favorable outcomes when they vote for political parties committed to bringing development to their constituencies. Referred to as *collective action*, this act of coming together can introduce a host of challenges. If the expected costs of political action are high or if they fall exclusively on a small group of entrepreneurs—whereas the benefits of policy change are equally distributed among actors—reform might never be initiated. Mobilizing relevant stakeholders, building coalitions, and making claims for policy change require time and dedication and can entail considerable political, financial, and fiduciary risks. The case study in appendix C will take the reader through all the trials and tribulations along the path of a real reform in the Philippines.

This chapter first introduces the major social dilemmas that citizens and groups face whenever they have to act together for a better development outcome. Going up a level of abstraction, we explore the concept of public goods. In a very broad sense, public goods are the final development goals for which actors and stakeholders have to come together in the first place and from which all of them benefit. The chapter then explores how different groups in society might be more or less able to overcome pro-development collective action problems and discusses the possible implications for policy making (see figure 3.1).

**FIGURE 3.1 Conceptual Map of Collective Action Problems**

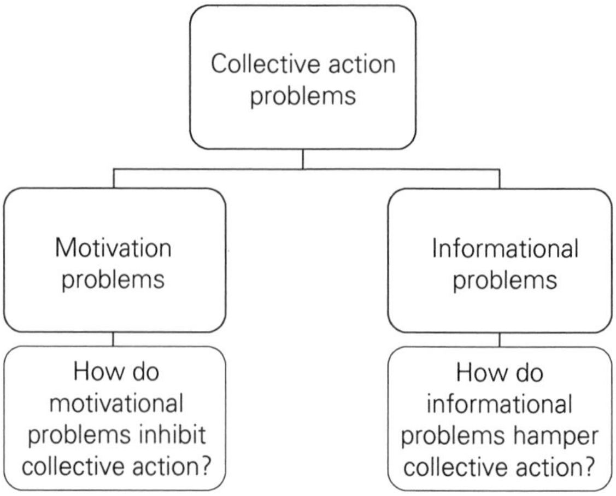

*Source:* Authors.

## Objectives of Chapter 3

By the end of this chapter, readers should be able to do the following:

- Grasp the concept and typology of private, public, and club goods and how they relate to development
- Understand why social dilemmas occur in development with respect to the production and maintenance of public goods or common-pool resources
- Explore the implications of collective action problems
- Think about some concrete factors that may facilitate or inhibit collective action
- Be familiar with major modes of collective action
- Link collective action obstacles to real-life situations.

## Collective Action Problems: At the Heart of Development

The title of this section paraphrases Elinor Ostrom, the recent Nobel Prize winner in economics, who argues that collective action is the answer to the *why* question (Ostrom 2010). Development deals primarily with the production of public goods, ranging from provision of basic water and electricity to the release of information about the way governments raise taxes and allocate spending to their constituents. Individuals and organizations often face several *social dilemmas* whenever the time to join forces and act together comes. These dilemmas refer to the mismatch between individual and group incentives to participate in the production of a public good. The logic is quite straightforward: if someone else incurs the costs of pro-development action while I derive full benefits, why would I contribute in the first place? Therefore, the individual's incentives not to pay the costs but to reap the benefits turn out to undermine the general interest of the group. Consequently, development efforts are often derailed by short-term self-interest that prevents reform from reaching ultimate outcomes. For instance, if citizens cannot act collectively to sanction corruption and abuses of political power, relationships of accountability fail, and distribution of public goods such as basic education and health suffers. In contrast, at the local or national level, effective collective action, through which actors articulate claims for public goods and monitor implementation, often translates into better development outcomes. Motivation is not the only source of social dilemmas. Large discrepancies in the information available to citizens, voters, or stakeholders make coordination and alignment of individual and group incentives hard to achieve.

**FIGURE 3.2 Impact of Individual and Collective Incentives on a Public Good**

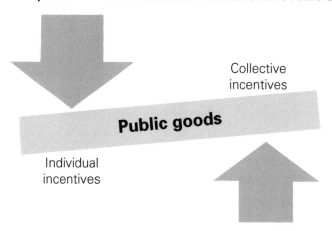

*Source:* Authors.

Figure 3.2 illustrates the impact of the two sets of incentives (individual and collective) on the production of a public good or the maintenance of a common-pool resource. Individual incentives resulting from short-term self-interest tend to undermine development, whereas collective (or group) incentives to act together lead to a superior outcome. This mismatch (or misalignment) between *individual* and *collective* incentives is the central *social dilemma* that hampers efforts to act jointly for the common good.

To allow for a better understanding of such a mismatch and its consequences on development, this chapter will introduce in greater detail the key concepts of public goods and social dilemmas and will present some of the factors that exacerbate or inhibit collective action problems.

## What Are Public Goods?

The term *public goods* refers to goods and services that simultaneously meet the following criteria:

- They are *nonrivalrous,* meaning that one individual's consumption of the good does not reduce the quantity or quality of that good or service for other participants in its consumption.
- They are *nonexcludable,* meaning that individuals cannot be stopped from consuming the good, even if they pay nothing toward the cost of providing the good.

**TABLE 3.1 Goods Quadrant—Public Goods versus Club (toll) Goods, Common-Pool Resources, and Private Goods**

| Difficulty of excluding potential beneficiaries | Rivalry of use | |
|---|---|---|
| | **High** | **Low** |
| High | *Common-pool resources or common goods:* for example, lakes, irrigation systems, fisheries, forests, annual budgets, intergovernmental fiscal transfers in federal systems | *Public goods:* for example, peace and security of a community, public safety, national defense, knowledge, fire protection, air, government transparency, corruption reduction or eradication |
| Low | *Private goods:* for example, food, clothing, general consumption goods | *Club (toll) goods:* for example, theaters, private clubs, day-care centers |

*Source:* Adapted from Ostrom (2005, 24). Ostrom Elinor. *Understanding Institutional Diversity.* 2005 © by Princeton University Press. Reprinted by permission of Princeton University Press.

- The pure public goods are also *nonexhaustible,* meaning that the good cannot be depleted by consumption (Samuelson 1954). Examples of pure public goods are air, natural landscapes, and national defense.

Goods or services that do not meet at least the first two characteristics listed above are called private goods, meaning either that their consumption is competitive or that only those who pay can consume them. Table 3.1 introduces a typology of goods based on two dimensions: *excludability of use* (can members prevent noncontributors from access to the good or service?) and *rivalry or subtractability of use* (if some users participate in the unrestrained consumption of the good, will this diminish other users' consumption?) (Ostrom 2005).

Most goods and services, however, are never purely public or private but fall somewhere in between. If group members who contributed to the production of the goods have the power to exclude noncontributors from using the goods or services, these are often labeled *club goods.* Sometimes, club goods are provided on a large social scale and resemble public goods. Other times, the club size is so small that they are de facto private goods.

Diagnosing the development problem implies thinking first about the good to be produced or maintained and its nature. It is well worth keeping in mind that the good or service may constitute a variety of tangible or intangible outcomes (national defense, water, electricity, information provided by governments to citizens, knowledge, popular protests demanding greater accountability, and so on). In chapter 1, we briefly discussed the difference between INSTITUTIONS (with capital letters) and institutions (lower-cased) (Banerjee and Duflo 2011). To paraphrase the authors, we could also think of PUBLIC GOODS that fulfill the conditions above. They are the broadest and most general examples of nonexcludability, nonrivalry, and nonexhaustibility of use that all of us recognize. This type includes the following:

- Clean air
- Universal primary education
- Universal health care
- National defense
- Knowledge
- Transparency of government
- Corruption-free bureaucracy
- Economic growth
- Development.

In the broadest possible sense, economic growth and development are public goods. Therefore, pro-development policy reforms require concerted action and the coordination of many different actors. Their effects are beneficial over the medium or long term for all participants, even if they entail short-term costs.

In some cases, policy goals and outcomes that intuitively resemble public goods still generate competitive or excludable behavior among participants. For example, in its pure state, universal primary education is often designed as a public good. However, school location, staffing policies, or delays in teachers' salaries make it de facto a club good, since certain constituencies who lack access to schools are excluded from its benefits. If school building and staffing occur only in areas of the country that provide political support for the incumbent party, other regions or localities will be deprived of access to education. Similarly, national defense is a public good since everyone benefits from security, but some actors—for example, government contractors—derive substantial private benefits from it (Aranson and Ordeshook 1985; Bueno de Mesquita et al. 2002). Often, if not always, public policies are mixtures of private and public goods.

As an analytical starter, the following questions might be useful:

- What is the good to be produced or maintained?
- Who are the producers of the good?
- Who benefits from the consumption of the good?
- How does it score on the three dimensions: *nonrivalrous, nonexcludable,* and *nonexhaustible?*
- Is the good or service private, public, or club?
- What are the costs and benefits of public good production or common-pool resource maintenance?

- Are they concentrated (incurred by a narrow subgroup only) or diffused (spread out widely in the group or population at large)?

Diagnosing development problems implies clarifying first the *what* of reform. The answers to this question can take many forms and shapes, including underproduction of the public good or inadequate maintenance of a common-pool resource. Once we grasp *what* exactly is being underproduced or undermaintained, we can then analytically move to understanding the *individual* and *group incentives* surrounding the good or service.

## What Factors Inhibit Collective Action?

Two general categories of factors lead to the collective action problem or to the difficulty groups have in mobilizing effectively for policy change. First are *motivational problems:* if somebody else can provide the public good without contributions from those who will benefit, there is always the temptation to free ride. Free riding means participating in the consumption but not in the production of the good. Second are *information problems,* meaning either that groups lack crucial information or that one group of stakeholders derives power from having more information than others (Ostrom 2010; Gibson et al. 2005).

### Motivational Problems and the Temptation to Free Ride

The incentive to free ride—or, simply put, to reap benefits without incurring costs—occurs for a variety of reasons. In some circumstances, as rational choice theory would predict, it is a simple matter of individual morality. In such situations, the free rider is a typical case of noncompliance with the rules of the group or other community norms. In other cases, however, even if individuals (or groups) are willing to participate in the production of public goods, they might not have the necessary resources to do so. For example, the poor can rarely afford to make the initial individual investment that a public good requires, irrespective of their rational calculations, incentives, or sense of morality (McKean 2000). Not paying water fees, for example, could mean either classic free riding or the inability of individual water users to afford the fee.

Collective action, or the act of mobilizing stakeholder groups to produce or maintain a good, is also challenging because it entails additional types of investments: pooling of costs and pooling of preferences. The former suffers from the inherent free-rider incentives just discussed. The latter dimension implies that, in addition to the individual motivation to contribute or not to the collective efforts, the way in which all preferences of actors get aggregated to produce policy outcomes can obstruct or promote certain modes of collective action. Preference aggregation depends not only on resources but also on the similarity of views and goals, as well as on information available to groups and individuals in society. Often, the poor fail to mobilize and effectively claim public goods precisely because they lack information about other groups that might have common interests. In addition, poverty—understood as the number of people whose income is lower than a given threshold—is in continuous flux. Some poor households, neighborhoods, or generations manage to escape it; others fall into it despite not being born poor (Krishna 2010). These differences in social mobility across groups and individuals sometimes induce significant heterogeneity of policy interests and goals, lack of cohesion, and overall disincentives to act jointly for specific policy outcomes. In other contexts, even if collective action happens and groups of actors decide to pursue reform together, divergent views with respect to either final policy goals or the very process of reaching them can easily dismantle coalitions. As we will see in the next chapter, institutions arise to solve collective action problems (albeit not always pro-development collective action) and to facilitate cost and preference pooling.

Let us briefly unpack the two categories of collective action problems. Motivational problems usually stem from a high individual ratio of costs to benefits induced by the size and heterogeneity of the group trying to mobilize (Olson 1965, 48 for the first three categories):

- The larger the group, the smaller the fraction is of the total benefit an individual receives from cooperating.
- The larger the group, the less likely it is that some subgroups in society will mobilize to obtain the public good, given the ratio of costs to benefits they would incur.
- The larger the group, the greater are the organizational costs (in the absence of coercion or other incentives from third parties).
- The more heterogeneous the assets, preferences, information, stakes, or identity of the participants, the less likely it is that collective action will be successful. For example, the poor and the rich, or members of different ethnic groups, more often than not fail to cooperate in reaching policy goals that might be beneficial to all.

As a result, large numbers of the poor or diffuse citizens are less likely to solve their collective action problems than, say, corporate interest groups. The discrepancy is indeed at the very heart of development, as it leads to skewed outcomes.

## Information Problems

Information problems, in contrast, plague groups of all sizes. *Information asymmetries* occur when an actor has information that others do not have. In this context, stakeholders who know more tend to have significant bargaining advantages over other groups and, hence, have high stakes in conserving such discrepancies. Voters often lack basic information about the electoral process, rules, procedures, political candidates, and policy options. Low turnout generated by missing information prevents groups from electing the candidate or party that would best represent them in legislatures and is thus a manifestation of a collective action problem. Opaqueness of budgetary processes and general lack of transparency about government activities impede the coordination of civil society or opposition groups around policy issues that could trigger greater accountability. A later chapter is dedicated entirely to informational constraints in policy change.

In addition to missing information, *moral hazard* and *adverse selection,* two special cases of information asymmetries that will be elaborated in chapter 7, can be serious obstacles to collective action. Moral hazard refers to a situation in which the better-informed individuals or actors engage in risky actions for an organization or collective precisely because they do not bear the full costs of such actions. Leaders of political parties, social movements, or reform teams do not always know enough about the real incentives and stakes of the rank and file within their group. This lack of information about the true actions of the members of an organization often does not allow leaders to adequately monitor commitment to the movement or party. For example, in many countries legislators may win an election because of their association with a party with a reputation for competency, prudence, and the like. However, if after the election such legislators can support risky bills and easily change political parties for opportunistic reasons, without penalty or negative career consequences, the collective action capacity of parties to pursue policies in parliaments is greatly reduced, and volatility increases.

Adverse selection refers to circumstances in which, for example, the leaders of organizations or coalitions have no way of properly assessing their new recruits' or members' true degree of individual commitment to the organizational goals. In cases of adverse selection, the actors who lack ideological or organizational commitment are also paradoxically more likely to join. For example, if a civil society organization offers concrete material benefits to all the new recruits to a citizen group advocating social accountability, as opposed to only the ones who prove commitment, it might attract members who are not interested in collective action per se and greater accountability but rather in the short-term tangible handouts. In this case,

adverse selection during recruitment may attract high numbers of participants with low true commitment to collective action.

Acquiring the necessary information to act collectively is costly. Political
parties, for example, reduce significantly the voters' cost of collecting information about policy platforms and electoral candidates, as well as the
politicians' costs of disseminating information to voters during campaigns
(Aldrich 1995; Kitschelt 2007, 525). Imagine a world without parties: individual politicians would have to bear the entire informational costs of campaigns during the process of running for office, and individual voters would
have to gather information on all candidates' policy positions, with very limited or nonexistent prior knowledge of them. In this sense, parties solve informational and coordination problems and thus facilitate collective action.
Papua New Guinea is one of the very few countries that has democratic competition without political parties.

## Social Dilemmas of Delivering Public Goods

Political economists commonly use three closely related models to demonstrate the social dilemmas of cooperation between individuals and groups in
society for achieving the delivery of public goods: *the prisoner's dilemma, the
tragedy of the commons, and the so-called logic of collective action.* Think of
these models as metaphors for human interaction. They are short parables
that illustrate the strategic reasons underpinning an important puzzle: why
cooperation for public goods and development does not occur even when it
is clear that it would make everybody better off. In fact, we play varieties of
the prisoner's dilemma game, and we face tragedy-of-the-commons challenges in our daily lives: in the family, at work, and in social settings. In large
communities, these problems only get worse—especially in the absence of
institutions that can correct for misaligned incentives.

### Prisoner's Dilemma

The prisoner's dilemma refers to a situation in which actors achieve suboptimal outcomes because they distrust each other in a strategic environment.
The exercise of the next chapter will explain in greater detail why prisoners
are the main characters of the story. A basic setup for a two-player prisoner's
dilemma game demonstrates that in the absence of institutions that can shift
the equilibrium, two individual actors decide not to cooperate to produce
the good that would have benefited them both collectively. The prisoner's
dilemma is an often-used analytical model that helps us understand why in-

dividuals or groups do not cooperate in the realization of optimal development or reform outcomes (producing or maintaining the good). The Game Theory 3.1 exercise following this chapter demonstrates how this concept applies to a community of farmers deciding to cooperate on joint irrigation work. Despite the fact that contributing to the building of an irrigation system would have benefited both farmers, neither of them trusts that the other will want to incur costs while she could just reap benefits, and the system is never built. This behavioral deadlock is especially prevalent in cases in which there have been no previous interactions or trust-building mechanisms developed between the two farmers. Additionally, large perceived differences among potential cooperators may induce a focus on dissimilarities rather than a search for common grounds. For instance, to give a real world example, in Tamil Nadu, India, and Guanajuato, Mexico, farmers who belonged to irrigation organizations were significantly more likely to cooperate for water conservation if they perceived each other as equals in landholding and social status (Bardhan and Dayton-Johnson 2007, 123).

## Tragedy of the Commons

The tragedy of the commons is a multiplayer prisoner's dilemma and illustrates a scenario in which many actors attempt to maximize their *individual* consumption of the good. However, by doing so *collectively*, they deplete or exhaust the good, with negative results for everyone. The tragedy of the commons usually plagues the use and maintenance of common-pool resources as diverse as the environment; forests, lakes, and open land; fish and wildlife; budgetary processes in parliaments; and intergovernmental fiscal arrangements in federal or decentralized systems. As an explanatory tool and diagnostic, the tragedy of the commons is particularly useful in cases in which the long-term *maintenance* rather than the production of the good is at stake.

We use the management of fisheries to illustrate this collective action problem. Many local communities around the globe depend on fishing for their livelihood. Individual fishermen have incentives to overuse resources. If they fail to cooperate by setting and enforcing consumption ceilings, they reduce the overall population of fish. For example, in Bodrum, Turkey, and in the Bay of Izmir several obstacles impeded such cooperation in the 1980s: overcrowding, quick gain from fishing, high demand associated with the tourism industry, and, above all, the lack of a viable institution that would mediate conflict between competing groups. In Bodrum, for example, the rules that prevented overfishing were not enforced by the Ministry of Agriculture. In addition, the time horizons and stakes of the fishermen groups were too large and too heterogeneous. Because they could not mobilize to enforce compliance with fishing rules, the result was a depletion of fish and an overall decline in the industry. By contrast, the Alanya community found innovative ways to solve its collective action problem. How? In the 1970s, the fish population reached low levels, and violent conflicts among local fishermen erupted. Therefore, a local co-op experimented with a trial-and-error system of allocating fishing licenses and monitoring compliance. Every year, the lists of fishing sites were endorsed by all individual fishermen and stored with the local mayor and police. Second, a lottery decided on the assignment of fishermen to a specific site. Third, to provide equal access to the most productive fishing sites, between September and January each fisherman had to move east each day and rotate the lot. This local arrangement managed to mediate disputes, enforce norms of fairness, prevent overcrowding, and optimize the capabilities of each site (Ostrom 1990, 19, 144–146).

### The Logic of Collective Action in Small and Large Groups

The logic of collective action[1] alludes to a similar mismatch between individual and collective incentives and explains theoretically why large groups in society lack effectiveness and power when they attempt to mobilize politically. According to this logic, group effectiveness relies on members' assessment that sufficient individual gain will come to them through participation or that free riders (those who do not share the cost of producing the good) will not receive the same level of benefits: that is, for collective action to succeed, the gains that result from collectively advocating for a policy outcome must significantly exceed the costs of mobilization.

This misalignment of individual and group incentives means that only certain groups that derive high individual benefits with lower administrative costs of mobilization (business lobbies, for example) are likely to mobilize successfully and pursue favorable outcomes. In contrast, diffuse groups of citizens affected by development policies or reform are less likely to mobilize. Hence, the power, resources, and intensity of the actors' preferences will be severely unbalanced. As a consequence, the final outcome may be skewed toward groups that can effectively solve collective action problems.

The electric power sector in India provides an example (Lal 2006). It is estimated that up to three-fourths of poor Indian households, especially in the rural areas, lack access to electric power. What are the observable causes? The public sector owns 90 percent of electricity production, is politically captured, and is plagued by severe rent seeking and corruption. Regressive subsidies benefiting large farmers contribute to a large sector deficit, estimated to have reached up to 1.5 percent of gross domestic product. Reform attempts began in the early 1990s and have been at the top of electoral party platforms ever since. Despite these efforts, severe underdelivery of electricity still persists.

In the federal system of India, most of the political obstacles related to electricity provision occur at the state level, where rich farmers benefit disproportionately from subsidies at the expense of all other users. The reliance on electric pumps for irrigation varies dramatically among states (12 percent in Rajasthan; 67 percent in Punjab), but across the board, medium and large farmers who own more than two hectares of land and benefit from subsidized electric pumps have tended to block reforms that would lead to the reduction of subsidies. Surveys have consistently indicated that users (including small farmers) would be willing to pay realistic electricity prices if the quality of delivery were adequate.

Despite high political salience and users' willingness to contribute to the production and maintenance of the public good, vested interests (large farmers) have traditionally blocked effective change that would entail subsidy reduction. What explains their success? First, big farmers are more politically consequential than the poor. As landowners and notables in their communities, they have the capacity to deliver many votes for the incumbent parties in exchange for benefits such as subsidies. Second, large farmers are better organized than the rural users who have a lower socioeconomic profile; therefore, they manage to lobby and secure subsidies at the expense of widely scattered rural communities that lack the capacity and resources to act collectively. Another similar collective action problem involving agricultural interests is discussed in Concepts in Practice 3.1.

These three theoretical constructs illustrate classic social dilemmas and emphasize the key idea that self-interested, rational individuals acting independently of each other have strong incentives not to cooperate (or to free ride) on the production or delivery of public goods (the prisoner's dilemma and the logic of collective action) and to deplete a limited shared resource (tragedy of the commons), even if long-term cooperation would be in their best interest. Accordingly, an individual will only rarely, contingent on the size of the group and the cost-benefit ratio, have incentives to join in the production of public goods. The immediate implication is that only powerful and cohesive interest groups are successful in achieving favorable policy.

## Identifying and Evaluating Collective Action Problems

When identifying a collective action problem in the course of a political-economy analysis, the analyst should do five things: (1) understand the type

**CONCEPTS IN PRACTICE 3.1**

## Prices of Agricultural Products in Sub-Saharan Africa

One of the seminal political-economy studies of agricultural policies in Africa found that the different potential for collective action of various stakeholder groups best explained the rural and urban differences in development (Bates 1981). In East African urban centers, oligopolistic industries and labor unions wanted high consumer prices for the manufactured goods they produced but low food prices, since 60 percent of the budget of an average urban dweller was spent on food. As a consequence, the state bureaucrats (representatives of marketing boards) offered farmers prices below the world market price, using the difference either as rents or for the political co-optation of well-organized urban interests. Thus, both urban labor and capital were allied against farmers and managed to lock in policies that favored them at the expense of rural areas. Among farmer groups, because of their weak capacity for collective action, only small farmers suffered the policy consequences. In contrast, larger farmers with

lobbying power managed to obtain generous subsidies from the state. This means that in countries with greater populations of large farmers (Côte d'Ivoire and Kenya, for instance) the agricultural policies were more favorable to the rural dwellers than in contexts characterized, paradoxically, by a more equal distribution of land among smaller farmers.

Why did small-scale farmers lack the capacity for collective action that would have enabled them to mobilize against the state and effectively demand change? First, the costs of political voice were too high, as small farmers tend to be more geographically dispersed and the state occasionally relied on coercion to enforce unpopular policies. Second, in some circumstances, these farmers have discovered alternative exit routes that allowed them to avoid the policy trap: the use of cross-crops that combined different crop prices, hedging financial risks, abandoning joint ventures that were not advantageous, and labor market migration, among others.

*Source:* Bates 1981.

of public good to be produced or maintained; (2) think analytically about the type of mismatch between individual and collective incentives to cooperate or join forces; (3) carefully examine the factors that led to the dilemma (motivational or informational) in the first place; (4) sift through the potential political-economic roots of these factors (does the motivational problem occur because of rational calculations, community or cultural norms, or discrepancy in resource endowments among individuals or groups?); and (5) consider whether correcting the collective action problem might lead to another similar dilemma (for example, will punishing noncompliant members of the group require a few compliant members to pay the full costs of enforcing the rules, whereas the benefits of enforcement extend to all?).

Often, adequate answers to these five questions have major implications for policy solutions. For example, if free riding occurs because of strictly rational considerations, monitoring and sanctioning might work well (Ostrom, Gardner, and Walker 1994). If, however, the root cause of free-riding behavior resides in poverty or, more broadly, in the incapacity (as opposed to lack of will) to contribute to the public goods, positive selective incentives for participation could do a better job of solving the problem.

On a more granular empirical level, research has identified a series of concrete factors that hamper mobilizational effectiveness and generate the logic of the collective action problem:

- *The number of interest groups.* Theoretically, the larger the number of interest groups, the more likely it is that they would offset each other's influence in shaping government policy. However, empirical research suggests that the number of such groups might not necessarily be a crucial factor. Many interest groups can receive policy concessions from the government if they are able to mobilize effectively (Bates 1981; Keefer 2004, 251).
- *Cohesion of the (economic) sector.* The less fractionalized the mobilizing group representing a certain sector, industry, or constituency is, the more likely it is to have an impact on policy (Frieden 1991, Keefer 2004, 252).
- *Magnitude of gains or losses caused by a potential policy change.* Higher stakes increase interest group effectiveness (Frieden 1991). For example, firms that are capital intensive, operate in natural resource extraction and management, and would incur high costs in redeploying their assets, have a stronger interest in acting collectively and deriving policy gains from governments (Bates 1981; Keefer 2004, 252).
- *The number of participants and the risks entailed by collective action.* As already argued, large groups do not often organize effectively to act in their shared interests. In many contexts, the poor or the consumers fail to influence public policy, despite their large numbers. Also, not all forms of collective action pose the same risks of participation. It is certainly less risky for individuals to take part in participatory budgeting exercises organized by civil society organizations in cooperation with municipal governments than to protest against corrupt political leaders who do not shy away from using force against contenders. Some rough estimations of the number of individuals who support a cause *and* choose to actively participate in contentious forms of collective action to achieve it (protests, demonstrations, and the like) suggest the so-called 5 percent rule: only 5 percent of all members of large social groups that would benefit over the long term from the outcome get involved, with the number of activists being overwhelmingly exceeded by bystanders (Lichbach 1998, 12, 17). In conclusion, smaller groups with high stakes have a greater likelihood of organizing effectively, potentially to the detriment of larger groups.

*Are individuals and groups thus doomed to be trapped in collective action dilemmas?* Despite both motivational and informational problems that lead to social dilemmas and plague collective action, some groups do manage to solve their incentive problems, organize, and attempt to lobby the government on behalf of their policy interests. Then the question becomes, When and under what conditions are these groups successful in obtaining their preferred policy result? The good news is that despite grim predictions, numerous studies confirm that several collective action problems are overcome every day (Ostrom 2000, Banerjee and Duflo 2011).

The examples of mobilizational incentives from India and Africa introduced above focused on powerful interest groups that manage to act jointly. These are not the only modes of collective action in town.

*Political parties*, for example, routinely aggregate policy and ideological preferences, information flows between voters and politicians, discipline members who do not comply with organizational rules, and mediate interaction between citizens and decision makers. *Social movement organizations* often rely on their core activists who manage to mobilize many participants in protests, demonstrations, or other forms of popular mobilization against bad governance. *Reform teams* sometimes develop as part of preexisting policy networks and bypass social dilemmas. For pro-development collective action, all these modes often build *coalitions*. How do these modes of collective action relate to accountability and a better provision of public goods (see Concepts in Practice 3.2)?

The subsequent chapters explore in depth how delegation or information constraints in organizations impede effective collective action for policy change. In addition, even when it occurs, agenda manipulation and lack of credible commitment might still prevent collective action from fully translating into the final development outcomes. Chapter 9 will review the broad repertoire of possible solutions to collective action problems in detail.


## Game Theory and Collective Action: Modeling Social Dilemmas with Nash Equilibria

Collective action problems can be understood and analyzed using the basic tools of game theory.[2] In essence, a collective action problem is a situation in which actors have no incentive to organize and obtain a favorable change in the status quo. That is, they are "stuck" in a suboptimal equilibrium. Game theory has a specific name for all situations, whether optimal or sub-

## Political Parties as Collective Action Problem Solvers

One of the greatest controversies in the political economy of development is whether democratization fosters development by ensuring that large groups of voters can hold policy makers to account. The fact that many East Asian countries appeared to pursue successful development outcomes despite having nondemocratic regimes that could, in theory, engage in arbitrary rule seems to partially refute this claim. The existence of institutionalized incumbent parties with clear rules of selection, succession, monitoring, and sanctioning created an alternative mechanism through which broad coalitions of stakeholders could act jointly and keep the unelected leaders accountable. More broadly, the existence of institutionalized parties has been linked by some studies to better development outcomes. In contrast, weak accountability of party leaders to their members and constituencies might not automatically foster development even in democratic contexts.

*Source:* Keefer (2011).

optimal, in which actors have no incentive to change their behavior: Nash equilibria.

## A Prisoner's Dilemma[3]

Two neighboring farmers grow a crop to feed their families, and if there is some surplus, they sell to the nearby market.[4] The farms are equidistant to a nearby river. If the farmers could build an irrigation system and bring water to the farms, then the crops they could grow and harvest would increase dramatically, and they would be able to send their children to a nearby school. If the irrigation system is built, neither farmer can be excluded from its use (free-rider problem). Furthermore, building the irrigation system is costly and would require both farmers to work together to build the ditch, if they were still to have time to grow their crops. If one farmer tries to build the irrigation system alone, she will succeed; but because she will not have time to grow any crops, she would not be able to feed her family.

The preferences of Farmer 1 (the farmers' preferences are symmetrical), based on the payoffs she receives, are as follows:

- If Farmer 1 does not help build the irrigation system but Farmer 2 does, Farmer 1 receives the benefit of the irrigation system but does not bear any of the costs. From a purely selfish perspective, this is the optimal outcome (highest payoff) for her. In this scenario, Farmer 2 bears the entire cost of the project but does not live to enjoy the benefits, as she had no time to tend to her fields.

- If Farmer 1 builds the irrigation system by herself, she bears the entire cost of the project but does not get to enjoy the benefits as she has no crops to harvest. Conversely, Farmer 2 enjoys the benefits of the irrigation system but bears none of the costs.
- If both Farmer 1 and Farmer 2 build the irrigation system, they both bear some of the costs (less time to grow their crops), but they both enjoy the benefits of higher crop yields.
- If neither farmer builds the irrigation system, they will enjoy a normal crop yield and incur no costs.

The diagram below conveys all this information but in a more concise format. There are two players, just as in the scenario of the two farmers. Each player has two options: cooperate or defect (not cooperate). The choices the players make determine their payoffs (benefits versus costs). To generalize the findings, the diagram uses the ordinal rankings of the players; a higher number denotes more utility—greater crop yield—allowing the farmer to buy more food for her family minus any costs associated with building the irrigation system and minus the initial loss of time tilling the field in order to dig the ditches.

|  | Cooperate | | Defect | |
|---|---|---|---|---|
| Cooperate | 3 | 3 | 1 | 4 |
| Defect | 4 | 1 | 2 | 2 |

Now let us think about how we can use the information to make predictions about what the farmers will do (hint: look back at the definition of the Nash equilibrium above).

Let's start with Farmer 1. Like any rational person, she wants to maximize her payoff (that is, maximize her crop yield and minimize her costs). However, she also knows that this outcome does not depend only on her actions but also on those of Farmer 2. Therefore, to decide what her optimal strategy should be, she needs to think about what Farmer 2 might do and condition her strategy on that expectation.

She can do this by running the following two-step thought experiment: if she knows that Farmer 2 would definitely build the irrigation system whether she herself cooperates or not, then her best action would be to defect (as she would get a payoff of four instead of three, the benefits of the irrigation system but none of the costs):

|  | Cooperate | | Defect | |
|---|---|---|---|---|
| Cooperate | 3 | 3 | 1 | 4 |
| Defect | 4♦ | 1 | 2 | 2 |

If she knows that Farmer 2 will definitely choose to defect, then her best action would also be to defect (a payoff of two versus a payoff of one):

|  | Cooperate | | Defect | |
|---|---|---|---|---|
| Cooperate | 3 | 3 | 1 | 4 |
| Defect | 4♦ | 1 | 2♦ | 2 |

Now let's think about Farmer 2. Like Farmer 1, she knows that her payoffs depend on the strategy of the other farmer. Through the same "thought experiment," it is possible to identify the strategy of Farmer 2. If she knows that Farmer 1 will definitely choose to build the irrigation system, then her best action would be to defect (as she would get a payoff of four instead of three):

|  | Cooperate | | Defect | |
|---|---|---|---|---|
| Cooperate | 3 | 3 | 1 | 4♦ |
| Defect | 4♦ | 1 | 2♦ | 2 |

If she knows that Farmer 1 will definitely choose to defect, then her best action would also be to defect (a payoff of two versus a payoff of one):

|  | Cooperate | | Defect | |
|---|---|---|---|---|
| Cooperate | 3 | 3 | 1 | 4♦ |
| Defect | 4♦ | 1 | 2♦ | 2♦ |

Given this scenario, both farmers have an incentive to defect, given how they expect the other farmer to react. As neither farmer can be made better off by unilaterally cooperating, this outcome constitutes a Nash equilibrium.

The prisoner's dilemma game is a simple but powerful tool for conveying how socially suboptimal outcomes can emerge from the rational behavior of individuals. For example, citizens in many countries would benefit if they could cooperate to fight corruption or perceived injustices. However, because every citizen would benefit from such an outcome, every citizen has an incentive to try and free ride—let others fight for change—and, therefore, nobody cooperates.

## Summary

This chapter has introduced collective action problems and explained how they can affect the provision of public goods. Given that some groups or modes of preference and cost aggregation may be more effective at overcoming collective action problems than others, unequal collective action capabilities can result in the persistence of skewed development outcomes. In addition to being symptomatic of underprovided public goods, collective action problems often plague many attempts at reform. This chapter helps policy entrepreneurs analytically identify and assess the costs, benefits, and feasibility of concerted action before they engage in the change process.

# Exercises for Chapter 3:
# Collective Action Dilemmas

## Exercise 3.1: The Unscrupulous Diner's Dilemma[5]

The facilitator explains the steps involved in the Unscrupulous Diner's Dilemma.

Steps in the exercise (time frame: ~40–45 minutes):
1. Read out instructions (1 minute)
2. Allow participants to read and answer (5–10 minutes)
3. Collect responses, tally responses, facilitate group discussion (10 minutes)
4. Class discussion (10 minutes)
5. Technical explanation (5–10 minutes)

Preparation and materials:
- Envelopes to be placed in the middle of the round table (one at each table)
- Pens should be available to all participants
- Copies of the handout of instructions
- Copies of the answer sheet
- Handout of key questions and group discussion
- Facilitator instructions

**NOTE: There are three different scenarios to be used. Each table works through one of the scenarios.**

Procedure:
1. The facilitator reads aloud the following instructions:
   I am going to distribute instructions and an answer sheet. Read the instructions and answer the questions on the answer sheet. Once you have read the instructions and completed your answers, place your answer sheet in the envelope in the middle of the table. DO NOT WRITE YOUR NAME ON EITHER DOCUMENT and MAKE SURE NO ONE SEES YOUR ANSWERS. Keep the instructions handy for the follow-up discussion. I will give you about 5–10 minutes to complete this.
2. The facilitator distributes the instructions handout and the answer sheet to all the participants.
3. The facilitator gauges the rate of completion of the assignment and gives participants a two-minute warning so that the activity can wrap up within its allotted 10-minute time frame. As part of the two-minute warning, the facilitator reminds participants that they should not write their

names on the answer sheet; when they have finished, they should put their answer sheet in the envelope in the middle of the table.

4. The facilitator explains:

   I will come around to collect the envelopes with the answer sheets and tally your responses. At the same time, I will give you a handout that includes two key questions. While I tally the responses on the answer sheets, please go ahead and discuss at your tables the two questions on the handout. Spend approximately 10 minutes in this discussion.

5. To tally the votes, the facilitator uses a blank answer sheet and notes for each option the total number of votes.

6. The facilitator walks around the room among the tables in a nonintrusive manner and pays attention to what is discussed. The facilitator notes a few comments from the tables that he or she can highlight as part of the transition to the lecture portion.

7. The facilitator gives the participants a two-minute warning to wrap up their discussion.

   A simple way to illustrate the tragedy of the commons is to remind participants of the coordination game (chapter 4). The suboptimal equilibrium (3,3) reflects a situation in which players do not cooperate (overgraze the commons), while the optimal equilibrium (4,4) represents a situation in which collective action problems are somehow resolved.

**Coordination Game**

|  | Cooperate | | Unilateral | |
|---|---|---|---|---|
| Cooperate | 4 | 4 | 1 | 1 |
| Unilateral | 1 | 1 | 3 | 3 |

8. The facilitator explains:

   Now that you have played the game and have had a chance to discuss with others at your tables some of the key underlying issues, let's find out the results of your individual decisions.

9. The facilitator announces the results and poses the following questions to the entire group:

   1. How many of you were surprised by the entire group's final tally?
   2. If yes, why?
   3. If no, why?

10. The facilitator then explains the case study activity.

11. The facilitator concludes with an explanation of the postexercise activity:

## Exercise 3.1: Instructions Handout 1

You and some acquaintances are at a restaurant and have decided to split the bill evenly among yourselves, regardless of what anyone ordered (splitting the bill = dividing the total bill by the number of people at the table). There are two items on the menu: (1) an expensive meal and (2) an inexpensive meal.

If you had to pay the full cost of the meal yourself, you would prefer the inexpensive meal to the expensive meal. However, if you think that one or two others around the table will choose the inexpensive meal and the rest might choose the expensive meal, you would prefer to buy the expensive meal because you will be paying the average cost of the entire meal.

The worst-case scenario, from your perspective, is that most other people or everyone else orders the expensive meal and you order the inexpensive meal, resulting in your paying a higher price for the inexpensive meal.

You know a few things about the other dinner guests:

- One dinner guest is on a diet and the inexpensive meal has a lower caloric content.
- Another dinner guest has health complications and does not like to eat too much, and the inexpensive meal is a smaller portion.

## Exercise 3.1: Instructions Handout 2

You and some acquaintances are at a restaurant and have decided to split the bill evenly among yourselves, regardless of what anyone orders (splitting the bill = dividing the total bill by the number of people at the table). There are two items on the menu: (1) an expensive meal and (2) an inexpensive meal.

If you had to pay the full cost of the meal yourself, you would prefer the inexpensive meal to the expensive meal. However, if you think that one or two others around the table will choose the inexpensive meal and the rest might choose the expensive meal, you would prefer to buy the expensive meal because you will be paying the average cost of the entire meal.

The worst-case scenario, from your perspective, is that most other people or everyone else orders the expensive meal and you order the inexpensive meal, resulting in your paying a higher price for the inexpensive meal.

You know a few things about the other dinner guests:

- Two diner guests are known to "enjoy their food" and will definitely be ordering the expensive meal.

## Exercise 3.1: Instructions Handout 3

You and some acquaintances are at a restaurant and have decided to split the bill evenly among yourselves, regardless of what anyone orders (splitting the bill = dividing the total bill by the number of people at the table). There are two items on the menu: (1) an expensive meal and (2) an inexpensive meal.

If you had to pay the full cost of the meal yourself, you would prefer the inexpensive meal to the expensive meal. However, if you think that one or two others around the table will choose the inexpensive meal and the rest might choose the expensive meal, you would prefer to buy the expensive meal because you will be paying the average cost of the entire meal.

The worst-case scenario, from your perspective, is that most other people or everyone else orders the expensive meal and you order the inexpensive meal, resulting in your paying a higher price for the inexpensive meal.

You know a few things about the other dinner guests:

- Two of the other dinner guests, who are close friends, are in financial difficulty, and having to split an expensive bill would certainly not help their finances.

## Exercise 3.1: Answer Sheet 1

Please indicate below, by ticking ($\checkmark$) the box next to the appropriate action, what you would like to do. PLEASE TICK ONLY ONE BOX.

| | |
|---|---|
| Buy the expensive meal | |
| Buy the inexpensive meal | |

Briefly explain why you decided to select one meal rather than the other.

| |
|---|
| |

**Once you have completed your answers, put them in the envelope in the middle of the table.**

## Exercise 3.1: Answer Sheet 2

Please indicate below, by ticking (√) the box next to the appropriate action, what you would like to do. PLEASE TICK ONLY ONE BOX.

| | |
|---|---|
| Buy the expensive meal | |
| Buy the inexpensive meal | |

Briefly explain why you decided to select one meal rather than the other.

**Once you have completed your answers, put them in the envelope in the middle of the table.**

## Exercise 3.1: Answer Sheet 3

Please indicate below, by ticking (√) the box next to the appropriate action, what you would like to do. PLEASE TICK ONLY ONE BOX.

| | |
|---|---|
| Buy the expensive meal | |
| Buy the inexpensive meal | |

Briefly explain why you decided to select one meal rather than the other.

**Once you have completed your answers, put them in the envelope in the middle of the table.**

## Exercise 3.1: Key Questions Handout – Group Discussion

In your group, discuss the following questions:

1. How did the fact that you were splitting the bill affect your decision to select one meal instead of the other?

2. How did the information you had about the other participants affect your decision?

## Notes

1. The logic of collective action was first introduced by Mancur Olson in 1965.
2. Readers interested in a more formal definition can consult the technical appendix (appendix B).
3. *Source:* Inspired from (Bardhan 1993).
4. Instructor note: If in a classroom setting, do exercise 3.1 (found at the end of the chapter) before having participants read this section.
5. *Source:* Inspired from (Gneezy et al. 2004).

## References

Aldrich, John H. 1995. *Why Parties? The Origin and Transformation of Party Politics in America.* New York: Cambridge University Press.

Aranson, Peter H., and Peter C. Ordeshook. 1985. "Public Interest, Private Interest, and the Democratic Polity." In *The Democratic State,* ed. Roger Benjamin and Stephen Elkin, eds., 87–177. Lawrence: University Press of Kansas.

Banerjee, Abhijit, and Esther Duflo. 2011. *Poor Economics: A Radical Rethinking of the Way to Fight Global Poverty.* New York. Public Affairs.

Bardhan, P. 1993. "Analytics of the Institutions of Informal Cooperation in Rural Development." *World Development* 21(4): 633–639.

Bardhan, Pranab, and Jeff Dayton-Johnson. 2007. "Inequality and the Governance of Water Resources in Mexico and South India." In *Inequality, Cooperation, and Environmental Sustainability,* ed. Jean-Maries Baland, Pranab Bardhan, and Samuel Bowles, 97–130. New York: Russell Sage.

Bates, Robert. 1981. *States and Markets in Tropical Africa: The Political Basis of Agricultural Policy.* Series on Social Choice and Political Economy. Berkeley: University of California Press.

Bueno de Mesquita, Bruce, James D. Morrow, Randolph M. Siverson, and Alastair Smith. 2002, "Political Institutions, Policy Choice and the Survival of Leaders." *British Journal of Political Science* 32 (4): 559–90.

Frieden, J. A. 1991. "Invested Interests: The Politics of National Economic Policies in a World of Global Finance." *International Organization* 45 (4): 425–51.

Gibson, Clark C., Krister Andersson, Elinor Ostrom, and Sujay Shivakumar. 2005. *The Samaritan's Dilemma: The Political Economy of Development Aid.* New York: Oxford University Press.

Gneezy, U., E. Haruvy, and H. Yafe, 2004. "The Inefficiency of Splitting the Bill." *The Economic Journal* 114 (495): 265–280.

Keefer, Phil. 2004. "What Does Political Economy Tell Us about Economic Development—and Vice Versa?" Policy Research Working Paper 3250, World Bank, Washington, DC.

———. 2011. "Collective Action, Political Parties, and Pro-Development Public Policy." *Asian Development Review* 28 (1): 94–118.

Kitschelt, Herbert. 2007. "Party Systems." In *The Oxford Handbook of Comparative Politics,* ed. Carles Boix and Susan C. Stokes, 522–54. New York: Oxford University Press.

Krishna, Anirudh. 2010. *One Illness Away: Why People Become Poor and How They Escape Poverty.* New York: Oxford University Press.

Lal, Sumir. 2006. "Can Good Economics Ever Be Good Politics? Case Study of the Power Sector in India." Working Paper 83, World Bank, Washington, DC.

Lichbach, Mark I. 1998. *The Rebel's Dilemma.* Ann Arbor: University of Michigan Press.

McKean, Margaret A. 2000. "Rational Choice Analysis and Area Studies." In *Beyond the Area Studies Wars: Toward a New International Studies,* ed. Neil L. Waters, 29–63. Hanover, NH: University of New England.

Olson, Mancur. 1965. *The Logic of Collective Action: Public Goods and the Theory of Groups.* Harvard Economic Studies. Cambridge: Harvard University Press.

Ostrom, Elinor. 1990. *Governing the Commons: The Evolution of Institutions for Collective Action.* Cambridge: Cambridge University Press.

Ostrom, Elinor. 2000. "Collective Action and the Evolution of Social Norms." *The Journal of Economic Perspectives* 14(3): 137–158.

———. 2005. *Understanding Institutional Diversity.* Princeton, NJ: Princeton University Press.

———. 2010. "Overcoming the Samaritan's Dilemma in Development Aid." Presentation at the Workshop in Political Theory and Policy Analysis, Indiana University Center for Study of Institutional Diversity, May 31, Bloomington, IN.

Ostrom, Elinor, Roy Gardner, and James Walker. 1994. *Rules, Games, and Common-Pool Resources.* Ann Arbor: University of Michigan Press.

Ostrom, Vincent. 1997. *The Meaning of Democracy and the Vulnerability of Democracies: A Response to Tocqueville's Challenge.* New York: Cambridge University Press.

Samuelson, Paul. 1954. "The Pure Theory of Public Expenditure." *Review of Economics and Statistics* 36 (4): 387–89.

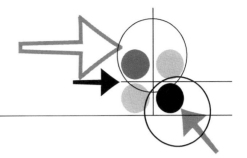

**CHAPTER 4**

# Theories and Mechanisms of Political Economy: Institutions and Equilibria

Pro-development reform entails some form of institutional change. This chapter explores the inner mechanics of institutions and the incentives that they generate. Why do institutional malfunctions persist? Why are they so durable if they generate obviously suboptimal outcomes? When do institutions change? What is the relationship between collective action and institutional change? The decisions that policy makers (politicians, bureaucrats) make, as well as the reactions of stakeholders (citizens, interest groups, and businesses, for example) to these decisions, are shaped by the rules or the institutional context in which this interaction occurs.

The "rules of the game" shape policy makers' choices (that is, Should I provide public goods, steal the money, or pander to key constituents?). They also constrain or boost the collective action potential of stakeholders. The policy landscape usually consists of formal and informal institutions, and both types of rules influence incentives for action. Therefore, by developing the ability to map the institutional context, reformers can identify the feasi-

**FIGURE 4.1 Conceptual Map: Understanding Institutions and Their Influence in Development**

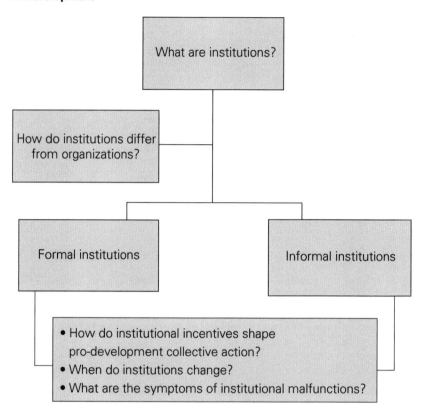

*Source:* Authors.

bility of different projects in light of the context-specific opportunities and constraints they face.

This chapter first defines institutions, links them to the collective action problem, distinguishes between different types of institutions (formal and informal), and offers theoretical explanations for their origins and change. Second, it introduces the basic tools of game theory, using the prisoner's dilemma to illustrate how the institutional context can determine which outcomes (equilibria) are viable. This overview of institutional analysis forms the basis of subsequent chapters that focus on how specific institutional factors—such as agenda setting, agency problems, information asymmetries, and credible commitment—affect collective action and policy outcomes.

## Objectives of Chapter 4

By the end of this chapter, readers should be able to do the following:

- Recognize institutions, organizations, formal institutions, informal institutions, institutional continuity and change, and the concept of equilibrium
- Understand the relationship among types of institutions, collective action, and development outcomes
- Link concepts of political economy to real-life situations.

## Institutions, Incentives, and Collective Action

In chapter 3, we explored why cooperation between individuals and groups in society does not occur, even when the potential gains from joint effort would make everyone better off. Social dilemmas stemming from the production and maintenance of public goods impede effective mobilization for economic development. Collective action problems occur, conceptually, in a world that lacks the right rules and incentives to make everyone participate. Institutions, or rules of interaction, arise for the very purpose of solving such collective action problems. They stabilize expectations and help actors realize the gains from cooperation. Simply put, institutions give actors the incentives to cooperate rather than opt out.

Nevertheless, as we will emphatically suggest again and again, just like collective action, not all forms of *institutions* have a positive impact on development. Powerful interests with plenty of resources and networks usually cooperate very well and build well-functioning institutions or rules that work to their advantage and block challengers. In development terms, the collective action potential of some groups and the institutions channeling it do not always lead to beneficial outcomes for all and often work against the poor. This fundamental problem explains skewed policies and outcomes.

Thus, for reformers, the search for the Holy Grail becomes a search for a specific kind of joint effort: the *pro-development type of collective action* that can lead to a better institutional equilibrium. When does it occur? Are there institutions that can help mobilization succeed? Can pro-development collective action occur within unfavorable institutional boundaries? Can a group navigate key institutions to help move an agenda forward?

Institutions are the larger conceptual umbrella here, because they can exist and thrive in the absence of pro-development collective action, whereas pro-development collective action cannot exist without institutions. Politi-

**FIGURE 4.2 Influence of Collective Action on Institutional Change**

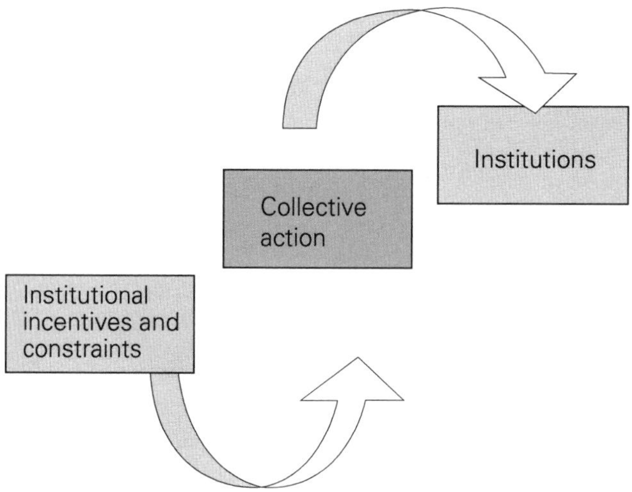

*Source:* Authors.

cal parties, civil society organizations, and protest movements need sets of rules to ensure cohesion and joint action. As the big conceptual context surrounding collective action, institutions can change dramatically, sometimes even in the absence of groups that can overcome collective action problems.

Nevertheless, this is not a one-way street. Even if the rules of the game significantly shape and confine the likelihood of pro-development mobilization, this handbook argues that successful collective action sometimes induces endogenous institutional change as well. Figure 4.2 illustrates this scenario.

To personalize this illustration, remember the 100 students who protested against the government led by emperor Bokassa in the Central African Empire (see the introduction to this volume). Their tragic fate set an example for many other potential protesters against abuses of power. In this case, brutal state repression dramatically increased the costs of direct action for similar groups or individuals who disagreed with the mandate to buy expensive school uniforms featuring a picture of the emperor. Therefore, in the vocabulary of political economy, the institution of autocracy diminished the potential for collective action by severely increasing the costs of protest.

North of the Central African Republic, many years later, a story with a similar beginning had a very different end. In the small rural town of Sidi Bouzid, on December 16, 2010, Mohamed Bouazizi, a street vendor supporting his family by selling fresh produce, was yet again (after many previous episodes) harassed by the local police who confiscated his wares because he could not pay a bribe. When he attempted to approach the governor to make a formal complaint, he was refused an appointment. In an economy that denied him any other alternative for survival, Bouazizi set himself ablaze in protest against the state. The country where this happened is Tunisia, and this episode catalyzed waves of protest that finally led to the toppling of Ben Ali's regime and ushered in the Arab Spring. In this case, despite autocratic rules banning dissent, effective and inspiring collective action led to profound institutional change.

Understanding the incentives of actors or stakeholders to support the provision of public goods or to promote change requires taking a step back to look at the rules that generate such incentives and constraints in the first place. Critical thinking about the origins and internal mechanics of rules or institutions can shed light on the conditions under which they are likely to change, as well as on the specific roles that economic and political actors can play during the change process.

Later in the chapter, tables 4.1 and 4.2 summarize a series of classic formal and informal institutions and link them to politicians' incentives and pro-development collective action. This list is not complete by any means, nor are the conceptual links as clear-cut. Its purpose is just to summarize some findings of the literature and engage the reader in systematic thinking about the effects of rules on outcomes. Since every policy reform or attempt at change is complex, in reality many rules must interact to produce successful collective action and positive development outcomes.

Institutions generate incentives for politicians and bureaucrats to pursue—or not—development and the provision of public goods. Understanding how institutions function and the incentives they generate matters. After all, policy reform in development entails fundamental changes of core rules. To identify those institutions that can help groups act collectively and achieve positive change, the following section will describe in detail what institutions are and how they generate incentives.

## What Are Institutions?

In the simplest possible conceptualization, institutions are the rules of the game. More formally, they can be defined as "rules, compliance procedures, and moral or ethical norms designed to constrain the behavior of individuals" (North 1981, 201–02.) All the components of this definition have implications for the origins, stability, and possibility of change. Please note, however, that the understanding of institutions as rules differs slightly from institutions as equilibria or norms (Crawford and Ostrom 1995). The focus on the rules of the game emphasizes an explicit sanction for noncompliance. By contrast, conceiving of institutions as equilibria relies on the evolution of shared expectations that certain actions automatically trigger unfavorable change in other actors' responses. The concept of institutions as norms rests on the internal sense of proper and improper behavior that constrains the actions of the actors (Crawford and Ostrom 1995, 583). This normative approach refers to the obligations and duties of the participants defined in a particular cultural context and reinforced through symbols, rituals, ceremonies, and the like.

Often, in everyday vocabulary, *institutions* and *organizations* are used interchangeably. Political economy, however, commonly imposes a conceptual distinction between them (North 1990). Before we go any further, the following clarification is in order.

***How Are Organizations Different from Institutions?*** Organizations bring together individuals or social groups with a common policy goal;[1] function according to their own rules, procedures, and culture; and seek to influence outcomes. They include political parties, bureaucratic units, firms, civil society groups, and international donor organizations, among many others. They are the players (actors or stakeholders) that interact strategically within the confines of the institutional context (North 1990).

Let us briefly explore the intersection of institutions and organizations. A trade union is an organization representing workers that tries to influence policy on such issues as wages or working conditions in a specific institutional context. In turn, the rules of the game resulting from the interaction among union, government, and employers shape the union's actual power and influence (cost of striking, the existence of closed shops, a formal policy-making role, and the like).

As suggested in chapter 3, organizations also facilitate collective action among individuals. Leaders of organizations monitor their boundaries, sanction free riding, and reward compliance. The internal institutional constraints on leadership matter very much for the organizational effectiveness of collective action. For example, if the rules governing the selection of leaders block challengers and make it harder for members to remove the incumbent, then accountability might be weak, and the "iron law of oligarchy" isolates the executive team from the rank and file (Michels 1911). At the other extreme, if the leadership is weak or rapidly changing, leaders might not be able to impose antishirking requirements on free riders. Political party discipline, strength, and cohesiveness have a lot to do with the organizational structure, leadership, and mechanisms of the parties as well as the internal accountability to members. A similar logic applies to civil society.

For a political-economy analysis, it is *also* important to assess whether organizations are monolithic or heterogeneous in their incentives, stakes, and

Understanding Policy Change

preferences. Often, different factions, divisions, units, and bureaus within the same organization have divergent goals and fail to act collectively.

After this clarification, we begin by mapping the institutional landscape. First, we will explore the inner logic of institutions consequential for development. Second, we look at how to recognize the main types of political-economic rules of the game and identify the incentives they produce.

***Institutional Mechanics: Inside the Machinery.*** *Institutions as equilibria.* The concept of institutions as equilibria implies that the development outcome they produce is self-enforcing. Once the outcome is achieved, no actor or stakeholder has an incentive to try and change it, even if it is far from his or her ideal policy preference (Weingast 2002, 682).[2] The conceptual focus is on the self-enforcing logic of institutions; that is, the parties to the pact must believe three things:

- They are better off accepting the outcome rather than rejecting it.
- Each actor will change his or her behavior when the other actors do so.
- All the individual actors will defend the gains of cooperation of the other participants (that is, no participant will be excluded from the benefits accrued in equilibrium).

Here is an example of a low institutional equilibrium from which actors did not have incentives to deviate. After the end of communism, many countries in Eastern Europe and Central Asia fell into a self-reinforcing "reform trap," whereby a predatory state raised taxes and diverted revenue away from the provision of public goods to satisfy politically powerful interest groups. As a result of the perceived misallocation of resources, many entrepreneurs and households began operating in the informal economy to avoid taxation. In turn, the expansion of the informal economy led to the further spiraling decline in tax revenue and provision of public goods. In an attempt to tackle the problem, some countries transitioned to a lower tax rate meant to stimulate the growth of the formal economy and increase tax revenue. Despite these policies, governments could not alter the institutional context by adopting the rule of law and effectively and credibly guaranteeing that the collected taxes would not benefit a narrow circle of elites. Firms operating in the informal economy were thus reluctant to participate in the formal economy. An equilibrium of low tax collection, heavy tax burden, and high corruption persisted because of this institutional configuration (Aslund, Boone, and Johnson 2002).

*Institutions as rules.* The concept of institutions as rules presupposes a third-party enforcer that can monitor and sanction noncompliant behavior of one or more participants. Traffic rules emerged as the result of coordination among participants and are enforced by the traffic police. This is a classic example of a rule-based institution. The absence or lack of capacity of the monitor or enforcer (that is, corrupt or inefficient police officers) alters the functioning of the institution. As the primary laws of the land, modern constitutions are the rules of the game par excellence. They arise from the strategic interaction of actors endowed with a certain distribution of power and enshrine expectations about how these arrangements will affect their power in the future. In most political systems, supreme or constitutional courts, as third-party enforcers, watch over constitutional rights and obligations. However, if the judiciary is not independent and strong, executives can interfere with its rulings, and the rules of the game are not enforced. This institutional malfunction can have detrimental consequences for development. Concepts in Practice 4.1 shows, in the case of access to basic water supplies in South Africa, how altering the rules of the game, and entrusting their enforcement to an independent third party, can provide disenfranchised groups with the institutional means for securing access to previously denied goods and services.

*Institutions as norms.* Institutions that have normative meaning within a specific cultural setting entail gains and costs of cooperation that are context specific. This mechanism is consistent with the previous understandings of institutions as equilibria or rules whenever the actors' stakes are clearly identifiable within a given cultural context. Norms themselves have often evolved from the strategic interaction of groups and individuals over long periods of time.

Historically, for example, tax rebellions in medieval Japan developed a leaderless pattern because the revolt leaders, if caught by authorities, were harshly punished (White 1995). Contributing to the evolution of community norms, in this case, the technology of law enforcement, created unique and enduring organizational structures and shaped the stakes of popular mobilization. Concepts in Practice 4.2 shows that cultural norms often define or constrain the sequence and protocol of actors' interactions, as well as the gains and losses derived from policy change.

As Concepts in Practice 4.2 illustrates, it is important for development analysts and practitioners to understand the specific normative meanings, dimensions, and gains or losses attached to policy reform by various stakeholder groups.

## Formal and Informal Institutions

A useful typology differentiates between formal institutions (those that exist in law or statute) and informal institutions (those without written rules or

## Constitutions and Individual Rights to Public Goods—Water Access and Health Care

Some constitutions around the world, attempting to redress severe and long-standing inequalities of access, have sought to grant all citizens basic rights to public services. South Africa, for instance, has a very high demand for water but the fifth-lowest water availability among the 41 Sub-Saharan African nations. Under these conditions of extreme resource scarcity, the apartheid regime concentrated the right of access in the hands of the white minority, which represented 13 percent of the population and used around 95 percent of the available water for agricultural irrigation on large farms. According to estimates, in the early 1990s, about 15.2 million South Africans did not have access to a basic water supply, and 20.5 million lacked access to basic sanitation (Mehta and Ntshona 2004, 4).

The postapartheid era made access to water and sanitation a policy priority, and the government instituted a policy that committed to providing universal access to a basic supply of safe water for all households. Thus, South Africa became the only country in the world that *constitutionally* guaranteed the right to basic drinking water and water for sanitation. Resetting the rules of the game and inscribing them in the constitution meant that poor citizens could take the local or national government to the Constitutional Court as the third-party enforcer if it reneged on this obligation. Indeed, the mere existence of legal grounds led many inhabitants of shantytowns to demand government account-

ability. In 2000, for example, residents of Walacedene—one of the poorest settlements of Capetown—won their class action suit in the Constitutional Court on grounds of the right to proper housing facilities. Similarly, in 2009, 5,000 poor inhabitants of Phiri, Soweto, made legal history as the first test case of the constitutional right to free water. The claimants won the case in the Supreme Court of Appeal but lost in the Constitutional Court (Danchin 2010).

Similarly, over the past 20 years, India, South Africa, and many countries in Latin America have begun guaranteeing the constitutional right to health care. This expansion of rights has translated into a wave of individual and class action litigation, as citizens have been able to demand that the public sector provide and cover the costs of specific medications and services. Despite the fact that the jury is still out on the fiscal and equity implications of health care litigation, citizens have often managed to demand the compliance of the executive with the rules of the game. In some cases, these formal rules enforced by the judiciary as an independent third party have led to dramatic and undeniable changes: universal lifetime access to basic HIV medication in India, increased health care coverage and benefits for all workers operating in the informal sector in Colombia, and preventing mother-to-child HIV transmission for the entire population of South Africa.

*Sources:* Mehta and Ntshona (2004); Danchin (2010); Yamin and Gloppen (2011).

formal structures that still determine outcomes). On the one hand, formal institutions such as constitutions and international treaties are drafted, debated, and voted upon during a long process through which all key actors set and clarify contractual expectations and ensure that the agreement they

### CONCEPTS IN PRACTICE 4.2
## Water Resource Management Reforms in Zimbabwe

In the late 1990s, several countries in southern Africa created decentralized water management institutions to increase the efficiency of water use and stimulate broader popular participation in resource management. Zimbabwe passed a water act in 1998 and began implementation two years later. This law promoted a new institutional configuration under the guise of integrated water management at the catchment level. Following technical trends in the international water management community, this institutional shift profoundly altered the way in which resources were managed and paid for in the localities. The former Water Resource Department became the Zimbabwe National Water Authority. Following the policy recommendations of the IMF Structural Adjustment Program, this new bureaucratic unit was supposed to operate along commercial lines and generate its own resources through user-fee collection for access to water.

Imposing such fees on consumption in rural areas often conflicted directly with local customs. For example, according to an analysis of the implementation of the reform, water is a God-given good for the Ndau community in Zimbabwe and is at the center of religious worship and ancestral beliefs. The owners of the water are the spirits of the ancestors, whereas the custodians are the tribal chiefs. Ndau beliefs about water access, ownership, and user fees were at odds with the new law and the central state's definition of resource ownership. Similarly, in several communal areas of Zimbabwe, traditional definitions of *community* (as settlements extending along entire rivers) directly contradicted the prescriptions imposed by the new law. As a result, significant numbers of users did not pay the fees the state expected to collect for water consumption.

In both instances, the preexisting rules of actors' interaction and the informal authorities that governed water consumption conflicted directly with state policy and undermined formal institutional change. By not engaging with local actors to understand the real stakes and rules of the community, reformers failed to anticipate the negative consequences of their policy.

*Source:* Nicol and Mtisi (2003).

reach will be binding. On the other hand, informal institutions—such as gender roles, family obligations, manners, and rules of appropriate behavior within a particular ethnic or faith-based group—may or may not be codified or written. Nonetheless, they produce strong compliance, sometimes even more so than written rules.

Why should we care about the complete institutional landscape of policy reform? Political economy brings politicians and political processes explicitly into development equations. The mechanisms or the rules through which political representatives are selected, monitored, and sanctioned generate individual or organizational incentives to provide public goods, engage in collective action, and shift (or not) development equilibria. These formal

**FIGURE 4.3 The Intersection of Formal and Informal Institutions**

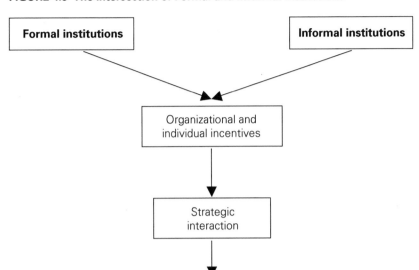

*Source:* Authors.

rules of selection often interact with the less visible territory of tacit expectations and lock in final outcomes. Understanding this intersection allows decision makers to correctly identify the feasible space for change, and avoid policy mistakes that harm more than help development. In the case of water management policy in Zimbabwe, for example, reformers ignored the informal rules of interaction at the local level, while expecting the formal rules designed by the central government in Harare to be fully enforced and to improve water management. Not taking into account informal institutions led to skewed incentives and outcomes: detrimental redefinition of traditional community boundaries and widespread noncompliance with the new policy.

Political-economy analysis should therefore take into account both categories and focus on the intersection of formal and informal institutions (as shown in figure 4.3).

***Formal Institutions.*** Most recognizable institutions of modern states—such as the form of government, the electoral system, and the arrangements ensuring political checks and balances—fall into the category of formal institutions. They are written or codified rules of behavior for all social, economic, and political actors. These sets of rules are sometimes called "parchment" institutions to denote their legalistic and codified character (Carey 2000).

But how effective are the rules or laws on paper in shaping economic, political, and social behavior? Especially in the case of the developing world, it has been widely recognized that not all written rules effectively govern behavior and that many effective individual incentives derive from tacit, unwritten rules (Carey 2000, 737). For example, the vast majority of countries have some sort of legislature with elected representatives who have a mandate given by their constituencies to enact legislation. However, some assemblies are merely "window dressing" forums that fulfill various purposes other than democratic representation. They can serve, for instance, as platforms through which powerful executive or hegemonic parties identify and co-opt political challengers. Similarly, in spite of relatively clear rules for the selection of the executive inscribed in constitutions, leaders often circumvent the legal constraints of their mandate. Instead, the real rules of access to power and allocation of scarce resources might reside in a narrow elite organized around the executive or the military, or they might entail mechanisms inherited from ethnic, kinship, or faith-based cleavages. By the same token, if the formal rules of representative democracy are weakly institutionalized and robust checks and balances on power are missing, executives have the space to abuse their mandate, build clientelistic voting networks, and consolidate a hard-to-defeat incumbency advantage.

Here are some examples of classic formal rules associated with the political process that have been found to generate incentives regarding the provision of public goods and collective action for reform:

- Political regime types (for instance, democracy versus authoritarianism)
- Federalism and decentralization
- Presidential versus parliamentary systems
- Bicameral versus unicameral legislature
- Executive-judiciary relations
- Electoral laws such as *proportional representation* (PR) (voting rules through which political candidates run for election on party lists and in which the number of votes received translates into the number of seats in the legislature) or *single-member district plurality vote* for candidate selection ("winner-take-all" systems in which only the candidate who wins the most votes at the constituency level gets elected).

Table 4.1 links these institutions to political incentives for pro-development collective action.

**TABLE 4.1 Political Incentives for Development and Collective Action Opportunities Induced by Formal Institutions**

| Formal institutions | Political incentives for provision of public goods. | Pro-development collective action: opportunities and constraints. |
|---|---|---|
| *Regime type* | | |
| Democracy | Elections provide accountability mechanisms. | Political parties, interest groups, and social movements are allowed. |
| Autocracy | Less or no direct accountability; repression; potential existence of alternative mechanisms of institutional checks and balances in some states. | Difficult for groups to pursue development agendas if they are not aligned with the priorities of political leadership. |
| Hybrid regimes | Partial accountability relations. | Some reforms can be pursued; "approved" parties are allowed to function, as long as they do not threaten the core distributive logic of the regime. |
| *Federalism* | | |
| Federations or decentralized systems | Regional interests are well represented; regional and local governments might overspend and engage in common-pool resource dilemmas; in some cases, if accountability is less clear, decentralization creates opportunities for corruption. | Political party cohesion and discipline might be lower since politicians have incentives to satisfy regional governors and not national party leaders; implementing policies could entail cooperation from both the center and subnational units, making cooperation more costly. |
| Unitary or centralized systems | National-level institutions shape political incentives. | Some parties might be more cohesive; national-level trade unions and business lobbies can pursue agendas more effectively than in decentralized systems; likely to act against decentralization reforms, for example. |
| *Executive-legislative relations* | | |
| Parliamentary system | Incentives for common-pool resource behavior in the budget process to satisfy individual constituencies; independent parliamentary behavior versus party discipline might depend on the type of coalition necessary for cabinet formation. | Collective action for lasting policy changes might depend on the relationship between the cabinet (minority versus majority) and legislature, cabinet duration, etc.; cabinet minority in some cases has induced lower party discipline. |
| Presidential system | Strong presidential powers; ability to use decrees; control of the budget process. | Collective action is contingent on the political relation between the head of state and legislature: if from the same party and high party discipline, effective reform; if not, potential policy stalemate. |

*(table continues on next page)*

**TABLE 4.1** *continued*

| Formal institutions | Political incentives for provision of public goods. | Pro-development collective action: opportunities and constraints. |
| --- | --- | --- |
| *Type of legislature*<br>Unicameral legislature | | Smaller coalitions necessary to pass reforms. |
| Bicameral legislature | Sometimes it allows greater representation of regional or occupational interests that balance out purely political incentives; traditionally designed to balance out the liberal popular chamber with a conservative counterpart (like the United Kingdom). | It increases the size of the coalitions and time required to pass pro-development laws; potential policy stalemate if ideologically divergent chambers. |
| Executive-judiciary relations | The degree of judiciary independence might give incentives to the judiciary to behave strategically and preempt conflicts with the executive. | Without judicial independence, collective action of groups trying to challenge executive decisions is reduced. |
| *Constitutional review rules*<br>Approval by ordinary majority | | Collective action for major changes or amendments of the constitution becomes easier. |
| Approval by supermajority | | More difficult to acquire the necessary majority for change. |
| *Electoral rules*<br>Single-member plurality | It creates incentives for politicians to pursue personalized constituency service (pork barrel politics; in some cases, clientelistic exchanges); some studies argue that it reduces corruption because it strengthens personal accountability.[a] | First-past-the-post systems are likely to have a lower number of parties (usually two major parties) but are less disciplined. |
| Proportional representation | Since politicians are elected based on party lists, it might decrease direct accountability to voters; it allows greater representation and a higher number of parties. | Coalitions and policy trade-offs are common; collective action for reform depends on party discipline, coalition size. In some cases, PR coalitions are fragile because of the high number of parties and policy divergence. |
| Closed-list proportional representation (party leaders decide on the order of candidates on the ballot) | Politicians have to cater to party leaders rather than local constituencies. | Less accountability to voters (some studies argue that they produce higher corruption levels), but also likely to increase party discipline for pushing reforms through. |

**TABLE 4.1** *continued*

| Formal institutions | Political incentives for provision of public goods. | Pro-development collective action: opportunities and constraints. |
|---|---|---|
| Open-list proportional representation (Voters have a say in terms of deciding the order in which candidates appear on the ballot) | More direct accountability as voters decide on the rank of candidate nomination. | This electoral rule generates a mix of accountability to voters and national party leaders. Its effects on collective action opportunities and party discipline might be contingent on other factors. |
| *Districting rules* District magnitude | The smaller the district, the higher the candidate competition for a representative seat. | It might personalize constituency benefits (pork barrel, clientelistic handouts) and reduce party cohesion at the national scale. |
| Overlap between local and national electoral districts | Might create incentives for or against decentralization. | If districts overlap, then legislators might fear that the mayors or governors of decentralized units would want to undermine their interests;[b] they might resist or oppose fiscal decentralization. |
| *Cabinet formation/ Coalition type* Concentration of executive power (minority cabinets or minimum winning coalition) | Either a minimal winning coalition or an undersized coalition forms the cabinet. | The collective action effect related to policy reform depends on the support of the legislature for the cabinet (low for undersized cabinets, higher for minimal winning); the minimal winning coalition cabinets could entail less policy concessions than oversized coalitions. |
| Sharing of executive power (oversized cabinets) | More parties than necessary form the government. | Potential coalition fragility, factionalism, policy trade-off. |
| *Interest group system* Pluralism | No major interest group coordination; labor, business, and government do not meet regularly to set wages, etc. | Many small organizations, no umbrella associations (i.e., business associations, large labor unions, no tripartite agreement), less influence in policy and reform. |
| Corporatism | Involves the incorporation of coordinated interest groups in policy formation (labor, business); some studies found better macroeconomic performance, others debate findings.[c] | The collective action potential of these interest groups to promote or block policies is very high (usually peak umbrella associations, large, few in numbers at the national level). |

*(table continues on next page)*

**TABLE 4.1** *continued*

| Formal institutions | Political incentives for provision of public goods. | Pro-development collective action: opportunities and constraints. |
|---|---|---|
| *Political party systems* | | |
| Two-party systems | Politicians appeal with policies to satisfy the median voter. | Produce single-party cabinets that are more stable than coalition governments and, according to some, more effective for policy making.[d] |
| Multiparty systems | Better representation of the preferences of a diverse electorate. | Generate coalition governments that are often fragile and nondurable. |
| Party discipline and cohesion | Organizational incentives to comply or not comply with national party leaders and policies. | Strong party discipline can effectively block or promote pro-development reforms. |
| Intraparty selection rules and competition | Some studies argue that intense intraparty competition might lead to clientelism.[e] | Collective action for public good provision through parties might be hampered by intraparty factionalism. |

*Source:* Authors; selected examples of formal institutions in democracies come from Lijphart 1999.

a. Persson and Tabellini (2005).
b. Eaton, Kaiser, and Smoke (2010).
c. Lijphart (1999).
d. Lijphart (1999).
e. Carey and Shugart (1995); Golden and Chang (2001).

Sometimes, even small changes within the same family of formal institutions (for example, the rules governing the election of political candidates) can lead to different outcomes related to the provision of public goods. Concepts in Practice 4.3 illustrates the effects of variations of electoral laws on the provision of public goods and economic reform in Brazil and República Bolivariana de Venezuela. As we will see, there is no easy answer, recipe, or immediate causality, as the effect of such rules is often complex. Therefore, mapping the web of core institutions governing the policy domain of interest allows reformers to identify the real origin or locus of skewed incentives, come up with correct diagnostics, and design feasible strategies of action.

Written, codified institutions often interact with unwritten, less formalized shared expectations of behavior among actors or stakeholders. These normative templates are called informal institutions. Development outcomes are in many cases the products of such interaction. Ignoring what lies behind the immediately visible landscape, as well as the real power relations underpinning and sustaining formal rules, and attempting to export blueprints of formal institutions on grounds that they functioned elsewhere can lead to either ineffective or detrimental outcomes. To paraphrase Luiz Carlos Bresser Pereira, a former Brazilian minister, "Institutions can be at most imported, never exported" (Przeworski 2004, 540).

**CONCEPTS IN PRACTICE 4.3**

## Effects of Electoral Laws on Public Goods in Brazil and República Bolivariana de Venezuela

Proportional representation is a voting method commonly used for national and local elections in which the number of votes won by a political party translates into a proportional number of seats in legislatures. For example, if a party wins 20 percent of votes nationally, it obtains roughly 20 percent of the seats in the parliament. The procedure through which political parties list candidates for elections and decide on their order on the ballot is also consequential for the final result.

The "open-list" proportional representation rules give voters direct influence over the order in which political candidates appear on the ballot, as they can alter the ranking of candidates on party lists (individual mandate). In contrast, in "closed-list" PR systems, party leaders, not voters, decide on the order.

How do these rules affect the provision of public goods? In Brazil, for example, open-list PR led to the creation of pockets of voters supporting individual candidates who offered either "pork" (narrowly targeted private goods to a specific constituency) or bribes for votes delivered en masse by local party bosses. These incentives led to very weak parties, individualistic deputies, and strong municipal party bosses. Thus, because of the fragmentation, weakness, and lack of cohesion in the party system, the incumbent president always needed governing coalitions that were hard to obtain and stabilize in order to pursue reform agendas. This volatility of reform coalitions at the center subsequently translated into increased corruption, pork barrel politics at the

district level, and reform deadlock (Ames 1999, 2001).

In República Bolivariana de Venezuela, in contrast, a closed-list system of proportional representation has been singled out as one of the factors leading to reform deadlock (Crisp 2000). In 1984, falling oil prices, large foreign debt, and declining real wages led to a crisis in a country previously commended for its stability and growth. The government, led by Jaime Lusinchi in collaboration with a small group of bureaucrats and a few interest groups, was in charge of navigating the necessary package of reforms. In the process, the executive immediately started to rule by decree, structured and dominated the legislative agenda, and consolidated unprecedented power. However, despite this wide-ranging political mandate, no significant reforms were undertaken. On the contrary, several policies solidified the vested interests of powerful groups to the detriment of diffuse groups of citizens.

How can this puzzle be explained in a democratic polity in which a vibrant legislature and an anxious public could have prevented the reform deadlock? Part of the explanation lies in the closed-list proportional representation rule (surviving until 1993) that made political candidates dependent on the central leadership of the party for their selection, not directly on voters. This institution created individual incentives for high party discipline, no opposition majority, and, overall, an ineffective congress unable to challenge a powerful president and interest groups. In the absence of a vocal civil society, reform was stalled.

***Informal Institutions.*** Informal institutions are social norms, conventions, or context-specific prescriptive templates of behavior. Unlike formal rules, they are usually unwritten and function outside official channels (Helmke and Levitsky 2006). Formal institutions, because of their legalistic and codified nature, are relatively easy to identify. Constitutions, laws, decrees, organizational charts, and electoral laws stipulate rights, responsibilities, future contingencies, and the monitoring technology that ensures compliance.

Tacit, informal rules or norms are sometimes trickier to pin down and analyze. Here are several rules of thumbs with respect to how to (or not to) identify them (Helmke and Levitsky 2006, 6–10):

- Informal institutions entail *shared* social expectations of behavior, as well as some form of external punishment for noncompliance.

- Not all unwritten behavioral patterns are informal institutions. For example, if bureaucratic corruption is tolerated or even encouraged by central state authorities and if there is an underlying expectation or tacit norm in the wider public sector community that bribes should be extracted, corruption becomes the informal rule of the game. If, however, bureaucrats solicit bribes in response to low public sector salaries, corruption is just a behavior triggered by the lack of adequate incentives.

- Informal institutions are often conflated with cultural values and informal organizations that have usually been overlooked by Western-centric institutional analyses (for example, tribes and clans). However, caution is needed in identifying and analyzing them. Sometimes, even if the *informal organization* (say, a particular ethnic tribe, for example) is a stakeholder in a reform process, it does not mean that the shared expectations *within* the group automatically shape the policy stakes and affect the broader process of policy change. If, nevertheless, the reform stakes assessed by this group are derived from common expectations of costs and benefits, the informal institutions are at work. As the example related to water management reforms in Zimbabwe showed, the informal institutions of the Ndau ethnic group that normatively defined concepts of ownership and property rights related to water had a direct impact on policy implementation. The mere incorporation of the same ethnic group in the list of local stakeholders for another policy (say, decentralization reforms) for which the group does not have a priori shared expectations, however, does not qualify as an informal institution.

- Some institutions that might be perceived as informal by the analysts are in reality highly formalized. Many African countries have created constitutional structures and responsibilities for traditional authorities (customary councils, chieftaincy committees, and the like) for different purposes: the unification of customary laws across regions, compiling and registering lines and succession of authority, coordinating customary policies with the regulatory framework of the central or local governments, institutionalizing patronage networks, and so forth. In Yemen, for example, the political survival of the incumbent party and the president traditionally depended on alliances with key tribal leaders. The Department of Tribal Affairs, a bureaucratic agency, pays stipends to 5,000 tribal sheikhs all across the country. In addition to this formal recognition, a parallel network awards government jobs to either family members or close allies of tribal leaders (Egel 2010; ARD 2006).

Similarly, in the 1990s, several Latin American countries codified and formalized indigenous laws to achieve better compliance with national policies. Treating them as informal ignores an entire political process of codification, formalization, and official recognition of these rules by the central state.

Strong informal rules of behavior can either undermine or dominate formal institutions. The interaction between the two types of rules of the game often explains development outcomes, as well as the success or failure of policy reform.

Sometimes, by eroding or circumventing written rules, conflicts between informal rules of behavior and formal institutions can have negative effects and block change. For example, even if the legal framework gives women equal rights (such as the right to vote or participate in the labor market), patriarchal, societal, ethnic, or family norms can de facto provide disincentives for acting on such rights (social stigma, exclusion, or physical punishment). In some cases, top-down reforms aiming to replace traditional institutions that regulate behavior with formal rules derived from "best practices" end up being either ineffective or counterproductive.

Informal institutions can also play a positive role by providing strong rules and mechanisms of accountability in cases where formal institutions are weak or missing. In China, for example, despite the lack of development funds in the villages and the absence of democratic mechanisms of accountability, some rural units perform better than others in delivering public goods. The cause of such variation in development outcomes lies in strong unofficial rules and norms that effectively stabilize expectations of actors. Villages with solidary social groups, such as temples or villagewide lineages (clans), typically provide more public goods. Concepts in Practice 4.4 considers some of the factors that led to this puzzling variation in development across rural localities.

Given that institutional weakness characterizes many developing countries (Bardhan 2002), the relevance of informal institutions and of their interaction with the formal rules of the game is essential for development policies and reforms.

## CONCEPTS IN PRACTICE 4.4
# Informal Institutions in China

A study conducted in four rural provinces in China that surveyed 316 villages showed that development funds rarely reach the villages since counties and townships prefer to invest their resources in infrastructure projects that connect localities rather than providing public goods inside the villages. Village governments are nevertheless responsible for irrigation, garbage collection, road maintenance, and primary education, with very few financial resources at their disposal. Despite resource scarcity across the board, the production and maintenance of public goods vary significantly in these rural localities. What explains this divergence in development outcomes? The study found that informal institutions—specifically, village solidary groups such as temples or clans—lead to superior delivery and maintenance of public goods.

For these informal institutions to provide incentives to village officials to perform, they have to meet two criteria: (1) they need to be encompassing, meaning that they must apply to everyone under the village jurisdiction; and (2) they need to include the officials as members. According to this argument, if officials and group members share a similar code of moral conduct and ethical obligations, their incentives are more likely to be aligned, with positive consequences for development. These informal codes of duties and responsibilities can derive from many sources: for example, similar religious beliefs (in the case of village temples) and family- or kin-related codified behavior (in the case of clans). Interestingly, in the Chinese context, the variation in development outcomes seems to be best explained by the joint effect of the two criteria. While village temples cover all the inhabitants of the village, including the officials responsible for public goods, village churches are encompassing but not embedded: they provide social services to a large segment of the village population but rarely include officials since they are nonindigenous institutions. In contrast, subvillage lineages, by definition, do not encompass the entire village population, although they might include the locality official. According to the study, village temples and villagewide lineages that are *simultaneously* encompassing and embedding score higher in governance indicators than villages featuring informal institutions that lack one of the two criteria (sublineages that include just a segment of the population or village churches). The findings demonstrate that, in certain contexts, informal mechanisms of accountability can lead to better development outcomes even in the absence of formal electoral alternatives.

*Source:* Tsai (2007).

Although understanding the political-economy environment surrounding reform—especially the configurations of informal and formal institutions—is challenging, it is crucial for a successful outcome. Following are some examples of informal institutions relevant in many parts of the world (Helmke and Levitsky 2006, 276–280):

- Political clientelism or patronage
- Informal rules of bureaucratic meritocracy (Singapore has the same postcolonial bureaucratic legacies as the Philippines and Indonesia but has unspoken norms of strong meritocracy)

- Unwritten norms of bureaucratic coordination between agencies
- Informal rules of interaction between bureaucrats and private sector companies that participate in public procurement processes (for example, Amakudari or "descent from heaven" practices in Japan, whereby retiring civil servants obtain lucrative jobs in companies for which they secured public contracts in the past)
- Blackmail and regulatory uncertainty (Kuchma in Ukraine, Fujimori in Peru)
- Informal interparty or executive-legislative consultations.

For a brief summary of the incentives provided by informal institutions and their impact on collective action for development, see table 4.2.

Sometimes, the causal effect of formal or informal institutions on development outcomes can be more complex than initially thought. Unintended consequences or specific interactions of many institutional layers skew the original goals. Concepts in Practice 4.5 presents an example of such unintended consequences in the case of regulations governing labor relations and the development outcomes they generated in Indian states.

## Institutional Origins, Stability, and Change

### Why Do Institutions Exist?

Generally two major explanatory frameworks seek to account for the origins and evolution of institutions: demand-side and supply-side approaches. Demand-side approaches tend to emphasize that institutions are designed to help (some or all) stakeholders enhance their ability to alleviate collective action problems: "Institutions arise in part to help create the conditions for self-enforcing cooperation in an environment where there are gains from cooperation but also incentive problems that hinder a community's ability to maintain cooperation" (Weingast 2002, 674).[3] Thus, for example, compulsory trade union memberships (closed-shop agreements) were established so that individual workers could not free ride on the efforts of a union to secure better working conditions for all workers in a factory.

Supply-side approaches tend to emphasize how the unintended consequences of institutions may alter the relative power of stakeholders in unforeseen ways and independently of the original raison d'être on which the institution was founded. For example, closed-shop agreements, by providing a union with significant power to disrupt production in an industry, could enable it to make political demands that have nothing directly to do with ensuring that workers' salaries or working conditions meet certain stan-

**TABLE 4.2 Incentives of Informal Institutions and Their Impact on Collective Action for Development**

| Informal institution | Political incentives to provide public goods | Pro-development collective action: opportunities and constraints |
|---|---|---|
| Political clientelism/patronage | It generates incentives for politicians and parties to cultivate personalized relations with local notables, intermediaries, organizations for distribution of clientelistic handouts, and vote monitoring. | Clientelism and political machines are very effective with respect to vote turnout and collective action since they mobilize large numbers of voters; they also commonly undermine programmatic policies and public good provision. |
| Unwritten norms of bureaucratic coordination | They give incentives for cooperation across agencies, irrespective of political affiliation. | Facilitate bureaucratic collective action at the policy formulation and implementation stage. |
| Regulatory uncertainty | In some environments, it creates incentives for corruption and self-refraining of opposition members from challenging the executive. | The fear and anticipation of arbitrary implementation of laws and regulations (for example, discretionary tax collection or inspections) reduce the collective action potential of opposition to the executive. |
| Rules of career advancement in bureaucracy and engagement with the private sector (for example, the Japanese Amakudari or "descent from heaven" system) | They give incentives for collusion between bureaucrats and private companies. | According to studies, they reduce the general level of oversight and increase risk taking from companies; they can hamper pro-development collective action. |
| Informal rules of interparty consultation | Informal consultation forums or caucuses across party lines might increase incentives for policy cooperation; create incentives for accountability (programmatic or clientelistic) to voters for individual politicians. | Facilitate bipartisan coalition formation and consolidation; prevent conflicts; it might entail policy trade-offs. |
| Clans, lineages, ethnic faith-based group norms | Give incentives to politicians, voters, and bureaucrats to stick together. | These norms are usually very effective at solving in-group collective action problems; high ethnic fractionalization or in-group/out-group competition for scarce resources reduces the potential for collective action, and, according to some studies, leads to public good underprovision.[a] |

*Source:* Authors.
a. Alesina, Baqir, and Easterly (1999).

**CONCEPTS IN PRACTICE 4.5**

## Labor Regulations in India

The relatively low rate of manufacturing growth in India stands in stark contrast to the manufacturing growth of neighboring East Asian states, as well as to India's own service and information technology industries. What explains this relatively poor performance? The role of formal institutions and how they affect the business environment could be one plausible, although by no means the only, factor, which may help explain part of this empirical puzzle. Many of the laws and regulations governing industry in India are set at the center and apply to all the states (the cornerstone legislation being the Regulation and Development Act of 1951). However, the regulation of industrial relations is a concurrent issue in which both the central and the state governments have the ability to "change the rules of the game" by altering legislation. Thus, while in 1947 virtually all Indian states had the same regulatory framework for industrial relations (governed by the Industrial Disputes Act of 1947), over time each state was able to change this act, in every jurisdiction.

In short, while all Indian states began with the same legal-institutional framework, by tracking the state-level reforms of the 1947 act over a period of 35 years, we can examine how those changes in the formal legal rules of the game affected final outcomes (economic growth, formal employment, and poverty rate). By coding whether each reform of the 1947 act, at the state level, was pro-employer, neutral, or pro-employee, the authors of this study were able to identify whether marginal changes in the formal regulatory environment had a significant effect on development outcomes. The authors found that pro-worker amendments were associated with reduced output, reduced formal employment, less investment, lower productivity, increased employment in the informal economy, and higher urban poverty rates. Thus, changing the rules of the game in a legally "pro-worker" way had the perverse effect of reducing the opportunities for formal employment and the betterment of living conditions.

*Source:* Besley and Burgess (2002).

dards. Thus, unions may lobby for subsidies to declining industries or for perpetuating jobs and benefits at the expense of the taxpayer (see, for example, North 1990 or Hayek 1962).

Irrespective of their genesis, for institutions to survive they must reach a self-enforcing equilibrium.[4] As already suggested, this means that the actors should be better off by obeying the rules, that they should change their behavior in response to other parties doing so, and that they will effectively counter attempts or political transgressions to change the rules of the game.

## When Do Institutional Equilibria Change?

Self-enforcing institutions embed and lock in context: power discrepancies among social groups, economic development, state capacity, and many other background conditions (North 1981, 18–50; 1990). Therefore, the prospects for profound change are likely to be shaped by significant shifts in the following factors:

- Power endowments of major actors
- Demography
- Technology
- Property rights
- Global economic production, distribution, and exchange
- International and domestic political competition
- Ideology.

***Change in Power Endowments of Actors.*** Institutions formalize and preserve preexisting power configurations; they reflect the underpinning balance of power between political groups in society. Historically, institutions (especially INSTITUTIONS, or the core societal rules of interaction) developed around certain power configurations and were created to preserve those power discrepancies.[5] Because these rules simultaneously shape collective action and development outcomes, changing them is always challenging and often impossible.

Here is an eloquent metaphor that captures the difficulty of major institutional change. In an influential article pondering the causal link between institutions and development outcomes, the author draws a comparison that all sport fans can relate to, and poses the following conundrum. Let's say that two teams play basketball (or any other sport for that matter), but one of them has a significant height advantage over the other team. The rules of the game and the referees—as third-party enforcers—are designed to be impartial. The conceptual problem here, the analyst argues, is that *independently* of all institutional guarantees designed to insure objectivity, the taller team is still more likely to win. It also follows, according to this line of argument, that the rules that would bring the game closer to fairness, for example lowering the basket, will not change in a world in which the taller or more powerful players make the rules, precisely because their team derives advantages from the status-quo (Przeworski 2004, 529). Therefore, major institutional change occurs only when the underlying balance of power changes.

One example of such institutional shifts comes from the historical evolution of succession and inheritance rules and provides an interesting illustration. Throughout the Middle Ages, primogeniture (or the right of succession granted exclusively to the first-born son) coexisted with a single-income source available to the household (usually land assets). Progressively, as the income alternatives diversified (the rise of industry, manufacturing, and the like), the bargaining power of the other siblings increased and ultimately succeeded in establishing more equal rules of succession and property division. Historians have shown that the main explanation behind equality-versus-first born favoritism inheritance rules in the 19th century was the availability of multiple sources of income for household members (Knight 1992, 169).

In more contemporary settings, transitions from autocracy to democracy occur when the nondemocratic coalition revolving around the political leader (that is, the military, one-party regime elites, powerful bureaucrats or notables, and broad societal groups that support the nondemocratic regime) fear defeat or replacement, have depleted the resources that bought political support, or have lost an open conflict with contenders.

Lower-case institutions also change when the power endowments of major actors in society shift. South Africa, for example, pursued a comprehensive decentralization policy at the beginning of the 1990s. Anticipating electoral defeat by the transition incumbent (the African National Congress, or ANC), the two establishment parties (the National Party dominant in the Eastern Cape Province and the Inkatha Party with a strong support base in Kwa Zulu Natal) pushed for enhanced fiscal and decision power in the regions to try to preserve some political gains, despite the loss at the national level. The ANC accepted the plan within the context of the transition pact. Years later, when the party consolidated, it withdrew support from decentralization to weaken the opposition parties in the provinces and internal party rivals. The government dramatically reduced the number of local governments, from nearly 900 to 238, in a process of amalgamation officially justified as a bureaucratic measure meant to address the precarious capacity problems of local governments. As some analysts pointed out, the policy marked a reassertion of centralized control underneath an administrative guise (Eaton, Kaiser, and Smoke 2010, 54).

Understanding institutional change as such has policy implications for reformers because it reveals the limits and perils of institutional engineering. If the underlying power relations are essential for equilibria, then just adopting or importing formal institutions that worked elsewhere can either fail to produce any results or do more harm than good.

***Demographic Change.*** Increases or decreases in population or changes in the demographic structure alter economic demand and production capabilities and create potential for changing the previously prevailing rules of distribution. For example, gender-friendly policy reforms in postgenocide Rwanda illustrate how institutions changed to reflect shifting demographics (Powley 2005). In October 2003, Rwanda found itself with the most gender-balanced legislature in the world, with women holding 48.8 percent of the seats. Prior to the civil war and genocide of the mid-1990s, they had never held more than 16 percent of the seats in the legislature. This puzzling reversal was partially caused by the massive demographic change triggered by the ethnic conflict that claimed over 800,000 lives. In the immediate aftermath of the genocide, the entire population was 70 percent female (women and girls).

To this day, the legacy of gender imbalance persists. In a postconflict situation in which women survived their husbands and sons, they had to acquire new skills rapidly and assume new gender roles. Into the organizational vacuum, multiethnic women from nongovernmental organizations (NGOs) such as Pro-Femmes stepped in, advocated for ethnic reconciliation, and advised the government on gender-friendly policies. The inclusive, reconciliatory, and gender-sensitive constitution adopted in the postconflict period, coupled with the role of women NGOs in fostering national reconciliation, was critical in raising the political profile of prospective female politicians. The greater formal representation of women resulted in the formation of a women's caucus and the passage of legislation that sought to promote women's issues, including the right of women to inherit land (1999), which had previously been prohibited. Thus, while Rwanda faced many developmental and political challenges, the change in the demographic composition of the broader population, as well as of the legislature, still had a clear and visible effect on policy-making priorities.

***Technological Change.*** The introduction of new technology increases efficiency, productivity, and power, thereby altering the relative costs of advocating for a new structure of redistribution. For example, with the increased ability of developing countries to use electronic transfers to send benefits to recipients rather than going through bureaucratic intermediaries, the discretionary power and potential for corruption of the public sector apparatus may be reduced. Over the past 10 years, the Internet and social media (such as Facebook and Twitter) have radically transformed social movements, popular protests, and political party appeals and fundraising and have thus facilitated collective action and empowered marginalized groups of citizens.

***Change in Property Rights.*** Property rights are, broadly speaking, rules "defining ownership, use, rights of income and alienability of resources and assets as expressed in laws and regulations" (North 2005, 57). They emerge as a result of an ongoing negotiation between the rulers of a state and its constituents and specify the duties and obligations of the ruler with respect to the assets (land, labor, capital) of individuals and companies. Changes in the specification or enforcement of the system of property rights can trigger institutional change.

***Changes in Global Production, Distribution, and Prices.*** For Nobel Prize–winning economist Douglas North, changes in tastes and in the ratio of the prices of the factors of production are the most important drivers of incremental institutional change. In medieval Europe, for example, the plague caused dramatic changes in the land-labor ratio and triggered an important resetting of political and economic rules. Similarly, changes in the relative prices of work, leisure, and contraception have modified the structure of the family unit and have altered behavior (North 1990, 84).

***Shifts in Domestic and International Political Competition.*** The intensity and robustness of political competition will limit the monopoly power of the state. Shifts in either international or domestic competition can trigger institutional change (North 1990).

According to increasing evidence in many developing countries, greater political competition has led to the creation of independent regulatory agencies, oversight institutions, civil service reforms, and ombudsmen (Geddes 1994; Grzymala-Busse 2006; O'Dwyer 2006). If political parties are uncertain about their electoral future when taking office, the argument goes, they have incentives to build in oversight institutions and public bureaucracies that will not punish them if they lose elections.

Following the transition from communism, some Eastern European countries (Estonia, Hungary, Lithuania, Poland, and Slovenia) adopted relatively fast civil service reforms and established independent supreme audit institutions or public procurement agencies. Others (Bulgaria, the Czech Republic, Latvia, and Slovakia) took almost 10 years to initiate a similar process of institution building. Paradoxically, some of the laggard state reformers like the Czech Republic were well ahead of other countries in market reforms as well as in prospects for accession to the European Union. What explains this puzzle? A study found that robust political competition among parties limited the discretion of executives who might have wanted to use state coffers to maintain their incumbency. Fearing replacement in future elections and potential retaliation if the opposition were to take power, incumbent politicians created relatively neutral monitoring and oversight institutions that could not be colonized by political rivals and that would guarantee a level playing field (Grzymala-Busse 2006).

***Major Ideological Shifts.*** The power of ideas to transform institutions has long been noted and documented (Hayek 1978). The transition from capitalism to communism and vice versa triggered profound changes across many institutions: property rights were reconfigured through waves of nationalization and privatization, the type of political regime was transformed overnight, and individual incentives were considerably altered. To understand the powerful exogenous impact of such ideological shifts, just imagine the sweeping capacity of some states to modify preexisting social norms that had survived for centuries, as well as the very fabric of property rights and basic social interactions. For example, Mao's China banned the practice of women's foot binding overnight. At the other end of the spectrum, post-Communist regimes attempted to reverse the logic of land property rights following decollectivization but in the process interfered with the society's understanding of kinship and family networks (Verdery 2003). As Concepts in Practice 4.6 will show with respect to Estonia's transition from commu-

---

**CONCEPTS IN PRACTICE 4.6**

## The Power of Ideas and Tax Reforms

Mart Laar, a historian by training, became prime minister of newly independent Estonia in 1992. During his first term as prime minister, from 1992 to 1994, he pursued a radical change in economic policies that saw Estonia's economy transformed from a part of the USSR to one of the most liberal market economies. A particularly contentious component of this reform policy was the implementation of a flat rate on income meant to simplify the tax code, increase revenue (decrease tax evasion), and help cement Estonia's reputation as a business-friendly country. Eventually, Estonia's flat-tax example was emulated by many other formerly Communist countries, including Bulgaria, Latvia, Lithuania, Romania, the Russian Federation, Slovakia, Ukraine, and, most recently, Hungary (Bemis 2011).

How did Estonia become Eastern Europe's pioneer in the flat-tax revolution? Western institutions such as the European Union did not support the flat tax, and in fact the International Monetary Fund initially gave the proposed reform a very cool reception. Instead, the idea came from Milton Friedman's book, *Free to Choose,* which advocated a flat tax and was the only economic text that Mart Laar claimed to have read. Thinking Friedman's idea logical, Laar simply implemented it.

Following transition, many Estonian economists thought that the imposition of such radical economic policies was unworkable. Laar, however, assumed that rapid privatization and the flat tax reforms inspired by Friedman's work have already been tested, successfully adopted, and well routinized in many Western countries. In his own words, his reform team 'walked on water' not knowing it to be impossible (CATO 2006).

In this way, a major element of Milton Friedman's fiscal policy prescriptions became the cornerstone of tax policy in most of Eastern Europe and the former USSR—not because of the prescriptions of the economics profession, but because of the reading priorities of a historian.

*Source:* CATO Institute (2006); Bemis (2011).

nism in the early 1990s, shifting ideologies and theories can have a big impact on reform opportunities and processes.

## The Other Side of the Coin: Institutional Resilience, Path Dependency, and Critical Junctures

One theoretical perspective[6] departs from the idea of institutions as "self-reinforcing equilibria" and focuses instead on particular historical junctures that have led to lasting arrangements. In this account, the resilience of seemingly underperforming institutions sheds light on the long-lasting mechanisms of the reproduction of rules, despite shocks that could have disrupted them (Thelen 1999).

This concept, often called *path dependence*, means that outcomes and patterns are locked in for long periods of time, making reversal of the processes hard or impossible (Pierson and Skocpol 2002). Even if the rules to which the stakeholders subscribe stall development, they survive because of the reinforcing feedback mechanisms that generated suboptimal incentives for the actors in the first place.

An often quoted example is the development of the so-called QWERTY typewriter keyboard at the end of the 19th century (David 1985).[7] Despite the later invention of more efficient alternative products,[8] QWERTY still became the most commonly used keyboard on the market because a number of factors converged to lock it in as the predominant choice. Once a critical mass of consumers started using it, the switching costs (the time one would need to invest in learning a new typing system and transitioning to a new keyboard) were prohibitively high. In addition, the larger the pool of consumers using QWERTY, the more profitable for specialized stores to sell QWERTY typewriters or computers and the more useful for new users to learn this style as opposed to direct competitors like the Dvorak keyboard. Economists often call this reinforcing process "network externalities" or "external increasing returns."

This analytical perspective emphasizes the role of history, temporal sequences, macro political-economic contexts, and complex configurations of structural conditions over long periods of time. The story of the QWERTY typewriter might have some lessons for development as well.

As shown in Concepts in Practice 4.7 with respect to the rise of neo-patrimonialism in Africa, a legacy of weak institutions and strong tribal and ethnic loyalties can generate powerful incentives that perpetuate ethnicity-based patronage even when it is clearly suboptimal for development.

**CONCEPTS IN PRACTICE 4.7**

## Neo-Patrimonialism in Africa and Historical Legacies

After decolonization, many African states inherited weak political institutions. This void created the space for elites associated with governments to rely on patronage. Thus, the state became neo-patrimonial, combining modern bureaucracies with traditional patron-client networks built on the exchange between political support and concrete material benefits for narrow pockets of elites. This pattern of rule significantly constrains the possibilities for policy change to this day.

Other long-lasting historical legacies have also led to highly resilient structures of political influence. In former settler colonies like Kenya, Namibia, and Zimbabwe, the early European farmers established powerful interest groups whose political clout is still observable today in agricultural policy making.

*Source:* Van de Walle 2001.

### Institutional (In)stability

Institutions are stable or resilient when they survive major economic and political changes and endure over longer periods of time (Levitsky and Murillo 2006). As much as path dependency and long periods of time might be responsible for locking in some very resilient underperforming institutions and the bad equilibria they generate, if institutions attempt to solve coordination and collective action problems and to stabilize actors' expectations, sudden changes and high volatility can also have a negative effect on beliefs, expectations, and preferences. If constitutions, legislatures, supreme courts of justice, or laws change overnight or if the civil service is staffed with incumbent party supporters following each election, then societal actors will fail to make long-term investments, with immediate consequences for economic development. As Concepts in Practice 4.8 below illustrates, the lack of institutional predictability creates a vicious circle that some call the "instability trap" (Helmke and Levitsky 2006; Levitsky and Murillo 2009), perpetuating a self-reinforcing trajectory of weak institutions over a long period of time.

## Symptoms of Institutional Failure: Lack of Enforcement

Institutions generate pro-development incentives when they function properly. In the real world, rules vary on how consequential they are for policy

## Lifespan of National Constitutions around the Globe

In the entire universe of national constitutions, on average, institutional arrangements last 19 years. The range of variation is huge: the U.S. Constitution, drafted in 1789, has survived for more than 220 years; at the other extreme, the Dominican Republic and Haiti together account for about 7 percent of the global number of constitutions because of their dramatic instability.

Let us take a quick look at the island of Hispaniola—a true "constitutional graveyard" (Elkins, Ginsburg, and Melton 2009, 180–185). During the 20th century, both the Dominican Republic and Haiti, the two countries sharing the tiny island, oscillated between democratic and autocratic regimes. The wide polarization between incumbents and oppositions increased the stakes of staying in power. Accordingly, when one of the parties came to office, it changed the constitution to set rules that would favor it politically. Paradoxically, during periods of strong executive rules in both countries (the Trujillo years in the Dominican Republic or the Duvalier regime in Haiti), presidents did not just make amendments—the easier path—but rather rewrote the legal document completely. This self-reinforcing constitutional death pattern created a spiral of all-or-nothing gains that, in turn, fed a climate of severe political and economic instability.

*Source:* Elkins, Ginsburg, and Melton (2009).

outcomes. Most reforms are attempts to remedy one form or another of institutional failure or malfunctioning. If actors ignore the rules of the game, believe that the rules are unfair, or think they themselves will not be sanctioned for noncompliance, the rules fail to produce incentives of any kind.

Good enforcement and some degree of stability are symptoms or manifestations of well-functioning institutions (Levitsky and Murillo 2009). Enforcement refers to the degree of actors' compliance with the rules of the game.

## Weak Institutional Enforcement

Many developing countries are characterized by weak formal institutions, created intentionally or unintentionally. In some cases, the actors who wrote the rules genuinely want to enforce them, if they have the capacity to do so. More often, they lack either the capacity or the will to enforce them (Levitsky and Murillo 2009, 120).

A weak civil service or a limited reach of the central state into remote regions of a country, for example, has been found to severely curtail the state's ability to monitor and sanction deviation from the rule of law. Some studies suggested that, in the 19th century, the Peruvian state, because of its unwillingness to challenge local hierarchies, had limited reach in the countryside and therefore failed to effectively raise taxes. This failure significantly hindered the development of the rural regions relative to their urban counterparts. In contrast, Chile was able to exercise more effective control over its rural areas and, therefore, has been able to craft and implement more successful development projects in both rural and urban regions (Soifer 2006).

Why is it that Chile and Mexico had a greater state capacity than Colombia and Peru, despite their shared cultural and institutional legacies? One historical factor affecting the capacity and effectiveness of the state seems to have been the ability and willingness of key elites in Chile and Mexico to use national bureaucrats to make and implement local policies, thereby freeing decision making from the grip of entrenched local patrons. While such a policy has its limits—bureaucrats' incentives were not necessarily fully aligned with those of local populations—they were effective in ensuring that national policies (infrastructure projects, tax collection) were implemented more effectively than when local power barons could capture national resources with little oversight on how these funds were used.[9]

In general, lack of political incentives is a key factor in weak institutional enforcement. Many governments in the developing world often adopt "window-dressing" institutions in order to comply with the donor community's conditions on borrowing but never plan to enforce them (Levitsky and Murillo 2009, 120). This is known as the Potemkin (or "fake") village phenomenon. Politicians usually lack incentives to build "real" villages because citizens cannot act collectively and sanction them for deviation, preferring instead to pocket the money allocated for development projects.

In other cases, weak institutional enforcement is the product of the bargaining strategies of political actors. For example, even if initially Brazil and South Africa could not guarantee enforcement of certain racial- and gender-equality rights inscribed in their constitutions, human rights activists still pushed for their official inclusion in the legislation, hoping that they could become effective at a later point in time (Htun 2003; Levitsky and Murillo 2009, 121).

Weak institutional enforcement, in some cases, is also the product of demand-side factors such as societal compliance (or lack thereof). High socioeconomic inequality can hamper systematic enforcement. In the early 1990s, Brazil and South Africa were two of the most unequal societies on earth. Despite the similar degree of income inequality, the ability of the state to collect taxes and implement fiscal policies varied remarkably. South Africa was able to collect taxes effectively and ensure that even rich citizens complied. Conversely, in Brazil rich elites were able to exempt themselves from most direct taxation, ensuring that the tax burden fell disproportionately on the poor.

One of the reasons that tax compliance was so different in the two countries stemmed from the social cleavages characterizing these societies. In South Africa, as a result of the solidarity between rich and poor whites, the rich were more willing to comply with the tax demands of the state. Conversely, in Brazil, where official discrimination was prohibited—although it was pervasive in practice—the rich felt less solidarity with any segment of the rest of the population. Thus, paradoxically, it was easier to establish fiscal policies that sought to redress past injustices against the Black population in South Africa (following the 1994 transition to democracy) than in Brazil, where fiscal compliance by the rich continues to be erratic and the state thus relies on more regressive and distortionary forms of taxation.[10]

Sometimes, the core logic of certain institutional arrangements stems from weak compliance. In many low- to middle-income countries, as public sector jobs decreased and incumbent politicians failed to credibly commit to generating employment for young college graduates, the informal economy became a necessary exit opportunity for the unemployed. Any attempts to reduce it by formalization met strong political discontent and resistance (Hibou 2006).

Similarly, in some contexts, selective enforcement of institutional rules is a powerful strategic tool of political co-optation or punishment. In Ben Ali's Tunisia, for example, access to bank credits or development subsidies for entrepreneurs was often granted based on personal relationships with key political actors, not on market criteria (Hibou 2006).

In general, clientelistic political systems, in which the incumbent party channels benefits only to its own voters, function on a logic of weak institutional enforcement of formal rules. Symptoms of weak institutional enforcement may include:

- Weak capacity (lack of resources)
- Weak political will
- Eroding informal institutions (clientelism)
- Adopted institutions that fail to achieve equilibrium because they do not fit the underlying distribution of power in society
- High stakes of the game (socioeconomic inequalities or wide political polarization).

The underlying causes of institutional failure are also the obstacles to collective action that we will be exploring in depth in the following chapters, which include information discrepancies, absence of credible commitment on the part of politicians, agency problems, institutional manipulation, and other forms of imperfections that erode the capacity of citizens to act effectively.

To sum up, taking into consideration the factors discussed in this chapter, when conducting a political-economy analysis, the researcher should ask the following questions about institutions and organizations:

- What are the formal and informal rules governing your policy domain of choice?
- Are they enforced or not? Why?
- Are they durable? Did they survive any major exogenous shocks in the recent past?
- Why does stability vary across different institutions?
- What is the analytical link among institutions, incentives, and the potential for pro-development collective action in your policy area or sector?
- Can you identify organizations involved in a project you have worked on or a public policy issue you are interested in?
- How did the institutional context in which these organizations operate affect their ability?
- Did the rules of the game make it easier or more difficult for each individual organization to achieve its goal?
- Are these organizations monolithic in preferences and reform stakes?
- Which organizational subunits would gain most from the passing of a certain piece of legislation? Do they benefit or not from the current rules?

Institutions affect how actors interact with each other, determining the outcomes of a social situation. Therefore, for a better knowledge of policy consequences, it is essential to understand the logic of strategic interaction between actors. This process will enable us to think about how different institutions, by altering the nature of this interaction, can affect outcomes. Game theory provides the tools by which we can study the interaction of actors in different institutional contexts. The core ingredients of a game follow.

## Modeling the Role of Institutions with Game Theory[11]

Let's recall the game introduced in chapter 3, dealing with the collective action problem two farmers faced. Because each farmer had an incentive not to cooperate (but to defect), both farmers were collectively worse off because they could not cooperate on building an irrigation system for both farms. Institutions can potentially mitigate such collective action problems by providing mechanisms to reconcile the interests of individuals with those of the group.

Assume, as in chapter 3, that the two farmers would benefit from constructing an irrigation system for their farms. Furthermore, assume that they now live in a country with a very robust and efficient legal system that enables them to write contracts with each other. Specifically, if the farmers enter into an agreement to construct an irrigation system jointly, but one of them does not cooperate (that is, the farmer defects), the courts will speedily and efficiently fine the noncooperating (defecting) farmer, effectively taking her crop yield and using it to compensate the farmer who did not renege on her agreement.

Assuming that the farmers have entered a legal agreement to cooperate and build the irrigation system; the preferences of the first farmer (the farmers' preferences are symmetrical) are based on the payoffs she would receive, as follows:

- If the first farmer reneges on her construction commitments but the second farmer does not renege, the first farmer is fined, losing all her crops. The second farmer bears the costs of the irrigation system, but she also has enough food to sustain her family (due to the fine) and subsequently benefits from the existence of the irrigation system.
- If the first farmer builds the irrigation system but the second farmer reneges on her construction commitment, then the first farmer bears the full cost but also receives compensation (able to feed her family) and the benefit of the irrigation system. The second farmer loses all her crops (due to the fine).
- If both the first and the second farmer build the irrigation system, they both bear some of the cost (less time to grow their own crops), but they both enjoy the benefits of higher crop yields.
- If both farmers renege on the agreement, the agreement is rendered void, and they both have a normal yield (equivalent to the fine).

The diagram below shows these payoffs. Cooperation is now a strictly dominant strategy; that is, both farmers will cooperate regardless of what they think the other farmer will do.

|  | Cooperate[b] | | Defect[a] | |
|---|---|---|---|---|
| Cooperate[b] | 3 | 3 | 2 | 1 |
| Defect[a] | 1 | 2 | 1 | 1 |

a. *Defect* here refers to noncooperation.
b. "Cooperate, cooperate" for both farmers is the equilibrium of the game, denoted by the asterisk.

## Summary

The outcomes of the political process depend on how the institutional context determines the feasible courses of action that different stakeholders can take. Therefore, being able to map and analyze the institutional context can significantly increase the value added of a political-economy analysis. By identifying the formal and informal institutions and the conditions under which they may change, a researcher can anticipate the equilibria that exist or that may emerge. As the next few chapters will demonstrate, specific institutional settings can engender various opportunities and challenges to stakeholders' ability to realize their own agenda. The reformer will thus be able to identify how some rules may empower stakeholders either to support or to oppose a reform proposal or set project priorities appropriately.

# Exercises for Chapter 4: Theories and Mechanisms of Political Economy: Institutions and Equilibria

## Exercise 4.1: The Prisoner's Dilemma Game[12]

The facilitator explains the steps involved in the Prisoner's Dilemma.

Steps in the exerciser (time frame: ~40–45 minutes):
1. Read out instructions (1 minute)
2. Allow participants to read and answer (5–10 minutes)
3. Collect responses, tally responses, facilitate group discussion (10 minutes)
4. Lecture (10–15 minutes)
5. Class discussion (10 minutes)

Preparation and Materials:
1. Envelopes (A4 size) to be placed in the middle of the round table (one at each table)
2. Pens should be available to all participants
3. Copies of the instructions
4. Copies of the answer sheet
5. Copies of the key questions handout and group discussion
6. Facilitator instructions

Procedure:
1. The facilitator reads aloud the following instructions:
   I am going to distribute instructions and an answer sheet. Read the instructions and answer the questions on the answer sheet. Once you have read the instructions and completed your answers, place your answer sheet in the envelope in the middle of the table. DO NOT WRITE YOUR NAME ON EITHER DOCUMENT and MAKE SURE NO ONE SEES YOUR ANSWERS. Keep the instructions handy for the follow-up discussion. I will give you about 5–10 minutes to complete this.
2. The facilitator distributes the instructions handout and answer sheet to all the participants.
3. The facilitator gauges the rate of completion of the assignment and gives participants a 2-minute warning so that the activity can wrap up within its allotted 10-minute time frame. As part of the 2-minute warning, the facilitator reminds participants that they should not write their names on the answer sheet; when they have finished, they should put their answer sheet in the envelope in the middle of the table.

4. The facilitator explains:

   I will come around to collect the envelopes with the answer sheets and tally your responses. At the same time, I will give you a handout that includes two key questions. While I tally the responses on the answer sheets, please go ahead and discuss at your tables the two questions on the handout. Spend approximately 10 minutes in this discussion.

5. To tally the votes, the facilitator uses a blank answer sheet and notes for each option the total number of votes.

6. The facilitator walks around the room among the tables in a nonintrusive manner and pays attention to what is discussed. The facilitator notes a few comments from the tables that he or she can highlight as part of the transition to the lecture portion.

7. The facilitator gives the participants a two-minute warning to wrap up their discussion.

8. The facilitator explains:

   Now, that you have played the game and had a chance to discuss with others at your table some of the key underlying issues, I will go ahead with a mini-lecture to talk about the technical aspects in relation to the conceptual aspects that you addressed in your discussions. In fact, I noted the following key words being used at several tables:

   a. Trust

9. The facilitator presents the lecture beginning with the announcement of the final overall tally by entering the results on the first slide. The facilitator ends the lecture by posing the following questions to the entire group:

   a. How many of you were surprised by the entire group's final tally that I shared at the beginning of the slide?

   b. If yes, why?

   c. If no, why?

## Handout Exercise Set 4.1: Instructions Handout 1

You and a colleague (whom you do not know well) have been arrested after committing a crime. Upon arrest you were separated (there is no way to communicate with him or her). You are now in a police cell and the police negotiator informs you that they are willing to offer you the following deal, which is simultaneously also being offered to your colleague (you can assume this information is true):

- If you confess to the crime and your colleague does not confess to the crime, you will receive a reduced sentence of 1 year in prison, while your colleague will receive a full sentence of 12 years in prison.
- If you do not confess to the crime but your colleague does confess to the crime, you will receive a full sentence of 12 years in prison while your colleague will receive a reduced sentence of 1 year in prison.
- If you both confess to the crime, you will both receive a reduced sentence of 6 years in prison.
- If neither one of you confesses, you will both receive a reduced sentence of 3 years.

## Handout Exercise Set 4.1: Answer Sheet 1

Please indicate below, by ticking (√) the box next to the appropriate action, what you would like to do. PLEASE TICK ONLY ONE BOX.

| | |
|---|---|
| Confess to the Crime | |
| Do Not Confess to the Crime | |

Please indicate below, by ticking (√) the box next to the appropriate action, what you would like to do. PLEASE ONLY TICK ONE BOX.

| | |
|---|---|
| He/she will confess to the crime | |
| He/she will not confess to the crime | |

Briefly explain why you decided to pursue one action rather than the other.

| |
|---|
| |

**Once you have completed your answers, put them in the envelope in the middle of the table.**

## Handout Exercise Set 4.1: Key Questions Handout 1 —
## Group Discussion

In your group, please discuss the following questions:

1. What do you expect the result of the game/tally to be among all participants across all tables? Why do you think this is the case?

2. How does taking into account someone else's behavior affect your
   decision?

## Notes

1. This distinction is specific to the new economic institutionalism.
2. *Self-enforcing equilibrium* has the following characteristics: (1) best strategy among the feasible strategies for all players; (2) any change in behavior triggers change in the other players with inferior outcomes; and (3) actors have the capacity and willingness to punish deviant behavior.
3. See also North (1984, 1990).
4. See the separate subsection for the concept of self-enforcing equilibrium.
5. Various institutionalism schools operate with different assumptions related to how "endogenous" (embedded in preexisting social relations and power configurations), or "exogenous" (actors have well defined ex ante preferences) institutions are. The Rational Choice School, for example, assumes for the most part that institutions are exogenous (Weingast 2002).
6. Historical institutionalism.
7. For a critique of this interpretation of the QWERTY narrative, see Liebowitz and Margolis (1990).
8. The Dvorak Simplified Keyboard, invented in 1936, was technically superior to QWERTY on many indicators such as finger motion, typing time, and the like.
9. Adapted from Soifer (2006).
10. See Lieberman (2003).
11. *Source:* Inspired by (Bardhan 1993).
12. *Source:* Inspired by (Gibbons 1992).

## References

Alesina, Alberto, Reza Baqir, and William Easterly. 1999. "Public Goods and Ethnic Divisions." Policy Research Working Paper 2108. World Bank, Development Research Group, Washington, DC.

Ames, Barry. 1999. "Approaches to the Study of Institutions in Latin American Politics." *Latin American Research Review* 34 (1): 221–36

———. 2001. *The Deadlock of Democracy in Brazil: Interests, Identities, and Institutions in Comparative Politics.* Ann Arbor: University of Michigan Press.

ARD. 2006. "Yemen Corruption Assessment: Technical Report." USAID, Washington, DC.

Aslund, Anders, Peter Boone, and Simon Johnson. 2002. "Escaping the Under-Reform Trap." Staff Working Paper 48, International Monetary Fund, Washington, DC.

Bardhan, P. 1993. "Analytics of the Institutions of Informal Cooperation in Rural Development." *World Development* 21 (4): 633–639.

Bardhan, Pranab. 2002. "Decentralization of Governance and Development." *Journal of Economic Perspectives* 16 (4): 185–205.

Bemis, T. 2011. 'Flat-tax countries include Bulgaria, Mongolia, Iraq,' Market Watch, *The Wall Street Journal website,* http://blogs.marketwatch.com/thetell/

2011/10/25/bulgaria-mongolia-guernsey-among-the-23-flat-tax-countries/. Web accessed: 6/18/2012

Besley, Timothy, and Robin Burgess. 2002. "Can Labor Regulation Hinder Economic Performance? Evidence from India." *Quarterly Journal of Economics* 119 (1): 91–134.

Carey, John. 2000. "Parchment, Equilibria, and Institutions." *Comparative Political Studies* 33 (6/7): 735–61.

Carey, John M., and Matthew Soberg Shugart. 1995. "Incentives to Cultivate a Personal Vote: A Rank Ordering of Electoral Formulas." *Electoral Studies* 14 (4): 417–39.

Cato Institute. 2006. "Individual Liberty, Free Markets, and Peace: Mart Laar's Biography." Cato Institute Website, http://www.cato.org/special/friedman/laar/.

Crawford, Sues E. S., and Elinor Ostrom. 1995. "A Grammar of Institutions." *American Political Science Review* 89 (3): 582–600.

Crisp, Brian F. 2000. *Democratic Institutional Design: The Powers and Incentives of Venezuelan Politicians and Interest Groups*. Palo Alto: Stanford University Press.

Danchin, Peter. 2010. "A Human Right to Water? The South African Constitutional Court's Decision in the *Mazibuko* Case." *EJIL: Talk!*, http://www .ejiltalk.org/a-human-right-to-water-the-south-african-constitutional-court%E2%80%99s-decision-in-the-mazibuko-case/.

David, Paul A. 1985. "Clio and the Economics of QWERTY." *American Economic Review* 77 (2): 332–37.

Eaton, Kent, Kai Kaiser, and Paul Smoke. 2010. *The Political Economy of Decentralization Reforms: Implications for Aid Effectiveness*. Washington, DC: World Bank.

Egel, Daniel. 2010. "Tribal Diversity, Political Patronage and the Yemeni Decentralization Experiment." Unpublished manuscript, http://www.cgdev.org/doc/events/Post-Doc%20Seminars/Daniel_Egel.pdf.

Elkins, Zachary, Tom Ginsburg, and James Melton. 2009. *The Endurance of National Constitutions*. Cambridge: Cambridge University Press.

Geddes, B. 1994. *Politician's Dilemma: Building State Capacity in Latin America*. Berkeley: University of California Press.

Gibbons, R. 1992. *A Primer in Game Theory*. Harlow: Prentice Hall.

Golden, Miriam A., and Eric C. C. Chang. 2001. "Competitive Corruption: Factional Conflict and Political Malfeasance in Postwar Italian Christian Democracy." *World Politics* 52 (July): 588–622.

Grzymala-Busse, Anna. 2006. "The Discreet Charm of Formal Institutions: Post-Communist Party Competition and State Oversight." *Comparative Political Studies* 39 (10): 1–30.

Hayek, Friedrich A. 1962. *Rules, Perception and Intelligibility*. Oxford: Oxford University Press.

———. 1978. *Constitution of Liberty*. Chicago: University of Chicago Press.

Helmke, G., and S. Levitsky, eds. 2006. *Informal Institutions and Democracy: Lessons from Latin America*. Baltimore: Johns Hopkins University Press.

Hibou, Béatrice. 2006. *La Force De L'obéIssance: Economie Politique De La RéPression En Tunisie*. Textes à L›appui Histoire Contemporaine. Paris: Découverte.

Htun, Mala. 2003. *Sex and the State.* New York: Cambridge University Press.

Knight, Jack. 1992. *Institutions and Social Conflict.* Cambridge: Cambridge University Press.

Levitsky, Steven, and María Victoria Murillo. 2009. "Variation in Institutional Strength: Causes and Implications." *Annual Review of Political Science* 12: 115–33.

Lieberman Evan. 2003. *Race and Regionalism in the Politics of Taxation in Brazil and South Africa.* Cambridge, UK: Cambridge University Press.

Liebowitz, S. J., and Stephen E. Margolis. 1990. "The Fable of the Keys." *Journal of Law and Economics* 33 (1): 1–25.

Lijphart, A. 1999. *Patterns of Democracy.* New Haven: Yale University Press.

Mehta, Lyla, and Zolile Ntshona. 2004. "Dancing to Two Tunes? Rights and Market-Based Approaches in South Africa's Water Domain." Research Paper 17, Institute of Development Studies, University of Sussex.

Michels, Robert. 1911. *Political Parties: A Sociological Study of the Oligarchical Tendencies of Modern Democracy.* Piscataway, NJ: Transaction Publishers.

Nicol, Alan, and Sobona Mtisi. 2003. "Politics and Water Policy: A Southern Africa Example." *IDS Bulletin* 34 (3): 41–53.

North, Douglass C. 1984. "Government and the Cost of Exchange in History." *Journal of Economic History* 44 (2): 255–64.

North, Douglas. 1981. *Structure and Change in Economic History.* New York: Norton.

———. 1990. *Institutions, Institutional Change, and Economic Performance.* New York: Cambridge University Press.

———. 2005. *Understanding the Process of Economic Change.* Princeton: Princeton University Press.

O'Dwyer, Conor. 2006. *Runaway State-Building: Patronage Politics and Democratic Development.* Baltimore: Johns Hopkins University Press.

Olson, Mancur. 1981. *The Rise and Decline of Nations: Economic Growth, Stagflation, and Social Rigidities.* New Haven: Yale University Press.

Persson, Torsten, and Guido Tabellini. 2005. *The Economic Effects of Constitutions.* Cambridge: MIT Press.

Pierson, Paul, and Theda Skocpol. 2002. "Historical Institutionalism in Contemporary Political Science." In *Political Science: State of the Discipline,* ed. Ira Katznelson and Helen V. Milner, 693–721. New York: W.W. Norton.

Powley, E. 2005. "Women Hold Up Half the Parliament." In *Women in Parliament: Beyond the Numbers,* ed. F. Ginwala and A. Karam. Stockholm: International Institute for Democracy and Electoral Assistance.

Przeworski, Adam. 2004. "Institutions Matter?" *Government and Opposition* 39 (4): 527–40.

Soifer, H. D. 2006. *Authority over Distance: Explaining Variation in State Infrastructural Power in Latin America.* PhD Dissertation. Cambridge, MA: Harvard University Press.

Thelen, K. 1999. "Historical Institutionalism in Comparative Politics." *Annual Review of Political Science* 2 (1): 369–404.

Tsai, Lily. 2007. *Accountability without Democracy: Solidary Groups and Public Goods Provision in Rural China*. Cambridge: Cambridge University Press.

Van de Walle, Nicolas. 2001. *African Economies and the Politics of Permanent Crisis, 1979–1999*. Cambridge: Cambridge University Press.

Verdery, K. 2003. *The Vanishing Hectare: Property and Value in Postsocialist Transylvania*. Ithaca: Cornell University Press.

Weingast, Barry. 2002. "Rational-Choice Institutionalism." In *Political Science: State of the Discipline,* ed. Ira Katznelson and Helen V. Milner, 660–92. New York: Norton.

White, James. 1995. *Ikki: Social Conflict and Political Protest in Early Modern Japan*. Ithaca, NY: Cornell University Press.

Yamin, Alicia, and Siri Gloppen, eds. 2011. *Litigating Health Rights: Can Courts Bring More Justice to Health?* Cambridge: Harvard University Press.

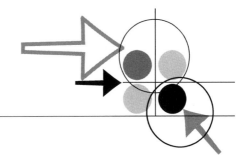

**CHAPTER 5**

# Collective Choice and Agenda Setting

Collective decision making often entails making a choice between several different viable alternatives. Sometimes, how decision makers present and compare these alternatives—that is, how they set an agenda—can determine which policy alternative is chosen, regardless of merit. In many policy-making contexts (especially in legislatures), the final decision can depend on the agenda-setting power of certain actors rather than on the inherent desirability of any of the possible choices faced.

Specifically, agenda setting is an institutional mechanism (see chapter 4) that mitigates the collective action problems faced by some or all of the individuals or groups with a stake in policy outcomes (see chapter 3). Agenda setting can facilitate collective action by helping groups economize on information; by allowing a subset of the group to develop specialist knowledge (for example, committees in legislatures, such as foreign affairs, public finance, defense, etc.); and by promoting group cohesion (for example, cohesion of a political party can be strengthened if committee appointments and membership are based on seniority or on a record of disciplined adherence to party policy).

**FIGURE 5.1 Agenda-Setting Conceptual Map**

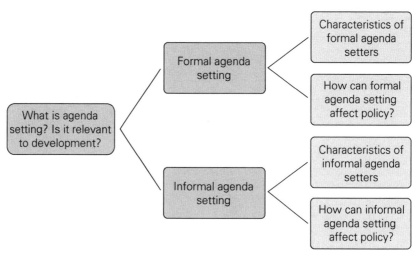

*Source:* Authors.

Therefore, understanding the role of agenda setting can help reformers both identify powerful agenda setters who might help or hinder their reform proposals, and design institutions to take into account future agenda-setting dynamics.

Normatively, the mere existence of agenda setting raises fundamental questions about the ways in which majority will translates into concrete policy outcomes. Of course, it is also important to note that the absence of agenda-setting mechanisms can also present challenges. Specifically, the lack of agenda control can generate information problems and a lack of cohesion among stakeholders. Learning about agenda setting is also relevant because in everyday development work the absence of such institutional mechanisms can lead to a lack of coordination, a weak detection and monitoring capacity, and, subsequently, suboptimal organizational outcomes. Therefore, it is useful to acquire the analytical tools that help understand the origins, organizational location, and probability of change associated with specific institutional problems (see figure 5.1).

This chapter uses the concept of *agenda setting* to show how a development practitioner can recognize and use institutional rules to alter policy outcomes. Reformers should ask themselves the following questions:

- Among the variety of rules governing the policy domain of interest, which ones are most relevant for change?
- Are these rules enforced?

- What strategic tools can be used to navigate existing formal and informal rules to bring the policy outcomes closer to the ideal goals?
- Who is responsible for scheduling the order in which policy proposals are submitted for debate and voted on according to the organizational procedure?

## Objectives of Chapter 5

By the end of this chapter, readers should be able to do the following:

- Identify the relevant formal and informal agenda-setting institutions that govern the policy domain
- Understand how agenda setting can induce changes in the final outcome irrespective of the distribution of stakeholder support for a certain policy alternative
- Explore potential positive or negative effects on policy change and reform caused by the absence or existence of agenda-setting power.

## What Is Agenda Setting?

Agenda control, or setting, refers to how the *process* of decision making affects outcomes irrespective of the substantive merit of each policy proposal.[1] The sequencing of decision making, the timing of voting procedures, and the skillful use of rules that govern the form in which bills or amendments are brought up for legislative debate are classic examples of agenda setting and will be explored in depth throughout this chapter. An often-quoted example illustrates the point: John Dingell, a former Democratic representative in the U.S. Congress, once said, "I'll let you write the substance . . . and you let me write the procedure, and I'll screw you every time."[2] The tremendous political power held by the Committee on Rules in the U.S. Congress since the 1880s is clear evidence that the use of voting rules in policy making matters significantly for the final legislative results.

The importance of agenda setting first came to prominence in the 1950s and 1960s as scholars in political science increasingly began to question the received orthodoxy that the raw power (number of voters, seats in parliament, and the like) of a group translated directly into an increased ability to influence outcomes. One of the major criticisms of this "classical pluralist" approach was that it did not take into account the ability of certain groups— not necessarily the largest groups but those that could overcome collective action problems most effectively—to use their superior capabilities to set the agenda and manipulate outcomes in their favor (Riker 1981).

We can think of agenda setting as having two dimensions (Bachrach and Baratz 1962): the first dimension is the choice between the alternatives on offer, and the second is the ability to determine what the choices are in the first place. Because agenda-setting individuals or groups may well not be the same as those who exercise the most power when deciding among alternatives, the importance of institutional rules and procedures governing the selection and scheduling of policy proposals can be significant.

The following sections briefly explain the process through which the policy preferences of stakeholders are aggregated to generate collective policy, thereby making it easy to see how strategic agenda setters might be able to use their power to influence outcomes.

### From Individual Preferences to Collective Choice

Individuals and organizations have different interests, stakes, and incentives in policy change. For example, let's assume that a local council has to deliberate over and vote on the location of a bridge. At the council, each of the three districts is represented by a councilor elected by the voters from that district, with each district having an equal number of votes on the council. One community might prefer the bridge to be built in its own district, but if that is not possible, it will prefer that the bridge be built in the neighboring district, rather than the district that is farther away. Another community, depending on its geographical location, will order its preferences differently. *Collective choice* is the process that converts such heterogeneity of policy positions into concrete outcomes.

*Agenda setting* (that is, the use of preference-aggregation rules such as voting) intermediates the way in which individual preferences translate into collective choice. Thus, agenda setting helps solve a fundamental problem characterizing majoritarian decision-making settings,[3] namely, the fact that the aggregation process through which individual choices become policy decisions leads to instability or "cycling" among multiple possible equilibria (Riker 1981; Shepsle 1989).

One of the most consequential institutions in many legislatures around the world is the use of committees to filter legislation. Committees develop specialist knowledge of a policy topic and have the power to select bills for debate in the legislature. As a consequence, few bills reach the floor. Committees limit the number of policy proposals to a more manageable number, although they may also have the effect of limiting the ability of the full legislature to amend bills. In this way, the existence of committees plays a critical role in ensuring that the workload of legislatures remains manageable.

The agenda-setting powers of legislative committees often translate into concrete development outcomes. Let's take a look at an example of "handing out the pork" in the German parliament (Stratmann and Baur 2002). Because committees decide which bills are voted on in the full legislative chamber or how the content of proposed legislation is altered, many committees have the power to ensure that the final version of a bill is closest to the interests of their (majority) membership. It has long been known that, because of these agenda-setting powers, election-seeking politicians may attempt to obtain committee positions through which they can use this power to further the interests of their own constituents. For example, in the case of the German Parliament, in which the elections of some members are determined by a constituency plurality (first past the post) rule and others under proportional representation (or through party lists), there is significant self-sorting on committees as politicians jockey to provide rents to their voters. Thus, unsurprisingly, committees that allocate spending to certain geographical areas are dominated by politicians elected from constituencies, while committees that allocate spending independent of geography but whose expenditure can be targeted to diffuse groups across the country are dominated by legislators elected by party lists. This desire to obtain relevant committee membership highlights the importance of agenda setting as a mechanism to please core voters and secure reelection.

## Cycling

To return to our example of the new bridge to be constructed, assuming four policy alternatives ($x$ = *bridge construction in District 1*, $y$ = *bridge construction in District 2*, and $z$ = *bridge construction in District 3*), three groups of voters have the following ranking of preferences (notation $P$ to be read as voter from District 1 prefers $x$ to $y$, $y$ to $z$, $x$ to $z$, etc.):

Voter from District 1: $x$ P1 $y$ P1 $z$
Voter from District 2: $y$ P2 $z$ P2 $x$
Voter from District 3: $z$ P3 $x$ P3 $y$

We need a majority (50 percent plus one, in this case, two voters) to agree on their rankings of individual preferences in order to aggregate them optimally in the final ordering of the group preference. What alternative ranking would win two votes? Notice the unstable equilibria for $x$, $y$, and $z$. No matter how hard one tries to find a sequence of $x$, $y$, and $z$ that would aggregate the will of the majority best, the efforts will fail (for the entire group, $x$ P $y$ P $z$ P $x$ P $y$ P $z$ P $x$). Therefore, $x$, $y$, and $z$ form a *cycle* (Johnson 1998).

Sometimes in efforts to aggregate preferences, some policy alternatives will win independently of the sequencing of the voting or the ordering of any other alternative. This concept is often referred to as a *Condorcet winner*.[4]

Unlike alternatives that are subject to cycling, a Condorcet winner is an alternative that can defeat each of the other alternatives in any pairwise majority vote. In this case, if our voters preferred a fourth alternative *w* (say, a bridge built at the joint border of all three districts) *that defeats x, y, and z in all three cases described above*, then *w* is a Condorcet winner.

As Concepts in Practice 5.1 explains in more detail, this problem of identifying the majority-preferred outcome in the presence of cycling is a major

■

**CONCEPTS IN PRACTICE 5.1**

## Optimum Outcomes and Constraints

Given cycling, what is the major dilemma a policy maker faces when trying to identify the majority-preferred outcome? As Nobel Prize–winning economist Kenneth Arrow formally demonstrated (Arrow 1951), no voting system can aggregate individual preferences in a way that satisfies the basic criteria of fairness. Therefore, it is impossible to know whether an outcome reflects the will of the majority or is the product of agenda manipulation by politicians.

Arrow's famous (im)possibility theorem has had a profound effect on our understanding of the normative implications of collective decision making. It has proved that no voting system can aggregate individual preferences in a manner that does not violate at least one of the following three conditions, which are often identified as being inherently desirable (fair) in collective decision making:

- If every individual in a group prefers alternative *x* to *y*, then the group will also prefer *x* to *y*.

- If every individual's preferences for alternatives *x* and *y* remain the same, the group preferences will also remain the same (even

when individual preferences for other alternatives change, say *w*).

- There is no dictator who can impose his or her preferences on the group. This means that if one person in the group cares intensely about having the bridge built in District 1, she cannot unilaterally impose her will so that the entire group prefers the same location for the infrastructure project.

While it is beyond the scope of this work to formally show how Arrow's theorem is proved, its implications for social choice are clear: in theory, the fact that there is no aggregation method that satisfies all three conditions at the same time implies that no voting procedure is ideal for reflecting the "will" of the majority. Thus, as Riker (1981) showed, the nonexistence of such an "objective" social optimum enables political entrepreneurs who can manipulate agendas to impose their private preferences on society. In other words, group decisions (public policy outcomes) may reflect the private preferences of the most adept political manipulators rather than the "will of the people."

preoccupation of social science, as it makes it difficult to argue that, even if a benevolent policy maker exists, he or she can actually know what is "best" for society.

### Why Agenda Setting?

Given the inherent instability of aggregation (reflected in the previously introduced concept of cycling and the general impossibility theorem), it has been argued that agenda setters (the committee system in some legislative institutions, for example) can (1) eliminate or prioritize policy alternatives and (2) strategically instrumentalize the voting power of political actors in a way that leads to the so-called structure-induced equilibrium (Shepsle and Weingast 1984, 1987; Riker 1986; Ordeshook and Schwartz 1987; Tsebelis 1994, 1997). Simply put, by manipulating voting procedures, strategic agenda setters can structure the political debate in such a way that they are more likely to get what they want (Pollack 1997, 121–122).

## Types of Agenda Setting

Often, in political economy, agenda setting refers to two distinct processes, formal and informal. Most of the official voting rules briefly described below fall into the category of *formal agenda setting*. The locus of agenda control and the political power of the agenda setter depend on the following factors (Pollack 1997):

- *Initiative rules.* Every legislative body has an idiosyncratic set of actors endowed with the right to initiate legislation. For example, in the U.S. Congress, specialized committees have disproportionate power over legislative proposals. In the European Union, the European Commission holds the right as the sole initiator of legislation.

  In the case of the Philippines public procurement reform, documented in greater detail in appendix C, the ability to initiate a new bill rested with specific committees in the legislature. In 1998, during the early days of reform attempts, when President Joseph Estrada was facing corruption allegations and had incentives to give legislative priority to a "clean" public procurement bill, his office needed to identify a member of Congress who was willing to sponsor the proposal and who belonged to a committee that would be sympathetic to the reform. The Budget Department's Legislative Liaison Office, keeping a low profile to avoid attracting open opposition to the reform attempt, found an influential member of the Committee of Public Works who was interested in the reformers' proposal.

The congressman who decided to sponsor the bill had previously initiated a legislative proposal on sanctions for violations of government contracting regulations and agreed to substitute the procurement package for his original initiative. Only two weeks before a legislative recess, he managed to use his influence with the Rules Committee to introduce the bill for debate with unprecedented speed, despite not being scheduled, and to bring it to the floor when most opposing legislators were absent and a neutral quorum was met.

- *Voting rules.* Under majority voting, a strong agenda setter can structure the decision process in a way that ensures a stable equilibrium close to its desired policy. Many times, in both parliaments and organizations, *the choice of the voting rule* can have profound implications for the final policy outcome. We have already suggested in previous chapters that the electoral rules through which political representatives are selected (on national party lists or through a "winner-take-all" system at the district level) may give politicians different incentives to offer clientelistic or universalistic public goods to their constituents. Similarly, legislatures, political party congresses, caucuses, organizations, or coalitions often employ various voting methods that count and aggregate individual preferences differently.

  In *one-vote systems*, all members of an organization pick only one among all possible options. In our bridge construction example, the voters of District 1 choose option *x*. In *ranked or preferential systems*, voters get to rank their options and assign points according to the rank. According to one such rule (Borda counting), District 2 voters will give a score of 3 to *y*, a score of 2 to *z*, and a score of 1 to *x*. In the end, the sum of total votes obtained by all alternatives decides the winner.

  In *rated voting systems*, voters can assign any grades or points within a range (say, 0 to 10) for all three options (District 3 voters could assign a score of 10 to *z*, 7 points to *x*, and 1 point to *y*). In our case, a Borda voting system will give the same number of 6 points to all options. In other cases, however, because ranked or rated voting systems are more sensitive to the averages of preferences across districts, they might lead to the selection of broadly acceptable policy options as opposed to those simply preferred by the majority. If agenda setters can select organizational voting rules, they are likely to influence the final outcome and either empower or bypass majorities. The interactive exercise at the end of this chapter will show how *the voting sequence*, or the order in which these three bridge construction site alternatives are submitted for majority decisions, can render a winner desired by the agenda setter.

- *Amendment rules.* Sometimes, amendment rules require just 50 percent plus one vote; other times, it is easier to accept an agenda setter's full bill proposal than it is to amend it. The European Commission is a case in point. Because of the unanimity rule governing its amendment powers, it is virtually impossible to amend its proposals.

In many legislatures around the world, committee rules with respect to who can propose, how, or in what shape or form amendments can go to the floor of the assembly for debate are numerous and granular. Their level of detail and technicality is often discouragingly complex for anyone not intimately acquainted with the legislative process. The standing U.S. Senate Manual of rules, orders, laws, and resolutions for the 112th Congress is a huge tome of no less than 1,429 pages detailing the minutiae of senators' work, protocols, and procedures. As we will see in the next section of this chapter, in some legislative assemblies, even small changes in rules affecting the order of amendments to bills, or the form in which the amendment is proposed (for example, if it is to be included in the original text of the bill or kept separate) can lead to policy outcomes that are quite different from what the majority really prefers.

For reformers, this factor can be both bad and good news. On the one hand, the high level of complexity makes the legislative process intimidating and difficult to navigate. On the other hand, the devil is in the details. Sometimes, paradoxically, key amendments to preexisting laws and regulations or consolidation of scattered regulations might be more important for providing quick gains to reformers than submitting for debate an entirely new bill that would meet open opposition.

In 2001, in Kenya, during the last days of the Moi administration, the public procurement system was plagued by severe corruption and colonized by entrenched political patronage networks. A reform team decided to tackle the challenge. The reformers' initial instinct was to prepare a new procurement act, make the attempt politically salient, and garner public support for reform. They were instead advised to take advantage of amendment procedures to the preexisting Exchequer and Audit Act rather than making their efforts public and attracting intense opposition from vested interests. As a result, as part of an omnibus act clarifying the implementation of the Exchequer and Audit Act, the Kenyan legislature passed a new set of public procurement regulations that unified all the disparate acts governing procurement and created key institutions; thus, the reform team bypassed the fierce opposition it would have generated by passing a new law.

The Philippines public procurement reform features a similar trajectory. In 2001, the reform team took a step-by-step approach and first persuaded President Arroyo to pass an executive order that consolidated all previous procurement regulations, despite the fact that this act did not allow amendments to the preexisting laws. This first step created a sense of policy ownership in the executive's office. In a second stage, the reform team garnered public support through the activities of a nongovernmental organization, Procurement Watch, and promoted the bill as a broader omnibus package designed to ensure transparency and not just a narrow change in the workings of public procurement. Thus, by building support incrementally, the reformers were finally able to gain sufficient leverage in both chambers of the legislature to ensure passage (see appendix C).

- *Heterogeneity of actors' preferences.* Often, the policy arena has a complex web of institutions, each having its own voting rules. In some legislative bodies, if the two chambers that need to jointly pass a bill have directly antagonistic interests (say, the majorities are held by two opposing political parties), the agenda setter (as the initiator of legislation) will refrain from even formulating the proposal in the first place. In the case of the Philippines procurement bill, the supporters' first attempt at passage in 1998 was obstructed because, while it passed in the lower house, the Senate had different political priorities and did not consider the bill. Whereas the congressman who sponsored the proposal in the lower house was a representative of the opposition and tried to distance himself from a president facing a corruption scandal, the chairman of the relevant Senate committee was closely associated with the president, did not have incentives to promote the bill, and strategically blocked it. Passage was finally assured after an election, which produced a more balanced distribution of party seats and a unified opposition party presence in both chambers. Subsequently, this new configuration allowed the reformers to identify a small number of pivotal supporters, from both the majority and opposition parties, to champion the bill, thereby allowing the media to portray its passage as a bipartisan effort (see appendix C).

- *The impatience (or time horizon) of the various actors to change the status-quo.* In many legislative settings, for example, as long as the agenda setter's proposal is better than the status quo, even if far from other actors' ideal or preferred policy, the bill could still pass. However, if the latter anticipate that the agenda setter is impatient to push the legislation (or has a short time horizon because of reputational or electoral risks), they can engage in a series of proposal rejections, until the agenda setter brings the policy closer to their preferences.

This type of strategic voting caused by different time horizons reduces the power of the agenda setter (Pollack 1997). In contrast, if the other decision makers are impatient, the influence of the agenda setter increases significantly (Shepsle 1989; Pollack 1997, 124). The same logic applies to many legislative agenda-setting processes as well. To go back to the case of the Philippines procurement bill, the need for President Estrada, who faced a corruption scandal and the possibility of impeachment, to pass a law that tried to minimize corruption in public procurement became attractive five months before an election. As a result, the president became a key supporter of the bill in order to boost his reelection prospects and thus increased the agenda setter's bargaining position. Unfortunately, by the time the bill had reached the Senate, many of its members were busy trying to bolster their own reelection prospects and were able to outlast the president (see appendix C).

## How Do Formal Rules Influence Outcomes?

As a sophisticated setting of agenda control, the U.S. House of Representatives has a vast range of rules for the *order, content, and form* in which amendments to legislative bills can be debated by the majority of members. This institutional setting allows the powerful Committee on Rules to "set the agenda" either by eliminating certain alternatives right from the beginning or by ordering their vote in a way that produces a result different from what another ordering alternative would have produced, even under conditions of sophisticated voting.

*Order or sequencing of voting* can alter the final outcome dramatically. The results change for alternative amendment voting agendas: for example, given a set of three proposals ($x, y,$ and $z$), an agenda setter decides on pitting $x$ against $y$, the winner of which is pitted against $z$ out of all three sequencing possibilities. The two discarded sequences are $x$ being pitted against $z$, the winner of which is pitted against $y$; and $z$ being pitted against $y$, the winner of which is pitted against $x$.

Below are some examples of rules governing *the content of policy proposals* that can yield different policy results (Patty and Penn 2008).

- *"Closed" or restrictive voting rules* in some legislatures (including the U.S. Congress) allow only certain policy amendments to reach the floor for debate.
- *"Open" rules*, in contrast, allow any germane legislative amendments to be debated, thus aligning more closely with the majority will.
- *Ordered open rules*, as a subset of the previous category that combines effects of both *content* and *order*, prespecify the order in which these amendments are considered (Patty and Penn 2008; Krehbiel 1991; Olezsek 2007).

However, even if some rules are more open to policy alternatives than others, they still allow ample room for strategic manipulation by agenda setters. This aspect raises important questions about the design of collective choice institutions, as well as about their outcomes (Patty and Penn 2008, 20; Dummett 1984).

For example, in the case of open rules, even if all amendments are submitted for debate, *the form of submission* will still alter the result. In some cases, the committee on rules will consider amendments to a specific piece of legislation that would first be fully incorporated or printed in the original bill and sent out for debate as a substitute bill, instead of simply being submitted as disparate individual amendments. However, this version of the amended piece of legislation is also pitted against the unamended original bill when voted on the floor. What is the reason for the inclusion of the original bill as well? Despite the seeming redundancy, studies show that in such cases, the outcomes differ fundamentally, depending on whether the original bill is included or not. When the original bill is included, the floor is more likely to choose the substitute bill as is. In the other case, the substitute bill will be chosen only after being amended on the floor by the majority (Patty and Penn 2008; Bach and Smith 1988).

By anticipating the voting outcome, the strategic agenda setter (in this case, the Committee on Rules in the U.S. House of Representatives) is thus able to deliberately select specific voting rules that would bring the policy content closer to its ideal point.[5]

## Informal Agenda Setting

While formal agenda influence is conferred by clear and codified decision-making rules, for *informal agenda control,* the agenda setter must be a skillful policy entrepreneur who, under conditions of imperfect information[6] and legislative impasse or polarization, can construct "focal points" for bargaining and bypassing obstacles. Rather than deciding on voting rules as in the case of formal agenda setting, the entrepreneur just offers an idea that can rescue the bargaining process when there is no other equilibrium (Garrett and Weingast 1993; Pollack 1997, 125).

Informal agenda-setting power requires policy creativity. The interesting thing about it is that many actors (lobbyists, legislative committees, influential individuals, media representatives, and civil society organizations, among others) can be policy entrepreneurs, unlike the formal agenda setter, whose role is clearly inscribed in institutional codes.

Regardless of whether agenda setting is formal or informal in nature, the tools of agenda manipulation are often similar (Riker 1981, 1986):

- *Heresthetics* can broadly be defined as the attempt by an individual policy entrepreneur or a cohesive group to try and manipulate the context or structure of a decision-making process to ensure a more favorable outcome.
- *Rhetoric* is the art of using language effectively to inform, persuade, or manipulate an audience.
- *Agenda control* means using formal legislative rules of proposal and amendment to obtain favorable voting outcomes.
- *Strategic voting* means using voting procedures to control outcomes.
- *Manipulation of dimensions* involves redefining a situation to create a stronger coalition.

Informal agenda-setting power also closely relates to the concept of *leadership*, as individuals who can persuade supporters of a reform to form a viable coalition or can use their influence at strategic moments can be critical to achieving policy goals. Some studies have identified three main factors that, combined, can generate a "policy window" for an innovative entrepreneurial idea that could serve as a key bargaining point (Kingdon 1984, 165–167; Pollack 1997):

- The identification of the problem
- The proposal of feasible and acceptable policy alternatives
- Political changes (alternations of political parties in the legislature, upcoming elections, and the like).

The confluence of these three simultaneous processes could possibly lead to a viable alternative to policy deadlock.

## What Are the Characteristics of a "Good" Formal and Informal Agenda Setter?

*The formal agenda setter* has to have a thorough understanding of the rules, the anticipated policy outcomes, and the strategic behavior of the major actors involved in the decision-making process. However, institutional power is often already assigned to the agenda-setting bodies and recognized by all participants from the very beginning. Concepts in Practice 5.2 offers an example of the power of formal agenda setting and the way in which it was used in Latin America to align development policy outcomes with presidential mandates.

CONCEPTS IN PRACTICE 5.2

## The Power of Formal Agenda Setting: Using the Presidential Veto to Make Policy in Uruguay

Traditionally, the ability of the president of Uruguay to influence lawmaking has been considered weak. While the president can veto a law passed by Congress, it is possible for the legislature to override such a veto, albeit with a three-fifths majority. Therefore, the conventional wisdom was that, when there was consensus, Congress would be able to get its way because the president's ability to stop legislation could be circumscribed.

However, this understanding of the relative power of the president and Congress does not take into account the agenda-setting power of the former. The president of Uruguay is not only able to veto legislation, but also to make 'amendatory observations'—that is changes to a bill after it has been approved by Congress. The implications of this amendatory power are that, in effect, the president has conditional agenda-setting power that enables him or her to alter final legislation. The president effectively sets the agenda by proposing to Congress an

amended version of the law, which can then be approved by a simple majority. Therefore, if Congress is better off accepting the president's amendment by a simple majority rather than overriding the veto, which requires a three-fifths majority, the president can influence policy outcomes through her agenda-setting power.

The agenda-setting power of the president of Uruguay was clearly evident in the passage of the Five Year Budget Bill (2000–2004), which saw the president significantly modify the act with respect to tax policy, salaries, the school curriculum, benefits, and funding. As Congress faced a 30-day deadline to pass the new bill and a supermajority is required to override the president's proposals, support to drop the president's proposals was sufficient only to eliminate 6 of a total of 34 amendments. In short, by setting the agenda, the president was able to significantly modify the final outcome of the policy-making process.

*Source:* Tsebelis and Alémán (2005).

Unlike the formal agenda setter, the *informal agenda setter* requires less clear and more eclectic skills, and his or her influence or power may vary. Studies have attempted to identify a set of basic features: the person usually possesses considerable authority as a policy expert or negotiator, patience and other skills necessary for navigating a complex institutional landscape (Kingdon, 1984, 188; Pollack 1997, 126). Influential policy networks of technical experts, coupled with incomplete information available to the political representatives, have often led to legislation proposed and passed without any amendment from legislators (see the Philippines case study on procurement in appendix C for further elaboration).

As Concepts in Practice 5.3 will now show with respect to the election of Abraham Lincoln in 1860, the roles of informal agenda setting and issue manipulation have long been effectively used by political entrepreneurs to further policy goals.

---

CONCEPTS IN PRACTICE 5.3

### The Power of Informal Agenda Setting: Using the Issue of Slavery to Get Elected

Sometimes being able to identify an issue that resonates with voters but is neglected by the establishment can help propel a seemingly marginal or extreme candidate into office. During the 1850s, attempts to dislodge the Democratic Party from power in the United States resulted in failure because the party had solid electoral support from both northern farmers and cotton planters in the South given its support for free trade, making it easier for these groups to export goods to Europe. As a result, industrialists (in the North) were isolated in their support for tariffs and hence protection from their European competitors.

How were the Democrats dislodged and the Republicans, under Abraham Lincoln, brought to power? Abraham Lincoln was able to use the issue of slavery (agenda setting) to divide the Democrats' coalition. Following the Missouri Compromise of 1820, the issue of slavery had become increasingly important to parts of the electorate for a variety of reasons (for example, westward expansion, the rise of the abolitionist movement, and so forth). By emphasizing this issue during his election campaign, Lincoln was able to create a new winning coalition that pitted northern farmers and industrialists against southern planters. In this way, by setting the electoral agenda, Lincoln was able to win the election of 1860. The U.S. Civil War of 1861–65 resulted in the abolition of slavery across the United States.

*Source:* Riker (1981).

---

## Agenda Setting as a Strategic Tool for Policy Making: A Note on Positivist and Normative Angles

So far, we have argued that agenda setting intermediates the aggregation of individual preferences in collective choice, bypassing cycles. In addition, and perhaps more important from the point of view of the general development practitioner, agenda setting is a *strategic tool* for pursuing policy or political goals.

Normatively, agenda setting as a policy tool can be used for both "good" and "nefarious" purposes. In some contexts, skillful manipulation of formal rules or the use of informal channels of political influence and communication can block any attempt to advance pro-development reform and act against positive change.

As will now be seen in the case of election rigging in a post-Communist context, framing and manipulating the issue of the fairness of the electoral process, by preemptively making allegations about the motives of election monitors, can detract from the real question of whether elections were held in a fair manner in the first place (see Concepts in Practice 5.4).

In other circumstances and institutional settings, a reform-minded agenda setter (for example, the head of the committee on rules or budgets in the national legislature) or a talented policy entrepreneur who manages to substantively influence the agenda at the right time can be crucial for pro-development policy change.

The Philippines case study in appendix C will illustrate in greater detail the key importance of agenda setters for the overhaul of the corrupt public procurement system in the Philippines. Despite unfavorable conditions for the passage of a bill targeting the vested interests that had blocked previous attempts at public procurement reforms, change agents skillfully located and co-opted a potential agenda setter—the chairman of an influential com-

---

CONCEPTS IN PRACTICE 5.4

## Agenda Manipulation in Competitive Authoritarian Elections

Nondemocratic regimes rely on a combination of coercion and persuasion to remain in power. In particular, competitive authoritarian regimes need to become adept at persuading the public that their rule is beneficial and better than any alternative the opposition can offer.

For example, in a recent election, opposition groups were allowed to monitor voting irregularities and even publish their findings through the electronic media. However, in anticipation of the opposition's possible allegations of ballot irregularities, rumors were circulated before the election that the opposition was planning to publish a list of alleged irregularities that it had already manufactured. Thus, when the opposition parties promptly published their list of irregularities after the election, some media outlets questioned the speed and the authenticity of the findings. The regime managed to diminish the credibility of the opposition's initial charges of voting irregularities and shifted the debate (agenda) toward the trustworthiness of the opposition rather than the tactics of the government.

*Source:* Schatz (2008).

mittee in the legislature (Committee for Public Works). Taking advantage of the absence on a particular voting day of members of Parliament opposed to reform, the agenda setter pushed the bill to the floor and managed to circumvent entrenched interests while acting within the prerogatives and legal constraints of his position.

## Summary

Policy outcomes are not always a reflection of the mobilization potential of large groups or majorities. Because of cycling, it is possible for strategically minded agenda setters, with either formal or informal power, to influence the decision-making process to further their agendas. Understanding how agenda setting works in a specific decision-making context is, therefore, critical in knowing how and under what conditions certain reforms may become feasible. Considering the dynamics of agenda setting in the design of new institutions is undeniably important.

# Exercises for Chapter 5: Collective Choice and Agenda Setting

## Exercise 5.1: The Agenda-Setting Game[8]

The facilitator explains the steps involved in the Agenda-Setting Game.

Steps in the exercise (time frame: ~25 minutes):
1. Read out instructions (1 minute)
2. Allow participants to read and play game (10–15 minutes)
3. Class discussion (10 minutes)

Preparation and materials:
1. Pens should be available to all participants
2. Copies of the Group Briefing handouts
3. Copies of the Head Official handout

Procedure:
1. The facilitator explains:

   For the following activity, at each table, you are going to be voting officials from three different districts, and you will need to decide where to build a new bridge. One of you will be the head official responsible for facilitating and recording the votes. Before I pass out the handout that includes the detailed briefing for the activity, please decide who the head official will be at each table. Once you do that, go around the table to indicate if you are in District A, B, or C. I will now go ahead and distribute the handouts.

2. The facilitator goes to each table and hands out Exercise 5.1, the Group Briefing handout, to all participants. In addition to this handout, the person selected as head official also receives Exercise 5.1: Head Official Briefing handout.

3. The facilitator asks the participants to read the detailed briefing and invites them to ask questions about the task at hand, if they have any.

4. The facilitator gauges the rate of completion of the assignment and gives participants a 2-minute warning so that the activity can wrap up within its allotted 10-minute time frame.

5. The facilitator asks the head official from one of the tables to report out the result of Scenario 1, then asks another table to report out the result of Scenario 2, and a third table to report out the result of Scenario 3. Then the facilitator poses the following questions for an overall group discussion:
   • How did the head official's agenda affect which outcome prevailed?
   • What, if anything, does this tell us about the role of institutions?

After the class game, the facilitator explains the logic of agenda setting by providing the technical explanation for agenda setting (Duch 2009, 1).

*"How do committees decide? How do decision-making procedures influence outcomes?*

Assume a set of alternatives and a set of committee members. It's simple if there are two options. If there are three alternatives, $x, y, z$, we might imagine a process such as

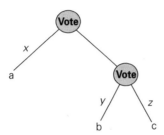

We describe processes such as these as *binary agendas* as at each stage of voting the choice is between two options. For example, at the first stage we consider whether we want to adopt $x$ or not. The number of terminal histories is at least the number of alternatives, and each alternative is associated with at least one terminal history." (ibid, 2009, 1–2)

*Three alternatives: A, B, and C, and three voting blocs of equal size in the city council. The preferences for the bridge construction project are ranked as follows:*

*Bloc 1 (33 percent): A > B > C*
*Bloc 2 (33 percent): B > C > A*
*Bloc 3 (33 percent): C > A > B*

*Here are the diagrams for results depending on the voting sequence:*[7]

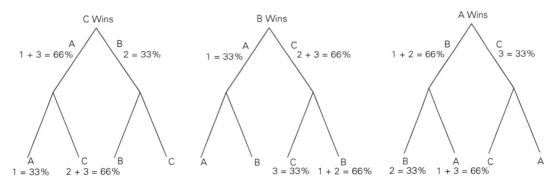

## Exercise 5.1: Group Briefing Handout

You are officials in three different districts and must decide on where to build a new bridge. Decision making is by majority voting. That is, a decision can be made only if more than 50 percent of the officials vote for it. Further-more, decisions are made using pairwise comparisons: that is, any two alternatives are put to the vote at any one time. There is a head official running this meeting who *does not vote* but sets the agenda. Each district represented has only one vote even if there are multiple officials from each district. Thus, for example, if District A has two people at your table and District B has three people, both districts still have only a single vote.

You represent one of the three districts (Districts A, B, or C) and would like to see the bridge built in your district. Failing that, you would rather see that the bridge is built in the adjoining district to yours. This means that

- District A officials prefer A>B>C
- District B officials prefer B>C>A
- District C officials prefer C>B>A.

The head official conducted an initial vote, and based on the preferences of each district, no location obtained a majority as each location has an equal vote (33.3 percent support).

For a proposal to be accepted and pass the 50 percent plus threshold, two of the three groups must actually vote in favor of the proposal.

The head official at each table will announce a legislative agenda with three different scenarios. Each scenario will have two stages. In the first stage, all districts will have the opportunity to vote between *two* possible locations. In the second stage, the winning location of the first stage will be up against the remaining location.

# Exercise 5.1: Head Official Handout

1. After all participants at the table have reviewed the Group Briefing handout, explain that there will be two rounds of voting based on three scenarios.
2. Explain that you will read out the voting scenario so that participants can decide how to vote.
3. Remind them that if there are multiple officials present from one district, that district still has only a single vote.
4. Record the first-round vote results.
5. Conduct the second-round vote.
6. Record which location wins for Scenario 1.

Once this has been done for Scenario 1, repeat the process for using Scenarios 2 and 3.

## Scenario 1

*First-Round Vote:* Vote between District A and District B.

What is the outcome of the first round?_____

*Second-Round Vote:* Vote between the [district that won in the first round vote] and District C.

What is the final outcome? _____

## Scenario 2

*First-Round Vote:* Vote between District A and District C.

What is the outcome of the first round?_____

*Second-Round Vote:* Vote between the [district that won in the first round vote] and District B

What is the final outcome?_____

## Scenario 3

*First-Round Vote:* Vote between District C and District B.

What is the outcome of the first round?_____

*Second-Round Vote:* Vote between the [district that won in the first round vote] and District A.

What is the final outcome?_____

## Notes

1. In fact, agenda manipulation can ensure that the "best collective outcome" does *not* become policy.

2. "I'll let you write the substance and you let me write the procedure, and I'll screw you every time." See Regulatory Reform Act: Hearings on H.R. 2327 Before the Subcommittee on Administrative Law and Governmental Relations of the House Committee on the Judiciary, 98th Cong. 312 (1983) (Patty and Penn 2008, 2).

3. For purposes of clarity, a majoritarian system is one in which public decisions require the consent of at least 50 percent plus one of voters.

4. The name comes from Marquis de Condorcet, a French philosopher who, in 1785, wrote a treatise entitled *Essay on the Application of Analysis to the Probability of Majority Decisions,* where he defined the concept and explained for the first time the paradox of social choice and preference aggregation.

5. An "ideal point" refers to the policy desired by a certain actor, and any departures from it decrease his or her utility or overall gain.

6. Defined as a situation in which one actor (the agenda setter) has information that other actors do not possess.

7. The game and diagrams illustrating the "paradox of voting" are adapted from Poole (2011), http://voteview.com/paradox_of_voting.htm.

8. *Source:* (Duch 2009) and (Poole 2011) .

## References

Arrow, Kenneth. 1951. *Social Choice and Individual Values.* New Haven: Yale University Press.

Bach, S., and S. S. Smith. 1988. *Managing Uncertainty in the House of Representatives: Adaptation and Innovation in Special Rules.* Washington, DC: Brookings Institution Press.

Bachrach, Peter, and Morton Baratz. 1962. "The Two Faces of Power." *American Political Science Review* 56 (4): 947–52.

Duch, Raymond. 2009. "Formal Analysis Lecture Notes." Nuffield College: Oxford, http://www.raymondduch.com/course/hilary2009/formalanalysis/lecture_2009_06.pdf.

Dummett, Michael. 1984. *Voting Procedures.* New York: Oxford University Press.

Garrett, G., and B. Weingast. 1993. "Ideas, Interests, and Institutions." In *The Role of Ideas in Foreign Policy,* ed. Judy Goldstein and Robert Keohane, 173–206. Ithaca: Cornell University Press.

Johnson, Paul. 1998. *Social Choice. Theory and Research.* Thousand Oaks, CA: A Sage University Paper.

Kingdon, J. W. 1984. *Agendas, Alternatives, and Public Policies.* London: Longman.

Krehbiel, Keith. 1991. *Information and Legislative Organization.* Ann Arbor: University of Michigan Press.

Oleszek, Walter. 2007. *Congressional Procedures and the Policy Process*. Washington, DC: CQ Press.

Olson, Mancur. 1965. *The Logic of Collective Action: Public Goods and the Theory of Groups*. Cambridge: Harvard University Press.

Ordeshook, P. C., and T. Schwartz. 1987. "Agendas and the Control of Political Outcomes." *American Political Science Review* 81 (1): 179–99.

Patty, J. W., and E. M. Penn. 2008. "Amendments, Covering, and Agenda Control: The Politics of Open Rules." Manuscript. Washington University, St. Louis.

Poole, Keith. 2011. *The Paradox of Voting (The Condorcet Paradox)*. Houston: University of Houston, http://voteview.com/paradox_of_voting.htm.

Pollack, Mark. 1997. "Delegation, Agency, and Agenda Setting in the European Community." *International Organization* 51 (1): 99–134.

Riker, William. 1981. *Liberalism against Populism: A Confrontation between the Theory of Democracy and the Theory of Social Choice*. Long Grove, IL: Waveland Press.

———. 1986. *The Art of Political Manipulation*. New Haven: Yale University Press.

Schatz, Edward. 2008. "Transnational Image Making and Soft Authoritarian Kazakhstan." *Slavic Review* 67 (1): 50–62.

Shepsle, Kenneth. 1989. "The Changing Textbook Congress." In *Can the Government Govern?* ed. John Chubb and Paul Peterson, 355–68. Washington, DC: Brookings Institution.

Shepsle, Kenneth, and Barry Weingast. 1984. "Uncovered Sets and Sophisticated Voting Outcomes with Implications for Agenda Institutions." *American Journal of Political Science* 28 (1): 49–74.

———. 1987. "The Institutional Foundations of Committee Power." *American Political Science Review* 81 (1): 85–194.

Stratmann, Thomas, and Martin Baur. 2002. "Plurality Rule, Proportional Representation, and the German Bundestag: How Incentives to Pork-Barrel Differ across Electoral Systems." *American Journal of Political Science* 46 (3): 506–14.

Tsebelis, G. 1994. "The Power of the European Parliament as a Conditional Agenda Setter." *American Political Science Review* 88 (1): 128–42.

———. 1997. *Bicameralism*. Cambridge: Cambridge University Press.

Tsebelis George, and Eduardo Aléman. 2005. "Presidential Conditional Agenda Setting in Latin America." *World Politics* 57 (3): 396–420.

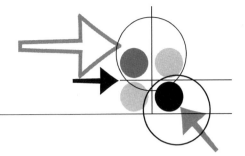

**CHAPTER 6**

# Delegation Problems and the Principal-Agent Relationship

Accountability implies a well-functioning relationship of delegation among citizens, politicians, and bureaucrats. Voters elect representatives and expect them to fulfill the policy mandate for which they were elected. Politicians enact laws and regulations but leave the implementation to bureaucracies. As chapter 2 suggested, mismatched incentives of these actors in fulfilling their tasks on any leg of the accountability triangle generate delegation problems. In turn, the noncompliance of delegates with the tasks of their mandate is consequential for public good delivery. Whenever politicians or bureaucrats shirk their duties, without adequate monitoring and penalties, corruption and poor governance thrive.

More pragmatically, to achieve an outcome—say, the realization of a development project or a reform target—the actors concerned with reaching this goal, known as *principals*, must often delegate tasks to those who can help implement the objective, referred to as the *agents*. Given the need for delegation and the fact that the interests of principals and agents do not always fully converge, a host of "principal-agent problems" arise, particularly the possibility that agents will shirk their duties. For example, bureaucratic and political agents do not always have incentives to allow their principals to scrutinize their use of taxpayers' money, even though the country may have passed freedom of information legislation that gives citizens the right to do so. As a result, some agents actively obstruct the effective implementation of these laws.

In general, the principal-agent problem, as the key analytical backbone of delegation, is very helpful in understanding a wide variety of relationships, including those between legislators (the principals) and bureaucrats (the agents); voters (as principals) and politicians (as agents); members of civil society or political party organizations and their leaders; employers and employees. Delegation and principal-agent relations are at the heart of political, bureaucratic, and social accountability. The position in the delegation chain and the scope of information about the task to be performed generate the sets of incentives for actors. But as we all know, delegation processes occur in all sorts of organizations. Political parties, civil society groups, or coalition leaders often entrust member recruitment, treasury tasks, or organizational expansion to agents. In these cases, shirking has negative consequences for the collective action potential of these groups and acts as a constraint on joint efforts to achieve policy change.

This chapter introduces readers to the challenge of delegation, to issues surrounding the principal-agent relationship, and to the different types of institutionally induced incentives (sanctioning and monitoring) that can sometimes mitigate conflict of interests between the two (see figure 6.1). Therefore, the chapter provides a basis for diagnosing the delegation challenges inherent in many projects and public policy-making contexts.

The central dilemma that this chapter addresses is how to get the politician or bureaucrat (the agent) to act in the best interests of voters and citizens (the principal), when the former has an informational advantage and interests that diverge from those of the latter.

**FIGURE 6.1 Delegation and Principal-Agent Conceptual Map**

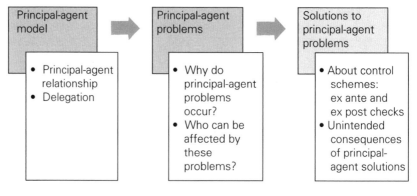

*Source:* Authors.

# Objectives of Chapter 6

By the end of this chapter, readers should be able to do the following:

- Understand the reasons for delegation, along with its potential benefits and pitfalls
- Describe various strategies for monitoring and sanctioning agents
- Recognize how the competing agendas of principals and agents may make one or the other more receptive to reform goals
- Learn to explore analytically the relationship among political institutions, collective action, and principal-agent problems and solutions.

# Delegation

Principal-agent relationships are inextricably related to the concept of *delegation:* that is, the resolution of a boss (the principal) to transfer consulting, decision, or implementation power to a worker (the agent). Given private information that favors agents and gives them incentives to shirk their duties on the mandate given by the principal, political economists have attempted to find answers to several theoretical questions. Why delegate in the first place?

## Why Do Bosses Willfully Give Up Control and Delegate?

The classic answer of delegation focuses on knowledge discrepancies between the principal and the agent. It is argued that actors who are more knowledgeable about the operational context will make better choices. More recent theoretical accounts focus less on the better outcome or better choice and more on how delegation can make "the outcomes *less risky*" (Bendor and Meirowitz, 2004, 294). The information and expertise about specific policies that the agent possesses or acquires can hedge against the risk of random shocks that could prevent the busy or less informed principal from achieving her target. Under conditions of uncertainty over how exactly policies will translate into outcomes, for instance, principals are likely to delegate tasks to agents, irrespective of how risk averse or risk prone they are. As the distance between the outcome uncertainty known by the bureaucracy, on the one hand, and by politicians, on the other, increases, delegation is more likely, and the mandate will be broader (Epstein and O'Halloran 1994, 1999; Bawn 1995). The risk rationale is central to the relationship between politicians as principals and bureaucracies as agents (Bendor and Meirowitz 2004, 294). Uncertainty over their own electoral fortune also makes incumbent political principals more likely to protect their bureaucratic agents from future interference. Thus, *political uncertainty* is also crucial to the nature and scope of the delegation mandate (Huber and Shipan 2006, 269) (Moe 1989).

Given that the delegation problems are inherent in a principal-agent relationship and occur when agents have an informational advantage over their boss, it is important to ask, Who will the principal trust enough to have as his or her agent? Bureaucrats know more about policy implementation than politicians. From the point of view of the executive and the incumbent political party, however, irrespective of their technical expertise and competence, not all bureaucrats are equally trustworthy. In empirical tests, given equally qualified agents, principals will choose the one that is the closest ideologically to them because principals care not only about "objective" competency but also about the realization of their own electoral agenda (the "ally principle") (Huber and Shipan 2006). The mandates of agencies (that is, bureaucratic units) often depend on the partisan game. The delegation mandate is likely to be narrower and leave less policy discretion to the agents in cases in which the policy preferences of politicians and bureaucrats do not converge. In situations of high policy conflict between the legislature and the executive and divided government, the delegation mandate contains less bureaucratic autonomy and less policy discretion, as politicians fear divergence. Now, let us see in more detail how and why delegation happens.

## How Does the Process of Delegation Occur?

Once principals have selected an agent, they also have to choose both *the degree of discretion* (how broad or narrow and how generic or specific the agency instructions should be) and *the estimate of the probability that the agent will shirk and get caught*. The precision with which the principal defines the tasks to be completed by the agent establishes the limits of action or the scope of the delegation mandate.

There are many cross-national studies of the principal-agent problem and the degree of policy discretion given to agents (measured as the level of detail in statutes or laws defining the authority and jurisdiction of bureaucratic agencies). The main findings can be summarized as the following:

- Presidential systems seem to be able to control bureaucracies better than parliamentary systems.
- Agents will have more limited discretion in an environment characterized by high policy conflict, high legislative capacity, and no bicameral

polarization, as well as when the legislative majority cannot rely on non-statutory factors.

- Coalition and minority governments are more likely to write policy details into statutes, thus restricting the agent's discretion. Anticipating fragility (short time in office), they have incentives to bring the policy preferences of the bureaucrats closer to their political agenda (Huber and Shipan 2002).

In addition to looking at how much policy discretion the agent has, some studies also classify types of delegation according to other criteria (Strøm, Muller and Bergman 2003, 64–66):

- *Direct versus indirect delegation.* In parliamentary regimes, for example, the voters elect legislatures, who then elect the prime minister and the cabinet, who further delegate authority to bureaucratic agencies (a form of indirect delegation). In presidential regimes, both the president and the legislatures are directly elected (direct delegation).
- *Singularity or plurality of agents and principals.* In parliamentary institutions, each agent (implementation unit) corresponds to one principal (the specific cabinet minister directly accountable to the Prime Minister who is accountable to the legislature), whereas in presidential regimes, the bureaucratic agent has at least two principals (the legislature and the president).
- *Competition between different agents' delegation mandates.* To use the same example of the two distinct institutional settings, in parliamentary contexts, there is no overlap between agents' jurisdictions: the ministry of education and the ministry of health do not directly monitor or compete with each other; in contrast, in presidential contexts, some bureaucratic agencies place bids for policy implementation whose winner is selected by the legislature and/or presidency; the system of checks and balances also allows agents to crosscheck mandates.

Sometimes, particularly in settings with strong authoritarian legacies, delegation is rare altogether, because top-level politicians usually make policy decisions and are not always comfortable with bureaucratic discretion or autonomy. As Concepts in Practice 6.1 shows, administrative reform in Iraq, a country with a top-down chain of command, entailed developing a middle tier of bureaucrats who could perform basic tasks such as data collection.

Acquiring a grasp on when, how, and why delegation occurs in organizations and institutions of political representation is an essential step in understanding why problems arise. Now, let's go up a level of abstraction. The following section will introduce in more detail the principal-agent theory and

**CONCEPTS IN PRACTICE 6.1**

## Solving Delegation Problems and Data Collection in the Iraqi Pension System

In 2009, the government of Iraq requested the World Bank's assistance in implementing a unified pension law. The law aimed to increase the number of Iraqis contributing to and benefiting from the social protection programs and creating enrollee contribution systems. However, the World Bank and the Iraqi National Board of Pensions quickly realized that, to achieve successful implementation, the team and the organization itself would have to address serious delegation challenges. A top-down culture in the bureaucracy was prevalent, top bureaucrats were reluctant to delegate tasks, and authority was highly concentrated. Teams and staff worked in silos, and collaboration was rare. Procedures in place were old and inefficient, and managers did not receive constant training.

To address data collection by first addressing delegation problems, reformers created a new pension team (with a mix of members from different offices) that had the task of collecting as much relevant pension data as possible in a short time. As a result, the team was able to come up with new managerial and data-gathering mechanisms that increased efficiency. Besides compiling data on beneficiaries of social protection, they also decided to renew, simplify, and standardize the documentation requirements of the National Board of Pensions, making the rules clear to all. Communication was also improved between pension officers and teams. Moreover, more training helped team members better understand and use new technology and innovative methods to increase their confidence when executing tasks. Overall, these solutions successfully addressed delegation problems, created a managerial middle level that was previously missing, and boosted the organization's performance.

*Source:* World Bank (2011).

discuss the actors' incentives in play. Having them in mind can help readers think of potential mechanisms for solving this type of constraint.

## The Principal, the Agent, and Their Incentives

Technically, the principal-agent relationship is built on two major assumptions: The boss wants an agent who is capable and willing to perform his tasks well - - the voter prefers a competent to an incompetent legislator; and second, the contract is feasible precisely because both parties prefer the superior option of delegating and working to one in which the boss retains full control of all tasks and the delegate shirks his duties (Bendor, Glazer, and Hammond 2001, 237–238). Democracy and elections, for example, function under the assumption that the interests of the citizenry, bureaucracy, and politicians are fully aligned However, two sets of problems—agency losses and slippage—can emerge (Pollack 1997, 108).

The first problem—agency loss—is inherent in any delegation relationship because principals and agents often have conflicting interests (Kiewiet and McCubbins 1991, 5). For example, voters as principals would like to see their preferred policies enacted by politicians as agents, but the latter also face incentives to shirk and opportunistically maximize rents instead of public goods in the absence of constraints designed to keep them in line with their mandate. The same logic applies to most organizational dynamics between rank and file members and leaders.

Moreover, beyond classic shirking, a second dynamic called *slippage* is induced by the institutional setup and structure of delegation (Pollack 1997, 108). Slippage often occurs when independently of the agent's propensity to shirk or comply, the black box of the decision making process within the agency, or the informal norms of policy implementation, lead to outcomes that are not aligned with the principal's mandate.

## What Are the Main Technical Features of a Principal-Agent Model?

A principal-agent model is essentially about how the different tasks, attributes, and roles of the principal and his or her agents shape delegation outcomes. Thus, the principal-agent dynamic involves at least two actors and has several standard features (or core assumptions) (this section builds heavily on Miller 2005, 205–06; Holmstrom 1979; Shavell 1979):

- *Information asymmetry*. This refers to any situation in which one actor has more information than another (the concept will be discussed in detail in chapter 7). Gathering complete information is expensive for the principal, one of the reasons for which delegation occurred in the first place. Legislators do not have the time and resources to actually monitor the daily routine of bureaucrats to make sure that they comply with their mandate. Even if at the end of the fiscal year, specialized legislative committees will assess the policy outcomes of an implementation agency, they will still not be able to clearly understand the major causes of underperformance: is it because of the economic context (for example, a crisis), the lack of coordination among various agencies, or a bureaucrat's inadequate effort?
- *Risk asymmetry*. When the agent's preferences and risks are not aligned with those of the principal (for example, the agent may be more risk

averse than the principal), the agent has a propensity to shirk his or her duties (see the Principal-Agent Game at the end of this chapter).

• *The "unified" principal initiates the principal-agent relationship, by delegating tasks to the agent.* This means that even in cases of multiple principals (several institutional veto points such as parliament, executive, and bicameral legislature, as opposed to just one legislative chamber, for example), the "unified" principal (that is, all the institutional veto points jointly) acts based on an aggregated set of preferences and decides to delegate tasks to the bureaucracy. Individual principals have a mechanism for agreeing on a unified strategy or on the process by which one or all of them will come to a decision.

• *Backward induction and common knowledge.* In many situations, the principal-agent dynamic has a sequential nature. Usually, the principal selects the agent (stage 1); the agent performs an action (stage 2); the principal observes and reacts to the final outcome (stage 3). It is usually assumed that both the principal and the agent know the structure of the game (stages), the payoffs, and the probability of outcomes; and the principal can see the agent's best response function down a "game tree"—that is, how a typical agent will react if the incentives are changed.

• *Ultimatum bargaining.* The principal makes a "take it or leave it" offer to the agent in delegating power to him or her, or not (Miller 2005; Sappington 1991). If the principal can correctly calibrate her offer, she may be able to ensure that the agent has an incentive to deviate only minimally from the principal's optimum preferences.

## What Are the Results of the Principal-Agent Dynamic?

If the probability of detecting the agent's shirking is low enough through the monitoring process and the sanctions attached to shirking are insignificant, the principal will choose not to delegate at all, and the agent will shirk if delegation occurs. However, if delegation does take place, the principal and the agent will bear certain consequences and tradeoffs in terms of risk transfer and efficiency—both the principal and the agent may be overwhelmed with their tasks.

***The Problem of Multiple Chains of Principals and Agents.*** In an analysis of a principal-agent relationship in a particular context, it is also useful to think of it as embedded in a broader ecosystem of principal-agent transactions. For example, the legislature is the principal and the revenue administration is the agent in one such mechanism, given that politicians specify the delegation mandate of bureaucratic agencies.

However, the legislators are elected by voters, who confer a certain electoral mandate on them (the platform on which candidates ran) and thus create another principal-agent relationship. If outcome-based incentives such as performance bonuses for tax collectors (the solution to the first principal-agent relationship) lead to coercive and abusive taxation, the negative outcome is transferred to the second principal-agent transaction: the voters will attempt to stop such abuse by formulating claims to their elected representatives, who, in a circular turn, will attempt to shift the incentives of the tax collection agency to limit abuse (again, the first principal-agent transaction). Thinking about the whole chain of principal-agent transactions, rather than analyzing them in isolation, can lead to a more sophisticated design of outcome-based incentives and monitoring techniques, as well as promoting greater accountability of politicians, bureaucrats, and voters.

## Who or What Will Make Sure That the Agent Complies with the Mandate? Solving Delegation Problems

The classic solutions to principal-agent problems are related to incentives given to the agent in exchange for committing to perform the tasks with due diligence, as well as to different types of monitoring or control mechanisms to detect the agent's deviations from the mandate conferred upon her by the principal. Because these are broad solutions that apply to the whole range of delegation issues, we will also briefly mention them in the next chapter, which explores information asymmetries as a subtype of larger principal-agent problems.

### Incentives to Achieve the Outcome Desired by the Principal

Outcome-based incentives are often used to overcome the problems inherent in a principal-agent relationship. For example, performance bonuses for bureaucrats and high sanctions for low effort are common techniques that encourage compliance with the agent's mandate. In some countries, for example, tax officers receive individual bonuses depending on the total revenue that they manage to collect. However, while outcome-based incentives are central to the principal-agent relationship, they can also generate unintended consequences. As in the example of tax or customs officers, the incentive of individual performance bonuses can lead to individual opportunism (abusive extraction) as well as to a lack of coordination among the many agents (tax collectors), with overall negative consequences for revenue collection and perceptions of procedural fairness.[1]

## Monitoring and Control Schemes

The principal can employ several different control schemes to prevent the agent's shirking. However, one should keep in mind that despite all precautions, an agent might at times choose to disobey and avoid delegation problems (Bendor and Meirowitz 2004, 302). Having said that, the control mechanisms can help minimize incentives for the agent to disobey the principal and thus are considered potential solutions for delegation problems that typically arise in development.

Depending on the sequencing of monitoring and sanctioning, there are two types of checks: ex ante checks, which are forms of controls put in place *before* the actual principal-agent transaction takes place, and ex post checks, which are put in place *after* the transaction. Examples of ex ante checks include

- *Contracts.* Detailed contracts that specify the aligned goals of principals and agents.
- *Recruitment screening and selection.* For example, electoral candidates may have to prove themselves first in the political party hierarchy; similarly, the head of a bureaucratic agency is often a civil servant with a long career in the bureaucracy (Kiewiet and McCubbins 1991, 27–31; Strøm 2000; Strøm, Muller, and Bergman 2003).

*Ex post control schemes.* Oversight is legislators' usual instrument for controlling bureaucratic information. According to *the probability of detection* embedded within the principal-agent relationship, oversight mechanisms can take two forms: (1) so-called "police patrols," in which the cost is high since it requires the principal to perform routine or random observations (monitoring) of the principal-agent relationship; and (2) "fire alarms," in which the mechanism of accountability implies that informed second parties (that is, oversight bureaucrats) or informed third parties (policy consumers or groups of citizens) send signals to the principals about the deviation of the agent (McCubbins, Noll, and Weingast 1987; Lupia and McCubbins 1994).

As opposed to ex ante checks, ex post monitoring occurs either during the delegation process itself (as with the "fire alarms" and "police patrols" discussed above) or at the end of it (through official reports and audits). Some authors argue that such controls are inferior to ex ante oversight mechanisms because some principals might gain from the agent's noncompliance (for example, the political party of the executive, but not the majority party in the legislature in cases of divided government). Therefore, in some cases, the interested principals have incentives to allow shirking (McCubbins, Noll, and Weingast 1987, Bendor, Glazer, and Hammond 2001, 246).

In addition to the mechanism of detection, *the penalty for shirking* is also consequential for the quality of the relationship. Studies have found that delegation will be equivalent to abdication (the principal simply gives up) when the penalties for lying and shirking are too weak and where agents (bureaucracies) perceive the ideological or policy compatibility and overlap between fire-alarm institutions and current legislators as weak, given that the cost of monitoring and sanctioning is high (Lupia and McCubbins 1994). An example of how some of these controls may help is presented below in Concepts in Practice 6.2.

CONCEPTS IN PRACTICE 6.2

## Can Politicians Directly Control Bureaucrats? Evidence from Tax Agency Reform in Argentina

Reforming Argentina's tax collection agency was an important priority for the first Menem administration (1989–95). Legislators in many developing countries face significant hurdles in controlling the bureaucracy. In this context, the control over the tax agency was particularly lax, and its losses were financed through loans. The attempts to correct agency losses and improve the principal-agent relationship interacted with political incentives: members of the parliament faced increased difficulties in maintaining their offices because of political violence and the overall instability of the democratic process. The closed electoral lists rendered the politicians' careers dependent on party leaders, cultivated strong party loyalty, and provided disincentives for particularistic benefits. In addition, elected officials in Argentina operated within cohesive parties that were not responsive to interest groups that could have acted as informed and interested third parties activating "fire alarms" in cases of bureaucratic non-

compliance. Therefore, they had to rely on costly routine "police patrol" checks on the tax agency.

This complex context shaped the nature of policy change targeting the legislative oversight of the bureaucracy. Specifically, the tax authority was ultimately reformed to take into account the fact that legislators could not rely on interest groups to alert them to the actions of the bureaucracy; instead, because "deck-stacking" (or cumbersome evidentiary procedures imposed on the agency) was very expensive, politicians chose to focus on streamlining the agency's internal procedures, simplifying the organizational hierarchy, and reducing the general organizational costs of oversight such as auditing and hearings. Therefore, even though interest groups were less likely to be able to incentivize individual legislators to alter the behavior of bureaucrats, legislators could more easily and directly monitor the activities of the tax agency.

*Source:* Eaton (2003).

Ex post mechanisms have two major categories of effects on the principal-agent problem that shape the scope of the mandate that the principal gives the agent (Huber and Shipan 2006):

- *The substitution effect.* Strong ex post monitoring will give incentives to the politicians to write a more discretionary statute of delegation (Huber and Shipan 2002; Bendor and Meirowitz 2004).
- *Political Uncertainty.* Uncertainty about the future preferences of the politicians (due to changes in the legislature after elections) requires the right balance of ex ante and ex post auditing mechanisms so that politicians can 'lock in' their policy preferences. Generally, if current politicians fear that their successors will renege on their preferred policy, they will be more willing to grant bureaucrats less discretion when delegating (Moe 1989). It is also important to keep in mind that the type of monitoring tools chosen by the principal induces strategic behavior on the side of the agent (Huber and Shipan 2006, 260–269).

In general, monitoring is less onerous when there is close ideological proximity between bureaucrats and governments. According to the ally principle—that is, the degree of policy conflict between politician and bureaucrats—if the policy-ideal points of the principal and those of the agent converge, delegation will be more extensive.

Some studies also argue that monitoring effectiveness and the type of monitoring devices differ significantly between parliamentary and presidential regimes. In parliamentary regimes, prime ministers (acting as agents) are often screened intensely by the legislatures, and they have already gained their reputation by climbing the incumbent party ranks. Therefore, strong ex ante checks are in place. In contrast, presidential regimes often bring in an agent (the president) who is an outsider and with whom the principals in the legislature might not be well acquainted. In presidential regimes, ex post checks (such as impeachment procedures or referendums) prevail as mechanisms of ensuring compliance with the mandate (Strøm, Muller, and Bergman 2003).

As many of the chapters of this handbook emphasize, the slippage or agency problems among citizens, politicians, and bureaucrats do not depend exclusively on the quality of monitoring or the particular incentives adopted. Like everything else in the political-economy universe, principal-agent relations do not exist in an institutional void. The incentives to shirk or not to shirk also depend on a host of other contextual rules of the game that may completely alter the initial intention of policy designers. For instance, one of the most common recipes recommended by international donors for reforming corrupt and inefficient tax administrations was the creation of semiautonomous revenue agencies to replace the more conventional central tax offices. Not surprisingly, evaluations of the performance of such organizations across Latin America and Africa showed mixed results: they were not a delegation panacea and worked as intended only in contexts characterized by strong political commitments (Minh Le 2007). Again, synergistic, complementary institutions matter for the final development result. Therefore, the practitioner should develop a holistic understanding of the institutional web of the policy-making environment before acting.

Finally, since collective action is at the heart of development and the guiding principle of our narrative, how do delegation and better bureaucratic accountability relate to the ability of citizens to mobilize? What constraints do principals or agents place on the space and capacity for the collective action of voters? Concepts in Practice in 6.3 suggests one of the many potential theoretical answers.

## Analyzing Principal-Agent Dilemmas Using Game Theory

Some of the basic intuitions of the logic of delegation can be conceptualized through a simple game. Before a discussion of the details of the game, it is critical to introduce a new solution concept—*backward induction*.

Backward induction is a method for solving games in which there is a limited number of moves and players make decisions sequentially (Shor 2005). First, one has to identify the optimal or best strategy of the last player, and then work 'backwards' determining the optimal strategy of the second last player, etc., until the optimal strategies of all players have been worked out (ibid).[2]

For example, let us look at a game in which an agent (who has already been appointed to a policy-making position by taxpayers) is assumed to be solely concerned with maximizing her private income. She has a choice over whether to use the position either to maximize her income by being corrupt (rent maximizing) or to minimize her income by being honest (rent minimizing). Given these preferences and choices, it might seem as if the agent will always choose to pursue a rent-maximizing course of action.[3]

## Principal-Agent and Collective Action

If politicians determine the rules that govern the civil service—for example, the level of bureaucratic professionalism and the degree of transparency in the budgetary process—then it becomes possible to understand under what conditions politicians have an incentive for ensuring that the civil service is an efficient organization as opposed to being simply a mechanism for distributing jobs to supporters, with scant regard for the quality of public service provision.

Using a large dataset, the authors of one study found that the existence of programmatic political parties—that is, those that do not rely on patrons to organize voters but can instead be held directly accountable by voters—is much more likely to favor a transparent and efficient civil service than parties that depend on patrons

to deliver goods to core voters (such parties are beholden to the demands of patrons for private goods).

In short, if voters can overcome collective action problems directly and hold political parties to account for the management of the civil service through programmatic party organizations, higher standards and less corruption may be the outcome. If, however, political parties are beholden to patrons, then narrow clientelistic concerns will dominate resource allocation. Thus, who the politician's principal is (voters or patrons)—which itself depends on the outcome of collective action (can voters organize into programmatic parties and keep them programmatic?)—determines the nature of the principal-agent dynamic, as well as the overall quality of service delivery.

*Source:* Cruz and Keefer (2010).

However, what if the agent can potentially be removed from office by taxpayers who have the ability to detect rent extraction and punish any agent who engages in such an activity? In this case, an agent who is more concerned with keeping her position will have an incentive to pursue a rent-minimizing agenda because she faces a trade-off: stay compliant and keep the post (payoff of 3) or try and rent maximize and eventually get caught and removed from office (payoff of 2).

In short, by looking down the game tree, agents can anticipate the reaction of the taxpayers to their different strategies (rent maximize; rent minimize) and can, therefore, select the strategy that will make them better off in the end. Thus, backward induction can be used to find the solution for this type of game (known as the "subgame perfect" Nash equilibrium) (see figure 6.2).

**FIGURE 6.2  Decision Making in a Sequential Form Game**

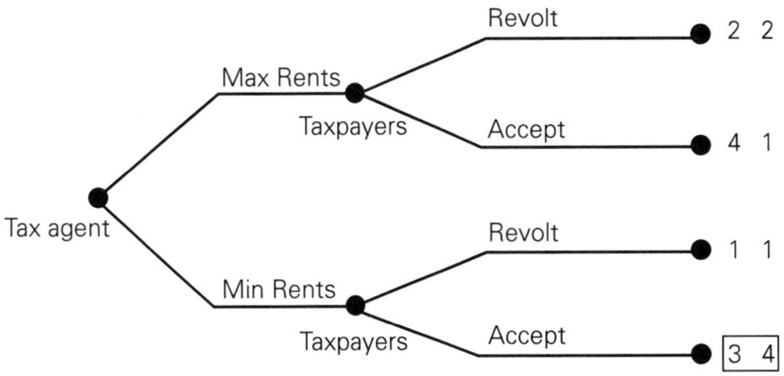

*Source:* Authors.

## Summary

The need to delegate tasks to politicians and bureaucrats can have significant effects on the implementation of a project's objectives because of the potential conflict of interest between principal and agent. Understanding the logic of principal-agent delegation and the tools that might, under certain conditions, mitigate this conflict is therefore a critical component of a good political-economy analysis. Grasping principal-agent dynamics makes it easier to identify some of the implementation challenges, to think about informational discrepancies between actors and groups in society and the unintended consequences of delegation, and to explore attempts to remedy the consequences. By understanding the components and logic of a principal-agent relationship, the development practitioner will be able to do the following:

- Make better-informed decisions about delegating tasks within his or her organization
- Introduce the most effective monitoring and incentive mechanism within concrete institutional contexts
- Recognize entry points for reforms (that is, who is more likely to have incentives aligned with the reform goals: the principal or the agent? Why?

# Exercises for Chapter 6: Principal-Agent Theory, Delegation, and Accountability

## Exercise 6.1: The Principal-Agent Game

The facilitator explains the steps involved in the Principal-Agent Game.

Steps in the exercise (time frame: ~40–45 minutes)

1. Read out instructions (1 minute)
2. Allow participants to read and answer (5–10 minutes)
3. Collect responses, tally responses, facilitate group discussion (10 minutes)
4. Class discussion (10 minutes)
5. Technical explanation (10–15 minutes)

Preparation and materials

a. Envelopes to be placed in the middle of the round table (one at each table)
b. Pens should be available to all participants
c. Copies of the Instructions handouts
d. Copies of the Answer Sheet
e. Copies of the Key Questions handout
f. Facilitator instructions

**NOTE: There are three different scenarios (one for each separate table). If there are only two tables, then Scenarios 1 and 3 should be used. If there are more than three tables, one or more of the three scenarios can be used again.**

Procedure:

1. The facilitator reads aloud the following instructions:
   I am going to distribute instructions and an answer sheet. Read the instructions and answer the questions on the answer sheet. Once you have read the instructions and completed the answer sheet, place your answer sheet in the envelope in the middle of the table. DO NOT WRITE YOUR NAME ON EITHER DOCUMENT and MAKE SURE NO ONE SEES YOUR ANSWER. Keep the instructions handy for our follow-up discussion. I will give you about 5–10 minutes to complete this.
2. The facilitator distributes the Instructions handout and Answer Sheet to all participants. **See Note above on the three scenarios**.
3. The facilitator gauges the rate of completion of the assignment and gives participants a 2-minute warning so that the activity can wrap up within its allotted 10-minute time frame. As part of the 2-minute warning, the

facilitator reminds participants that they should not write their names on the answer sheet; when they have finished, they should put their answer sheet in the envelope in the middle of the table.

4. The facilitator explains:

    I will come around to collect the envelopes with the answer sheets and tally your responses. At the same time, I will give you a handout that includes two Key Questions. While I tally the responses on the answer sheets, please go ahead and discuss at your tables the two questions on the handout. Spend approximately 10 minutes in this discussion.

5. To tally the votes, the facilitator uses a blank Answer Sheet and notes for each option the total number of votes.

6. The facilitator walks around the room among the tables in a nonintrusive manner and pays attention to what is discussed. The facilitator notes a few comments from the tables that he or she can highlight as part of the transition to the technical explanation portion.

7. The facilitator gives the participants a two-minute warning to wrap up their discussion.

8. The facilitator explains:

    Now that you have played the game and had a chance to discuss with others at your tables some of the key underlying issues, let's find out the results of your individual decisions.

9. The facilitator announces the results and poses the following questions to the entire group:

    1. How many of you were surprised by the entire group's final tally?
    2. If yes, why?
    3. If no, why?

## Exercise 6.1: Instructions Handout 1

You are an extremely busy executive working in a field you are passionate about. You have several important projects whose deadlines are all coming up. You know that if you were not under a time constraint, you could complete all the projects yourself. Given the time constraints, you have the following choices:

1. Try and complete all the projects yourself, doing a satisfactory job overall.
2. Delegating one project to an assistant, allowing you to complete all the other projects extremely well but forcing you to accept whatever quality outcome your assistant produces.

You know that your assistant is an extremely competent employee who wants to impress you, as she will soon be up for promotion.

## Exercise 6.1: Instructions Handout 2

You are an extremely busy executive working in a field you are passionate about. You have several important projects whose deadlines are all coming up. You know that if you were not under a time constraint, you could complete all the projects yourself. Given the time constraints, you have the following choices:

1. Try and complete all the projects yourself, doing a satisfactory job overall.
2. Delegating one project to an assistant, allowing you to complete all the other projects extremely well but forcing you to accept whatever quality outcome your assistant produces.

Your assistant is new, so you are unsure of how well he or she will be able to complete the project. However, it is relatively easy for you to monitor the work, so that if he or she seems to be falling behind you would know almost immediately.

## Exercise 6.1: Instructions Handout 3

You are an extremely busy executive working in a field you are passionate about. You have several important projects whose deadlines are all coming up. You know that if you were not under a time constraint, you could complete all the projects yourself. Given the time constraints, you have the following choices:

1. Try and complete all the projects yourself, doing a satisfactory job overall.
2. Delegating one project to an assistant, allowing you to complete all the other projects extremely well but forcing you to accept whatever quality outcome your assistant produces.

Your assistant is extremely incompetent. He or she was hired only because he or she is a relative of the big boss upstairs. If the assistant does a bad job, there will be no consequences for him or her.

## Exercise 6.1: Answer Sheet 1

Please indicate below, by ticking (√) the box next to the appropriate action, what you would like to do. PLEASE TICK ONLY ONE BOX.

| | |
|---|---|
| Do all the work yourself | |
| Delegate some of the work to your assistant | |

Briefly explain why you decided to pursue one action rather than the other.

| |
|---|
| |

**Once you have completed your answers, put them in the envelope in the middle of the table.**

## Exercise 6.1: Answer Sheet 2

Please indicate below, by ticking (√) the box next to the appropriate action, what you would like to do. PLEASE TICK ONLY ONE BOX.

| | |
|---|---|
| Do all the work yourself | |
| Delegate some of the work to your assistant | |

Briefly explain why you decided to pursue one action rather than the other.

**Once you have completed your answers, put them in the envelope in the middle of the table.**

## Exercise 6.1: Answer Sheet 3

Please indicate below, by ticking (√) the box next to the appropriate action, what you would like to do. PLEASE TICK ONLY ONE BOX.

| | |
|---|---|
| Do all the work yourself | |
| Delegate some of the work to your assistant | |

Briefly explain why you decided to pursue one action rather than the other.

<br><br><br><br><br><br><br><br><br><br><br><br>

**Once you have completed your answers, put them in the envelope in the middle of the table.**

## Exercise 6.1: Key Questions Handout—Group Discussion

In your groups, please discuss the following questions:

1. What are the main reasons people are giving for the action they have taken?

2. How does the information you have on the way in which your assistant was selected and your ability to monitor him or her affect your answer? (If applicable)

3. How does the information you have on the way in which you can monitor your assistant's progress affect your answer?

4. What does the example suggest about the importance of information asymmetries in determining decisions to delegate?

## Notes

1. U4 Anti-Corruption Resource Center, "Revenue Administration and Corruption," http://www.u4.no/themes/pfm/Revenueissue/revenue5.cfm#7.
2. Shor, M. 2005. "Backward Induction," Dictionary of Game Theory Terms, Game Theory.net, <*http://www.gametheory.net/dictionary/ url_of_entry.html*> Web accessed: 6/18/2012.
3. Inspired by the congressional dominance literature as summarized in (Muller 2003, 386–405).

## References

Bawn, Kathleen. 1995. "Political Control versus Expertise: Congressional Choices about Administrative Procedures." *American Political Science Review* 62–73.

Bendor, J., A. Glazer, and T. Hammond. 2001. "Theories of Delegation." *Annual Review of Political Science* 4 (1): 235–69.

Bendor, J., and A. Meirowitz. 2004. "Spatial Models of Delegation." *American Political Science Review* 98 (2): 293–310.

Cruz, C., and P. Keefer. 2010. "Programmatic Political Parties and Public Sector Reform." Paper presented at the American Political Science Association annual meeting, July 19, Washington, DC.

Eaton, K. 2003. "Can Politicians Control Bureaucrats? Applying Theories of Political Control to Argentina's Democracy." *Latin American Politics and Society* 45 (4): 33–62.

Epstein, D., and S. O'Halloran. 1994. "Administrative Procedures, Information, and Agency Discretion." *American Journal of Political Science* 38 (3): 697–722.

———. 1999. *Delegated Powers: A Transaction Cost Politics Approach to Policy Making under Separate Powers*. Cambridge: Cambridge University Press.

Holmstrom, Bengt. 1979. "Moral Hazard and Observability." *Bell Journal of Economics* 10: 74–91.

Horn, M. J. 1995. *The Political Economy of Public Administration: Institutional Choice in the Public Sector*. New York: Cambridge University Press.

Huber, J. D., and C. R. Shipan. 2002. *Deliberate Discretion: The Institutional Foundations of Bureaucratic Autonomy*. New York: Cambridge University Press.

Huber, John and Charles Shipan. 2006. "Politics, Delegation, and Bureaucracy" in *The Oxford Handbook of Political Economy*. Ed. Barry R. Weingast and Donald A. Wittman, 256–271. Oxford: Oxford University Press.

Kiewiet, D. R., and M. D. McCubbins. 1991. *The Logic of Delegation: Congressional Parties and the Appropriations Process*. Chicago: University of Chicago Press.

Lupia, Arthur, and Mathew McCubbins. 1994. "Who Controls? Information and the Structure of Legislative Decision Making." *Legislative Studies Quarterly* 19 (3): 361–84.

McCubbins, Mathew D., and Terry Sullivan. 1987. *Congress: Structure and Policy: Political Economy of Institutions and Decisions*. New York: Cambridge University Press.

McCubbins, Mathew, Roger Noll, and Barry Weingast. 1987. "Administrative procedures as instruments of political control." *Journal of Law, Economics, and Organization* 3:243–77.

Miller, Gary J. 2005. "The Political Evolution of Principal-Agent Models." *Annual Review of Political Science* 8 (1): 203–25.

Minh Le, Tuan. 2007. "Combating Corruption in Revenue Administration: An Overview." In *The Many Faces of Corruption: Tracking Vulnerabilities at the Sector Level,* ed. Jose E. Campos and Sanjay Pradhan, 355–38. Washington, DC: World Bank.

Moe, T. M. 1989. "The Politics of Bureaucratic Structure." In *Can the Government Govern?* ed. J. Chubb and E. Peterson, 267–329. Washington, DC: Brookings Institution Press.

Muller, D. 2003. *Public Choice III.* Cambridge: Cambridge University Press

Powell, B., and G. Whitten. 1993. "A Cross-National Analysis of Economy Voting: Taking Political Context into Account." *American Journal of Political Science* 37: 391–414.

Sappington, David E. M. 1991. "Incentives in Principal-Agent Relationships." *Journal of Economic Perspectives* 5 (2): 45–66.

Shavell, Steven. 1979. "Risk Sharing and Incentives in the Principal and Agent Relationship." *Bell Journal of Economics* 55–73.

Shepsle, K. A. 1992. "Bureaucratic Drift, Coalitional Drift, and Time Consistency: A Comment on Macey." *Journal of Law, Economics, and Organization* 8 (1): 111.

Shor, M, .2005. "Backward Induction," Dictionary of Game Theory Terms, Game Theory.net, <*http://www.gametheory.net/dictionary/ url_of_entry.html*> Web accessed: 6/18/2012

Strøm, K. 2000. "Delegation and Accountability in Parliamentary Democracies." *European Journal of Political Research* 37 (3): 261–90.

Strøm, K., C. Wolfgang Muller, and T. Bergman. 2003. *Delegation and Accountability in Parliamentary Democracies.* Oxford: Oxford University Press.

Tsebelis, George. 1999. "Veto Players and Law Production in Parliamentary Democracies: An Empirical Analysis." *American Political Science Review* 591–608.

Weber, Max. 1918. "Science as a Vocation." Speech at Munich University, http://www.ne.jp/asahi/moriyuki/abukuma/weber/lecture/science_frame.html.

World Bank. 2011. "Accelerating Reforms within Iraq's National Board of Pensions," http://siteresources.worldbank.org/INTMENA/Resources/QuickNote51.pdf >.

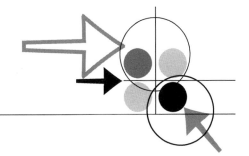

# CHAPTER 7

# Causes and Effects of Information Asymmetries in the Policy-Making Process

The role of information in fostering pro-development collective action is crucial. *Information asymmetry* refers to any situation in which one individual, group, or actor has some information that another actor does not possess. Significant information asymmetries among voters, politicians, and bureaucrats can lead to ineffective representation and undermine the ability of voters to monitor and sanction noncompliance through elections. The magnitude of information asymmetries varies widely around the world. For instance, the 2005 Latino Barometer opinion survey found a large percentage of respondents agreeing with the statement that "politics is so complicated that people like us often do not know what is happening." The variation across countries was also substantial, ranging from 40 percent in República Bolivariana de Venezuela to 69 percent in El Salvador and 68 percent in Paraguay (Taylor-Robinson 2010, 15).

Information problems are not confined to developing countries only. Significant information asymmetries characterize all electorates in all countries. Studies done in the United States, for example, show that the Gini coefficient of the distribution of political information across U.S. voters is around 0.60. This indicator takes values between 0 (indicating equally distributed information across all voters) and 1 (indicating that only one person knows what is going on in policy making) (Converse 2000, 333). In the absence of strong technologies of political commitment and monitoring, this information asymmetry significantly reduces effective collective action and leads to less accountable forms of political representation.

Despite persistent information asymmetries, in some contexts well-functioning institutional mechanisms of monitoring and precommitment (politicians' ability to commit to a certain course of action in the future) can substitute for this gap and make sure that development is not entirely derailed. As a political columnist has suggested, "Never overestimate the information of the electorate, but never underestimate its intelligence" (Mark Shields, cited in Converse 2000, 331). In other contexts, attempting to correct information asymmetries can have unintended consequences and can even hamper pro-development collective action. This chapter will explore in greater detail the complicated and often nonlinear relationship between information asymmetries and collective action.

Chapters 3 and 4 showed how collective action capabilities and the institutional context can determine the ability of different stakeholders to translate their latent preferences into actual policy outcomes. However, because policy is made by politicians and bureaucrats (whose interests may only partly align with those of voters), it is important to consider how they strategically use information flows and gaps to garner support, get elected, or get promoted. To be sure, some participants in economic or political markets simply have more information than others. For example, bureaucrats may know the true cost of providing a publicly financed good and service, but voters and elected officials may not, thereby providing an opportunity for bureaucrats to push for a larger budget than is justified by their outputs. Even if laws and regulations clearly establish the procedural blueprint for budget formulation and approval, some ministries or bureaucratic agencies may have greater informational resources that give them advantageous bargaining positions in a given institutional environment. Thus, even when institutions function relatively well, actors (as stakeholders) have different degrees of knowledge about the details of the transaction, the process, or the real policy outcome.

Information asymmetries are important to understand because they influence the likelihood of change. Voters or policy consumers need information, first and foremost, to evaluate the performance, motives, or competence of the policy producers. Reformers need to acquire information about other stakeholders with similar policy positions in order to build lasting coalitions. As one of the major ingredients of accountability and effective collective ac-

**FIGURE 7.1 Conceptual Map of Information Problems and Asymmetries**

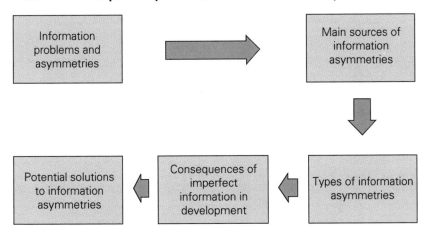

*Source:* Authors.

tion, information that is available and interpretable by all participants in economic transactions—voters, politicians, and bureaucrats—is crucial for development. The availability, transparency, and interpretability of information in the process of policy change can make substantive differences in the final outcome. In fact, under certain conditions, even small amounts of informational correctives can have large effects on development outcomes.

While information is critical, it is not a panacea. Under certain conditions, it may actually increase the divergence of interests between stakeholders and policy makers, if the latter resort to pandering or concealing their true agenda in the short run so that they may remain in power long enough to pursue a private agenda at a later point in time. In other circumstances, as we will see, keeping a low profile, bypassing full contestation, and avoiding a politically polarized environment benefit reform teams. This chapter introduces the concept of information asymmetries as part of a broader family of economic and political market imperfections (see figure 7.1).

## Objectives of Chapter 7

The analytics introduced in this chapter will help development practitioners to:

- Understand information problems and asymmetries
- Develop an intuitive understanding of the strategic origins of informational imperfections

- Diagnose the scope and type of information problems within their own policy change process and linking chapter concepts to relevant life situations
- Reflect on the relationship between information asymmetries and collective action in their own work
- Identify the most context-appropriate strategy for correcting such imperfections.

## The Political Economy of Information

As noted above, information asymmetries arise when a systematic discrepancy exists between the information available to the different market participants or contractual parties. Simply put, one actor knows more than the others. Producers know more about their own products than consumers, sellers know more than buyers, and employees know more their own abilities in the workplace than employers.

In economics, the earlier general equilibrium theories were derived from three main assumptions: perfect information among market participants in transactions; a complete set of markets (that is, all buyers and sellers were able to trade goods and services with everybody else without incurring transaction costs); and no enforcement problems (contracts are fully enforced) (Arrow and Debreu 1954). In this theoretical universe, institutions and collective action did not matter at all. Supply and demand were solely responsible for market equilibrium. However, as the 2001 Nobel Prize winning team (George Akerlof, Michael Spence, and Joseph Stiglitz) argued, markets suffer from imperfect information problems, which in turn significantly affect the nature of transactions. Because some parties have more information about their own ability to fulfill the contractual obligations, their actions and choices convey some sort of signals to the other market participants. In return, these participants react to such informational cues (Stiglitz 2000, 1444; Stiglitz 2002, 460). For example, when a firm offers a three-year guarantee on an electronic appliance, it signals product confidence to consumers in addition to its commitment to absorb the risk of paying for maintenance if the appliance breaks. The price of the product, per se, does not convey all necessary information (Stiglitz 2002, 468).

Firm managers also have incentives to increase information asymmetries between them and consumers to gain or retain market power. Corporate governance, finance, and organizational design are key domains where managers and firm employees have more information than shareholders and consumers, as well as incentives to perpetuate this lack of transparency. One of the key theoretical contributions of this seminal body of work demonstrates that markets alone do not give incentives to participants to disclose information about their characteristics and activities in the absence of institutions that oblige them to do so. Therefore, explicitly incorporating information problems into the analysis has changed the paradigm in modern economics.

Similar (if not larger) information gaps apply to political markets as well. Governments and politicians, by definition, know more about their own competence, policies, and regulations than do citizens. In extreme cases, they do not share anything with the opposition or voters. In some countries, for example, the annual budget document sent to parliaments for review has no more than a few pages. In the recent past, several severe financial crises with worldwide development consequences were triggered by governments' lack of fiscal transparency: the 1997 Asian financial crisis or the more recent case of Greece in the Euro Area.

Information problems are much more acute in the case of governments than in the case of firms. Lack of transparency or "sunshine" conceals mistakes, corruption, and abuses of power. Moreover, in economic markets, customers can switch to another product if firm managers use secrecy to cover mismanagement or abuse. In politics, the exit opportunity, especially when the executive perpetuates information asymmetries, is always difficult and often impossible (Stiglitz 2002, 487–488). Information about political representatives' behavior and policies also has distributional consequences. Because in many ways such information is a scarce good, it empowers some groups that have access to it at the expense of others.

We have already suggested that lack of voter information (due to voter characteristics or a lack of government transparency) is one of the most important sources of information asymmetry in politics. Even in developed contexts, lack of knowledge about candidates' characteristics, as well as the manipulation of voters' decisions through political campaigning and advertising, give electoral advantage to special interests that can mobilize more effectively to extract favorable policies through behind-the-scenes lobbying, advertising, and the like (Grossman and Helpman 1996). Given that voters cannot adequately monitor the behavior of politicians in contexts with high information asymmetries, politicians can extract rents with little risk of being sanctioned. Therefore, the informational discrepancies among various stakeholders have profound implications for institutions, accountability relations between citizens and governments, the collective action potential of stakeholders, and ultimately policy outcomes. Let us also recall from chapter 3 that public information and transparency provided by governments to citizens is a public good and the benefits extend to everyone in society (Stiglitz

2008). Precisely because it is a public good, it also suffers from some of the inherent collective action problems discussed earlier, such as free riding. As we will see in this chapter, citizens want government transparency, but sometimes the costs of individual participation for obtaining it exceed the benefits.

## Where Do Information Asymmetries Come from? Types of Information Problems

Information problems originate in principal-agent relations, a topic that chapter 6 explored in greater depth. This relationship, which characterizes all processes of delegation (say, from politicians to bureaucrats or from voters to politicians), generates so-called agency problems. Simply put, one of the participants in the transaction (the one who delegates, or the voter) runs the risk of not having the delegatee (say, the legislator representing his or her district) fulfill its obligations. While incentives generated by principal-agent relationships are broader than informational problems, transparency constitutes a crucial component of agency issues.

Two central issues lie at the core of the concept of information asymmetries (Stiglitz 2000, 1447):

- *The problem of selection.* Identifying the characteristics of political participants.
- *The problem of behavior.* Identifying divergent or skewed incentives embedded in the relationship between actors. For a more detailed discussion of monitoring and enforcement, see also chapter 9

Both types of information problems refer to the negative consequences of information asymmetries between two groups of actors (say, voters and politicians). We will now present several examples.

*Self-Selection.* "Self-selection is the process through which individuals reveal information about themselves through the choices they make" (Rothschild and Stiglitz 1976; Stiglitz 2000, 1450). The typical insurance example of self-selection is the following: an insurance company does not know the real likelihood of an accident for the individual seeking insurance. However, if the latter chooses to purchase an insurance package with a higher deductible than other alternatives available, the insurer can infer from this choice that the individual assesses himself as less likely to have an accident in the short run. As another example, governments often do not know the real economic ability of taxpayers, but for tax purposes, it bases its assessment of their capacity to pay on what it can observe (such as wealth, income, or, as in medieval Europe, the number of house windows). This process of self-selection in regard to taxation is crucial in developing countries, where governments are less likely to observe the real income of market participants because of large informal economies or undeclared wealth and income. Hence, they cannot impose an effective income tax schedule (Stiglitz 2000, 1451). As Concepts in Practice 7.1 below illustrates, the role of self-selection in bureaucracies can be a powerful factor in shaping organizational outcomes.

***Moral Hazard.*** Moral hazard occurs when one actor has incentives to take a higher risk because he is not bearing the full costs of his actions. Typical examples of moral hazard also come from the insurance market. Homeowners' insurance, for example, generates incentives either to be careless about home safety or, in more extreme cases, to file insurance claims for a loss that never actually occurred. Because insurers cannot monitor behavior adequately, they have to find ways to reduce moral hazard by taking indirect preventive measures (for example, installing sprinklers, in the case of home insurers, or setting up institutions that prevent blatant corruption of politicians, in the case of voters) (Arrow 1971; Stiglitz 2000, 1453; 2001).

---

### CONCEPTS IN PRACTICE 7.1
## Individual Characteristics and the Working Environment in Bureaucracies

In large and complex institutions, the ability to realize goals or collective mandates requires the interaction and coordination of a large number of individuals, not all facing the same incentives. The development of an administrative and management system generates incentives for political control (hierarchies). Such mechanisms, in turn, affect who is most likely to rise to the top and make decisions. As Friedrich Hayek noted with respect to the public sector at large, the management of big organizations tends to favor the advancement of those with a relatively unscrupulous "political" personality. Even though these people may not be as technically competent as others, or as cooperative, they are essential to the realization of the organization's goals. Thus, paradoxically, the self-selection process generated by the growth of an organization can undermine its long-term productivity, as resources are diverted to the private agendas of administrators less closely aligned with the organization's mission, than more technically competent and cooperative personality types.

*Source:* Hayek (1944).

---

Moral hazard types of information asymmetries characterize all relations between voters, political representatives, and bureaucracies. Voters do not know how the legislators they elect in their district will actually behave in the legislature. Therefore, once elected and "insured" for at least one term of office, politicians have incentives to behave opportunistically, engage in corruption, and deviate from their mandate, in the absence of effective monitoring. While the risky action is undertaken by politicians, often voters are the ones incurring the costs, and the relationship of accountability suffers.

Another example of moral hazard comes from the historical relationship between imperial centers and provincial notables. Let's imagine a feudal world with a center and many vassal kingdoms. If a central government gives authority to local rulers to raise taxes on its behalf, that government incurs the potential risk of making enough resources available to the local or regional rulers to mobilize armies against the center and claim political power. Therefore, the center has often imposed a lower tax rate on the provinces than it would have done in the absence of the moral hazard problem. Voluntarily limiting its own tax-collection capacity has also, paradoxically, limited the military threat posed by its local agents. The Ottoman Empire during its classical age (1453–1600s) is a case in point. Through the "fief system," the sultan had incentives to implement provincial taxes below what he could have feasibly extracted, given the possible armed resistance that provincial elites could have mounted once they had accumulated enough resources. This central dilemma of dual delegation of taxation and coercion also characterized administrations in medieval Europe, Japan, and Persia (Karaman 2009, 692).

Moral hazard problems also characterize more contemporaneous federal arrangements or decentralized institutions around the world. If local or regional governments in decentralized systems anticipate bailouts from the central government in case they overspend, they lack incentives not to engage in overspending in the first place. The incentives, in this case, generate a collective action problem, because subnational units can engage in a version of the tragedy of the commons by "overfishing" the total amount of transfers from the center. Since the likelihood of bailouts leads subnational governments to engage in strategic behavior vis-à-vis the central government, moral hazard problems have profound consequences for the design of intergovernmental transfers.

Correcting moral hazard incentives is not an easy task. Furthermore, attempts to correct moral hazard incentives can create even more serious problems. In an effort to prevent such incentives, for example, health insurance companies set up complex systems to screen for preexisting conditions but in the process exclude many from qualifying for insurance in the first place.[1]

***Adverse Selection.*** Another prevalent form of information asymmetries, closely related to moral hazard, is adverse selection. Adverse selection, to return to our insurance examples, refers to a situation in which the actors who pose the highest risk are also the ones most likely to enter an insurance contract. For example, smokers are more likely than nonsmokers to buy health or life insurance, but, at the same time, they are generally more likely to actually incur the health risks associated with smoking. Therefore, this problem is the "adverse" self-selection of a higher-risk group into the insurance contract.

One of the classic examples of adverse selection made famous by Nobel Prize winner George Akerlof refers to the market for "lemons" or bad used cars (Akerlof 1970). Buyers want a quality product but are not sure if the car they are about to buy is bad or good since they cannot observe and thoroughly evaluate all product dimensions. Therefore, consumers expect to pay an average price that is lower than the real value for a good used car. The sellers of good cars will thus lose in this transaction and have incentives to withdraw from the market. Because only the bad cars stay up for sale, a downward spiral of lower prices and lower-quality products results in a market dominated by bad cars. Eventually, this process could result in the disappearance of the market altogether as consumers are unwilling to pay anything at all for the substandard products on offer.

Adverse selection problems in politics have a similar logic. Assume there are two kinds of politicians: one who is interested in keeping voters happy through policies and another who is running for office just for the high salary, opportunities for corruption, and side payments. In the absence of information about performance in office, reputation, or the like, voters will not know what kind of politician a candidate is. Especially under conditions of high monetary incentives for members of legislatures, it is likely that more candidates from the second group will run for office. Uninformed voters who cannot tell the two types apart will be more likely to vote for an opportunistic candidate, given that they are more likely to run for office, and the overall quality of political representation will go down. This dynamic has important consequences for accountability and the provision of public goods (Mattozzi and Merlo 2007). The process of adverse selection can sometimes make voters accept clientelistic payments or enter patronage networks, as they are skeptical of the overall competence of their political representatives.

### The Repertoire of Solutions to Problems of Information Asymmetries

Two possible solutions for correcting information asymmetries in the principal-agent relationship relate to monitoring and incentive pay (Stiglitz 2000, 1454).

*Monitoring* the behavior of bureaucrats and politicians to prevent moral hazard and adverse selection problems can be done by the media, civil society, and oversight institutions. One example is public account committees (PACs). The ability of bureaucrats to implement public policy without direct oversight can result in incentives for corruption and waste. Oversight bodies that undertake random or targeted audits can mitigate such tendencies. In European countries, the power of parliamentary PACs, whose role is to scrutinize the use of public funds, has had varying degrees of success (Buzaljko et al. 2010). Specifically, countries with more powerful PACs, such as Denmark, waste less public funding than countries in which the powers of the PACs are severely circumscribed, such as Greece. Concepts in Practice 7.2 illustrates a case of bureaucratic oversight in Ghana, where such institutions corrected information asymmetries and significantly improved public finances.

*Incentive pay* for the agent (that is, incentive pay for bureaucrats or political representatives) is one of the classic prescriptions of civil service reforms. Paying civil servants high wages while also having a clear mechanism for rewarding or punishing bureaucratic performance has sometimes been suggested as a good way to tackle corruption and inefficiency. Singapore pays some of the highest salaries for civil servants and politicians in the world. These salaries, combined with a tough penal system and reward bonuses for delivering long-term economic growth, may be one of the reasons behind the success of Singapore and its relatively low rate of corruption, according to some studies (Behnke et al. 2008).

However, a caveat is in order: as the adverse selection example showed in the case of political candidates for office, high material rewards for politicians can attract the least ideal candidates who do not enter politics to provide public goods and boost development but rather to enjoy the spoils of office. Organizations that solve collective action problems such as political parties or civil society organizations face similar challenges, as their leaders are not often able to gauge the degree of commitment to the group of new adherents to the cause. Selective incentives linked to actual performance in office or in the organization might under certain conditions do a better job of solving adverse selection problems, as they can discourage nonperformers.

**CONCEPTS IN PRACTICE 7.2**

## Taming the Bureaucracy through Broadcasting: The Case of Ghana's Public Account Committee

Ghana's 1992 constitution gave parliament oversight over the executive. To supervise public finances, a public account committee was established. The committee was headed by a member of the opposition and was responsible for scrutinizing public finances, as in most Commonwealth countries (former U.K. colonies).

Formally, the 25-member committee had the power to call for "persons and papers"—that is, all government officials and documents it considered necessary for fulfilling its obligations and effectively scrutinizing the use of taxpayers' money. However, in practice, the public account committee's powers were severely diminished because many members did not feel compelled to attend meetings and the committee's recommendations were not implemented.

Starting in 2005, a concerted effort was made to increase the committee's effective-

ness and to ensure that its hearings could be held in public where they would receive media attention. The public account committee began holding public meetings in 2007, and the first such hearing became a major media event. The presence of the media—especially the private media, which did not stop broadcasting when ministers were called to answer potentially embarrassing questions about public financial management—not only ensured high attendance but also led to the uncovering of irregularities in payments and public procurement.

Thus, the use of the media to televise and disseminate information about the actions of the bureaucracy ensured, for the first time, that legislative oversight significantly affected the behavior of the executive.

*Source:* Sallas-Menshah (2011).

## Broader Implications of Information Asymmetries

Information asymmetry problems can have profound implications for the role of institutions. According to traditional paradigms, marginal or incremental changes in information were not supposed to dramatically affect actors' beliefs and equilibria. Nevertheless, because of the major role that information asymmetries play in the strategic interaction of different actors (such as voters, politicians, and bureaucrats), we now know that even small amounts of information can have large consequences for institutional equilibria (Stiglitz 2000, 2002). Because of the significant difference that corrective information can make for markets, firms, and consumers, we recognize that some degree of regulation is necessary for market efficiency (Shapiro and Stiglitz 1985). In political markets, transparency and freedom of information laws, along with demands for increased accountability, can alter significantly the relationship between the government (as agent) and the citizens (as principals).

Disclosure or freedom of information laws that oblige public authorities to provide information to the general public are sometimes powerful tools for correcting information asymmetries. Some countries, such as Thailand, incorporated them into the constitution. Others joined the wave of global adopters. Unfortunately, laws on paper are not enough. As we will see later in this chapter, voters and citizens must be able to solve collective action problems and act upon them to keep the executive accountable and solve moral hazard or adverse selection problems.

## Correctors of Information Asymmetries: The Role of the Media, Civil Society, and Donors

Lack of information, as well as lack of commitment to deliver on campaign promises on the part of elected politicians, renders accountability relations problematic. Information asymmetries make monitoring difficult and can induce politicians to focus on very narrow constituencies through targeted exchanges as opposed to providing public goods. Alternatively, as the example presented in Concepts in Practice 7.3 shows, solving information asymmetries can incentivize politicians to provide previously undersupplied public goods. Mass media has a crucial role to play in the process. Increased transparency can encourage collective action and public participation built around demands for better performance from the government.

In line with the Indian example, several studies have found newspaper circulation and media freedom to be inversely correlated with the level of corruption and positively correlated with the security of property rights (Adsera, Boix, and Payne 2003; Brunetti and Weder 1999; Ahrend 2002). Countries with more vibrant media seem to have, on average, more accountability, fewer governance problems, and more robust political turnover (Besley and Prat 2001). Furthermore, strengthening the capacity of the media can make it easier for voters and elected officials to control the executive because it helps reveal the "true" character of the politicians with more accuracy.

Sometimes information collected and disclosed by donors or other members of the development community in collaboration with domestic media also had an immediate effect on correcting asymmetries. A famous study conducted in Uganda in 1995 attempted to trace central education spending to the final recipients of funds: individual schools. Shockingly, only around 20 percent of total allocations ever reached them. After the negative publicity following the release of these findings, the government started to share month-to-month information on disbursements to local districts. In addi-

**CONCEPTS IN PRACTICE 7.3**

## Feeding the Starving: The Role of the Media in Generating Incentives for Politicians to Respond to Famines and Flood Damage

India is an ideal case study of how elections and the role of the media can interact to influence officials' incentives to take certain actions. Despite the variation in political competition across the country—with some states more dominated by a single party than others—and wide differences in the availability of local-language newspapers, it is possible to observe how a more competitive political system and a more vibrant media might enhance transparency, affect the actions of elected officials, prevent moral hazard, and make officeholders more responsive or accountable in implementing development policies.

Using data from 1958 to 1992, a study identified the extent to which variations in political competition and the circulation of the local newspapers affected the public distribution of food and calamity relief to marginalized groups most at risk of hunger in times of famine. The study found that representative democracy and the presence of free and independent regional presses were significant factors in ensuring the protection of vulnerable citizens because these elements increased public visibility of relief action or lack thereof.

*Source:* Besley and Burgess (2002).

tion, as a result of an ambitious national newspaper campaign that followed this first Public Expenditure Tracking Survey, when the same study was repeated five years later, 80 percent of the funds reached their beneficiaries. The school headmasters, acting on this information, successfully claimed their share of development funds whenever they did not fully receive them (Banerjee and Duflo 2011, 236–37; Reinikka and Svensson 2004, 2005).

Paradoxically, in this particular instance, the information-correction mechanism has also led to a rethinking of the entire principal-agent relationship embedded in the process of decentralization that, in turn, contributed to the reversal of the initial reform. The public revelation of dramatic inefficiencies in allocation of the education fund to the localities created an opportunity for bureaucratic agencies opposing decentralization to recentralize. As a result of this new information that became available in 2002, the revised fiscal decentralization strategy significantly restricted the fiscal autonomy of local governments. Until that point, Uganda, together with South Africa, was the leading adopter of decentralization reforms in Sub-Saharan Africa (Eaton, Kaiser, and Smoke 2010, 57–58). The indirect role that increased transparency played in the process of reform reversal sheds light on some of the potential unintended consequences of information correctives. It also calls attention to the strategies employed by some segments of the bureaucracy that used the newly available evidence to consolidate their position and recentralize.

In addition to the availability of news sources, patterns of media ownership and their implications for overall transparency also matter significantly. Some cross-national studies have shown that state ownership of the media generally correlates with higher corruption (Djankov et al. 2003). Other recent in-depth case studies have analyzed the impact of commercial liberalization of Chinese media on regulatory implementation and argued that this process has helped reinforce the state's legitimacy rather than challenging it (Stockmann and Gallagher 2011). Private media outlets effectively bolstered the state narrative of a proworker bias in judicial cases related to labor conflicts, and boosted the overall confidence in the legal system.

In addition to mass media, civil society organizations have a crucial role to play in promoting transparency. In some cases, the executive has private information that voters do not possess and has moral hazard incentives. In other cases, the government itself lacks the capacity to collect crucial data from citizens that could help provide public goods more effectively. Sometimes, civil society intermediaries provide key solutions to these bidirectional information problems. The government of Bangladesh, for example, responded much more promptly to the floods of 1998 than it did to a similar natural calamity that had occurred 10 years earlier, in 1988. During the 1988 floods, the government attempts to distribute emergency relief, food and water were severely curtailed by a poor distribution network, weak engagement with civil society organizations, and a general lack of information about the specific needs of victims across the damaged areas (Beck 2005, 11). These factors, coupled with pervasive and institutionalized corruption, resulted in a severe misallocation of resources. Shelters were built in sub-optimal locations, and some victims even had to pay rent.

The 1998 floods affected approximately 68% of the country and directly impacted around 30 million people (ibid, 3). Despite a disaster magnitude comparable with the previous episode and higher population densities, the death toll was 60 percent lower. Why? The role of civil society organizations turned out to be critical in facilitating a more effective response to the crisis. First, the NGOs had effective local distribution networks. Second, they were better able to collect crucial and timely information about the victims' needs, especially as the advent of mobile phones and GPS devices facilitated this effort (Beck 2005, 11–14; Young et al. 2000). The government coordinated with thousands of NGOs, took advantage of their information collection and distribution capacity, and finally ensured a significantly better response compared to 1988.

## The Role of Technology in Correcting Information Asymmetries

Let us recall the discussion from chapter 4 about the role that major technology shifts have had on institutional change. Technology is increasingly being used to help stakeholders correct information asymmetries, to monitor the provision of public goods and services in a principal-agent relationship, and to solve collective action problems. Many organizations are using technological innovations to oversee public service delivery, to measure its impact on development around the world, and to create platforms and virtual communities of citizens with interests in development issues. Concepts in Practice 7.4 describes how these technologies have been applied to improve outcomes in both developed and developing countries.

---

**CONCEPTS IN PRACTICE 7.4**

## Using Technology to Monitor the Provision of Public Goods

Some development programs are using cell phones to track whether promised goods have arrived at their destination. Others are using technology on a bigger scale, developing programs like Mapping for Results, which monitors where World Bank aid goes and to whom.[a] Moreover, whether it is to express their discontent or to share their data and exchange their stories, citizens are increasingly using technology to learn, communicate, and solve collective action problems for institutional change. The role of Facebook or Twitter for mobilizational efforts is well established by now. The Arab Spring is a case in point.

Technology also allows better monitoring of agents by principals and the efficient correction of information asymmetries. A recent study[b] presents an analysis of cases from Brazil, Chile, India, Kenya, and Slovakia, where technology interventions seem to have increased the accountability of public organizations, expanded their services, and improved their outcomes.

For instance, in Kenya, a free technology platform was created to allow the monitoring of the 2010 constitutional referendum and presented a space for citizens to report acts of violence (by webmail or mobile phones). The platform became so popular that it had 45,000 users.[c] In the case of India, a technology tool was created to track the behavior of political leaders throughout their time in office, showing when and how citizens solicit information from their officials.[d] Another study developed in India[e] shows that using cameras to monitor teachers' attendance could contribute significantly to a reduction in teacher absenteeism. This study financially rewarded teachers who proved, with a camera, their attendance at school. While many factors are involved in increasing accountability, these and many other studies suggest that technology can certainly become helpful in the process of correcting information asymmetries between citizens (as principals) and bureaucrats and politicians (as agents).

a. See http://maps.worldbank.org/.
b. Fung, Gilman, and Shkabatur (2011).
c. See http://www.ushahidi.com/about-us.
d. See http://www.transparency-initiative.org/wp-content/uploads/2011/05/impact_case_studies_final1.pdf.
e. See Duflo and Hanna (2006), http://www.hks.harvard.edu/inequality/Seminar/Papers/Duflo06.pdf.

---

## Can Transparency Have Unintended Consequences?

Despite the normative halo surrounding transparency in development circles, in some cases full information availability and policy contestability have created pitfalls. Under certain circumstances, induced transparency (as a corrective mechanism for information asymmetries) may distort outcomes or provide disincentives for collective action and claims making:

- More transparency might cause excessive politicization, with potentially negative consequences for legislative outcomes (Heald 2003).
- In some cases, increased transparency might lead to decreased efficiency of high-quality service providers in the public sector. In general, teachers and health workers unions have mobilized against transparency. Increased visibility of performance may attract more service users. Paradoxically, unlike in the private sector, under conditions of rationing and budget constraints, this phenomenon might put high pressure on high performers and decrease overall efficiency of operation (Gavazza and Lizzeri 2007).
- More transparency might encourage low-competency incumbents who do not stand a chance of being reelected to give up trying to appease voters and pursue a strategy of aggressive short-term rent extraction (Besley 2006).
- Transparency can also induce politicians to keep costly preelectoral promises at the expense of policy flexibility and prevent "good" candidates from running for office in the first place (Geraats 2005).
- Sometimes, a certain degree of secrecy or low visibility may lead to better allocation of resources or reform outcomes, because those that would lose from reforms will not be able to coalesce around a clear and highly visible target and block the attempt at change.
- As a result of transparency laws aimed at correcting information asymmetries, the process of requesting information may entail high costs or risks for the actors involved. It can sometimes allow autocratic incumbents to target those who are seeking information as political opponents.
- Information symmetries between the executive and private firms competing for public procurement contracts may, under certain conditions, cause collusion, with negative consequences for the bidding process (Olken 2007).

Given that the effects of any attempt to correct information asymmetries are contingent on specific contexts and preexisting institutions, the analyst should be cautious when selecting the solution, and explore its potential unintended consequences.

**FIGURE 7.2 Influence of Transparency, through the Media, on Government**

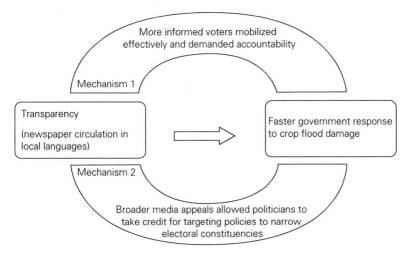

*Source:* Authors.

In addition to theoretical or conceptual mechanisms, empirical evidence may also require a careful selection of indicators and interpretation of findings. Figure 7.2 presents an example of increased transparency that might have unintended consequences. Using the example of connecting higher newspaper circulation in India with faster government response to crop flood damage and famines, let us think systematically about the different ways in which we could interpret the results (this point was developed by Keefer 2004, 266, based on Besley and Burgess 2002).

Whereas mechanism 1 in figure 7.2 is aligned with the general hypothesis that increased transparency leads to better development outcomes through collective action, mechanism 2 demonstrates an alternative explanatory route for the empirical finding. This second explanation suggests that, independent of collective action and popular claims for greater accountability, local politicians might want to target the affected political constituencies because of the high policy visibility that allows them to take immediate credit for reelection purposes. At the same time, they can reduce the delivery of public goods or programmatic spending in other "less visible" domains (education, health, or districts not affected by crop damage, for example). Therefore, the causal relationship among indicators of transparency, collective action, and observed policy outcomes should always be interpreted with caution.

# Understanding the Nonlinear Relationship between Information Asymmetries and Pro-Development Collective Action

Does transparency or the correction of information asymmetries always facilitate pro-development collective action? Under what conditions do they fulfill that role? Does newly acquired information always bolster the potential of reform groups to mobilize? Analysts and reformers interested in understanding the political economy of information should carefully think about all possible causal configurations and contingencies.

It needs to be emphasized that robust accountability of politicians to citizens or voters entails two components: transparency and collective action. Government transparency by itself does not always trigger public participation that automatically translates into socially beneficial policies. Freedom of information laws on paper, without accompanying mechanisms that ensure that citizens know their rights and can collectively act upon them to solicit information, do not mean much. In fact, sometimes they could even be detrimental in the short run when claiming these rights attracts political retaliation from powerful incumbents. This outcome is most obvious in nondemocratic regimes where the cost of acting on existing laws (often adopted at the pressure of international donors) and requesting sensitive data on, say, public expenditure is prohibitively high for individuals and groups.

Even in the case of democratic polities, it may be difficult for transparency alone to increase accountability, assign individual responsibility, or effectively sanction officials in contexts in which the performance of individual legislators in office is difficult to gauge. If political parties are weak and fail to solve their own collective action problems, it is not easy for elected officials to provide anything other than redistribution to a narrow set of partisan supporters to be reelected, whatever their individual competence. For example, evidence from Benin suggests that increased access to information, through broader radio reception, has not heightened demand for better public education, possibly because of the weakness of the national party system and inadequate complementary mechanisms of accountability (Keefer and Khemani 2011). Increased access to information did, however, induce some behavioral changes.

In general, the relationship between information asymmetries and collective action is under theoretical scrutiny, but it seems to be more nuanced than a simple linear dynamic through which transparency always positively and unconditionally affects pro-development collective action. Synergistic institutions of accountability might be necessary to complement increased transparency for positive outcomes.

The following vignettes tell four different stories about this relationship. The first case shows how citizens mobilized successfully, collected data, and increased transparency. Despite these accomplishments, in the absence of complementary accountability mechanisms, they could not align politicians' incentives with their policy goals. As a result, basic water services remained underprovided in rural South Africa (*collective action and transparency, but no results*). The second story is equally pessimistic and shows that in Peru's legislature a higher degree of transparency and increased accountability of individual legislators to constituencies paradoxically reduced the collective action potential of opposition to the corrupt Fujimori government (*transparency, no collective action, no results*).

The third vignette is more optimistic. Despite death threats, a high-ranking bureaucrat in the Nigerian government decided to disclose key public finance data in national newspapers and thereby increased accountability (*no collective action, transparency, and concrete results*). The fourth instance, also optimistic, shows how a team of Kenyan reformers kept a low profile to avoid open political confrontation with powerful vested interests and was able to change key regulations governing a very corrupt and clientelistic public procurement system (*collective action, no transparency, and results*).

The puzzling variation in the capacity of key driving factors such as transparency and collective action to produce tangible development outcomes shows that, in these four stories, there was no necessary or sufficient condition for reform success. Both transparency and collective action might need to interact with other specific sets of incentives and institutions to generate robust and lasting accountability relations between voters and politicians.

## Information, Collective Action, and Water Access in Rural South Africa

A project initiated by a civil society organization in a small South African municipality involved local governments, tribal elders, and citizens in an exercise meant to facilitate community assessment of water services and demand policy action from the state agencies responsible for implementation (Hemson and Buccus 2009). The community first participated in training workshops to learn how to use scorecards and then collected actual information on water sources, conditions, and access throughout the municipality.

Empowered by the newly acquired information, the community appealed to the local officials who were initially interested in the project, recognizing that the local council would have never obtained these valuable data without this ambitious effort of community mobilization and collective action. Despite this first enthusiastic feedback, however, the election time was approaching, and internal divisions within the African National Congress (the incumbent party) created competition between two tiers of local government. Therefore, to avoid signaling incompetency to the upper tier, an elected official blocked the dissemination of the data showing problematic water management, and the problems of water services were never addressed. In this case, although effective collective action led to information correction, the outcome was suboptimal, because of electoral incentives and lack of robust political accountability.

### Transparency and Collective Action—Trade-Offs in Peru's Legislature

The Peruvian Congress under Fujimori provides a counterintuitive story in which the correction of information asymmetries and increased capacity of voters to monitor the performance in office of their political representatives led, paradoxically, to weaker collective action among the opposition parties and, as a result, to the political dominance of a corrupt party and head of state (Carey 2003). This vignette reveals the benefits of nonlinear thinking that would a priori suggest that transparency and information asymmetries automatically solve pro-development collective action problems. In 1997, at the advice of the Inter-American Development Bank, the Peruvian Congress bought an electronic vote-counting machine to replace hand counts prone to mistakes and irregularities. Initially, legislators opposed the technological upgrade, fearing that their votes would be on record. Ultimately, with buy-in from the incumbent party, the machine was purchased, voting began to be recorded, and the media took full advantage. Newspapers and TV stations began to report on the performance in office of individual legislators (number and type of bills, for example).

Paradoxically, close to the year 2000, when Fujimori's party had a narrow majority in parliament, this technological upgrade that increased transparency also gave individual politicians incentives to cater to their local constituencies rather than to act collectively as a party. All of a sudden, it became possible for voters to identify the extent to which their representative had "brought home the bacon"—that is, provided her supporters with goods and services. As a consequence, the opposition parties became fragmented and lacked discipline and cohesiveness, whereas the incumbent party—under the strong leadership of Fujimori—behaved as a compact voting bloc and locked in opportunities for vetoing all reforms that attempted to dismantle its patronage and corruption. Information asymmetries between politicians and voters were indeed corrected, but in this case greater transparency came at the expense of opposition legislators and undermined their effective collective action.

## Risky Disclosure of Key Budget Information in Nigeria

In Nigeria, in 2004, under conditions of severe budgetary opaqueness and high political stakes associated with the oil revenues, finance minister Okonjo-Iweala started to publish the state-by-state central transfers to the 36 state governments in national newspapers each month. This public disclosure made some of the state governors particularly uncomfortable (Vallely 2006). As a result of her commitment to enhance fiscal transparency, the minister made many political enemies and even received a number of death threats. Similar consequences of information disclosure affect many journalists around the world every day. In cases like this, because of the high individual cost of action and claims making, generating transparency is a public good and suffers from collective action problems. As already argued, if the benefits of information on revenue and spending extend to all citizens but the prohibitively high costs fall on only a handful of individuals (for example, death threats or actual political persecution), the fight for information is not likely to take place. It is precisely in these settings that leadership, activism, and entrepreneurship become necessary to undertake risks and open up the path to the collective action needed to correct information asymmetries. The Nigerian junior finance minister is a good example of these requirements.

## Strategic Obfuscation, Collective Action, and Reform in Kenya

The case of Kenya we mentioned in chapter 5 demonstrates that, quite counterintuitively, reform sometimes has better chances under conditions of relative opaqueness.[2] In 2001, during the last days of the Moi administration, the incumbent party was desperately trying to use government funds to finance its patronage networks to maintain power. Public procurement turned out to be one of the main venues of funding the party through the discretionary award of contracts to private firms and individuals. A small circle of Kenyan reformers decided to make the issue salient, increase its visibility, and garner public support. According to the conventional wisdom corroborated by the advice of international donors, making the issue salient and initiating a national debate that would help coordinate unorganized reform supporters from different segments of society would weaken resistance and opposition

## The Consequences of Information Asymmetries on Development Outcomes

How can we formally conceptualize the persistence of suboptimal equilibria due to information costs? One way is to think of political and market imperfections as leading to suboptimal equilibrium outcomes (that is, "steady states"; see appendix A and chapter 3). A good equilibrium is one in which the outcome is the most favorable possible. Conversely, a bad equilibrium is one in which, for some reason (such as information asymmetries or costs) resources are being inefficiently allocated.

At the most abstract level, it is possible to conceptualize the existence of "good" and "bad" equilibria using the tools of game theory. As the table below shows, two players can choose to either cooperate or not cooperate. There are two Nash equilibria in this game (cooperate, cooperate) and (don't cooperate, don't cooperate). It is not possible to deduce, a priori, which equilibrium emerges. However, if information costs between players affect their ability to coordinate, then it becomes possible to establish the conditions under which the optimal or suboptimal equilibrium is most likely to emerge.

For example, two civil society organizations might benefit from jointly promoting a certain issue, thereby, raising public awareness and mobilizing resources in favor of their agendas

to policy change. Animated by this impulse, the reformers approached the permanent secretary in the Ministry of Finance.

They were in for surprising advice. The strategy suggested to them was exactly the opposite. Instead of becoming easy targets of political vengeance

(cooperate, cooperate as equilibrium). If only one group tries to promote the issue, both groups will lose out, because the issue will be publicly perceived as lacking significant and joint support. If both groups do not cooperate, the issue will be considered a low priority but will not be neglected as if it were an issue that had been poorly supported by only one group (don't cooperate, don't cooperate equilibrium).

If the ability of these two groups to coordinate their strategies depends on the cost of information they face, then changes in information costs can have a profound effect on whether the optimal (cooperate, cooperate) or the suboptimal (don't cooperate, don't cooperate) equilibrium emerges. For example, each group might need to gather information on the size, mobilization capacity, commonality of interests, competency of the leadership, and influence of the other group before it decides whether to try and coordinate in pressing a common cause. However, obtaining such information can be costly. Therefore, as information costs fall (or rise), the ability of the two groups to communicate effectively and jointly coordinate increases (or decreases); and, in turn, the result increases (or decreases) the possibility that the higher equilibrium outcome will emerge.

| | Cooperate | | Don't Cooperate | |
|---|---|---|---|---|
| Cooperate | 4 | 4 | 1 | 1 |
| Don't Cooperate | 1 | 1 | 3 | 3 |

*Source:* Inspired from (Cartwright et al 2009).

under conditions of making open claims, they were advised to proceed as "quietly" as possible through procedural channels. Taking the advice, the group of reformers identified a package of implementation rules (an omnibus bill) that would automatically follow the legislative vote on the annual budget, ensuring the precision and scope of regulatory implementation. Circumventing debate altogether with help from within the bureaucracy, the team—to its surprise—was able to insert the desired amendments as if they were yet another strictly technical regulation. As a result, crucial reforms that would never have succeeded if the issue had been clear and open to contestation to all political actors passed because of strategic obfuscation. Our Philippines case study paints a similar portrait (see appendix C).

As illustrated by the above examples, solving information asymmetries and enhancing transparency can sometimes help or jeopardize reform coalitions and their opportunities to generate change. Information sharing allows coordination, joint action, and trust-building among members of reform teams. Sometimes, as we have seen, disclosure and transparency may have unintended consequences. By understanding this nuanced relationship between correctives to information asymmetry and the potential for collective action, development practitioners can identify the best feasible strategy for achieving results (see Concepts in Practice 7.5).

## Summary

Information asymmetries and the incentives they generate are crucial constraints to pro-development collective action and policy change. Problems of missing information, moral hazard, or adverse selection pose serious problems for the accountability of political representatives to voters and often lead to suboptimal delivery of public goods. However, the relationship between transparency and collective action, on the one hand, and development outcomes, on the other hand, is nonlinear and might be contingent on parallel accountability mechanisms, monitoring devices, or institutional features. Accounting for nonlinearity allows practitioners to think in a context-specific way about the theoretical and empirical path leading from transparency to tangible development reforms.

### Notes

1. We are grateful to Margaret Levi for this point.
2. WBI and CommGap, "Political Economy Analysis to Action: A Global Learning Event," June 2010, Washington, DC.

# References

Adsera, Alicia, Carles Boix, and Mark Payne. 2003. "Are You Being Served? Political Accountability and Quality of Government." *Journal of Law, Economics, and Organization* 19 (2): 445–90.

Ahrend, Rudiger. 2002. "Press Freedom, Human Capital, and Corruption." Working Paper 2002-11, DELTA, Paris.

Akerlof, George A. 1970. "The Market for 'Lemons': Quality Uncertainty and the Market Mechanism." *Quarterly Journal of Economics* 84 (3): 488–500.

Arrow, Kenneth J. 1971. "A Utilitarian Approach to the Concept of Equality in Public Expenditure." *Quarterly Journal of Economics* 85 (3): 409–15.

Arrow, K. J., and G. Debreu. 1954. "Existence of an Equilibrium for a Competitive Economy." *Econometrica* 22: 265–90.

Banerjee, A., and E. Duflo. 2011. *Poor Economics: A Radical Rethinking of the Way to Fight Global Poverty.* New York: Public Affairs.

Beck, T. 2005. "Learning Lessons from Disaster Recovery: The Case of Bangladesh. Disaster Risk Management." Working Paper Series 11. Washington, DC: The World Bank.

Behnke, Kathrin, Alexander Hamilton, Leo Pagnac, and Paulina Terrazas. 2008. *The Dynamics of Legislative Rewards.* London: London School of Economics and World Bank.

Besley, T. 2006. *Principled Agents? The Political Economy of Good Government.* New York: Oxford University Press.

Besley, Timothy, and Robin Burgess. 2002. "The Political Economy of Government Responsiveness: Theory and Evidence from India." *Quarterly Journal of Economics* 117 (4): 1415–51.

Besley, Timothy, and Andrea Prat. 2001. "Handcuffs for the Grabbing Hand? Media Capture and Government Accountability." CEPR Discussion Paper, Center for Economic Policy Research, Washington, DC.

Brunetti, Aymo, and Beatrice Weder. 1999. "More Open Economies Have Better Governments." Economic Series 905, University of Saarland, Saarbrücken, Germany.

Buzaljko, Karolina, Anna Marlene Kanis, Alexandra Tamasan, and Frans Verkaat. 2010. "Public Financial Oversight: A Comparative Analysis of Parliamentary Committees across Europe." Maastricht Graduate School of Governance, Maastricht, Netherlands, and World Bank Institute, Washington, DC.

Carey, John M. 2003. "Transparency versus Collective Action." *Comparative Political Studies* 36 (9): 983–1006.

Cartwright, E., J. Gillet, and M. Van Vugt. 2009. "Endogenous Leadership in a Coordination Game with Conflict of Interest and Asymmetric Information." *School of Economics Discussion Papers,* No. 0913, University of Kent, http://hdl. handle.net/10419/50571' Web accessed: 6/18/2012.

Converse, Philip. 2000. "Assessing the Capacity of Mass Electorates." *Annual Review of Political Science* 3 (1): 331–53.

Djankov, D., C. McLiesh, T. Nenova, and A. Shleifer. 2003. "Who Owns the Media?" *Journal of Law and Economics* 46 (2): 341–82.

Duflo, Esther, and Rema Hanna. 2006. "Monitoring Works: Getting Teachers to Come to School." NBER Working Paper 11880, National Bureau of Economic Research, Cambridge, MA, http://www.hks.harvard.edu/inequality/Seminar/Papers/Duflo06.pdf.

Eaton, Kent, Kai Kaiser, and Paul Smoke. 2010. *The Political Economy of Decentralization Reforms: Implications for Aid Effectiveness.* Washington, DC: World Bank.

Fung, Archon, Hollie Gilman and Jennifer Shkabatur. 2011. *Impact Case Studies from Middle Income and Developing Countries,* http://www.transparency-initiative.org/wp-content/uploads/2011/05/impact_case_studies_final1.pdf.

Gavazza, A., and A. Lizzeri. 2007. "The Perils of Transparency in Bureaucracies." *American Economic Review* 97 (2): 300–05.

Geraats, Petra. 2005. "Transparency of Monetary Policy: Theory and Practice." *CESIfo Economic Studies,* Vol. 52 (March): 111–52.

Grossman, Gene, and Elhanan Helpman. 1996. "Electoral Competition and Special Interest Politics." *Review of Economic Studies* 63 (2): 265–86.

Hayek, Friedrich A. 1944. *The Road to Serfdom.* Chicago: University of Chicago Press.

Heald, D. 2003. "Fiscal Transparency: Concepts, Measurement and UK Practice." *Public Administration* 81 (4): 723–59.

Hemson, David, and Imraan Buccus. 2009. "The Citizen Voice Project: An Intervention in Water Services in Rural South Africa." *IDS Bulletin* 40 (6): 60–69.

Karaman, K. K. I. 2009. "Decentralized Coercion and Self-Restraint in Provincial Taxation: The Ottoman Empire, 15th–16th Centuries." *Journal of Economic Behavior and Organization* 71 (3): 690–703.

Keefer, Philip. 2004. "What Does Political Economy Tell Us about Economic Development and Vice Versa?" *World Bank Annual Reviews on Political Science* 7: 247–72.

Keefer, Philip, and Stuti Khemani. 2011. "Mass Media and Public Services: The Effects of Radio Access on Public Education in Benin." Policy Research Working Paper 5559, World Bank, Washington, DC.

Mattozzi, Andrea, and Antonio Merlo. 2007. "The Transparency of Politics and the Quality of Politicians." *American Economic Review* 97 (2): 311–15.

Olken, B. 2007. "Monitoring Corruption: Evidence from a Field Experiment in Indonesia." *Journal of Political Economy* 115 (2): 200–49.

Reinikka, Ritva, and Jakob Svensson. 2004. *The Power of Information Evidence from a Newspaper Campaign to Reduce Capture.* Washington, DC: World Bank, http://www.econ.worldbank.org/view.php? type=5&id=34028.

———. 2005. "Fighting Corruption to Improve Schooling: Evidence from a Newspaper Campaign in Uganda." *Journal of the European Economic Association* 3 (2/3): 259–67.

Rothschild, Michael, and Joseph E. Stiglitz. 1976. "Equilibrium in Competitive Insurance Markets: An Essay on the Economics of Imperfect Information." *Quarterly Journal of Economics* 90 (4): 630–49.

Sallas-Menshah, Samuel. 2011. "Engaging Civil Society: Ghana's First Public PAC Hearing." In *African Parliamentary Reform*, ed. Frederick Stapenhurst, Rasheed Draman, Andrew Imlach, Alexander Hamilton, and Cindy Kroon, 5–14. New York: Routledge.

Shapiro, Carl, and Joseph E. Stiglitz. 1985. "Equilibrium Unemployment as a Worker Discipline Device." *American Economic Review* 75 (4): 892–93.

Stiglitz, J. E. 2000. "The Contributions of the Economics of Information to Twentieth Century Economics." *Quarterly Journal of Economics* 115 (4): 1441–78.

———. 2001. "Challenges in the Analysis of the Role of Institutions in Economic Development." In *The Institutional Foundations of a Market Economy*, ed. Gudrun Kochendorfer-Lucius and Boris Pleskovic, 15–28. Bonn: German Foundation for International Development.

———. 2002. "Information and the Change in the Paradigm in Economics." *American Economic Review* 92 (3): 460–501.

———. 2008. "Fostering an Independent Media with a Diversity of Views." In *Information and Public Choice: From Media Markets to Policymaking*, ed. R. Islam, 139–52. Washington, DC: World Bank.

Stockmann D., and M. Gallagher. 2011. "Remote Control: How the Media Sustains Authoritarian Rule in China." *Comparative Political Studies* 44 (4): 436–67.

Taylor-Robinson, M. 2010. *Do the Poor Count? Democratic Institutions and Accountability in a Context of Poverty*. University Park: Pennsylvania State University Press.

Vallely, Paul. (2006, May 16). "Transcript of Interview with Mrs. Ngozi Okonjo-Iweala, Nigerian Finance Minister." *The Independent (UK)*. Retrieved April, 2012.

Young, R. and Associates. 2000. "Bangladesh: 1998 Flood Appeal: An Independent Evaluation." *Active Learning Network for Accountability and Performance in Humanitarian Action*. London: Overseas Development Institute. Available at: http://www.alnap.org/pool/files/erd-2859-full.pdf

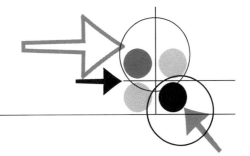

**CHAPTER 8**

# Credible Commitment

Credible commitment mechanisms that give different actors the incentives to follow through on the actions to which they are formally committed constitute an important ingredient for successful reform (see figure 8.1). Without "tying their own hands," leaders can violate or renege on their own agendas, and voters may be unable to oust incumbents who are pursuing bad policies.

Leaders can signal their credible commitment to specific policies by establishing some form of institutional limits on their power or by following through on their campaign promises.

The following examples introduce some of the conventional credible commitment mechanisms adopted in many countries:

- Control of budgets by parliaments can make it difficult, if not impossible, for leaders to violate key expenditure and macroeconomic commitments.
- An independent judiciary and politically insulated bureaucracies can help monitor and enforce policy commitments and deter politicians from colonizing institutions before or after elections.

**FIGURE 8.1 Conceptual Map of Credible Commitment**

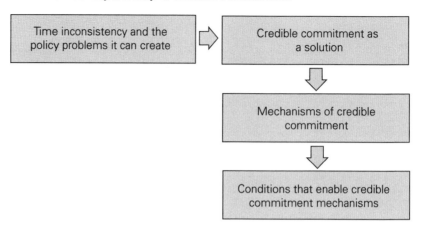

*Source:* Authors.

## Objectives of Chapter 8

By the end of this chapter, readers should be able to do the following:

- Explain the logic of credible commitment as a solution to time inconsistencies problems
- Think about the connection between collective action and credible commitment
- Explore how institutions may induce opportunities to make credible commitments
- Understand the role of independent third-party monitoring and enforcement
- Link the logic of credible commitment to real-life situations.

## The Problem: Time Inconsistency

The concept of "time inconsistency" or "dynamic inconsistency" refers to a change in the preferences of a decision maker that occurs between an initial policy promise and a policy decision that takes place later. Because politicians want to be reelected, their preferences might change over time. Without institutional guarantees, however, it is not possible for politicians today to ensure that they will take the same action in the future. Time inconsistency is often one of the key determinants of whether credible commitment problems exist.

As an example, politicians often campaign on reducing inflation in order to win elections. However, once they are in office, implementing inflation-reducing policies might have politically unpopular consequences, such as increased unemployment. Therefore, even if the initial preferences of the government policy makers were consistent with the goals of reducing inflation, once the time has come to implement them, they may lack incentives to follow through.

One of the classic examples of time inconsistency and credible commitment is quite familiar, drawing on the dilemma of Ulysses in Homer's *Odyssey*. On the one hand, Ulysses and his sailors want to hear the mesmerizing Sirens' song. On the other hand, Ulysses knows that once he hears it, it could be lethal. He would be tempted to swim toward them at the cost of his life. Therefore, Ulysses asks his crew to tie him to the mast of the ship. The hero instructs his sailors not to release him during the song even if, enchanted by the Sirens, he begs to be released. In other words, he designed a mechanism to protect himself from his own incentives to undertake a risky action at a later point in time (Elster 2000).

The concept of time inconsistency can also be applied to the issue of property rights, as it has significant consequences for investment and economic development. "Economic activities often involve time-inconsistent exchanges between the state and private agents" (Frye 2004, 455). For example, a government promises favorable investment conditions for a given company (such as preferential tax treatment or regulatory measures). However, once the company decides to invest, the government may renege ex post on the ex ante promises, despite written laws or agreements that stipulate differently. If the company could foresee the time-inconsistent behavior of the government, it would not invest in the first place (Frye 2004; Diermeier et al. 1997).

## What Is "Credible Commitment"?

The concept of credible commitment, closely related to "precommitment," refers to a situation in which politicians (and, more specifically, the government) "tie their own hands" against future discretionary use of state institutions for political or private gains. Given the time inconsistency problems illustrated above, commitment mechanisms block politicians from taking advantage of institutions for political purposes when their incentives may change (say, right before an election). For example, by making the judiciary independent, politicians may limit their own ability to engage in corruption even when they have strong career incentives to do so. Refraining from such politically gainful but socially detrimental behavior implies the design of strong rules of the game recognized by all actors concerned. Understood as such, credible commitment is a solution to the problem of time inconsistencies.

The creation of an independent central bank is another standard example of a commitment device because it stabilizes inflation rates and inflationary expectations by guaranteeing that populist governments will not engage in overspending right before elections. Similarly, civil service reform in a democratic system that would uproot corruption and clientelism presupposes that legislative parties are institutionally committed not to populate the bureaucracy with their party members when they have the chance (if they win the next elections). The logic of credible commitment can be applied to a whole variety of institutional choices through which politicians tie their own hands in different settings and policy domains: democracy, bureaucratic reforms, fiscal rules, and natural resource governance are just a few examples.

### What Are the Mechanisms of Credible Commitment?

External independent enforcement and mutual monitoring are the most obvious mechanisms for ensuring credible commitments (Schelling 1960; Bates 1988), especially when paired with clear rules of election, appointment, and decision making. When all parties recognize such institutional arrangements as "the only game in town" and when violations of the rules trigger sanctions, the effect is to stabilize expectations, reduce the uncertainties associated with the political process, and thus contribute to economic development.

Chapter 1 has already introduced the technical and political-economic dimensions of independent central banks. As Concepts in Practice 8.1 shows, the temptation of elected officials to manipulate the economy before and after elections can help explain why central banks were made independent in the first place.

Other examples of institutions created as commitment devices include the following:

- Independent courts of public accounts or supreme audit institutions
- Independent electoral commissions
- Civil service commissions.

Independence on paper, however, does not automatically translate into de facto insulation from political pressure. Although the presence of such institutions does signal a certain degree of commitment of governments and politicians to not interfering with elections, bureaucracies, or public budget-

Understanding Policy Change

## The Rise of Independent Central Banks

Since the end of World War II and especially since the 1970s, a growing number of countries have granted operational independence to their central banks, meaning that while politicians set inflation targets, the technocrats in the central banks implement them. As already discussed in previous chapters, the case for central bank independence is that elected officials are prone to abuse monetary policy to make voters feel better off just before an election by overinflating the economy. Thus, setting the central bank free from day-to-day political interference is a way of avoiding this outcome.

However, incentives generated by political institutions, and not by purely technical considerations, often explain the decision to commit or not. As some empirical evidence shows, political variables are good determinants of how fast a country adopted central bank independence. Countries with federal systems, in which political accountability and the attribution of responsibility for economic policy making were more fragmented, were among the earlier adopters. Unitary states, in contrast, in which attribution of inflation policy was clearer, were late comers.

In short, according to this study, federal institutions tend to dilute the clarity of macroeconomic tasks and potentially increase political temptations to manipulate monetary policy. Therefore, in such contexts, calls for credible commitment mechanisms were likely to be more imperative and finally led to the earlier adoption of independent central banks.

*Source:* Farvaque (2002).

ing for political purposes, that commitment might not be especially credible in the absence of robust political opposition in legislatures or adequate checks and balances. There may be nothing to impede a powerful executive from interfering in the work of these institutional devices without incentives to refrain. This dynamic is problematic because it raises the question of how many institutional safeguards are needed to ensure real credibility.

If independence on paper is not enough, what guarantees that the hands of the politicians are genuinely tied? What stops them from using the same institutions to tie their competitors' hands? To quote the eloquent words of Norwegian philosopher Jens Arup Seip, "In politics, people never try to bind themselves, only to bind others" (Elster 2000, ix).

The political-economy literature identifies several core mechanisms that ensure credible commitments. Discussion of some of these mechanisms follows.

***Constitutional Limits on Government Power.*** In 1688, following the Glorious Revolution in England, the establishment of Parliament as an institutional constraint on the power of the monarchy allowed the king to "commit" to the repayment of debts and the security of property rights (North and Weingast 1989).

***Guardian Judiciary.*** A guardian judiciary is an independent body that can prevent the government from violating the rights of investors and asset holders (Landes and Posner 1975). A strong and independent judiciary may enable the government to credibly commit to repaying its debts, as the constitutional power of the judges might be greater than the political incentives the executive might otherwise have.

***"Hostage" Mechanisms.*** A "hostage mechanism" as a means of inducing credible commitments occurs when the government agrees to allow one of its assets to be seized by a third party if it fails to adhere to its promise to other actors (Williamson 1983). Some studies outline what is needed to create an effective hostage mechanism: (1) the value of the asset has to be great enough so that the government has significant financial incentives not to allow its seizure; and (2) the asset needs to be held abroad so that the government has no control over the seizure (Haber, Razo, and Maurer 2003, 25).

An example of a successful hostage mechanism comes from República Bolivariana de Venezuela and has to do with the management of the foreign assets of Petróleos de Venezuela, the country's state-owned petroleum company.[1] The foreign assets function as a hostage mechanism because they can be seized if the government overextracts revenue from the company and fails to ensure the rights of foreign investors (Haber, Razo, and Maurer 2003). As the loss of such assets would hurt politicians and exceed any popularity or rents they would have otherwise obtained from the seizure, these assets act as a credible commitment against expropriation.

In addition, governments can also use a third party to enforce contracts and guarantee the rights of economic actors (Haber, Razo, and Maurer 2003, 26–32). However, the problem with implementing these rules or commitments in some countries (those that are resource dependent) is that they are often under authoritarian rule where a third-party mechanism would be ineffective and a constitution is unlikely to be upheld in the first place.

***Multiple "Veto Players" Systems.*** Another example of credible commitment mechanisms is illustrated in Concepts in Practice 8.2. This example shows how the number and configuration of veto players—different actors who have the power to block policy—can prevent sudden policy switches or reversals induced by shifting political incentives. The number of veto players, however, comes at the expense of a potential shortcoming: the same institutional device that prevents policy shifts and reversals that could be

## The Importance of Veto Players in Policy Making

"Veto players can be defined as individual or collective actors whose agreement is required for a change in the status quo" (Tsebelis 1995, 289). Two types of veto players are very common in political systems: "institutional veto players" (presidents, chambers) and "partisan veto players" (such as political parties) (Tsebelis 2002). Generally, as the number of veto players (with nonidentical interests) increases, the scope for policy change decreases: that is, the status quo—whether better or worse than a proposed alternative—is more likely to persist. For example, in the United Kingdom there are generally few veto players. The majority in Parliament can pass any legislation it likes without agreement from a strong executive or from any other major actor. Conversely, in the United States the president can veto legislation passed by Congress, and the Supreme Court can nullify (veto) legislation passed by Congress and approved by the president.

*Source:* Tsebelis (1995).

detrimental to development might also be responsible for blocking pro-development change.

In multiple "veto players" systems, achieving agreement over policy reversals requires the approval of several political actors rather than only one (executive, legislature, regional representatives, the general population through a referendum, and so on). Institutionalizing checks and balances that place limits on policy makers can signal some policy stability in the long run to members of the opposition, to voters, or to private investors. Policy stability can lead to greater investments and potentially to better development outcomes.

***Reputational Mechanisms.*** Reputation has also been shown to fill several roles with implications for establishing the credibility of commitment (Kreps and Wilson 1982; Mazaheri 2008; Milgrom and Roberts 1982):

- They often preserve contracts as well as other relationships of exchange between actors and firms, political parties and voters (North 1990; North and Weingast 1989).
- Reputation encourages or discourages transactions or political candidacies even before the actual occurrence (Greif 1994; Kollock 1994).
- Reputational signals serve as a blueprint for day-to-day interaction among firms, agents, bureaucrats, and other actors. They lock in expectations

that parties or governments will not renege on the initial policy promise under conditions of time-inconsistent behavior.

Reputation is most useful as a mechanism of credible commitment in political-economic contexts with high volatility and risk, high information asymmetries, little third-party enforcement (Kreps and Wilson 1982), scarce capital, and in highly personalized transactions between exchange agents (informal economy) (Geertz 1978).

## But How "Credible" Is a Credible Commitment?

Despite the conceptual appeal of "credible commitment" as a solution to the time inconsistency problems that actors face, the degree and "credibility" of a commitment that can be achieved through constitutions or third-party enforcers have been heavily debated. Some scholars have argued that creating multiple institutional veto points is neither a necessary nor a sufficient condition for credibility (Stasavage 2002a, 2002b). Specifically, it has been suggested that for credibility of commitment to be established, control of veto points by different political parties and the possibility of cross-issue coalitions are prerequisites.

Accordingly, with the example of 1688 England in mind, some studies have traced the evolution of interest rates on government debt over time and found that a country's credibility for not defaulting on its sovereign debt was not automatically triggered by the mere institutional existence of the Parliament, as an institutional veto point and a significant check on the power of the monarch. What seems to matter most for achieved credibility, in this particular account, was a cohesive cross-issue Whig coalition of government debt holders, characterized by a disciplined party organization and covering issues as diverse as religion, foreign policy, and finance. In contrast, the majority of land-owning interests represented in the Parliament would have not cared (and were even often against) sovereign debt repayment. By the same token, even if the Bank of England had been created to lead to commitment, as a nonpolitical institution, by itself, it would not have led to credibility without the debt holders' cohesive efforts to block any other actors' interference with its apolitical nature (Stasavage 2002a, 2002b). In 18th century France, the credible commitment to repay debts was never achieved because government debt holders were never represented in the parliament.

These two stories bring us back to the recurrent question of this handbook: how does credible commitment help or hinder pro-development collective action? What is the relationship between the two concepts? In the case of Great Britain, according to this account, the Whigs used well-documented devices to enforce voting cohesion and party discipline between 1688 and 1715. The collective action of this multi-issue coalition managed to enforce the credible commitment of debt repayment. In France, in contrast, the political coalitions that developed in the Assembly after the Revolution were highly unstable, and parties could not discipline their rank and file in pursuit of cohesive policies on government debt (Stasavage 2002b). In this instance, the collective action problem hindered the credibility of government commitment.

## Credible Commitment, Collective Action, and Development

The ability of groups to overcome collective action problems can be a critical factor in determining the extent to which credible commitments can exist. Collective action–induced credible commitment can facilitate good governance and hence development in several important ways (Keefer 2011, 3–5):

- *Mitigating rent-seeking.* The ability of citizens to remove low performance office holders depends on the existence of a credible alternative, accompanied by effective electoral sanctions. Collective action is essential in ensuring that citizens can replace incumbents with challengers who can credibly commit to providing public goods, and therefore is the cornerstone for incentivizing rent minimization amongst policy-makers.
- *Altering political incentives.* Politicians lack incentives to enact pro-development policies whenever citizens cannot act collectively to hold them accountable for reneging on their promises and diverting resources towards organized lobbies.
- *Affecting private investment.* Private investment will decrease if individual investors fear that government expropriation of their assets will not result in a collective response from other investors.
- *Restraining patronage.* The absence of a collective action–induced credible commitment can have implications for the provision of public goods. If political parties and individual politicians cannot commit to providing universalistic goods, such as health or education, then one possible outcome is the emergence of "patrons," who act as intermediaries between politicians and citizens (Keefer and Vlaicu 2008).

# The Importance of Collective Action–Induced Credible Commitment to Development: What the Data Say

One of the key puzzles in development is why the introduction of competitive elections in new democracies does not necessarily lead to less clientelism, corruption, and rent seeking activities (Keefer 2011). Although stable, well-established democracies do exhibit significantly less corruption than other regime types, this is not the case with young democracies.

One explanation for this puzzling phenomenon is that competitive elections do not, in and of themselves, create incentives for political elites to minimize rents. As noted above, if candidates (especially those associated with new and less established party labels) cannot credibly commit to a set of programmatic or universalistic policies that benefit a wide range of citizens, then voters will not believe any politicians who pledge that they will pursue a good governance agenda.

As Concepts in Practice 8.3 shows, because of a programmatic void, patronage networks filled the postauthoritarian political space in the Dominican Republic and led to inferior development outcomes (Keefer and Vlaicu 2008).

Concepts in Practice 8.4 offers another example of how political parties' lack of credibility in delivering public goods to all citizens affects a large number of developing countries. Many societies are deeply divided along

---

CONCEPTS IN PRACTICE 8.3

## Collective Action and Credible Commitment in the Dominican Republic

The Dominican Republic emerged as a democracy after the elections of 1966, following the assassination of Rafael Trujillo in 1961 and the ousting of a democratically elected leader by a military coup in 1962. The winner of these elections, Joaquin Balaguer, managed to remain in office after two more elections in 1970 and 1974, not because he established a reputation for providing good value for taxpayers' money but by building and exploiting the clientelistic network developed by Trujillo. This network included everything from the distribution of bicycles to village children, to the doling out of public sector jobs. This clientelistic modus operandi did not end with the election of the opposition to power (1978 and 1982). Given that the credible commitment mechanism was still lacking, the opposition similarly relied on patronage networks to remain popular.

## Political Responses to the AIDS Epidemic and Ethnic Affiliations

AIDS epidemics affect a large percentage of the population in many African countries. Yet some governments are more prompt than others in presenting the contagion as a public health issue and in implementing policies to contain it. Why? Recent studies have found that in countries with clearly defined ethnic cleavages, the HIV epidemic was not perceived as a shared threat to the nation but instead was framed as a threat to a specific group. In such circumstances, the response of the government to the epidemic was slow and indecisive.

Irrespective of the ethnic group in power, institutions based on clear ethnic boundaries tended to shift the blame for the spread of the disease, creating social stigma and ultimately putting in place less effective policies for addressing national pandemics. In contrast, in contexts with more blurred lines of ethnicity, policy advances were more likely. South Africa and Brazil, two countries where the evolution of the pandemic was similar, illustrate this large difference in policy outcomes. Whereas the Brazilian government built bureaucratic capacity and a relatively autonomous agency to address HIV early on in the 1980s, the South African National AIDS Council, a comparable organization, saw the light only in the year 2000, and its authority is still not widely recognized (Gauri and Lieberman 2006; Lieberman 2009).

ethnic, linguistic, or religious lines. Because of their weak commitment to delivering universalistic policies across such cleavages, politicians often send identity-based signals to voters and mobilize them along ethnic or religious issues. This tendency becomes a vicious circle, as deeply fragmented societies fail to cooperate to provide public goods to the detriment of economic development (Varshney 2001; Chandra 2004; Miguel and Gugerty 2005).

## Modeling Credible Commitment as a Challenger Game[2]

To further help readers understand the implications of credible commitment to reform and development, this section will present two games that illustrate how credible commitment, or the lack of it, can affect outcomes.

First, consider a case in which two players cannot credibly commit to a specific course of action. Say, for example, that an incumbent politician has two strategies he or she can pursue, given the existence of a challenger candidate. The incumbent can either fight the election campaign (by raising and expending resources) or give in. Conversely, the challenger can decide either to enter the race or to stay out.

In the normal-form simultaneous-move game below, neither actor can commit, a priori, to a specific course of action. However, given the assumption of complete information, the challenger candidate can anticipate that "give in" strictly dominates (see definitions in chapter 2) "fight" for the incumbent. Therefore, the challenger will enter the contest (the Nash equilibrium is *give in; enter*).

|  | Enter | | Stay Out | |
|---|---|---|---|---|
| Fight | 1 | **1** | 3 | **2** |
| Give In | 2 | **4** | 4 | **3** |

However, what if the incumbent can credibly commit to fighting before the challenger has a choice of whether to enter or not? Say, for example, the incumbent can spend his or her time in office cultivating links with supporters and engaging in preemptive campaign financing. This situation can be modeled as an extensive-form game (below). Here, the outcome associated with the subgame perfect Nash equilibrium[3] is *fight; stay out,* because the incumbent can anticipate that if he or she does not credibly commit to fight (in the first stage), the challenger will have an incentive to enter (in the second stage), obtaining a payoff of 4 instead of 3. However, if the incumbent fights in the first stage, the challenger will elect to stay out (challenger payoff of 2 versus 1). In such a setting, the incumbent is better off than before, because by credibly committing to fight, he or she gets a payoff of 3 instead of 2 (in the first game).

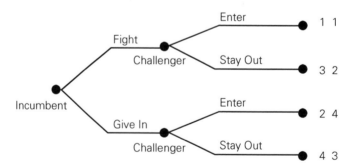

## Summary

Many policy change initiatives require those involved in decision making to be able to credibly commit to certain actions. Why should citizens pay taxes if their governments cannot commit to not expropriating them as private rents? By critically evaluating and understanding the problem of credible commitment, as well as its relationship with the capacity for collective action of various groups, reformers can identify any commitment-related problems they may face and evaluate whether, in light of these problems, the project remains feasible.

## Notes

1. http://www.stanford.edu/class/polisci313/papers/MonaldiFeb04.pdf, 2–4.
2. *Source:* Inspired by (McCarty and Meirowitz 2006).
3. For simplicity and exposition purposes, the sub game perfect equilibria do not include off-path analysis.

## References

Bates, R. H. 1988. *Toward a Political Economy of Development: A Rational Choice Perspective.* Berkley: University of California Press.

Chandra, Kanchan. 2004. *Why Ethnic Parties Succeed.* Cambridge: Cambridge University Press.

Diermeier, D., J. M. Ericson, T. Frye, and S. Lewis. 1997. "Credible Commitment and Property Rights: The Role of Strategic Interaction between Political and Economic Actors." In *The Political Economy of Property Rights: Institutional Change and Credibility in the Reform of Centrally Planned Economies,* ed. David Weimer, 20–41. Cambridge: Cambridge University Press.

Elster, Jon. 2000. *Ulysses Unbound: Studies in Rationality, Precommitment, and Constraints.* Cambridge: Cambridge University Press.

Farvaque, Etienne. 2002. "Political Determinants of Central Bank Independence." *Economics Letters* 77 (1): 131–35.

Frye, T. 2004. "Credible Commitment and Property Rights: Evidence from Russia." *American Political Science Review* 98: 453–66.

Gauri, V., and E. S. Lieberman. 2006. "Boundary Institutions and HIV Policy in Brazil and South Africa." *Studies in Comparative International Development* 41 (3): 47–73.

Geertz, C. 1978. "The Bazaar Economy: Information Search in Peasant Bargaining." *American Economic Review* 68 (2): 28–32.

Greif, A. 1994. "Cultural Beliefs and the Organization of Society: A Historical and Theoretical Reflection on Collectivist and Individualist Societies." *Journal of Political Economy* 102 (5): 912–50.

Haber, S. H., A. Razo, and N. Maurer. 2003. *The Politics of Property Rights: Political Instability, Credible Commitments, and Economic Growth in Mexico, 1876–1929.* Cambridge: Cambridge University Press.

Kasara, K. 2007. "Tax Me If You Can: Ethnic Geography, Democracy, and the Taxation of Agriculture in Africa." *American Political Science Review* 101 (1): 159–72.

Keefer, Philip. 2011. "Collective Action, Political Parties, and Pro-Development Public Policy." *Asian Development Review* 28 (1): 94–118.

Keefer, Philip, and Razvan Vlaicu. 2008. "Democracy, Credibility, and Clientelism." *Journal of Law, Economics, and Organization* 24 (2): 371–406.

Kollock, P. 1994. "The Emergence of Exchange Structures: An Experimental Study of Uncertainty, Commitment, and Trust." *American Journal of Sociology* 100 (2): 313–45.

Kreps, D. M., and R. Wilson. 1982. "Reputation and Imperfect Information." *Journal of Economic Theory* 27 (2): 253–79.

Landes, William M., and Richard A. Posner. 1975. "The Independent Judiciary in an Interest-Group Perspective." *Journal of Law and Economics* 18 (3): 875–901.

Lieberman, E. 2009. *Boundaries of Contagion: How Ethnic Politics Have Shaped Government Responses to AIDS*. Princeton: Princeton University Press.

Mazaheri, Nimah. 2008. "An 'Informal' Revolution: State-Business Conflict and Institutional Change in Iran." *Middle Eastern Studies* 44 (4): 585–602.

McCarty, N., and A. Meirowitz. 2006. *Political Game Theory*. Cambridge, MA: Cambridge University Press.

Miguel, Edward, and Mary Kay Gugerty. 2005. "Ethnic Diversity, Social Sanctions, and Public Goods in Kenya." *Journal of Public Economics* 89 (11/12): 2325–68.

Milgrom, P., and J. Roberts. 1982. "Predation, Reputation, and Entry Deterrence." *Journal of Economic Theory* 27 (2): 280–312.

Monaldi, F. 2001. "Sunk-Costs, Institutions, and Commitment: Foreign Investment in the Venezuelan Oil Industry." Unpublished manuscript, Stanford University, Department of Political Science.

North, D. 1990. *Institutions, Institutional Change and Economic Performance*. Cambridge: Cambridge University Press.

North, D. C., and B. Weingast. 1989. "Constitutions and Credible Commitments: The Evolution of the Institutions of Public Choice in 17th Century England." *Journal of Economic History* 49 (4): 803–32.

Schelling, T. C. 1960. *The Strategy of Conflict*. Cambridge: Harvard University Press.

Stasavage, David. 2002a. "Private Investment and Political Institutions." *Economics and Politics* 14 (1): 41–63.

Stasavage, David. 2002b. "Credible Commitment in Early Modern Europe: North and Weingast Revisited," London, LSE Research online, http://eprints.lse.ac.uk/227/1/credible_commitment.pdf.

Tsebelis, George. 1995. "Decision Making in Political Systems: Veto Players in Presidentialism, Parliamentarism, Multicameralism, and Multipartyism." *British Journal of Political Science* 25 (3): 289–326.

———. 2002. *Veto Players: How Political Institutions Work*. Princeton, NJ: Princeton University Press.

Varshney, Ashutosh. 2001. "Ethnic Conflict and Civil Society: India and Beyond." *World Politics* 53 (3): 362–98.

Williamson, O. E. 1983. "Credible Commitments: Using Hostages to Support Exchange." *American Economic Review* 73 (4): 519–40.

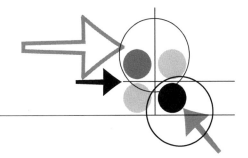

**CHAPTER 9**

# Solutions to Collective Action Problems

Collective action is the engine of change. Reform occurs when individuals and groups act together, share information, and keep politicians and bureaucrats accountable. Pro-development mobilization is not easy, and institutional constraints often act against reform. Lack of information, motivational factors, missing mechanisms for credible commitment, delegation problems in organizations with unaccountable leaders, and institutional manipulation against policy reform all stifle attempts to effectively mobilize and change the status quo.

Fortunately, despite grim predictions, pro-development collective action does happen. Groups manage to mobilize in spite of formidable obstacles. Sometimes they make history. Mohamed Bouazizi, a street vendor in a rural town in Tunisia, became the catalyst of the previously unthinkable Arab Spring; the city of Porto Alegre in Brazil has a vibrant civil society that actively monitors municipal spending and has built more schools in 10 years than were ever thought possible; in the Indian state of Uttar Pradesh, a low-caste political party significantly increased the electrification rate of villages; and a coalition of bureaucrats, nongovernmental organizations (NGOs), youth groups, and leading politicians took advantage of institutional opportunities and reformed a corrupt system of public procurement in the Philippines.

How do good results come about? The honest answer is that nobody really knows why good things happen despite unfavorable odds, but we can do our best to look at a repertoire of classic solutions to collective action problems that have been identified in a very rich and diverse body of knowledge that cuts across all social sciences. Let us see what it has to offer future change agents.

Chapter 3 introduced the logic of the collective action problem and its major implications: the undersupply of public goods, the overuse of common resources, and the general inability of large groups in society to formulate claims for a better development outcome. We have also explored many modes of collective action that we encounter every day: social movements, political parties, interest groups, coalitions, and reform teams.

This chapter will wrap up the theoretical section of the handbook by examining in more detail specific ways in which collective action problems can be solved. The first section will explore some of the organizational and coalitional characteristics, as well as effective institutional arrangements that build and maintain collaborative efforts for public goods. The second section will deal with various monitoring and sanctioning mechanisms, trust, distrust, and selective incentives, and their effect on governance and development outcomes. Finally, the chapter will introduce the concept of leadership as a potential solution to collective action problems.

The chapter establishes a basis for helping change agents analytically sort through some of the ways out of key dilemmas that would otherwise hamper the realization of their agenda (see figure 9.1). By improving information flows, cultivating trust and communication among the members of a group or organization, and using different institutional mechanisms of monitoring and sanctioning, reformers might be able to overcome the problems that prevent the provision of public goods and effective pro-development action.

## Objectives of Chapter 9

By the end of chapter 9, readers should be able to do the following:

- Understand how different mechanisms can help resolve collective action problems.
- Explore organizational and coalitional features that lead to successful pro-development action.
- Think about potential institutional arrangements that govern effective joint efforts in development.

**FIGURE 9.1 Conceptual Map: Solutions to Collective Action Problems**

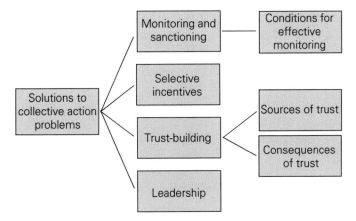

*Source:* Authors.

- Appreciate the importance of different monitoring techniques, trust building, selective incentives, and leadership, as well as their potential role in resolving collective action problems.
- Be able to link concepts of collective action solutions to real-life situations.

## When Do Mobilization and Production of Public Goods Occur?

We know that many successful cases of collective action have taken place despite the chronic misalignment between individual and group incentives postulated by theoretical work. Why and under what conditions does alignment happen? How do communities come together to regulate the use of common resources? How do individuals succeed in effectively mobilizing for policy change in high-risk political-economic environments? What roles do mutual trust, face-to-face interaction, and reciprocity play in facilitating successful collective action? How can organizations monitor and sanction noncompliant behavior of members, correct informational discrepancies, and delegate crucial coordination tasks to leaders?

The three central dilemmas of cooperation described in chapter 3—the prisoner's dilemma, the tragedy of the commons, and the logic of collective action—have been challenged on both theoretical and empirical grounds. Let us briefly review some of the reasons for optimism.

## Group Size Matters . . . but Not Always

Chapter 3 argues that the size of the group matters since it is much more difficult to pool risks, preferences, and organizational costs among many citizens as opposed to just a few. Large groups of diffuse citizens are less likely to solve collective action problems than small, more concentrated business lobbies. Theoretically, however, some researchers have shown that the large number does not always hamper collective action, as long as a subgroup of individuals cares intensely about providing a public good, even if all other members are free riders (Hardin 1971, 1995).

Smaller privileged subgroups (sometimes referred to as $k$-groups to indicate that they include only $k$ members out of a total of $n$ group members, with $k<n$), even as part of a larger and more diffuse group of interests, can solve collective action problems. Why? Because, as the argument goes, the ratio of benefits to costs for some individuals might be equally important, if not more important, than the sheer size of the group and the fact that majorities might not contribute. Concretely, some subgroups in society stand to benefit from providing the good, even without cooperation from other members, as long as they have strong preferences for the good and their individual benefits exceed the costs of the production of a public good or participation in it. For example, business associations have been shown to play a significant role in demanding anticorruption measures, increased bureaucratic accountability, and the preemption of the predatory behavior of the state in many post-Communist countries (Duvanova 2007; Pyle 2011). If we think of lower levels of corruption as a public good that benefits the society at large, then the mobilization efforts of business groups and associations might have positive spillover effects for all citizens in the long run.

Highly repressive autocratic contexts inhibit pro-development collective action because the costs of individual participation are prohibitively high. Often, challengers are killed, imprisoned, heavily penalized, or threatened. Despite such high individual risks compared to potential benefits, popular protests against corrupt politicians and bureaucrats often occur because a small number of activists or groups want change so intensely that the benefits of individual action far outweigh the costs if and when the final goal is reached. We have already mentioned the so-called 5 percent rule: some argue that roughly only about 5 percent of all citizens who would benefit in the long term from pro-development mobilization and protests get involved in contentious collective action. Because of the high costs of participation, the number of activists is usually overwhelmingly exceeded by bystanders (Lichbach 1998). In general, for reformers, identifying a nucleus of $k$-actors with high stakes and preferences who are able to drive the process of change on behalf of large groups of citizens can lead to a solution of collective action problems.

## Effective Modes of Collective Action in Development

Organizations, associations, networks, and coalitions that function well, commit to outcomes, share information, and are accountable to their members constitute effective modes of collective action in development. Mobilization is difficult in the first place, but what happens after it occurs the first time? How is it maintained, routinized, and institutionalized? The main forms or modes of institutionalized collective action are organizations that all of us recognize: political parties, labor unions, NGOs, social movement organizations, business lobbies, and the like. Organizations allow citizens or members with similar policy preferences to delegate the tasks of representation to leaders, activists, and political entrepreneurs to obtain policy benefits.

Chapter 3 has already introduced political parties as aggregators of preferences and costs. Political parties are in no need of introduction. They run for elections on policy platforms and strive to enact laws and regulations favorable to their constituents if they become incumbents. Civil society organizations engage in advocacy, build accountability platforms and coalitions, and partner with other major actors to push reforms forward. Unions aggregate the policy preferences of their members and are often effective in obtaining benefits for them from private employers or the public sector. Teachers' unions in India's Uttar Pradesh, for example, successfully blocked a policy aiming to place the firing, hiring, and absenteeism monitoring of teachers under the supervision of the village *panchayaat* (or assembly). Similarly, in Brazil, well-organized health workers were very influential in shaping the health care reform package, while teachers' unions in Argentina and Mexico mobilized and blocked decentralization reforms affecting education (*World Development Report 2004*, 8).

In some cases, organizations have certain *intrinsic features* that lead to greater success than others in pursuing common goals. Research seeking to find solutions to the tragedy of the commons, for example, studied many collectivities managing common-pool resources and identified some criteria that lead to their effectiveness in solving collective action: the total number of participants (the fewer, the easier the cooperation); the minimum number of contributors needed to initiate collective action; the decision makers' patience with respect to the consumption of the good; the homogeneity of stakeholder preferences, and finally, the existence of committed leaders among group members (Ostrom 1990, 188). These features do not exist exclusively in the case of collective action for common-pool resource management. Coalitions of political parties in parliamentary systems and reform teams face very similar constraints. They first have to decide on the number of members in the coalition; if parties or reformers want to maximize individual power or take full credit for policies enacted, they will opt for "minimal winning coalitions" that include the smallest possible number of participants (Riker 1962). But besides sheer number of members, power, or electoral credit taking, policy similarity and homogeneity of preferences also matter for coalitional stability. Especially in the case of ideological divergence among participants, coalitions face an informational problem: the uncertainty about future defectors. Therefore, to compensate for such uncertainty, coalition cabinets sometimes invite additional members. These policy criteria thus lead to the creation of oversized ruling or reform coalitions, meaning that they accommodate more members than are strictly necessary for enacting policies. A similar dynamic applies to minority cabinets that have to continually negotiate with other legislative parties, behaving like a de facto oversized coalition (Lijphart 1999, 62–90). Coalition size might come at the expense of reform effectiveness. Because more policy concessions are needed to keep a larger number of members happy, very large and participatory party or reform coalitions could become weak and lose momentum or focus.

Time horizons or the patience of individual members also matters for the stability of the coalition. Although some parties or reformers can afford to wait more than others in the face of upcoming elections, economic crises, or other exogenous shocks, the convergence of time horizons among participants can lead to successful collective action.

However, as we emphasized throughout the handbook, the mere existence of organizations or coalitions that pool costs and preferences does not automatically guarantee pro-development change. Without adequate *institutional mechanisms* that address the constraints discussed in previous chapters, organizations will fail to reach their goals. In a sense, parties, unions, NGOs, cooperatives, coalition governments, and reform teams are all plagued by a second-order collective action problem. Because members delegate decision making to leaders, they face principal-agent risks. The leadership may have incentives that are not fully aligned with the wishes of the rank and file. Furthermore, information asymmetries can lead to moral hazard, adverse selection, or severe lack of coordination among the members of the organization. Without information on free riding and shirking, noncompliant members cannot be sanctioned. They will thus fail to contribute to the joint action for policy change and reform. If organizations do not institutionalize mechanisms through which leaders "tie their own hands" and credibly commit to monitor and police shirking, the potential for collective action decreases. In the case of legislatures, party weakness, fragmentation, and lack of cohesion and discipline often lead to instability and high policy volatility within the coalition. Therefore, just as in the broader political-economic environment, well-functioning organizations need rules and mechanisms that correct for all these sets of constraints. As the chapter will discuss in the subsequent sections, *good monitoring and sanctioning techniques, adequate selective incentives for compliance, trust building, and leadership assets* are essential for dealing with collective action problems and deriving pro-development benefits.

## Institutional Arrangements and Types of Authority That Matter

Mobilization for public goods can occur through several broad institutional arrangements identified in the literature. Sometimes, they feature a top-down model of authority for decision making. Other times, dispersed and multiple institutional centers of authority, connected by policy networks, can lead to effective collective action solutions. Let's explore some of these arrangements:

- *Informal, tacit contracts or conventions.* In these informal arrangements, individuals or groups, following continuous interaction, agree that the long-term benefits of cooperation outweigh the short-term gains of noncooperation. This solution relies on the ongoing interaction among participants that allows for communication, trust, and common expectations of behavior. Organizationally, it may or may not require conventional forms of hierarchical leadership (Lichbach 1998).
- *Hierarchical context, or top-down monitoring and enforcement of sanctions for noncompliant members.* This institutional formula presupposes the existence of mobilizing organizations and leaders who can successfully police shirking and distribute selective incentives to solve the collective action problem. Governments can sometimes fulfill this role successfully; other times, communities find more effective solutions outside the public sector (Lichbach 1998, 167–170).
- *Polycentric governance arrangements.* The literature on the tragedy of the commons emphasizes the specific type and characteristics of institutional arrangements that can lead to increased intergroup cooperation. Instead of thinking about governance systems as *monocentric* (having only one central authority, say, the government or the state), researchers have argued that *polycentric* systems, in which multiple relevant actors play different authority roles in the absence of a central command center might lead to better policy outcomes. For example, in the world of common-

pool resource management, studies of the West Basin water systems in California showed that better outcomes were made possible because many initiative centers were involved in coordinating the regulation of water use. This broad participation, rather than a single peak national agency, brought civil society, businesses, politicians, and bureaucratic units together to coordinate regulation. The creative polycentric arrangement resulted in various legal agreements among producers and the development of innovative technology to increase the efficiency of water consumption (Ostrom 2010, 5–6).

In a similar spirit, other research shows that multiple and less conventional centers of authority for the provision of public goods can emerge through a variety of self-help groups organized around the mistrust of a corrupt state. Hometown associations in Nigeria, for instance, stepped in and provided a minimum threshold of public goods in the absence of a functioning local government. Civil society organizations representing informal miners built networks and coalitions and formulated effective claims against rent-seeking officials and industrial mining companies in the postconflict eastern part of the Democratic Republic of Congo (Fahey 2008). Networks of women's credit groups and self-help organizations successfully provided loans to individual members in Tanzania and Uganda (Gibbon 2001).

Apart from the concentration or diffusion of authority, effective solutions to collective action problems include at least one, and in most cases several, of the following four tools or devices: *monitoring and sanctioning, selective incentives to comply, trust building,* and *good leaders.* These mechanisms are central to well-functioning organizations and coalitions because they help solve principal-agent problems and correct information asymmetries, and they become widely accepted when leaders can credibly commit to using them systematically.

## Tools for Solving Collective Action Problems

### Monitoring and Sanctioning

Chapters 6 and 7 on principal-agent relationships and information asymmetries introduced the concepts of monitoring and incentives as forms of social controls undertaken to minimize agency costs and preempt adverse selection. This section also looks at monitoring and sanctioning as the main devices for alleviating or solving broader collective action problems. The previous chapters have presented various dilemmas: the tragedy of the commons (or the common-pool resource problem), the prisoner's dilemma, and the logic of collective action. Let us see if we can find ways to address their motivational and informational root causes.

***Discouraging Motivational Constraints and Achieving Coordination.*** Many convincing findings in the literature show that monitoring and sanctioning are necessary (although not always sufficient) for solutions to collective action. To give a concrete example, in the case of common-pool resource management, effective enforcement of institutional rules of lumber use is highly correlated with successful forest management around the world (Pagdee, Kim, and Daugherty 2006; Ostrom 1990; Ostrom and Nagendra 2006). In addition, among all potential solutions to common-pool resource problems, some studies have found regular monitoring and strict rule enforcement to be more important than any other alternatives (Gibson, Williams, and Ostrom 2005).

Beyond the maintenance of a common good, if we think of the prisoner's dilemma and the tragedy of the commons as metaphors of broader collective action problems that characterize political life, then similar solutions apply more widely. If voters have information and can monitor politicians' behavior or if corrupt legislators lose elections because of underperformance, then the poor can act collectively and achieve development outcomes. Monitoring and sanctioning are linked to most of the institutional constraints the previous chapters explored: credible commitment issues, independent oversight bodies, accountability, information asymmetries, institutional manipulation, and agency problems. Effective organizations, coalitions, and reform teams usually devise ex ante or ex post monitoring devices to make sure that members do not have incentives to opportunistically defect and that leaders do not shirk their duties toward the rank and file. Monitoring detects behavior and is the precondition for the other two concrete tools: sanctions applied to defectors and selective incentives targeted to high-commitment individuals and groups.

***Performing the Monitoring Task.*** Several different options can govern the selection of monitors. External parties such as independent ombudsmen, for example, can make sure that governments hear the voice of the citizens directly. Inside the executive, politicians can monitor the behavior of bureaucratic agencies to make sure that they comply with the policy mandate. Political party, union, and NGO leaders screen new recruits, often offer career incentives, and monitor their behavior within the organization. A community faced with collective action problems can also design self-regulatory monitoring devices. For instance, women's cooperatives in Nigeria, Nepali farmers, and artisanal miners in the Democratic Republic of Congo (DRC) have all found creative ways to police organizational and associational borders and ensure that free-riding or tragedy-of-the-commons–types of problems do not arise. The fishermen community in Alanya, Turkey, succeeded in avoiding overfishing partly because it involved the local mayor and police in the assignment and monitoring of fishing sites. But as the vignette from chapter 3 demonstrates, similar communities in Bodrum, Turkey, failed to effectively monitor individual behavior and did not solve the social dilemma that they were facing.

***Monitoring the Monitor.*** Can the monitor be trusted? This is an old philosophical puzzle. Collective action tools, unfortunately, have two inherent problems (Shapiro 2005, 280). First, many regulatory arrangements devised for the purposes of monitoring and sanctioning are also principal-agent relationships themselves. For example, politicians are the principals and monitors of bureaucrats but the agents of voters. If voters lack information and are unable to observe what political representatives do in office, politicians might collude with bureaucrats and engage in corruption; the chain of broken monitoring devices will then undermine accountability. In addition, it is both costly and difficult for an organization to delegate monitoring and sanctioning functions to a third party and to check regularly if the monitors themselves do not shirk or do not favor some members at the expense of others. Second, because the members of an organization or the community incur costs to obtain benefits, monitoring and sanctioning tools for overcoming collective action often induce a second-level (or second-order) collective action problem: why should I bear the costs of a neutral third-party monitor, when I can just wait for the benefits of organizational policing? As Elster (1989) puts it:

> Before a union can force or induce workers to join it must overcome a free-rider problem in the first place. To assume that the incentives are offered in a decentralized way, by mutual monitoring, gives rise to a second-order free-rider problem. Why, for instance, should a rational, selfish worker ostracize or otherwise punish those who don't join the union? What's in it for him? True, it may be better for all members than if none do, but for each member it may be even better to remain passive. Punishment almost invariably is costly to the punisher, while the benefits from punishment are diffusely distributed over the members. It is, in fact, a public good: To provide it, one would need second order selective incentives which would, however, run into a third-order free-rider problem. (40–41; Copyright © 1989 Jon Elster. Ed. *The Cement of Society. A Study of Social Order.* Reprinted with the permission of Cambridge University Press)

The important question, then, for reformers and leaders to answer becomes under what conditions will good and systematic monitoring and sanctioning tools work (Ostrom 2005; Coleman and Steed 2009).

Monitoring and oversight can also have unintended consequences or generate perverse incentives. For example, because excessive oversight can make individuals feel that they are not trusted, organizational members or leaders may alter their behavior negatively, making it more costly to engender cooperation (Frey 1997; Ostrom 1997). In general, however, monitoring and the possibility of sanctioning are essential tools for the correction of information asymmetries pervasive among participants in collective action. In addition, systematic policing and enforcement are ways in which organizational leaders commit to their members that they are solving the problems of free-riding or overconsumption.

***Selective Incentives.*** If good monitoring devices help organizational leaders detect member defection or give the rank and file the possibility of keeping leaders accountable, reward or punishment logically follows.

Selective incentives for individuals and groups are common ways to solve collective action problems, because they reward those who cooperate (positive incentives) or punish those who do not cooperate (negative incentives). Chapters 3 and 7 introduced the role of positive selective incentives in correcting adverse selection problems in an organization. The leadership of an NGO, for example, often cannot distinguish between the different levels of commitment to the common policy goal of the new recruits. Some are there for action; others for very tangible material rewards. As we know by now, information asymmetries (adverse selection in particular) lead to the prevalence of the latter category. This is not good news for any group that wants committed individuals who will not defect opportunistically the first time they can. Therefore, rather than giving all those who joined monetary rewards, it might be wiser to consider selective incentives rewarding good performance and directly incentivizing a high level of policy or reform commitment.

Selective incentives are a widely used tool for solving collective action problems. For instance, by publicly recognizing donors for their contributions, many public and civil society organizations can provide a (nonpecuniary) reward to those who contribute resources to their cause and boost their capacity to promote policies (an example is all the "named" chairs at universities or dinners that political candidates have with donors whose contributions exceed a certain threshold). In the case of coalitions, reform teams, or policy-seeking organizations, loyalty is an important asset, and leaders sometimes secure it through selective rewards to members who prove it.

Some studies have shown that positive (reward) and negative (punishment) selective incentives or sanctions might have different implications for collective action. Whereas positive incentives promote cooperation among a few members and cultivate an elite "club" of cooperators within the organization, the negative incentives induce unanimous cooperation. In spite of this finding, however, negative incentives also might cause some hostility among group members, which could undermine the cooperation and solidarity that the organization intended to promote in the first place (Oliver 1980).

To give an example of selective incentives at play in a bureaucracy, consider the case of Singapore. Several possibilities have been offered to explain its economic success: one of them has to do with bureaucratic incentives. In Singapore, well-performing civil servants receive some of the highest salaries in the world, but they also face credible and harsh sanctions for the abuse of public office. Furthermore, monitoring civil servants is relatively easy, given the country's small size (Behnke et al. 2008).

### Trust, Face-to-Face Interaction, and Communication

What is trust? Trust is a relationship between two parties that involves several critical elements (Levi 1998, 78–79):

- The first is the initial identification of the trusted and an evaluation of his or her trustworthiness: that is, the willingness and capacity to act in good faith with respect to a particular activity.
- The second is that the trust relationship must be maintained through repeated interaction between the two parties in order to confirm the trustworthiness component.

Trust applies to both individuals and institutions. Citizens' "trust" in an institution means that citizens (as principals in a principal-agent relationship) believe that the institutional rules and procedures effectively constrain the behavior of public officials (as agents) and render them competent and credible when acting in the best interest of the citizens.

Trust is essential to solving collective action problems. To act jointly toward the production of public goods or reform, members of a group, organization, or coalition must have some degree of confidence in both the real policy intentions of other members and their capacity to overcome motivational constraints and not simply free ride.

***Sources and Types of Trust.*** There are several families of explanations for the origins of trust (Levi 1998; Rothstein 2000). A cultural explanation argues that trust is closely related to information problems prevalent in society, with costly to fake cultural attributes acting as a signal of which strangers we can trust and to what extent. We trust other members of a social group based on the information we have about their behavior. Because of

**CONCEPTS IN PRACTICE 9.1**

## Case Study: Social Capital and Development

Trying to explain different development trajectories of countries has led some authors to consider the role of social capital—defined as the generalized level of trust and reliable informational exchanges emanating from an individual's social network (Woolcock 1998, 185)—in fostering growth and development. Given that development outcomes are associated with higher specialization and trade between individuals, firms, and government, the absence of trust can impose significant "transaction costs" on development. If, for example, private firms have to expend larger resources on guarding against physical or intellectual theft, then development will be limited.

For instance, Singapore was able to induce rapid socioeconomic development because of strong norms of trust and reciprocity that existed in the small city-state, while many parts of India have been unable to stimulate growth even when financial resources are available.

*Source:* Woolcock (1998).

different power endowments and the informational flows among various members of society, informational entrepreneurs (political parties, media, and the like) constantly engage in negotiating and communicating ideas about trust and the trustworthiness of groups, individuals, and organizations such as ethnic groups, religious associations, and political parties (Rothstein 2000, 488). Ideology, or the worldview of individual actors, is largely a script of trust relationships in society. Context-specific notions of morality also shape trust in groups by rewarding and punishing cooperators and defectors through a complex array of institutions (family traditions, regional or ethnic rules of behavior, informal honor codes, and religious norms, among others).

In this version of the story, trust can also result from *closely knit networks and associations* of individuals promoting members' loyalty (Levi 1998, 80). Seminal empirical studies have shown that greater participation in associations, or denser "social capital," is strongly associated with higher degrees of interpersonal trust and better development outcomes (Putnam 1993). Concepts in Practice 9.1 provides an example of the connection between trust and social capital, on one hand, and development outcomes, on the other.

Trust can be easier to facilitate when actors have to *repeatedly interact with each other or* engage *in face-to-face communication.* Preexisting passive social networks in the informal economy resulting from daily interaction have served as powerful infrastructure for mobilization in a variety of contexts. In 1980s' Iran, for instance, pro-poor movements started and succeeded in Tehran neighborhoods, in which informal vendors interacted in their everyday life, despite lack of organization and financial resources (Bayat 1997). Interestingly, before engaging in collective action, these vendors did not necessarily know each other personally. However, because they saw each other every day over long periods of time and developed passive social networks, they were ready to act when their livelihood was threatened by housing policies enacted by the government.

***Is Trust Always Good—Can Distrust Be Healthy?*** This section briefly addresses the normative assumptions about the inherent desirability of trust, distrust, and their context-specific impact on collective action, institutions, and compliance. It also looks at the virtues and pitfalls of both concepts (adapted from Braithwaite and Levi 1998; Levi 1998, 2006).

As commonly used, *trust* usually has a positive connotation. However, according to some scholars, "Trust is neither normatively good nor bad; it is neither a virtue nor a vice. . . . The act of trusting may have consequences productive for the individual, or not, and beneficial to her society, or not" (Levi 1998; Braithwaite and Levi 1998, 81).

The normative value of active trust or distrust with respect to pro-development collective action depends on specific situations. Some degree of generalized trust in other individuals, organizations, and state institutions can create virtuous circles of cooperation and solutions to collective action dilemmas. The payoffs (or stakes) of the game for individual players are certainly affected by their degree of trust or distrust. In the prisoner's dilemma game, cooperation does not occur primarily because the two participants do not trust each other.

Under some circumstances, a level of distrust among members can lead to efficient and cohesive organizations that solve collective action effectively. Because of severe negative consequences in case of noncompliance, members of some organizations will not have an incentive to defect or betray other members (for example, the Mafia) (Gambetta 1993; Levi 1998, 81). In some contexts, distrust might be somewhat beneficial for development outcomes because it could block the coordination of groups that, if they solved their collective action problem, would have a negative impact on society (ethnic cleansing, for example, or even vested interests that would otherwise join forces and stall development) (Hardin 1995).

***Tools of Trust Building.*** Trust is "a fragile commodity;" it requires long-term investments and repeated interaction between parties and can be relatively quickly dissolved (Braithwaite and Levi 1998, 81, 241). There are, however, some classic tools for building trust that development practitioners can use to change the stakes of the game and facilitate collective action.

Face-to-face interaction, communication, and talk about common problems have been proven in experimental settings to work well for building trust in small groups. Deliberative democracy, for example, as a form of direct engagement of citizens with policy making can promote understanding of complex issues, interpersonal trust, and possibly cooperation. Although direct talk, communication, and persuasion work well in relatively small groups, their applicability might be limited in broader social contexts because of high transaction costs (Elster 1998, Rothstein 2000, 481). In some circumstances, deliberation may open the door to persuasion and manipulation of the public agenda by skillful entrepreneurs. The example of trust and local leadership in Concepts in Practice 9.2 shows how trust can enable political entrepreneurs to implement their own agenda at the expense of their constituents.

## Leadership

Finally, good leaders can solve both informational and motivational problems. The puzzle, however, is how to keep leaders accountable to their orga-

---

CONCEPTS IN PRACTICE 9.2

### Leadership, Trust, and Participation in São Tomé and Príncipe

Political participation and deliberation have long been promoted on both normative and instrumental grounds as a means of fostering greater democratic accountability and democratic learning. However, skeptics have argued that such participatory mechanisms may be prone to influence and manipulation by charismatic leaders and powerful interest groups (see chapter 5 on agenda manipulation by political entrepreneurs). In 2004, the small country of São Tomé and Príncipe organized a national forum that offered groups of citizens the opportunity to debate and deliberate major economic issues. Using data from a unique field experiment in which leaders of policy debates were randomly assigned to communities, the researchers showed that the influence of individual leaders was a robust predictor of the policy priorities identified by the discussion group. Therefore, the results of this experiment are striking, as they demonstrate a clear leadership effect on priority setting. These findings suggest that while trust in a benevolent leader might minimize costs of providing public goods and build a more effective organization, trust in other types of leaders may simply make it easier for them to manipulate the agenda to realize their private gains. Thus, the intrinsic power of deliberation to foster democratic learning was certainly exceeded by the power of leaders to shape outcomes.

*Source:* Humphreys, Masters, and Sandbu (2006)..

---

nizational members and make sure that their interests do not diverge from their principal. In addition to monitoring, sanctioning, and trust building, leadership is a classic solution to collective action problems.

Traditional collective action problems like the social dilemmas introduced in chapter 3 assume that all group members have the same characteristics with respect to realizing group objectives. Conversely, various members of a group may have different preferences and skills sets. As a consequence of this assumption, there is a possibility that a subset of group members can create an incentive structure that enables the whole group to overcome the problem of collective action. In short, group members can be divided based on their preferences and skills sets, into "leaders" and "followers." The leader(s) of a group can be identified as those who can mobilize, coordinate, and design an organization that can successfully lobby in order to provide collective goods for its members (Colomer 1995, 227).

What types of leaders? Who can be a leader? Concepts in Practice 9.3 provides an example of the public perceptions of different types of leaders in the Democratic Republic of Congo and how this view can potentially affect development outcomes.

---

**CONCEPTS IN PRACTICE 9.3**

## Leaders in the Democratic Republic of Congo

A study of community leaders in postconflict situations looked at the coexistence of multiple types of leaders fulfilling different tasks in a community. A baseline survey in the DRC, for example, found that villagers preferred a dual leadership structure. According to the survey, respondents believed, on the one hand, that the traditional chiefs should have political authority and that, although community decisions should not be participatory, chiefs should be subjected to some accountability mechanisms. On the other hand, respondents wanted elected development committees rather than the traditional tribal chiefs to take the primary role in managing development funds.

A systematic pattern also emerged with respect to community trust in leadership for allocating development funds: the majority of participants across all four DRC provinces participating in the study tended to trust development committees, followed by village chiefs and then, distantly, NGOs. The balance of authority and trust between village chiefs and village-level elected development committees tilted toward the committees, with the exception of Haut Katanga, where village chiefs were more trusted for managing funds.

*Source:* Humphreys (2008).

*Leadership and Collective Action Problems.* Leaders derive benefits from their role as collective action facilitators. These rewards could come, for example, from the provision of a collective good or from the prestige or legacy that he or she may obtain from acting in this capacity. The implications are that groups that might have been unable to overcome collective action problems in the absence of a leader are able to do so, because leaders help coordinate, disseminate information to members, police organizational boundaries, and create a set of incentives that ensure that free-rider problems are overcome and that collective goods are subsequently provided. In a field experiment in Liberia, villagers involved in a community-driven reconstruction program (including the election of local leaders) exhibited stronger social cohesion than other similar communities. The experiment specifically explored whether newly created institutions, including directly elected leaders, promote social cohesion and collective action in a post-conflict context. The collective action capacity was measured through the outcome of a public game that allowed control communities to raise funds for their Community Driven Reconstruction program in Northern Liberia. Despite the fact that this study does not directly evaluate the impact of leaders on public participation, it shows that democratically elected committees with local legitimacy were able to solicit higher cohesion in their localities and better coordination for reconstruction efforts (Fearon, Humphreys, and Weinstein 2009). In other contexts, however, studies of community-driven reconstruction programs showed mixed results and unintended consequences with respect to members' access to leadership positions. For example, an NGO-funded program aimed at strengthening the capacity of indigenous women's organizations in western Kenya led, unexpectedly, to the selection of educated women in leadership positions instead of fostering equality of access for marginalized community members (Gugerty and Kremer 2008).

If the emergence of a leader is a viable possibility, then the next critical question to consider is, Who should be the leader? Ideally, from the perspective of the average group member, the best leader is the one who maximizes the realization of the collective good at the lowest possible cost. However, in practice, candidates for leadership will emerge according to the opportunity costs they face (salary, time constraints, and the like). In some circumstances, change agents may take turns, as leaders at times and followers at others, due to the diverse skill set that leadership requires, in addition to individual costs. A specific group might not be able to incentivize members of a high enough caliber to become group leaders, and, therefore, under certain conditions, leadership may not provide a solution to collective action problems. The rules of selection and succession also matter, since they shape leaders' power to credibly commit to the members of their group or association that they will not abuse the power or the organizational mandate.

When thinking about leadership as a solution to collective action problems, also consider how leaders can alter the subjective expectations of different groups to maximize their ability to take advantage of political opportunities that may further their cause. It is important for the analyst to distinguish carefully between an objective and a perceived evaluation of the costs of policy change or reform. For example, an objective analysis of the degree of government coercion or repression might show that the government is not open to policy change and is instead able and willing to repress or exclude groups that advocate for change. The subjective perception of mobilized groups might diverge, however (Kurzman 2004). The mismatch between the objective assessment of opportunities for action and groups' subjective perception can significantly affect the individual cost-benefit analysis of participation in collective action. It is the role of an effective leader to mitigate any subjective misperceptions about what the group can achieve.

## Conceptualizing Leadership, Trust, and Repeated Interaction through Games

It is easy to model these solutions to collective action problems using some of the substantive arguments made above.

### Solution 1: Leadership[1]

Recall in chapter 4 the discussion of games with multiple equilibria. Some theorists (for example, Calvert 1992) use coordination games to illustrate the potential significance of leadership. In the simple game below, two equilibria exist (cooperate; cooperate and unilateral; unilateral). However, it is not possible to deduce from the game which equilibrium emerges. The value added (of good leadership) might therefore be conceptualized as the process by which these players can coordinate on the better equilibrium, (cooperate; cooperate).

|  | Cooperate | | Unilateral | |
|---|---|---|---|---|
| Cooperate | 4 | 4 | 1 | 1 |
| Unilateral | 1 | 1 | 3 | 3 |

Of course, the existence of leadership is not the only mechanism that may allow players to achieve an optimal outcome, as we hope will become apparent from the class simulation.

### Solution 2: Long Time Horizons, Repeated Interaction, Trust[2]

Sometimes, if actors have to interact with each other over an indefinitely long period of time, they may have an incentive to behave differently from how they would act if they know they will interact for only a short time. How does indefinitely playing the prisoner's dilemma affect the equilibrium outcomes?

|           | Cooperate |   | Defect |   |
|-----------|-----------|---|--------|---|
| Cooperate | 3         | 3 | 1      | 4 |
| Defect    | 4         | 1 | 2      | 2 |

In a "grim trigger" strategy—that is, a player cooperates unless the other player defects, in which case the first player will also defect in the next round and every round thereafter—a player has to choose from a stream of (2,2,2,2,2.....) or (3,1,1,1,1.....). Which one is in a player's best interest? The answer depends on his or her discount factor. A discount factor is simply the present value of future payoffs. Generally, the discount factor is greater than zero but less than one. This reflects the fact that is generally assumed to prefer something today to the same thing in the future. For example, one dollar in a year is worth less than one dollar today. Calculating the discount factor allows us to calculate how "patient" the player must be to be incentivized to cooperate indefinitely (don't confess) rather than defect (confess). The result in this case is that

$$2 \geq \frac{3}{1-\delta^2} \text{ and } 2 \geq 3 - 2\delta.$$

Or, more simply, the discount factor satisfies the inequality:

$$\delta \geq \frac{1}{2}.$$

Therefore, the more patient an actor is (the more they value future payoffs from cooperation), the more likely he or she will be to desist from uncooperative short-term behavior.

## Summary

This chapter has focused on how a variety of different incentive structures or interventions may remedy the collective action problems identified in chapter 3. While many potential options exist to mitigate these problems, it is important to note that a number of them may have unintended consequences.

Furthermore, given that collective action is itself a public good, the establishment of institutional arrangements to remedy initial collective action problems may give rise to a host of new problems: namely, that the agents, leaders, politicians, bureaucrats, etc., who are responsible for resolving social dilemmas do themselves have an incentive to pursue their own agendas and bring about an additional collective action problem. By understanding the options they have, reformers will be able to identify a range of potential solutions, recognize viable opportunities, and use an appropriate combination of tools.

# Exercises for Chapter 9: Solutions to Collective Action Problems

## Exercise 9.1: The Prisoner's Dilemma with Different Time Horizons/Institutional Incentives Game[3]

The facilitator explains the steps involved in the Prisoner's Dilemma.

Steps in the exercise (time frame: ~40–45 minutes):
1. Read out instructions (1 minute)
2. Allow participants to read and answer (5–10 minutes)
3. Collect responses, tally Responses, group discussion (10 minutes)
4. Class discussion (10 minutes)
5. Technical explanation (10–15 minutes)

Preparation and materials:
- Envelopes to be placed in the middle of the round table (one at each table)
- Pens should be available to all participants
- Copies of the Instructions handout
- Copies of the Answer Sheet
- Copies of the Key Questions handout

Facilitator instructions:

**NOTE: There are three different scenarios (one for each table). If there are only two tables, then scenarios 1 and 3 should be used. If there are more than three tables, one or more of the three scenarios can be used again.**

1. The facilitator reads aloud the following instructions:
   I am going to distribute instructions and an answer sheet. Read the instructions and answer the questions on the answer sheet. Once you have read the instructions and completed your answers, place your answer sheet in the envelope in the middle of the table. DO NOT WRITE YOUR NAME ON EITHER DOCUMENT and MAKE SURE NO ONE SEES YOUR ANSWER. Keep the instructions handy for the follow-up discussion. I will give you about 5–10 minutes to complete this.
2. The facilitator distributes the Instructions handout and Answer Sheet to all the participants.
3. The facilitator gauges the rate of completion of the assignment and gives participants a 2-minute warning so that the activity can wrap up within its allotted 10-minute time frame. As part of the 2-minute warning, the

facilitator reminds participants that they should not write their names on the answer sheet; when they have finished, they should put their answer sheet in the envelope in the middle of the table.

4. The facilitator explains:

   I will come around to collect the envelopes with the answer sheets and tally your responses. At the same time, I will give you a Key Questions handout that includes two questions. While I tally the responses on the answer sheets, please go ahead and discuss at your tables the two questions on the handout. Spend approximately 10 minutes discussing these.

5. To tally the votes, the facilitator uses a blank Answer Sheet and notes for each option the total number of votes.

6. The facilitator walks around the room among the tables in a nonintrusive manner and pays attention to what is discussed. The facilitator notes a few comments from the tables that he or she can highlight as part of the transition to the lecture portion.

7. The facilitator gives the participants a 2-minute warning to wrap up their discussion.

8. The facilitator explains:

   Now that you have played the game and had a chance to discuss with others at your tables some of the key underlying issues, let's find out the results of your individual decisions.

9. The facilitator announces the results and poses the following questions to the entire group:
   ○ Were you surprised by the answers?
   ○ Alert the participants to the different scenarios at play and how these engender different levels of trust between participants.
   a. The facilitator then explains the case study activity.

## Exercise 9.1: Instructions Handout 1

You and a colleague have been arrested after committing a crime. You are both members of a criminal family (Mafia). Upon arrest, you were separated, and there is no way to communicate with him or her. You are now in a police cell, and the police negotiator informs you that they are willing to offer you the following deal, which is also simultaneously being offered to your colleague (you can assume this information is true).

1.  If you confess to the crime and your colleague does not confess to the crime, you will receive a reduced sentence of 1 year in prison while your colleague will receive a full sentence of 12 years in prison.
2.  If you do not confess to the crime but your colleague does confess to the crime, you will receive a full sentence of 12 years in prison while your colleague will receive a reduced sentence of 1 year in prison.
3.  If you both confess to the crime, you will both receive a reduced sentence of 6 years in prison.
4.  If neither one of you confesses, you will both receive a reduced sentence of 3 years.

You know that the criminal family you and your colleague belong to has a "zero tolerance" policy toward members who confess to crimes. In the past, family members who have violated this policy have subsequently fallen victims to "accidents." You are quite sure that the Mafia can infiltrate any witness protection programs and would have no difficulty finding you or your colleague in the future.

## Exercise 9.1: Instructions Handout 2

You and a colleague, who happens to be a very close and trusted friend, have been arrested after committing a crime. Upon arrest you were separated, and there is no way to communicate with him or her. You are now in a police cell, and the police negotiator informs you that they are willing to offer you the following deal, which is also simultaneously being offered to your colleague (you can assume this information is true):

1. If you confess to the crime and your colleague does not confess to the crime, you will receive a reduced sentence of 1 year in prison while your colleague will receive a full sentence of 12 years in prison.
2. If you do not confess to the crime but your colleague does confess to the crime, you will receive a full sentence of 12 years in prison while your colleague will receive a reduced sentence of 1 year in prison.
3. If you both confess to the crime, you will both receive a reduced sentence of 6 years in prison.
4. If neither one of you confesses, you will both receive a reduced sentence of 3 years.

You and your colleague or close friend have been through a lot together. You have known each other for many years and have an overlapping network of friends and associates.

## Exercise 9.1: Instructions Handout 3

You and a colleague have been arrested after committing a crime. Upon arrest, you were separated. You are now in a police cell, and the police negotiator informs you that they are willing to offer you the following deal, which is also simultaneously being offered to your colleague (you can assume this information is true):

1. If you confess to the crime and your colleague does not confess to the crime, you will receive a reduced sentence of 1 year in prison while your colleague will receive a full sentence of 12 years in prison.
2. If you do not confess to the crime but your colleague does confess to the crime, you will receive a full sentence of 12 years in prison while your colleague will receive a reduced sentence of 1 year in prison.
3. If you both confess to the crime, you will both receive a reduced sentence of 6 years in prison.
4. If neither one of you confesses, you will both receive a reduced sentence of 3 years.

You and your colleague are both relying on the services of an extremely competent lawyer who can mediate between the two of you and get you (both) to sign legally binding civil contracts.

This lawyer has just informed you that your colleague is willing to sign a contract stating that she did not commit the crime so long as you simultaneously do the same.

## Exercise 9.1: Answer Sheet Handout 1

Please indicate below, by ticking (√) the box next to the appropriate action, what you would like to do. PLEASE TICK ONLY ONE BOX.

| | |
|---|---|
| Confess to the crime | |
| Do not confess to the crime | |

Please indicate below, by ticking (√) the box next to the appropriate action, *what you think* your colleague will do. PLEASE ONLY TICK ONE BOX.

| | |
|---|---|
| He/she will confess to the crime | |
| He/she will not confess to the crime | |

Briefly explain why you decided to select one course of action over the other.

| |
|---|
| |

**Once you have completed your answers, put them in the envelope in the middle of the table.**

## Exercise 9.1: Answer Sheet Handout 2

Please indicate below, by ticking (√) the box next to the appropriate action, what you would like to do. PLEASE TICK ONLY ONE BOX.

| Confess to the crime | |
|---|---|
| Do not confess to the crime | |

Please indicate below, by ticking (√) the box next to the appropriate action, *what you think* your colleague will do. PLEASE ONLY TICK ONE BOX.

| He/she will confess to the crime | |
|---|---|
| He/she will not confess to the crime | |

Briefly explain why you decided to select one course of action over the other.

| |
|---|
| |

**Once you have completed your answers, put them in the envelope in the middle of the table.**

## Exercise 9.1: Answer Sheet Handout 3

Please indicate below, by ticking (√) the box next to the appropriate action, what you would like to do. PLEASE TICK ONLY ONE BOX.

| | |
|---|---|
| Confess to the crime | |
| Do not confess to the crime | |

Please indicate below, by ticking (√) the box next to the appropriate action, *what you think* your colleague will do. PLEASE ONLY TICK ONE BOX.

| | |
|---|---|
| He/she will confess to the crime | |
| He/she will not confess to the crime | |

Briefly explain why you decided to select one course of action over the other.

| |
|---|
| |

**Once you have completed your answers, put them in the envelope in the middle of the table.**

## Exercise 9.1: Key Questions Handout—Group Discussion

Once everyone around the table has completed his or her individual responses and placed them in the envelope, please discuss the following questions as a group.

1. What are the main reasons people are giving for the action they took?

2. Does the anticipated action of a person's colleague seem to be affecting how people choose whether to confess to the crime?

3. How does the additional information you have about your colleague, the broader context, or mediating parties affect behavior in this case?

Notes:

## Notes

1. *Source:* Inspired by (Calvert 1992, 7–24).
2. *Source:* Duch (2009) and inspired by Rothstein (2000).
3. *Source:* Inspired from (Duch 2009) and (Rothstein 2000).

## References

Bayat, Asef. 1997. *Street Politics: Poor People's Movements in Iran*. New York: Columbia University Press.

Behnke, C., A. Hamilton, L. Pagnac, and P. Terrazas. 2008. *The Dynamics of Legislative Rewards*. Washington, DC: World Bank Institute.

Braithwaite, Valerie, and Margaret Levi, eds. 1998. *Trust and Governance*. Russell Sage Foundation Series on Trust. New York: Russell Sage Foundation.

Calvert, R. 1992. "Leadership and Its Basis in Problems of Social Coordination." *International Political Science Review* 13 (1): 7–24.

Coleman, Eric A., and Brian Steed. 2009. "Monitoring and Sanctioning in the Commons: An Application to Forestry." *Ecological Economics* 68 (7): 2106–13.

Colomer, J. M. 1995. "Leadership Games in Collective Action." *Rationality and Society* 7 (2): 225–46.

Duch, R. 2009. "Formal Analysis Lecture Notes." Nuffield College: Oxford, http://www.raymondduch.com/course/hilary2009/formalanalysis/lecture_2009_06.pdf.

Duvanova, Dinissa. 2007. "Bureaucratic Corruption and Collective Action: Business Associations in the Postcommunist Transition." *Comparative Politics* 37 (4): 441–61.

Elster, Jon. 1989. ed. *The Cement of Society: A Study of Social Order*. Cambridge, MA: Cambridge University Press.

———. 1998. *Deliberative Democracy*. Cambridge Studies in the Theory of Democracy. Cambridge: Cambridge University Press.

Fahey, Dan. 2008. *Le Fleuve d'Or: The Production and Trade of Gold from Mongbwalu, DRC*. L'Afrique des Grands Lacs, Annuaire 2007–2008. Paris: L'Harmattan.

Fearon, J. D., M. Humphreys, and J. M. Weinstein. 2009. "Can Development Aid Contribute to Social Cohesion after Civil War? Evidence from a Field Experiment in Post-Conflict Liberia." *American Economic Review* 99 (2): 287–91.

Frey, Bruno S. 1997. *Not Just for the Money: An Economic Theory of Individual Motivation*. Cheltenham: E. Elgar.

Gambetta, D. 1993. *The Sicillian Mafia. The Business of Private Protection*. Cambridge, MA: Harvard University Press.

Gibbon, P. 2001. "Civil Society, Locality and Globalization in Rural Tanzania: A Forty-Year Perspective." *Development and Change* 32 (5): 819–44.

Gibson, C. C., J. T. Williams, and E. Ostrom. 2005. "Local Enforcement and Better Forests." *World Development* 33 (2): 273–84.

Gugerty, M. K., and K. Kremer. 2008. "Outside Funding and the Dynamics of Participation in Community Associations." *American Journal of Political Science* 52 (3): 585–602.

Hardin, E. 1995. *One for All: The Logic of Group Conflict*. Princeton: Princeton University Press.

Hardin, Russell. 1971. "Collective Action as an Agreeable N Prisoners' Dilemma." *Behavioral Science* 16 (5): 472–81.

Humphreys, Macartan, W. A. Masters, and Martin E. Sandbu. 2006. "The Role of Leaders in Democratic Deliberations: Results from a Field Experiment in São Tomé and Príncipe." *World Politics* 58 (4): 583–622.

Humphreys, Macartan. 2008. "Community Driven Reconstruction in the Democratic Republic of Congo. Baseline Report." Unpublished Manuscript. Columbia University. Available at: http://www.columbia.edu/~mh2245/DRC/report.pdf

Kurzman, C. 2004. "Can Understanding Undermine Explanation? The Confused Experience of Revolution." *Philosophy of the Social Sciences* 34 (3) (2004): 328–51.

Levi, Margaret. 1998. "A State of Trust." In *Trust and Governance*, ed. Valerie Braithwaite and Margaret Levi, 77–101. Russell Sage Foundation Series on Trust. New York: Russell Sage Foundation.

———. 2006. "Why We Need a New Theory of Government." *Perspectives on Politics* 4 (1): 5–19.

Lichbach, Mark Irving. 1998. *The Rebel's Dilemma*. Ann Arbor: University of Michigan Press.

Lijphart, Arend. 1999. *Patterns of Democracy: Government Forms and Performance in Thirty-Six Countries*. New Haven: Yale University Press.

Oliver, Pamela. 1980. "Rewards and Punishments as Selective Incentives for Collective Action: Theoretical Investigations." *American Journal of Sociology* 85 (6): 1356–75.

Ostrom, Elinor. 1990. *Governing the Commons: The Evolution of Institutions for Collective Action*. Cambridge: Cambridge University Press.

———. 1997. "Investing in Capital, Institutions, and Incentives." In *Institutions and Economic Development: Growth and Governance in Less-Developed and Post-Socialist Countries,* ed. Christopher Clague, 153–81. Baltimore: Johns Hopkins University Press.

———. 2005. *Understanding Institutional Diversity*. Princeton: Princeton University Press.

———. 2010. "A Long Polycentric Journey." *Annual Review of Political Science* 13 (June): 1–23.

Ostrom, E., and H. Nagendra. 2006. "Insights on Linking Forests, Trees, and People from the Air, on the Ground, and in the Laboratory." *Proceedings of the National Academy of Sciences* 103 (51): 19, 224–31.

Pagdee, A., Y.-S. Kim, and P. J. Daugherty. 2006. "What Makes Community Forest Management Successful: A Meta-Study from Community Forests throughout the World." *Society and Natural Resources* 19 (1): 33–52.

Putnam, Robert. 1993. *Making Democracy Work: Civic Traditions in Modern Italy*. Princeton: Princeton University Press.

Pyle, W. 2011. "Organized Business, Political Competition, and Property Rights: Evidence from the Russian Federation." *Journal of Law, Economics, and Organization* 27 (1): 2–31.

Riker, William H. 1962. *The Theory of Political Coalitions*. Vol. 578. New Haven: Yale University Press.

Rothstein, B. 2003. "Social Capital, Economic Growth and Quality of Government: The Causal Mechanism." *New Political Economy* 8 (1): 49–71.

Rothstein Bo. 2000. "Trust, Social Dilemmas and Collective Memories." *Journal of Theoretical Politics* 12 (4): 477–501.

Shapiro, Susan P. 2005. "Agency Theory." *Annual Review of Sociology* 31: 263–84.

Woolcock, Michael. 1998. "Social Capital and Economic Development: Toward a Theoretical Synthesis and Policy Framework." *Theory and Society* 27 (2): 151–208.

World Bank. 2004. *World Development Report 2004: Making Services Work for Poor People*. Washington, DC: World Bank.

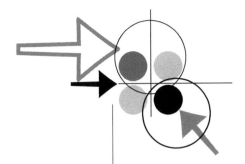

# PART II

Chapters 10 and 11 will attempt to bridge the gap between political-economy analysis and operational practice. This section explores strategies of "how to" systematically organize and implement analytical findings.

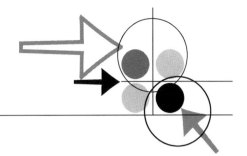

**CHAPTER 10**

# How to Conduct Political-Economy Analyses: First Steps

Now, we move from theory to practice. In this chapter, we use tools and mechanisms previously introduced to conduct political-economy analyses of real-life situations. The chapter will help readers identify and plan for specific factors—such as stakeholder interaction, informational, and motivational problems and other institutional constraints—that impede collective action and to create reform strategies that help realize their objectives. This kind of diagnostic addresses the *what*, the *why,* and the *how* of reform.

The first section of this chapter presents most of the political-economy analysis tools a reformer needs to do the following:

- Diagnose the need for change, or the *what* of the reform
- Understand the logic behind the problem, or the *why*
- Anticipate the costs and benefits of concrete reform paths
- Reflect on the change process itself and on the problems posing internal or organizational obstacles to change.

The structured process through which development practitioners gather and systematize information on the *what* and the *why* of policy change helps both to clarify why suboptimal development outcomes persist and to inform the priorities of the change process. Once reformers have carefully examined the policy costs and benefits and selected the reform path from a repertoire of possible solutions, they must shift to strategic thinking. Advancing reform goals means evaluating viable alternatives and anticipating stakeholders' reactions, intensities of preferences, resources, and so on.

## Objectives of Chapter 10

By the end of this chapter, readers should be able to do the following:

- Identify various types of stakeholders and the consequences (stakes) that reform could have for them
- Create maps of stakeholders, including the various groups and individuals that might support or oppose reform, and, as shown in figure 10.1, an estimate of the factors that determine the strength of their preference and their ability to mobilize collectively
- Assess the institutional context in which actors' interaction occurs
- Understand and incorporate into their analyses the sets of constraints on change their projects face
- Differentiate between various analytical instruments and techniques such as inferential and descriptive political-economy analysis.

**FIGURE 10.1 Conceptual Diagram of Political-Economy Diagnostics**

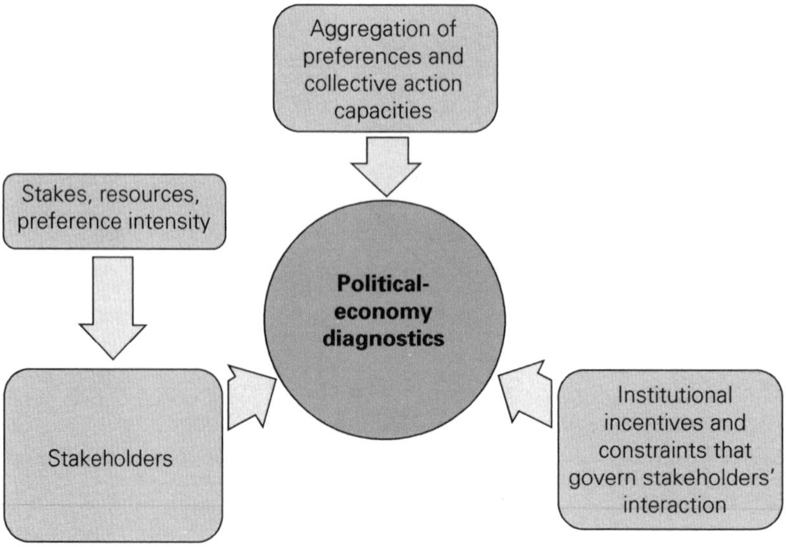

*Source:* Authors.

## Who Are the Stakeholders, and How Can Their Preferences Be Mapped?

*Stakeholders*—also sometimes referred to as the actors or players in a strategic game—are parties with identifiable interests in the process of reform. These can be *individuals* (for example, influential members of the opposition, the president, the prime minister, and civil society leaders, among others) or *organizations* (labor unions, administrative units, various factions within political parties or within the national legislature, donor agencies, and the like). The context in which stakeholders operate creates both opportunities and challenges for them as they seek to further their agenda.

It is often the case that to induce change, a coalition of stakeholders must come together and mobilize resources. In many circumstances, individual stakeholders may have little experience working with each other, and this lack of familiarity could potentially generate a host of coordination problems. Furthermore, the common goal of reform may spark disputes over the relative contributions of different coalition partners.

To preempt some of these challenges, reformers must first identify potential stakeholders, their comparative advantages, their stakes in the reform process, and the feasibility of producing a viable reform coalition. This process comprises two parts: (1) an inventory (or mapping) of the key stakeholders, their political influence, and the links between them; and (2) a grasp of the stakes in achieving or not achieving policy reform. What and how much will these actors win or lose? Keep in mind that there are different types of stakes and that not all of them are necessarily quantifiable.

### Stakeholder Mapping

There is a fine line between creating a comprehensive list of most or all actors with specific policy interests and simply identifying key stakeholders and mapping their preferences for analytical purposes. Thinking about the pertinent *aggregation* of preferences can help condense useful information and shed light on the coalitional potential of the stakeholders. Below are some examples of broad levels of interest aggregation and articulation:

- Socioeconomic class (defined in terms of income or wealth; for example, the rich, the middle class, the poor)
- Ethnic groups
- Faith-based groups
- Informal groups of well-connected individuals
- Rural versus urban interests.

The pertinent aggregation of preferences depends on the mobilization potential of individuals or organizations with vested interests in the reform process. Mobilization for policy action requires stakeholders first and foremost to solve their collective action problems. Passive preferences for reform or policy change, in the absence of collective action, do not create cohesive groups of stakeholders. As Amartya Sen (1977, 329) noted, "Commitment drives an all-important wedge between personal choice *(preference)* and personal welfare *(interest)*."

Thus, based on the capacity for collective action and the corresponding influence within the policy domain, two types of groups may exist: (1) unorganized or diffuse interests and (2) organized or concentrated interests. Therefore, the analyst must be very careful when specifying *latent interests or preferences* in society, as opposed to *articulated and mobilized interests* that hinge on solving collective action problems. One of the criticisms of analyses based on class (rich versus poor, for example) is precisely the lack of specification about how these interests become aggregated and mobilized in the first place and transform individuals into cohesive class-based political actors with homogeneous member preferences (such as rich, poor, and middle class).

There are two main analytical approaches that help analysts determine preferences and interest aggregation:

- *Inductive*, revealing subjective values or actual preferences derived from field work, interviewing actors intricately involved in the policy-making process on the ground, and survey work
- *Deductive*, revealing objective values or expected preferences that can be derived from theory based on the logical possibilities and precedents of preference articulation and interest aggregation.

An example of discrepancies in the two methods comes from case studies of financial liberalization in Japan. According to deductive expectations, in the 1980s Japanese consumers were believed to favor financial liberalization since such a reform was likely to trigger lower prices (access to higher-quality or lower-priced services because of increased competition). In practice, however, Japanese consumers actually mobilized against their own interests (narrowly defined) and opposed financial liberalization (Vogel 1999). What explained the passivism of Japanese consumer groups in light of their actual (material) interests? This failure to push for liberalization of bank deposit interest rates was not a collective action problem but rather, as inductive analysis demonstrated, a case of consumers with different lifestyle preferences who wished to preserve the availability of Japanese companies even more than they desired the benefits associated with a drop in prices for financial products.

To summarize, a good political economy diagnostic should clarify four steps before completing the list of stakeholders: *their policy preferences* (personal choices); *interest specification* (actors' awareness of how their preferences translate into personal welfare); *interest articulation* (what actors actually want, express and pursue regardless of their capacity to obtain it); and *interest aggregation* (collective action capacities for policy change).

Organizations that solve collective action by pooling preferences of individuals and groups who coalesce around common policy goals are often one of two types, each with its own strengths: (1) *single-issue organizations* (taxpayer associations, public sector labor unions, and the like), which have a focused, interest-based specialization and a good knowledge of the policy domain and may have already solved issues of coordination; and (2) *multi-issue organizations* (political parties, broad interest groups, labor federations, and the like), which have more power through formal policy channels and potentially more clout or perceived legitimacy in voicing demands for change.

The position of stakeholders vis-à-vis governments and the intensity of advocacy during the reform process places them in the following categories (Fritz, Kaiser, and Levy 2009, xiii):

- Demand-side versus supply-side stakeholders (government versus non-traditional, nonstate actors)
- *Reform champions* (powerful actors with high stakes in the policy process who facilitate collective action and advocate change), versus *reform opponents* (concentrated interests that derive benefits from the status-quo).

It is important to note that reform champions and opponents might have multiple policy agendas, as well as various collective action and coalition-building skills (*Idem*). After taking all these factors into account, the analyst should be able to identify the potential *winners and losers* of the reform process, as well as those for whom reform will be *neutral*.

## Stakes (or Payoffs)

*Stakes* refer to the consequences of the reform process for various stakeholders. The checklist presented in the next chapter uses the concepts of preferences, interests, payoffs, and stakes interchangeably to refer to gains and losses from policy outcomes. Expected consequences of policy change vary in substance, time frame, stakeholders' risk profile, and reform stages.[1]

There are different types of stakes, and not all of them are necessarily quantifiable. A typology of stakes may be relevant to actors in the reform process:

- *Monetary stakes or payoffs.* For example, if a reform will result in stricter taxpayer registration policies, taxpayers who engage in tax evasion or are active in the informal sector stand to see their profits reduced; therefore, we would expect some resistance from these individuals or groups.
- *Reputational costs and gains.* By successfully pioneering or implementing the reform, individual policy makers may enhance their reputations, thereby advancing their careers within a political party, bureaucracy, or international community. Some reputational costs and gains are specific to a given cultural context.
- *Audience costs and gain.*[2] When political leaders make commitments and do not follow through, their popular approval may diminish. In foreign policy, if leaders make empty war threats, they might suffer loss of credibility and approval with their domestic political constituency. Likewise, if during election campaigns politicians promise schools and roads but later renege on the promise, they might be punished in the next electoral round. Audience costs depend on the type of political system and on accountability relations.

Here are other important factors that shape actors' stakes:

- *Time horizon.* Depending on the situation, the differences between the short-term and the long-term gains perceived by stakeholders, as well as the period of time that actors can afford to wait without incurring major political costs, might be significant in the process of reform.
- *Stakeholders' risk profile.* Some key stakeholders will be more risk averse (less willing to take political risk by promoting a particular reform) than others who may be risk prone or risk seeking (more likely to put their reputations on the line for a successful reform outcome).
- *Reform stages.* Some actors or stakeholders will be interested primarily in the process of policy formulation; others will have most to gain from policy implementation. Mapping the stakes of policy change can tell us a lot about the magnitude of gains or losses stakeholders anticipate, but they do not paint the full picture yet. It is also crucial to know what resources stakeholders have, as well as what institutional advantages or constraints they face.

## The Role of Institutions

Having identified the relevant stakeholders and their preferences, the analyst must then understand how the institutional context determines the power of different stakeholders to promote their agendas. In other words, it is important to map the formal and informal institutions that govern a policy-making process to determine how the rules of the game may affect the ability of certain stakeholders to realize their policy goals. For instance, the ministry of education, because of its institutional location in the policy domain, will be more influential in pursuing reform than a civil society organization that advocates teachers' related causes. The institutional power of various stakeholders may or may not be associated with the financial resources at their disposal.

Below are some sample questions to help identify institutions for political-economy diagnostics:

- Is there any institutional malfunction? If so, is it caused by the formal or by the informal rules governing the interaction of various stakeholders?
- Do the rules that govern the domain of change reflect preexisting power relations between actors?
- What institution or rule generated the relevant suboptimal outcomes?
- Does the institutional context grant certain stakeholders special privileges, such as the ability to veto a reform or set the agenda?
- Once change agents understand the institutional map of reform, how can they navigate among institutions and surmount obstacles?
- Are there any opportunities for *formal* or *informal* agenda setting? By taking advantage of some institutional rules, can change agents circumvent entrenched interests that would block attempts at reform?
- How do the incentives generated by the rules of the game affect the collective action potential, resources, and reform stakes for stakeholders?

## The Role of Constraints

Apart from identifying relevant stakeholders and the institutional context in which they operate, change agents should also consider the constraints stakeholders face. Previous chapters have argued that understanding principal-agent problems, information asymmetries, or lack of credible commitment are crucial for pro-development collective action and change. Identifying such constraints can explain the *what* and *why* and provide clues about the *how* of reform. For instance, by recognizing a problem as one of institutional commitment to a certain policy action, reformers can work to establish the strong rules that remedy it. Ideally, the checklist in chapter 11 leads from evaluation and diagnostics to interventions that minimize corruption, enhance accountability, and foster good governance. When identifying these constraints, one can attempt to answer questions such as those below:

- Within the policy domain, what are the main modes of collective action—political parties, unions, institutionalized social movements, and the like—and how successful are they?
- What is the nature of the collective action problem: individual free riding, lack of trust, the size of the group, poor incentives, or large inequalities in financial resources between some members of the group and others? Can stakeholders overcome collective action problems? These two questions will also overlap with stakeholder mapping since collective action and preference aggregation will actually determine who the stakeholders are in the first place.
- Are information problems obstructing or facilitating collective action within the change process?
- What are the origins of these imperfections?
- Can the asymmetries be corrected? If so, what are the most effective corrective mechanisms?
- Can a functional principal-agent relationship be established between a reform coalition and those who implement the agenda?
- What are the most effective monitoring, sanctioning, or incentive tools that would prevent organizational leaders from shirking and enhance their accountability to the group members?
- Is a certain bureaucratic agency more corrupt than others due to inefficiently designed monitoring and sanctioning techniques used by the principal?
- Are there any *time inconsistency* problems that generate chronic mismatches between electoral promises of politicians and development results? What is the repertoire of potential mechanisms of credible commitment that the reform team could choose from?

By analyzing potential constraints, one can determine what is and is not feasible in a reform process.

## Methods and Instruments for Diagnostics and Analysis

How can the analyst capture the stakeholder preferences, interactions, and constraints? Because reform environments change continually, political information needs to be routinely gathered, updated, and examined with the final reform goal in mind. A continuous stream of information can help general development practitioners work effectively in fast-changing environments, adjust to evolving realities, and avoid the surprises that often derail the success and sustainability of policy reform. Political-economy analysis brings two analytical components to the table: descriptive and inferential.

## Modes of Analysis: Descriptive and Inferential Political Economy

The *descriptive* evaluation of stakeholders and stakes creates a "map" to guide reform efforts. Accurate mapping depends on continuously updated information gathered from media; from interviews with researchers, journalists, and politicians; or from more systematic sources, such as transcripts of parliamentary debate, surveys, official data for budgetary allocations, and so on. Given the potential bias embedded in various information streams and channels, multiple sources should be compared and cross-validated to ensure accuracy. For example, anecdotal evidence on public service delivery gathered from interviews with politicians or bureaucrats should be verified with hard data on budget allocations and with official documents on implementation of service delivery. This method, called *triangulation* in social science research, requires extra effort for political-economy analysts but simultaneously provides a broader and less biased picture of stakeholders (actors), stakes (payoffs), and institutions.

The *inferential* (or causal) component of political-economy analysis serves as the "compass" for policy interventions. Going beyond the *what*, it explores the heart of the *why*. By looking at the strategic interaction between actors, the inferential component of the analysis sheds light on institutional equilibria. Why do they occur and persist?

Unlike the descriptive component, for which information gathering is a relatively straightforward process once the problem has been defined, the inferential (or causal) analysis has a more ambitious mission:

- To identify the relevant institutions (or institutional features) for the given policy change
- To describe the incentives and the dynamic equilibria
- To allow for *comparative statics,* or *scenario analyses,* that illustrate how much the existing equilibrium would adjust if any key factor changed.

All political systems are complex, and the institutional landscape can be overwhelming for the general development practitioner. Political-economy analysis allows an inventory of relevant institutions and draws a distinction between proximate and distant causes of an inferior equilibrium.

Because institutions are interdependent, the scope of information required for the inferential component of the analysis exceeds the inputs necessary for descriptive analysis. For example, the key role of a certain committee in the national legislature interacts with policy incentives for its individual members within their own political parties, as well as with electoral laws and reelection goals. What dimension of the four influences described is the immediate cause of the committee's failure to support the proposed reform?

These complex interactions among multiple nested institutions require a plethora of political-economic information beyond the immediate scope of the proposed policy reform. For example, an inferential analysis might also look at how an upcoming change in the electoral system or the process of decentralization might affect opportunities to implement education or health reform by reconfiguring and realigning incentives and institutions.

Whereas descriptive political-economy analysis is heavily context specific, the inferential type draws on lessons learned in other contexts. In this sense, general reform practitioners should build repositories of political-economy studies done in other countries, in other sectors, or across nations. Reformers can use this theory-based reference to help identify institutions and other political-economic factors that have been found relevant in other countries or sectors and should thus be considered in the analysis at hand.

As we have seen, inferential political-economy analysis relies heavily on learning from external sources, whereas the descriptive analysis uses information gathered mostly in a specific context and time. Inferential political-economy analysis is the only method that allows us to sort through competing hypotheses or explanations and choose that ones confirmed by empirical data.

## Instruments for Identifying Stakeholders, Their Incentives, Constraints, and Interaction

How can we concretely identify relevant stakeholders? How can we measure their perceptions, preferences, resource endowments, and institutional position? As demonstrated in Concepts in Practice 10.1, one way is to develop a valid and consistent survey instrument that can capture the data. Although self-reporting in interviews has its pitfalls (strategic miscommunication or failure to recall events, for example), a well-designed survey can elicit proxies for the "real" preferences of stakeholders, as well as for their intensity, with an adequate degree of accuracy. Of course, other context-specific tools may be appropriate as well. For example, interviews or quali-

**CONCEPTS IN PRACTICE 10.1**

## Using a Survey Instrument to Map the Political Economy of Health Care Litigation

In many countries that have publicly financed health care systems, judicial review influences which treatments are available to the public (through priority-setting cases) and how health care professionals are held accountable (through negligence cases). Health care litigation can, potentially, affect both the efficiency and the equity of a health care system, but the net welfare effects are ambiguous. On the one hand, health care litigation can promote efficiency by incentivizing health care professionals to be mindful of patients—reducing waste and carelessness. However, the fear of lawsuits in malpractice cases may incentivize health care professionals to order unnecessary tests or procedures, to carry expensive insurance policies, and to spend too long on each patient—driving up costs and hence impairing the efficient allocation of resources.

Health care litigation may also have effects on equity. Because decisions about which medications are provided to the public sector are often made by bureaucrats in consultation with only the most organized interest groups, litiga-

tion may allow groups excluded from this initial decision-making process to obtain medication and treatment for their conditions. However, as the ability to litigate is unlikely to be equal for all groups, increased health care litigation may result in the skewing of resources toward those who can litigate and away from those who cannot (often the poor and marginalized).

To help understand the perceptions of different stakeholders on the net effect of health care litigation, a study identified and surveyed key actors involved in or affected by health care litigation (bureaucrats, patient groups, representatives of the medical profession, judges, pharmaceutical companies, academics, and journalists). This exercise allowed mapping the preferences of different stakeholders, the intensity of these preferences, the institutional rules governing the actors' interaction, and the perceptions of stakeholders of many different dimensions of health care litigation. In addition, the survey also assessed the extent to which the stakeholders communicate and collaborate with each other.

*Source:* Corduneanu-Huci, Hamilton, and Masses-Ferrer (2011).

tative case studies may provide critical insights into the political-economy context of reform.

## From Theory to Action

Regardless of the type of political-economy analysis in question, it is essential to consider how such findings might affect the agendas of relevant stakeholders and their incentive either to take ownership of or to oppose the implications of reform.

## Agenda Ownership

Political-economy analysis pays attention to context and identifies the spaces for feasible reform. Once the stakeholders, their interests, and their institutional influence have been mapped and the ensuing equilibria teased out, the next step in coalition building is to consider who *owns* the reform agenda. The key aim for the policy reformer should be to support the emergence and continuation of pro-change coalitions, "while accepting that these actors coordinated in coalitions of change, define the scope and precise direction of change they want to pursue" (Fritz, Kaiser, and Levy 2009, 20).

Ownership of the change agenda thus presupposes (1) *legitimacy* (that is, the acceptance or full recognition) of the authority for change; and (2) a *genuine belief* that the change will result in a better (welfare-enhancing) equilibrium. In short, stakeholders will become proactive only when they believe in, or own, the reform goals and the potential for change.

## Leadership

What do leaders do when faced with the fundamental problems and mechanisms that this handbook has presented so far—principal-agent issues, information asymmetries, market failure, collective action problems, and credible commitments, among others?

***Leaders as Coordinators and as Solvers of Political-Economy Problems.***
Leaders who can organize reform coalitions can be a critical component of realizing the reform process. Up until now, we have seen how important the interaction between actors can be in explaining outcomes. We have explored how rational actors may need to condition their behavior (strategies) based on how they anticipate that other actors will react or behave (as in the prisoner's dilemma). We have also looked at how such interactions can result in the emergence and persistence of suboptimal outcomes (as in the coordination game). We have seen that institutions might incentivize actors to alter their strategies, potentially changing the outcomes (the agenda-setting game, the principal-agent game, and the credible commitment examples).

A final, but potentially critical, concept we need to come back to is the role of leadership in explaining outcomes.[3] In many real-life situations, actors may be able to understand and anticipate how they, in cooperation with some or all other players, can change the environment (rules of the game) and thus generate different outcomes. This result may come about through a process of *leadership*.

In the broadest possible sense, leadership can be analytically construed as the ability to understand and alter the nature of interaction between actors. For example, the coordination game has two equilibria. Given this institutional context and the preferences of actors, it is not possible to predict, a priori, which equilibrium will prevail. However, if one of the players is known to be a good communicator and can convince the other player that coordination will be beneficial to both, a more accurate prediction of what will happen in the game may be possible. Thus, the incorporation of leadership into our thinking potentially increases our ability to analyze and predict outcomes.

However, it is important to remember that leadership is no panacea. Poor accountability mechanisms, or a conflict of interest between a leader and the majority of a reform coalition, can obstruct reform objectives. In contrast, sometimes, the ability of large groups to spontaneously organize and realize their objectives in a leaderless pattern can facilitate positive change.

## Summary

To understand how policy making works, and therefore how pro-development changes can occur, we must be able to identify and understand the stakeholders' incentives and stakes. The preferences, payoffs, and strategic interaction among different actors are vital in determining which proposals are feasible and which are not. Political-economy analyses allow reformers to identify who might help or hinder their reform process by drawing useful analytical maps that the reformers can then navigate.

## Exercise 10.1: The Leadership Game[4]

The facilitator explains the steps involved in the Leadership Game.

Steps in the exercise (time frame: ~40–45 minutes):
- Read out instructions (1 minute)
- Allow participants to read and answer (5–10 minutes)
- Collect responses, tally responses, group discussion (10 minutes)
- Class discussion (10 minutes)
- Technical explanation (10 minutes)

Preparation and materials:
- Envelopes to be placed in the middle of the round table (one at each table)
- Pens should be available to all participants
- Copies of the handout of instructions
- Copies of the answer sheet
- Copies of the Key Questions

Facilitator instructions:
1. The facilitator should read aloud the following instructions:
   I am going to distribute instructions and an answer sheet. Read the instructions and answer the questions on the answer sheet. Once you have read the instructions and completed your answers, place your answer sheet in the envelope in the middle of the table. DO NOT WRITE YOUR NAME ON EITHER DOCUMENT and MAKE SURE NO ONE SEES YOUR ANSWER. Keep the instructions handy for our follow-up discussion. I will give you about 5–10 minutes to complete this.
2. The facilitator distributes the instructions handout and answer sheet to all the participants.
3. The facilitator gauges the rate of completion of the assignment and gives participants a 2-minute warning so that the activity can wrap up within its allotted 10-minute time frame. As part of the 2-minute warning, the facilitator reminds participants that they should not write their names on the answer sheet; when they have finished, they should put the answer sheet in the envelope in the middle of the table.
4. The facilitator explains:
   I will come around to collect the envelopes with the answer sheets and tally your responses. At the same time, I will give you a handout that includes two key questions. While I tally the responses on the answer sheets, please go ahead and discuss at your tables the two questions on the handout. Spend approximately 10 minutes in this discussion.

5.  To tally the votes, the facilitator uses a blank answer sheet and notes for each option the total number of votes.
6.  The facilitator walks around the room among the tables in a nonintrusive manner and pays attention to what is discussed. The facilitator notes a few comments from the tables that he or she can highlight as part of the transition to the lecture portion.
7.  The facilitator gives the participants a 2-minute warning to wrap up their discussion.
8.  The facilitator explains:
    Now that you have played the game and had a chance to discuss with others at your tables some of the key underlying issues, let's find out the results of your individual decisions.
9.  The facilitator announces the results and poses the following questions to the entire group:
    1.  Were you surprised by the answers?
    2.  What does the answers say about the need for leadership?
    3.  What does this exercise suggest is the link between leadership and the institutional context?

## Exercise 10.1: Instructions Handout 1

You are part of a large team, which has been assigned a very important project whose outcome is critical for the organization.

The project has many components, and it makes sense that team members with specific skills specialize in different tasks. However, the project also requires coordination between team members to ensure that the end product is coherent. Therefore, it might make sense if someone assumed the responsibility of strategic oversight of the project.

You are one of the people who is on good terms with everyone on the project, and you also have a very clear idea of what the end product needs to look like.

Also, your organization has a well-established culture of using a team coordinator for large projects. In fact, all the other team members are used to working in a team with someone coordinating activities.

Furthermore, your organization has effective support mechanisms to facilitate this coordination role, providing dispute resolution mechanisms and support for a team coordinator who may face unanticipated difficulties in dealing with team dynamics.

## Exercise 10.1: Instructions Handout 2

You are part of a large team, which has been assigned a very important project whose outcome is critical for the organization.

The project has many components, and it makes sense that team members with specific skills specialize in different tasks. However, the project also requires coordination between team members to ensure that the end product is coherent. Therefore, it might make sense if someone assumed the responsibility of strategic oversight of the project.

You are one of the people who is on good terms with everyone on the project, and you also have a very clear idea of what the end product needs to look like.

However, you also know that no large project undertaken by the organization in the past has had a group coordinator. Therefore, you are unsure how your colleagues will react to your suggestion that you take on this role.

Furthermore, you know that one other member on the team very much enjoys "leadership roles" and would therefore make a huge fuss if anyone else thought he or she should have such a role.

## Exercise 10.1: Answer Sheet Handout 1

Please indicate below, by ticking (√) the box next to the appropriate action, what you would like to do. PLEASE TICK ONLY ONE BOX.

| | |
|---|---|
| Propose to act as team coordinator | |
| Propose nothing | |

Briefly explain why you decided to select one option rather than the other.

**Once you have completed your answers, put them in the envelope in the middle of the table.**

## Exercise 10.1: Answer Sheet Handout 2

Please indicate below, by ticking (√) the box next to the appropriate action, what you would like to do. PLEASE TICK ONLY ONE BOX.

| | |
|---|---|
| Propose to act as team coordinator | |
| Propose nothing | |

Briefly explain why you decided to select one option rather than the other.

| |
|---|
| |

**Once you have completed your answers, put them in the envelope in the middle of the table.**

### Exercise 10.1: Key Questions Handout—Group Discussion

Once those around the table have completed their individual responses and placed them in the envelope, please discuss the following questions as a group:

• What are the main reasons people are giving for the action they have taken?

• Does the organization's culture appear to be affecting people's answers?

• If so, what does that suggest about factors needed to achieve team coordination beyond the presence of a willing individual with the right skills?

Notes:

## Notes

1. While technically stakes and payoffs are analytically distinct—stakes refer to the anticipated consequences of a decision while payoffs refers to the consequence of an outcome of strategic interaction, they are both concerned with the potential monetary and/or non-monetary factors that affect decision maker's welfare and decision-making calculus.
2. See Tomz (2007).
3. See Solution 1: Leadership in Chapter 9 (page 264) for an exposition on how leadership can facilitate coordination.
4. *Source:* Inspired from (Calvert 1992) and (Rothstein 2000).

## References

Calvert, R. 1992. "Leadership and Its Basis in Problems of Social Coordination." *International Political Science Review* 13(1): 7–24.

Corduneanu-Huci, Cristina, Alexander Hamilton, and Issel Masses-Ferrer. 2011. "The Political Economy of Healthcare Litigation: Model and Empirical Application to Uruguay." Policy Research Working Paper 5821, World Bank, Washington, DC.

Duch, R. 2009. "Formal Analysis Lecture Notes." Nuffield College: Oxford, http://www.raymondduch.com/course/hilary2009/formalanalysis/lecture_2009_06.pdf.

Fritz, Verena, Kai Kaiser, and Brian Levy. 2009. *Problem-Driven Governance and Political-Economy Analysis.* Washington, DC: World Bank.

Rothstein, B. 2000. 'Trust, Social Dilemmas and Collective Memories,' *Journal of Theoretical Politics* 12(4): 477–501.

Sen, Amartya. 1977. "Rational Fools: A Critique of the Behavioral Foundations of Economic Theory." *Philosophy and Public Affairs* 6 (4): 317–44.

Tomz, Michael. 2007. "Domestic Audience Costs in International Relations: An Experimental Approach." *International Organization* 61 (4): 821–44.

Vogel, Stephen. 1999. "Can Japan Disengage? Winners and Losers in Japan's Political Economy, and the Ties That Bind Them." *Social Science Journal of Japan* 2 (1): 3–21.

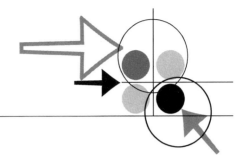

**CHAPTER 11**

# Recognizing Opportunity for Policy Change

This chapter takes the development of actionable political-economy analysis to the next level. It examines how outside events or "shocks"—such as a change of government, an economic meltdown, or a foreign crisis—can provide reformers with both opportunities and challenges for realizing their policy goals. A good political-economy analysis will not only create a framework for thinking about the *what,* the *why,* and the *how* of reform but also take into account such dynamic factors as anticipated events (reaction of vested interests or mobilization of supporters) and unanticipated events (natural disasters and the like). Finally, because the *when* of change also matters, a robust diagnostic should include recommendations for timing the initiation of reform.

Once the development practitioner has an understanding of the opportunities and challenges presented by outside events, as well as by stakeholders, it is possible to leverage momentum for action. For example, political scandals have sometimes enabled good governance campaigners to ensure the enactment of reforms (such as freedom of information acts or procurement laws) because of increased public support for such measures. Of course, a political scandal may also weaken the reform coalition if supporters of one cause are forced to resign because of their activities in an unrelated field.

In short, this chapter discusses the importance of timing and the other factors that practitioners should consider when deciding whether and when to push a reform forward. First, we examine how the timing of policy change can affect the success of a reform process. Second, we argue that a project must be responsive to changing dynamics, and we explore how political, social, economic, and international events affect project implementation on the ground. Third, we look at the effects of other factors, including concurrent reform policies, and how these may affect results. Finally, we bring together the insights of this chapter and those of chapter 10 into a comprehensive checklist for political-economy analysis, designed to help policy makers think systematically about the relevant political-economy factors and mechanisms that they need to consider before embarking on a project.

## Objectives of Chapter 11

By the end of this chapter, readers should be able to understand the following:

- The complexities of temporal sequencing and their relevance for political-economy analysis
- The temporal dynamics of the processes of reform
- The stages of project or reform implementation.

Learning how to conduct a political-economy analysis can empower readers to think about change in their own work.

## Time Frames for Reform: Timing, Sequencing, Pacing, and Maintaining Momentum

Certain moments in time are particularly auspicious for lasting change. In the parlance of political economy, these openings as often called critical junctures—unprecedented episodes of catalytic events that lead to the realignment of incentives and lift preexistent constraints on action. One example is the fall of the Berlin Wall in 1989, followed by the collapse of communism in Eastern Europe and eventually the dismemberment of the Soviet

Union. Critical junctures can be triggered by many factors: domestic and international conflict, geopolitical shifts, economic booms or crises, the discovery of new natural resources, global changes in economic conditions, major episodes of technological innovation or changes of political regimes. These openings may create unique opportunities for reforms that could lead to better development equilibria.

### Timing: Why Is Timing Important?

Public policy does not occur in a vacuum. Numerous factors may already be affecting public policy makers at the time a reforming coalition attempts to effect change. These factors can potentially make the policy-making context more or less conducive to a reform agenda. As noted in one report on policy change efforts, "The sequencing and timing of actions associated with policy reforms can also determine the level of tension and conflict, the duration, and ultimately the success or failure of reforms" (Social Development Network 2008, 2). Below are some timing factors that may help or hinder the effort of a reform coalition.

***Domestic Timing Factors.*** *Election cycles.* An election cycle is a crucial domestic factor that can significantly affect the success of reform efforts. As elections approach, office holders may be more willing or less willing to engage with policy proposals, depending on how those proposals may affect their electoral prospects.

An example of the effect of such timing on policy making comes from a study of pre- and postelection macroeconomic policy (Alesina, Cohen, and Roubini 1992). It has long been assumed that politicians have an incentive to try and make voters feel better off just before an election—leaving unpopular economic adjustment to the postelection period. This tendency can mean that projects with an immediate "feel good" impact may be favored in the run-up to an election, while funding for similar projects may dry up immediately afterward. Using data from 18 countries in the Organisation for Economic Co-operation and Development, the authors of the study find little evidence of pre-election attempts to boost growth or reduce unemployment (Alesina, Cohen, and Roubini 1992). However, the authors did find evidence that monetary policy is looser in election years and that public expenditure is also greater, which may make it easier to obtain credit for an upcoming project.

*Shifts in public opinion.* Shifts in public opinion may also affect the timing of reform efforts. Reforms often work best when they coincide with surges in public support. In certain contexts, public opinion polls are a useful mechanism for helping determine whether the timing is right to implement a reform. If a population expresses negative attitudes toward a proposed policy, then the reformers should consider either changing the policy or delaying the implementation of the reform and designing an effective communication strategy for garnering more support. Media events may alter the receptiveness of the public to the reform agenda by increasing or decreasing the saliency of the issue.

An example of the effects of public opinion comes from a study of how the spread of radio in the United States promoted relief efforts in the 1930s (Strömberg 2004). If voters have more information about what spending programs are available, they are more likely to demand that their elected representatives obtain that funding. The author of this study showed that the spread of radio had the effect of increasing the amount of relief funds that counties received during the Great Depression. Thus, more informed voters (those with a radio) were able to obtain more resources than the relatively uninformed voters (those without a radio), even when controlling for other characteristics. This finding suggests that voters with information may be more willing to mobilize and punish or reward incumbents based on the decisions they make. Public opinion support often provides significant help to reform champions in reaching their policy goals.

*Changes to policy-making structures.* Especially during the public policy–making process, the reorganization of bureaucratic departments or the inclusion of new stakeholders in decision making can alter the priorities and hence the attractiveness of fresh reform agendas.

An example of the participation of civil society in policy design in Brazil illustrates the point (Houtzager and Lavalle 2010). The formal inclusion of civil society actors in policy making in Brazil has altered local government priorities and activities. While this change in procedure has increased the overall ability of such groups to hold government to account and reduce administrative inefficiencies, it has also raised important questions about the new direction of public policy. The participation of civil society groups does not automatically guarantee that the interests of citizens, as opposed to the interests of those who control or lead these groups, are favored. Many of the civil society organizations now involved in decision making do not have mechanisms of accountability themselves since their leaders are not often elected or monitored. Therefore, if they fail to develop these mechanisms in the future, civil society groups may be just as prone to weak accountability and corruption as the policy makers they sought to curtail. Thus, while a change in the administrative process may shift policy priorities and open up reform possibilities, it does not guarantee a reduction of inefficiencies or necessarily ensure representation of marginalized groups of citizens.

**Economic Timing Factors.** *Changes in the economic context.* The growth of gross domestic product, inflation, and unemployment may alter the feasibility or the political desirability of different reform agendas.

Studies of socioeconomic development and corruption provide an example (Treisman 2007). Economic modernization and long periods of democratic government have been associated with less (perceived) corruption. The possible mechanisms behind this outcome are many, but to a certain extent they involve the ability of an increasingly informed citizenry to oversee incumbent politicians. Because informed voters can reward elected officials who facilitate the provision of public goods and punish officials who engage in rent seeking, pro-development reform agendas become more feasible and viable as the broader socioeconomic context improves.

Economic crises often open opportunities for change that have never existed before. For example, the decisions of some Latin American leaders to pursue drastic economic reform policies following crises in the 1980s and 1990s can be partially explained by the leaders' belief that voters were informed enough to know that the painful reforms were necessary for solving the structural causes of the crises. In addition, the likelihood of significant losses in the standard of living of the population in the absence of necessary reforms made the general public more sympathetic toward dramatic policy change (Weyland 2003). At other times, crises generate policy taboos. In periods of high inflation or unemployment, reform attempts that are likely to impose additional costs on the population (for example, food subsidy reductions) are likely to be highly contentious and short-lived.

*The budget cycle.* The availability of funds and the incentive structure surrounding allocations of resources may determine when it is feasible to make certain policy recommendations.

Budgeting in the public sector is an example. In many public organizations, budgets are allocated at the beginning of the fiscal year, and any surplus revenue is taken back at the end of this period. This cycle creates an incentive for individual agencies to spend any remaining budget toward the end of the fiscal year. The incentive may be particularly acute if a budget surplus is taken as a signal that too much money was allocated to the agency in the first place. Thus, projects that may not have been considered viable may suddenly receive funding, not because of a change in priorities but because of the political economy of the budget process. Major public sector organizations affected by such budgetary rules include the World Bank, many agencies around the world, and the U.S. Department of Defense. Studies have found that even if the formal rules and official policies of certain development organizations try to lower or eliminate the pressure to spend the entire budget allocations by the end of the fiscal year, many project leaders still face informal pressures to do so because of career advancement incentives. The case of the Swedish International Development Cooperation Agency has been well documented (Gibson et al. 2005).

*Public finances.* The state of public finances (budget deficit, public debt) may alter the feasibility or political desirability of different reform agendas.

Structural adjustment policies in Europe are an example. As a result of unsustainable public finances in much of the peripheral Euro Area in 2012, governments such as Greece, Ireland, and Portugal have had to implement austerity and structural adjustments to comply with the demands of donors (the International Monetary Fund and other member states of the European Union), just as other governments like Italy and Spain have had to stave off the need for such loans by reassuring investors that they can repay their debts. The situation has resulted in politically costly policies, including increased taxation, reduced public spending, and the deregulation and privatization of the economies (opposed by organized interest groups). The economic environment has obviously constrained certain projects (those dependent on public finance), but it may create opportunities for others (those restricted by the power of some vested-interest groups now losing their policy-making powers).

***International Timing Factors.*** *International "best practice" recommendations.* What is perceived as being the optimal policy modus operandi or outcome, according to the international academic or policy-making community, may aid or hinder a reform agenda.

One such example is the spread of central bank independence as a credible signal of sound monetary policy (Moser 1999). The spread of central bank independence in much of the world during the 1990s can be explained partly by the need of governments to credibly commit to limiting their role in manipulating monetary policy in favor of short-term political gain over long-term macroeconomic stability. As one would expect, this set of reforms diffused worldwide came about at least partly to signal a commitment to a sound and more long-term monetary policy. According to the author of this study, it is indeed the case that central bank independence is associated with increased foreign direct investment. In a context of credible macroeconomic conditions, credit constraints may also be eased, and budget cycles may be mitigated, making it easier for nongovernmental organizations and development agencies to access funds.

*International relations.* The state and shifts of diplomatic relations among various countries may alter the saliency or feasibility of different reform agendas.

Countries of strategic importance may sometimes receive international aid and support because of their geographical location or their abundance of resources (Lamb 1987). Foreign aid may provide significant financial support for development projects. However, it may also make politicians unresponsive and corrupt and enable them to bribe segments of the public with aid money. Such aid may be used in creating fake jobs and nepotistic networks that are antithetical to sustainable development. For example, the regime of Mobutu Sese Seko was the recipient of over half the U.S. aid to Sub-Saharan Africa in the 1970s, despite the regime's poor human rights record and massive corruption. The share of money that the United States allocated for the provision of public goods went instead to enrich the political elite, while the vast majority of the population remained in extreme poverty. Geopolitical changes, accompanied by sudden decreases or increases in strategic rent or aid flows, can carve spaces for domestic actors to formulate claims and initiate pro-development reforms.

Not taking into account how these exogenous factors may affect the desirability of a reform coalition's agenda can result in missed opportunities or the failure of the reform process. No matter how efficient the internal organization and activities of a reform coalition are, a host of factors influence public policy makers' incentives to accept, modify, or reject a reform initiative. Therefore, reformers must ensure that their proposals complement rather than work against such incentives whenever feasible.

In summary, timing and synchronizing a reform agenda to take into account the opportunities and challenges presented by the policy-making environment are keys to success.

## Pacing and Sequencing

The question of pacing and sequencing is closely linked to the concept of reform ownership. Once analysts diagnose the problem, they will often spend considerable time addressing collective action obstacles within the coalition or network of stakeholders, as well as building consensus around reform strategies. This slow process actually works in reformers' favor, as incrementalism can build political will and ownership of reform more successfully than radical policy changes imposed from the outside.

The right sequencing of reform steps can build in short-term political gains that broaden acceptance and pave the way for subsequent stages. If reform fatigue and weak political legitimacy are important obstacles to the change process, small and tangible outcomes on the ground (building schools or improving access to water in a relatively short time) can create community trust and generate a virtuous circle of electoral incentives for politicians to deliver similar results. More ambitious dimensions of reform, however, will need a longer time frame for consultation and implementation (Grindle 2002).

## Complementarity versus Trade-offs of Different Reform Areas

The temporal dimension of the reform process has consequences for the substance and scope of the reform as well.

*Complementarity of reform areas.* Certain policies will not be successful unless bureaucracies are strong and isolated enough from political pressures to implement them credibly. For example, decentralization without an adequate body of local civil servants who have both the capacity and the political incentives to execute the process will not lead to long-lasting positive effects. Therefore, the general development practitioner must identify the prerequisites of the desired reform and establish priorities among various change dimensions with a careful eye toward timing and sequence.

*Policy area trade-offs.* Feasible change usually implies trade-offs between policy priorities. Research has shown that in some contexts, crucial and heavily contested public administration reforms were possible only at the expense of maintaining "pockets of patronage" within the bureaucracy. In post-1985 Bolivia, for example, as well as in other Latin American contexts, civil service reforms and privatization of state-owned enterprises were possible because of the maintenance of underperforming bureaucratic enclaves that preserved the rents of key elites (Grindle 2007; Geddes 1996).

As argued, the *when* of reform—timing, pacing, and sequencing—can open new opportunities for reform and determine success. Thus, strategies related to timing, alongside diagnostics of stakeholder dynamics, play an important role in political-economy analysis.

But how can we bring together all the elements required to undertake a comprehensive political-economy analysis? The following section provides readers with a portable set of questions that can help them identify some of the critical elements and features of the decision-making context.

BOX 11.1

# Political-Economy Analysis: A Practical Checklist

Although every situation in which a political-economy analysis may be useful is unique, complex, and dynamic, a generic checklist of the basic mapping process used in the analysis is a good starting point. A political-economy analysis entails three major steps:

- Identifying the stakeholders and their preferences
- Identifying the rules of the game and the dynamics of interaction between stakeholders
- Identifying how institutional constraints such as information problems, lack of credible commitment, principal-agent relationships, and agenda-setting dynamics shape the proposed policy agenda and the collective action capacity of reform groups.

## Stakeholders and Their Preferences

Without exception, a prospective reform will benefit some individuals and groups while negatively affecting the agendas of others. Reformers must evaluate not just the actors and their preferences but also the intensity of those preferences and the ability of the stakeholders to collectively support or oppose the reform. The following questions serve as a guide:

- *Who are the relevant stakeholders?* Identifying the relevant actors requires an understanding of all the individuals or groups that may potentially benefit or lose from a change in the status quo.
- *What resources does each stakeholder have?* Resources include not only the physical endowments (funds, supporters, and cohesive and organized administration) but also the political and communication resources (ability to veto policy change, ability to alter public opinion). The stakeholders' agenda-setting power, capacity to overcome collective action problems, and ability to credibly commit, as illustrated in box table 11.1, must also be considered.
- *What is the intensity of stakeholder preference?* Stakeholders may be positively or negatively affected by a proposed change; likewise, they stand to gain or lose by maintenance of the status quo. The magnitude of this effect will determine how they are likely to respond to policy initiatives. Stakeholders that are only minimally affected (whether

**BOX TABLE 11.1 Comparison of Stakeholder Preferences and Resources**

| Stakeholder | Benefits from reform? | Resources | Intensity of preference | Incentive for mobilization (resources x intensity) |
|---|---|---|---|---|
| A | Yes | 2 | 0.2 | 0.4 |
| B | Yes | 3 | 0.1 | 0.3 |
| C | Yes | 2 | 0.1 | 0.2 |
| D | No | 8 | 1.0 | 8.0 |
| E | No | 9 | 0.9 | 8.1 |

*Source:* Authors.

positively or negatively) by the proposed change will probably be less willing to mobilize resources in favor of or against a reform than stakeholders who are more significantly affected.

One way to organize the information on stakeholders and their resources is to use a listing similar to that in box table 11.1. Such listings contain comparative information on the willingness of different stakeholders to mobilize for or against the proposed reform. In the example below, we assume detailed knowledge of stakeholder resources and incentives (it is certainly possible to use simple ranking if this information is not available). Therefore, the following numerical scales are used:

- The resources of stakeholders are given a numeric value from 1 to 10 (1 = *no resources*, 10 = *significant resources*).
- The intensity of stakeholder preference is given a numeric value between 0 and 1 (effectively, a discount factor, with 0 meaning the actor does not care much about the policy issue, whereas 1 implies that she cares intensely).

From the analysis above, it becomes apparent that even though there are more stakeholders in favor (A, B, and C) than against reform (D, E), the uneven resources and intensity of preferences mean that the stakeholders in favor of the status quo have greater incentives to mobilize against the reform (16.1) than those who favor the reform coalition (0.9).

While it is critical to identify the preferences of individual stakeholders, the greater weakness of one group of stakeholders does not mean that the advocates of the reform process should give up. Outcomes may depend far more on the interaction of stakeholders (as in the coordination game) than on their individual capacities.

## Institutional Incentives and Constraints

The configuration of institutions can play critical roles in the success of reforms. One of the things to think about, with respect to institutions, is the information dynamics that these create between stakeholders. As shown in box table 11.2, such information imperfections may take the shape of moral hazard and adverse selection problems that, in turn, may prohibit effective stakeholder mobilization or collaboration. Of course, if these pathologies are not too significant, it may cost more to fix them than to accept suboptimal mobilization.

As illustrated in box table 11.3, institutions will also affect the interaction of actors through the way they enhance or limit their ability to do the following:

- *Delegate tasks to each other* (principal-agent dynamic). Such delegation may allow stakeholders to specialize in the task at which they are most effective. However, if it is difficult to monitor each other, such set-ups may not be very effective in a coalition or organization. In addition, because members of organizations such as political parties,

**BOX TABLE 11.2 Information Imperfections: Costs and Benefits of Correction**

| Information imperfection | Magnitude of problem | Benefits of correction | Costs of correction | Correction advised? |
|---|---|---|---|---|
| Asymmetries | High | High | High | Yes |
| Moral hazard | Low | Low | High | No |
| Adverse selection | Low | Medium | High | No |

*Source:* Authors.

**BOX TABLE 11.3 Mechanisms, Priorities, and Solutions**

| Mechanism | Problem diagnosed? | Nature of malfunction | Priority of intervention | Solution |
|---|---|---|---|---|
| Principal-agent | Yes | Low monitoring capacity | High | Ex ante controls |
| Credible commitment | Yes | Lack of credibility | Medium | Third-party monitor |
| Collective action | Somewhat | Lack of leadership | Low | Identifying potential leaders |

*Source:* Authors.

**BOX TABLE 11.4 Institutional Stability and Agenda-Setting Opportunities**

| Institution | Type | Stability | Enforcement | Agenda-setting opportunity? (formal, informal) |
|---|---|---|---|---|
| A | Formal | High | High | Yes |
| B | Informal | Low | Low | No |
| C | Formal | Volatile | High | No |
| D | Formal | Low | Medium | Yes |
| E | Informal | High | Low | No |

*Source:* Authors.

nongovernmental organizations, and interest or citizens' groups delegate tasks to their leaders, they have to be aware of the leaders' incentives embedded in the principal-agent relationship. Shirking, or not being able to enforce some level of coordination and discipline among members, leads to problematic accountability relations and to diminished collective action potential of the group in general.

- *Credibly commit to a specific course of action.* Whether stakeholders can or cannot trust each other over a given time horizon can be critical as reforms usually require a multistage commitment.

*Institutional constraints.* Finally, institutional constraints may affect the very ability of a stakeholder to mobilize. Without mobilization, the actor will not be able to influence policy making.

Once all the different types of incentives generated by institutions are well understood, it is possible to assess their importance by examining how stable they are and whether the rules they entail are really enforced. Institutions may sometimes create incentives, but these may be so weak that they do not, in fact, influence outcomes. Generally, the more stable the context, whether due to the role of formal or of informal institutions, the less likely that the dynamics among stakeholders will suddenly or unexpectedly alter their preferences. The analysts and reformers should also be able to identify agenda-setting opportunities or obstacles associated with their own policy initiative (see box table 11.4).

## Between-Stakeholder Dynamics and Collective Action

At this point, the role of leadership and the timing of opportunities, following the process of rigorous mapping, can be critical. Therefore, the next step to consider in the political-economy analysis is how bringing the stakeholders together for reform might affect outcomes. Perhaps a broad coalition for reform (involving groups A, B, and C) would strengthen the ability to demand change and thus increase the possibility of success. Consider the following dynamics:

- How feasible will it be to facilitate dialogue and communication between the stakeholders?
- How feasible will it be to foster an environment conducive to the development of an appropriate leadership structure?
- Do different stakeholders trust each other? How willing are they to compromise with their ideal policy aspirations?

Having evaluated how to guide the dynamics between actors with a common interest to make the reform coalition viable, the reformer can now consider ways to use the external environment to further the reform agenda through adequate timing, pacing, and sequencing of major steps of action and milestones.

Only with an in-depth understanding of stakeholders and the institutional environment they operate in can reformers become well equipped to organize for reform and move forward strategically.

## Summary

Policy making often occurs in a context in which outside events may significantly alter the reformer's opportunities and constraints. Furthermore, stakeholders with different preferences and capabilities often pursue their own agendas and may not have an incentive to care about the public interest. Stakeholder identification and the analytical mapping of institutional dynamics and constraints in play enable reformers to organize critical information, helping them facilitate or foster collective action. By acknowledging the power of events and of actors' interaction, a development practitioner will be able to realize strategic opportunities, evaluate the complexities of policy shifts in a fruitful manner, and thus work effectively to achieve pro-development change.

### References

Alesina, Alberto, Gerald Cohen, and Nouriel Roubini. 1992. "Macroeconomic Policy and Elections in OECD Democracies." *Economics and Politics* 4 (1): 1–30.

Campos, J. Edgardo, and Vinay Bhargava. 2007. "Introduction: Tackling a Social Pandemic." In *The Many Faces of Corruption: Tracking Vulnerabilities at the Sector Level,* ed. J. Edgardo Campos and Sanjay Pradhan, 1–25. Washington, DC: World Bank.

Geddes, Barbara. 1996. *Politician's Dilemma: Building State Capacity in Latin America.* Berkeley: University of California Press.

Gibson, Clark C., Krister Andersson, Elinor Ostrom, and Sujay Shivakumar. 2005. *The Samaritan's Dilemma: The Political Economy of Development Aid.* New York: Oxford University Press.

Grindle, Merilee. 2002. *Good Enough Governance: Poverty Reduction and Reform in Developing Countries.* Cambridge: Harvard University Press.

———. 2007. *Going Local: Decentralization, Democratization, and the Promise of Good Governance.* Princeton, NJ: Princeton University Press.

Houtzager, Peter, and Gurza Adrian Lavalle. 2010. "Civil Society's Claim to Political Representation in Brazil." *Studies in Comparative International Development* 45: 1–29.

Lamb, David. 1987. *The Africans.* New York: Random House.

Moser, Peter. 1999. "Checks and Balances, and the Supply of Central Bank Independence." *European Economic Review* 43 (8): 1569–93.

Social Development Network. 2008. "The Political Economy of Policy Reform: Issues and Implications for Policy Dialogue and Development Operations." Report 44288-GLB, 2, World Bank, Washington, DC.

Strömberg, David. 2004. "Radio's Impact on Public Spending." *Quarterly Journal of Economics* 119 (1): 189–221.

Treisman, Daniel. 2007. "What Have We Learned about the Causes of Corruption from Ten Years of Cross-National Empirical Research?" *Annual Review of Political Science* 10 (1): 211–44.

Weyland, Kurt. 2003. *The Politics of Market Reform in Fragile Economies: Argentina, Brazil, Peru, and Venezuela.* Princeton, NJ: Princeton University Press.

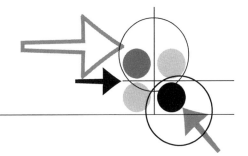

# APPENDIX A

# Fundamental Concepts in Game Theory

## Game Theory and Political-Economy Dynamics

To understand social and political dynamics in terms of a game, we need to learn a few basic definitions that will enable us to "read" the games presented in the book (readers interested in a more formal treatment can consult appendix B).

### Basic Concepts in Game Theory (a Gentle Introduction)

***Ingredients of a Game.*** All Games have the following five elements (Rapoport 1974 cited by Smith 2003); Rapoport (1974) and Smith (2003):

- *Rational players or actors.* That is, a player, faced with a choice between alternatives (e.g., *a, b, c*) can say (1) whether she prefers or is indifferent between two alternatives (e.g., *a>b* and *b>c*), this is defined as having complete preferences; and (2) that these complete preferences must be transitive (if *a>b* and *b>c*, then *a>c*). For example, citizens and politicians, incumbents and challengers, competing firms, etc.

- *Actions available to each player*. For example, confess/don't confess, cooperate/don't cooperate, or work hard/shirk.
- *Strategies*. This is the set (potentially a combination) of actions a player can pursue given how she expects or knows other players will react to her behavior. For example, a bureaucrat's strategies may include the following: (1) engage in increased rent-seeking activities if she anticipates that politicians will not be able to observe her behavior; or (2) minimize her rent-seeking activities if she anticipates that politicians will detect such activities and punish her for her actions.
- *Rules of Interaction*. Players do not usually operate in an institutional vacuum. Context matters as, for example, it determines what information players have, whether they make decisions simultaneously, whether they can communicate with each other, etc.
- *Outcomes or results*. For example, one possible outcome of a bureaucrat's pursuing a rent-seeking agenda is that her actions are detected and she loses her job.
- *Payoffs*. These are the utility accrued by each player as a result of each possible outcome. In other words, payoffs are the value or utility that players gain from different outcomes. The utility of an outcome depends on the costs and benefits it generates. Specifically, an outcome will be more favorable the larger the gap between the benefits minus the costs. Benefits and costs may be a variety of things—money, votes, fame, etc. Payoffs can be represented in different ways. When faced with a set of (discrete) alternative actions, as in table A.1, one simple way of representing the desirability of payoffs is to rank them in order, say from 1 to 4 (if there are four discrete choices). It is important to note that such ordinal rankings do not convey the magnitude of the difference between the alternatives but only their ordering. Thus, in the table below 4,000 votes is preferred to 3,000 votes, which is preferred to 2,500 votes, although the gap between these alternatives differs (3,000 is 1,000 less than 4,000 while 2,500 is 500 less than 3,000).

For example, a bureaucrat may receive a higher payoff if she pursues a rent-seeking strategy and is not detected (keeping her job) than if she pursues a rent-seeking strategy and is detected, resulting in her losing her job and facing criminal proceedings.

In the case of the Philippines procurement reform example, the payoffs to the general public of the passage of the bill were positive (less of their tax money was stolen). For corrupt officials, however, the payoffs are negative, as the bill would lead to fewer possibilities to generate illicit income from corrupt procurement dealings.

**TABLE A.1 An Illustration of Payoffs**

| Payoff (ordinal ranking) | Benefit-cost | Example (votes of a candidate) |
|:---:|:---|:---|
| 4 | Greatest | 4,000 votes |
| 3 | | 3,000 votes |
| 2 | | 2,500 votes |
| 1 | Smallest | 1 vote |

***Game Theory and Party Election Platforms.*** Let's illustrate the power of this solution concept by using a very simple example. The diagram below represents a normal form game in which two players can act simultaneously. In this case, let us assume the players are two political parties competing for office. Each party can decide on its own electoral platform. In this case, a party can run on either a promise to focus on domestic issues or a promise to engage in a pointless war with a friendly neighboring state.

Given that the electorate would never vote for a party that promised to embark on a ruinous war, both parties will avoid this issue. To see this, let's examine the payoffs for the first party (red). Knowledge of electoral preferences allows the parties to rank their electoral strategies based on how they will appeal to voters, given the other party's behavior. The optimal outcome (vote maximization) of a party is that it pursues the most popular policy and the other party pursues the least popular campaign strategy (highest payoff); the second most favorable outcome is that both parties pursue a popular campaign strategy; the third best alternative is that both parties pursue an unpopular campaign strategy; and the least favorable outcome, for any given party, is that it pursues an unpopular campaign strategy while the other party pursues a popular strategy.

Let's say the first party (light grey) believes that the second party (dark grey) will pursue a domestic electoral campaign. In this case, the first party would obtain a payoff of 3 if it also pursued a domestic campaign and a payoff of 1 if it pursued a war-focused campaign. If, alternatively, the first party believed the second party would pursue a war-focused campaign, it would obtain a payoff of 4 if it pursued a domestic campaign and a payoff of 2 if the party also pursued a war-focused campaign. In short, regardless of what strategy the second party chooses, the first party is always better off pursuing a domestically focused agenda (3> 1 and 4>2). Therefore, pursuing a domestic-focused campaign strictly dominated pursuing a war-focused campaign for the first party independently of the platform choice of the second party. Given that the preferences of the second party are identical to those of the first (a domestic-focused campaign strictly dominated a war-focused campaign), it is therefore possible to use the iterated elimination of strictly dominated strategies to find the unique solution to the game: namely, that both parties will pursue a domestically focused agenda.

|  | Domestic | | War | |
|---|---|---|---|---|
| Domestic | 3 | 3 | 4 | 1 |
| War | 1 | 4 | 2 | 2 |

## Reference

Game Theory Net. 2012. A resource for educators and students of game theory. Owen Graduate School of Management, Vanderbilt University: Nashville, Tennessee, http://www.gametheory.net/.

Rapoport, A. (ed.). 1974. *Game Theory as a Theory of Conflict Resolution*. Boston: D. Reidel Publishing Company.

Shor, M. 2012. Dictionary of Game Theory Terms, Game Theory.net, <http://www.gametheory.net/dictionary/ url_of_entry.html>

Smith S. 2003. "Game Theory." *Beyond Intractability*. Eds. Guy Burgess and Heidi Burgess. Conflict Information Consortium, University of Colorado, Boulder: Posted August (2003) < http://www.beyondintractability.org/bi-essay/prisoners-dilemma >

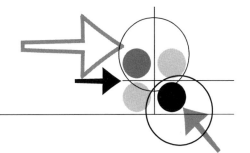

## APPENDIX B

# Technical Appendix

## Nash Equilibrium

Refers to a situation in which an action undertaken by a player is optimal given the actions of every other player. No player has an incentive to deviate from her course of action without the others doing so (Osborne 2003, 21).

## Weakly Dominated Strategy

Refers to any strategy that yields payoffs at least as great as any alternative strategy for a specific player. Such strategy results in a higher payoff for at least a subset of the strategy profiles of other players (Shor 2006a).

## Strictly Dominated Strategy

Refers to a strategy which yields a higher payoff for a player independently of the actions of any other players in the game (Shor 2006b).

# References

Osborne, M. 2003. *Introduction to Game Theory*. Oxford: Oxford University Press

Shor, M. 2006a. 'Weakly Dominated Strategies,' Dictionary of Game Theory Terms, Game Theory.net, <http://www.gametheory.net/dictionary/url_of_entry.html>

Shor, M. 2006b. 'Strictly Dominated Strategies,' Dictionary of Game Theory Terms, Game Theory.net, <http://www.gametheory.net/dictionary/url_of_entry.html>

Shor, M. 2012. "Dictionary of Game Theory Terms." Game Theory.net, http://www.gametheory.net/dictionary/url_of_entry.html

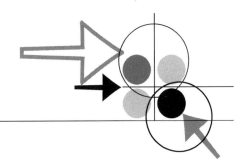

# APPENDIX C

# Political-Economy Concepts in Practice: Public Procurement Reform in the Philippines

Corruption has been identified as one of the major factors that can hinder development. Given a weak rule of law, the environment becomes more hospitable to corruption, thus significantly affecting economic growth and distributive outcomes. The following case study summary describes a public procurement reform in the Philippines that began in 1998 and was approved in 2003 (Campos and and Syquia 2005). This case illustrates how, in a highly complex political-economy environment, a group of reformers was able to form a coalition to advocate for policy change in the crucial area of public procurement transparency.

*Note:* This is a summary of the World Bank Policy Study by Jose Edgardo Campos and Jose Luis Syquia, *Managing the Politics of Reform: Overhauling the Legal Infrastructure of Public Procurement in the Philippines* (Washington, DC: World Bank, 2005).

The story begins when a group of policy entrepreneurs recognized that the weak rule of law and poor governance in the Philippines prevented growth and development. To address this challenge, the group identified a concrete reform goal: they would overhaul the regulations and operational procedures related to public procurement. Reaching this goal entailed overcoming many political-economy obstacles. The team first had to acquire a comprehensive understanding of the operational context. Then it had to create feasible and effective strategies for bypassing opposition. Indeed, their understanding of context enabled their successful strategy design; in turn, the strategies minimized the bargaining leverage of vested interests, allowing a comprehensive bill to pass in the legislature.

This reform presents a vivid example of how political-economy concepts, key identified constraints, and strategic solutions apply in practice. Given the richness of this case, the following summary will illustrate how the theoretical building blocks discussed throughout the handbook affect real-life scenarios and how using some of the existing political-economy tools can help change agents' understanding of their context and develop feasible and effective strategies to address constraints and achieve positive results.

## Identifying the Problem

According to Transparency International, in the early 1990s the Philippines was among the most corrupt countries of East Asia. Corruption took many forms, flourishing in many sectors of the country; procurement was one of the venues where corruption thrived (Social Weather Station, 2002). With contradictory procurement regulations that allowed opportunities to award corrupt contracts, companies winning public contracts were rarely the most efficient, qualified, or cost effective. By paying bribes to government officials, a company could earn a contract and deliver costly but poor services to the people. As a result, the general public received suboptimal services and goods.

## Timeline of the Reform Passage

Reform of government procurement in the Philippines involved multiple actors and occurred over a period of at least five years (see figure C.1) (Cabañero-Verzosa and Garcia 2009). The following sections integrate political-economy concepts to describe how passage of reform legislation was ultimately achieved.

## FIGURE C.1 Five-Year Timeline of the Philippines Procurement Reform

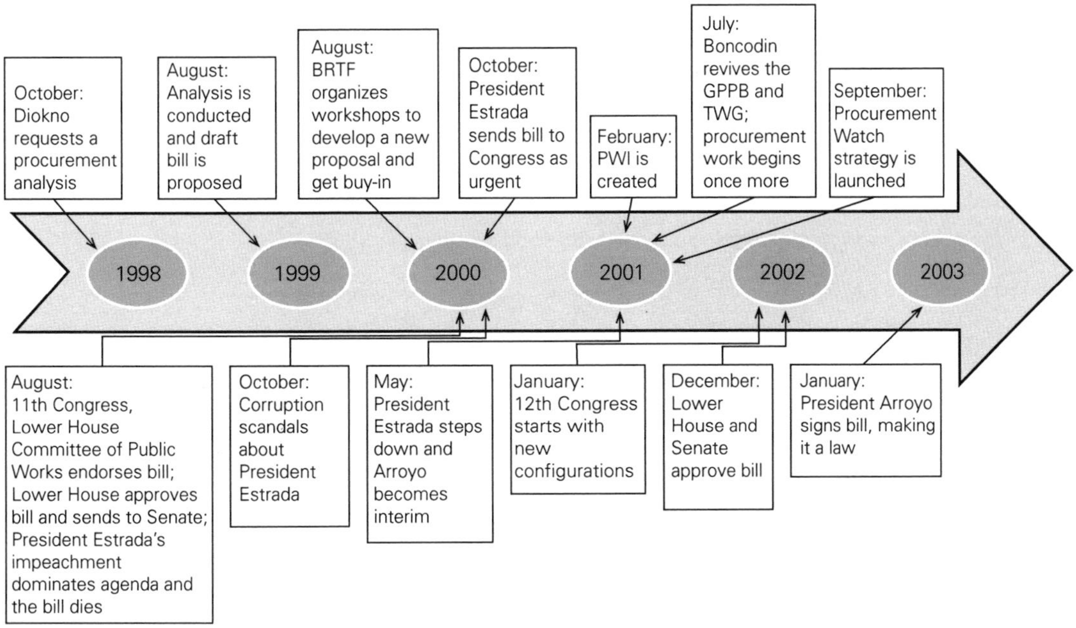

Graph adapted from Cabañero-Verzosa and Garcia 2009, 85.

## Round One

In 1998, Benjamin Diokno saw a window of opportunity for a reform path. As head of the Department of Budget and Management (DBM), Diokno understood how the existing rules and laws governing the procurement processes created opportunities for clientelistic bids. Determined to work toward a solution, he began by requesting the help of the U.S. Agency for International Development (USAID) in conducting an analysis to better understand the procurement system. Based on this study, the analysts would draft a bill to streamline the public procurement system.

With much enthusiasm, USAID hired two consultants to develop a rigorous analysis and draft a bill proposal. Soon a complication arose. Both consultants had previously worked in countries where top-down leadership was the most effective method of change. In the Philippines, by contrast, individualism is very strong. Because different agencies and bodies have differing incentives, it is difficult for them to come together with one voice. Perhaps based on prior experiences, the consultants failed to engage the DBM staff during the development phase of the analysis, which generated discontent and lack of support. In great need of buy-in, Diokno urged his Budget Reform Task Force (BRTF), and later the Technical Working Group (TWG), to organize a series of workshops where staff could critique the analysis and create their own draft of a procurement law. As BRTF expected, the workshops provided opportunities for staff and bureaucrats to participate and created a sense of ownership and support for the bill. This approach, used frequently throughout the entire reform effort, coincides with the chapter 7 strategies for solving information asymmetries and generating trust among coalition members (chapter 9).

The new collaborative draft was sent to President Joseph Estrada, who had a variety of incentives to support this bill. First, his campaign emphasized budget reforms and transparency. Second, he was facing corruption accusations that were increasingly threatening his incumbency. Presumably hoping to demonstrate a credible commitment (see chapter 8) to campaign promises in advance of the election, scheduled only five months away, the president gave legislative priority to the bill.

After gauging the president's interest in supporting the bill, the Budget Department's Legislative Liaison Office identified the congressional committee that would have the capacity and will to work towards reform. The team found the perfect match for the job and sent the draft to the Committee on Public Works. This decision stemmed from the fact that Congressman Neptali Gonzalez II, a member of the Committee, had previously initiated a related bill on government contracting regulations and sanctions for noncompliance. Acknowledging the similarities of both versions, Congressman Gonzalez II agreed to sponsor the legislation and substitute it for his original bill. Because this original draft was already scheduled for debate, the reform team was not only able to find a strong supporter, but was also able to insert the bill for prompt debate. It is also important to note, in line with our observations in Chapter 5, that during the initialization phase, the reform team kept a relatively low profile in order to prevent vested interests supporting the status quo from blocking their efforts.

Time dynamics were an important part of this decision, with reformers using windows of opportunity (see chapters 4 and 11) to incentivize politicians to commit. Specifically, the draft discussion coincided with highly publicized calls for the president's impeachment on allegations of corruption. Essentially, the team hoped that the bill's anticorruption flavor would motivate legislators to support the measure to increase their popularity and credibility with the general public. In addition, political competition generated by the upcoming election made politicians eager to distance themselves from the unpopular president by calling for reform. (Chapter 4 discusses the influence of political competition on the likelihood of institutional change.) Consequently, the proposed measure had immediate acceptance in the committee. Now that the influential Committee on Public Works had accepted to sponsor the bill, the next step entailed finding the right time to bring it to the floor of the Congress and secure approval. Congressman Gonzalez II, a seasoned agenda setter, was able to significantly influence the scheduling of the bills for floor debate, and waited until most opposing legislators were absent to introduce the Procurement Reform in Congress. This strategic move presents a powerful illustration of the agenda-setting mechanism discussed in chapter 5: reformers waited for the right time and took advantage of institutional rules governing voting in order to move forward. In this concrete case, agenda setting allowed for the bill to receive unanimous approval.

Once Congress had approved the bill, the draft went to the Senate, where majority floor leader Francisco Tatad worked to identify another committee willing to sponsor it. This time, in the second chamber, the senators were less eager to work on the bill, as the presidential impeachment trial as well as their individual incentives to survive electorally by credibly dissociating themselves from corruption allegations loomed high on the horizon. As a result of lack of interest in the legislation, the bill died in the Senate. This meant that during the next congressional session, the reform project would have to start from scratch to gather approval from both Lower House and the Senate. Figure C.2 details the involvement of various actors in the first round of legislation.

## Round Two

Significant changes occurred from the time of lost momentum until the beginning of the new Congressional session. In May 2001, President Estrada resigned. Vice president, Gloria Macapagal-Arroyo succeeded him as the interim president of the Philippines. The Lower House and the Senate reshuffled most influential positions. With these tectonic shifts in the background, Emilia Boncodin was now asked to serve as the DBM's secretary. Boncodin saw her appointment as a renewed opportunity to further the procurement bill, and thus asked undersecretary Laura Pascua, to manage the reform process. As a result, Boncodin and Pascua worked jointly to reactivate the Government Procurement Policy Board (GPPB) and to prepare an executive order that would consolidate the desired changes with a set of new rules governing consulting services. This strategy aimed at increasing support for the bill, especially from those who were promoted by the new administration. The team also decided to revive the Technical Working Group (TWG). After two months of intense weekly meetings held by the TWG, the GPPB approved the new draft. On October 8, 2001, and following GPPB's approval,

**FIGURE C.2 Round 1 Net Map: Who Influenced the Passage of the Procurement Reform Law?**

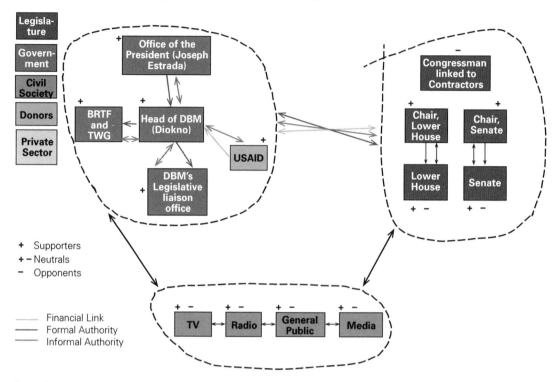

Source for the graphic tool: NetMap, Schiffer 2012.

interim president Arroyo, who signaled commitment to improving governance in the Philippines, signed Executive Order 40.

The effective delegation of tasks that is apparent in this round—particularly with regard to the various bureaucratic units, the DBM and GPPB—can be partially explained by a greater alignment in policy preferences between President Arroyo and the Lower House, than under the leadership of President Estrada. The work of the DBM helped create this preference alignment, which in turn translated into expanded delegation to the agency (see chapter 6 on the principal-agent theory). In other words, civil servants at the DBM, as reform actors, correctly identified the changing political space and were able to react effectively.

Several chapters of the handbook suggested that *monitoring and sanctioning* are essential solutions to collective action problems, correctors of information asymmetries in principal-agent relationships, and effective mechanisms of credible commitment. Neutral third parties can often fulfill effective roles of 'fire alarms' or 'police patrols' that make sure that ex-ante policy commitments are not reneged upon. Let's see what happens in the procurement reform story. While passing the bill was a major accomplishment, the BRTF and the Technical Assistance Team were aware of the important role that a nongovernmental organization would play in monitoring implementation and compliance with the law. To this end, Procurement Watch, Inc., established in 2001, had the main mission to "fight corruption in public procurement" (Campos and Syquia 2005, 6).

To develop credibility and build a platform among key stakeholders, the organization invited respected civil society representatives to become part of the Procurement Watch Board. Its staff became highly involved in the deliberations of the new bill. Eventually, Procurement Watch, in addition to playing the role of a third party monitor, also became an important vehicle for solving collective action problems among civil society representatives and bureaucrats interested in reform, stemming from missing information and lack of credibility (see chapters 3 and 9).

Collective action was realized through Procurement Watch's interaction with stakeholder groups and the media (see table C.1). Getting the omnibus procurement law passed required sufficient public support for the bill. Procurement Watch brought together the support of key civil society organizations and increased the salience of the issue related to corruption in public procurement through various media platforms: print, radio, and television.

**TABLE C.1  Stakeholder Map for the Philippines Procurement Reform**

| Stakeholder | Benefits from reform? | Resources | Intensity of preferences | Incentive for mobilization (resources × intensity) |
|---|---|---|---|---|
| Government reform teams | Yes | High | High | High |
| Donors | Yes | Medium | High | Medium |
| Investigative media | Yes | Medium | Medium | Medium |
| Big contractors | Yes | High | High | High |
| NGOs and CS | Yes | Low | Medium | Medium |
| General public | Yes | Medium-low | Medium-low | Low |
| General media | Yes | Medium | Low | Low |
| Church | Yes | Medium | Medium | Medium |
| Legislators linked to contractors | No | High | High | High |

*Source:* Authors.

Why this strategy? Chapter 7 discussed the example of increased government responsiveness to flood damage triggered by media exposure. It also suggested that media impacts political incentives on a two-way street. On one hand, an informed public is likely to formulate demands for greater accountability; on the other hand, increased issue salience and visibility attracts politicians because of electoral credit taking opportunities. In this case, Procurement Watch skillfully appealed simultaneously to both targets: the general public and individual politicians. The organization worked to educate civil society about the importance of the new legal changes and helped gain public support from major stakeholders such as youth (students and associations), the Catholic Church, private sector groups represented by chambers of commerce, media outlets, and civil society organizations (including the Transparency and Accountability Network). As a result, attempting to take advantage of increased visibility that media coverage could bring, individual politicians hurried to associate themselves with the procurement measure These partnerships brought enough public support (mobilization) to pressure lawmakers into considering the bill.

The reform team had to think strategically about its next steps, under conditions of a shifting political landscape in both Chambers of Congress. During the new administration, the two chambers of the legislature had a more balanced power distribution, but opposition was much more unified (see chapter 4). Reformers approached legislators from both major competing parties, the National People's Coalition Party and the Philippine Democratic Party, and convinced an influential senator to sponsor the bill jointly. This strategic arrangement allowed the media team to portray the bill as a bipartisan effort and successfully minimized the risk of interparty conflicts that would hinder the passage of the reform (Campos and Syquia 2005, 23).

During the opening debates taking place in the Lower House, Speaker Jose de Venecia firmly endorsed this version of the bill. Then, he entrusted the project to his colleague Congressman Rolando Andaya Jr., chairman of the Appropriations Committee. Congressman Andaya immediately decided to assign senior bureaucratic staff to the secretariat of the Congressional Technical Working Group, and requested that the technical assistance (TA) team be incorporated in the secretariat as well. After numerous work sessions, the Congressional Technical Working Group developed a draft submitted to the Lower House on May 16, 2002.

Once again, Congressman Gonzalez II was now waiting for the right time to introduce the bill to Congress (see chapters 5 and 11). Because several key legislators strongly opposed the reform, Gonzalez decided to wait five months to schedule the debate for a day when a majority of the quorum of the legislators in attendance favored the bill. His agenda setting strategy was again successful and the bill passed with a large majority.

Three different senators sponsored several versions of the bill in the Senate. To aid the passage, the TA team and the BRTF sought Senator Edgardo Angara's endorsement, given his status as a powerful member of the opposition and the leader of the legislative caucus. With the help of Senator Angara's chief of staff and chief policy adviser, the TA team arranged a meeting between Senator Angara and Secretary Boncodin. The meeting was highly successful, resulting in Senator Angara's endorsement. Senator Angara assigned his staff to work with the three entities—the TWG, the TA team, and Procurement Watch—to craft a Senate version of the new legislative project. He then submitted a comprehensive report which covered the new Senate Bill and attracted considerable media attention. Two months later, the Senate floor debated the bill, voted and approved it. Figure C.3 details the involvement of various actors in the second round of legislation.

**FIGURE C.3  Round 2 Net Map: Who Influenced the Passage of the Procurement Reform Law?**

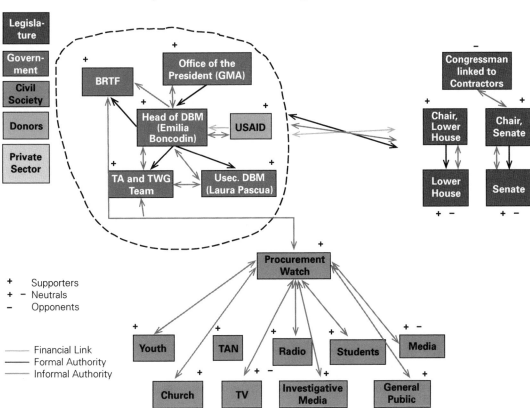

Source for the graphic tool: NetMap, Schiffer 2012.

Furthermore, given that two versions of the bill adopted in the two chambers required reconciliation, the Bicameral Conference Committee convened to consolidate them and negotiate differences. The resulting version was approved by both houses, with an added provision that emphasized implementation oversight for the law for an initial period of five years. This final version of the bill was signed on January 10, 2003 by President Arroyo. Thus, after a long saga, the Consolidated Procurement Reform Bill finally became law.

## References

Cabañero-Verzosa, C., and H. Garcia. 2009. *Building Commitment to Reform through Strategic Communication: The Five Key Decisions*. Washington, DC: World Bank.

Campos, J., and J. Syquia 2005. *Managing the Politics of Reform: Overhauling the Legal Infrastructure of Public Procurement in the Philippines*. Washington, DC, World Bank.

Schiffer, Eva. "Net-Map Toolbox. Influence Mapping of Social Networks." Available at: http://netmap.wordpress.com/. Last modified on May 9, 2012.

Social Weather Station. 2002. "Survey of Enterprises on Public Sector Corruption." Presentation at the Asian Institute of Management in Manila, Philippines, Intercontinental Hotel, March 21.

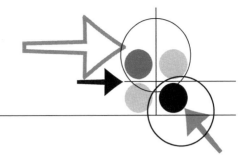

## APPENDIX D

# Political-Economy Homework Exercises

This homework is designed to reinforce the learning outcomes from the classes (especially with respect to coalition building), provide a benchmark on how to write a case study, and facilitate teamwork.

You will be randomly assigned into groups of five to complete the homework. It is important that you work on these exercises together. You will each be given a "character card." During some of the homework exercises, you will use the information on these cards to role play to illustrate the complexity of the coalition-building process. When the homework does not use the role-playing cards, you can assume that you are not trying to act in character. The materials needed include group instructions and character cards.

*Please note: Homework should be distributed after each relevant exercise. Do not distribute all homework together as this may affect the learning outcomes.*

# Exercise 1: The Commonwealth of Rationaltopia

Group Briefing: *Read this information as a group. Then each one of you should read your individual card for 2 minutes. After doing so, go around the table and individually discuss your character's policy preferences. Once this process is complete, fill in the answer sheet as a group.*

The Commonwealth of Rationaltopia is a developing country, which has been independent for the last 60 years. Since independence, the commonwealth has been characterized by the following:

1. *Structural changes in government.* Within only a few decades, the commonwealth has shifted from a parliamentary form of government, to a presidential form of government, to a semipresidential form of government, and now back to a full presidential system. The current president sees himself (or herself) as the leader of the nation and the region and is very keen to pursue a proactive defense and foreign policy. The president does not want to be entangled with the "petty" considerations of domestic politics.
2. *Clientelism in elections.* The parliament is hampered by infighting and deadlock. Each legislator seeks to provide supporters with benefits in the form of tangible material handouts throughout the electoral cycle. All seem to care about being reelected, but none seems interested in making long-term policy to benefit anyone beyond their supporters.
3. *An insulated bureaucracy.* In contrast to the legislature, the bureaucracy is a source of stability. While retention of bureaucrats has ensured that someone is responsible for enacting national policy, this insularity has also resulted in allegations of gross inefficiency and corruption.
4. *Divided civil society organizations.* While there are some very dynamic organizations in civil society, they tend to be split geographically (and therefore linguistically and religiously). Many organizations operate in either the south or the north of the country but not in both regions.
5. *Politicized private sector.* Although the developing status of the Rationaltopia means that there are some booming businesses (e.g., tourism, mining, and agriculture), other businesses, especially small businesses without political connections, are struggling to establish themselves. In particular, some members of the business community argue that political connection and not business acumen determines everything from how long it takes to get a business license to who gets selected for government procurement services.

## Participant 1: Character Card A

You are president of Rationaltopia. You have always known that you were destined for greatness. You feel that, no matter what domestic sacrifices have to be made, it is your duty to the people of Rationaltopia to maintain a strong military and a proactive foreign policy.

When it is your turn to speak, introduce yourself as the president of Rationaltopia. Try to convince everyone that your vision is sound and that the long-term benefits of pursuing an active foreign policy—such as security and good relations with neighboring states—are in everyone's interest.

## Participant 2: Character Card A

You are a member of parliament (MP). You are fed up with everyone blaming the inability of elected politicians to get along and develop coherent policy. You work very hard to make sure your supporters receive any benefits you can deliver for them. After all, isn't that your role—to look after the people who elected you?

When it is your turn to speak, introduce yourself as a member of parliament. Try to convince everyone that MPs, such as yourself, are doing a good job in looking after the people who voted for you. It is unfair to be branded irresponsible just because you don't want to divert resources away from your supporters. Everyone in Rationaltopia has the vote, so if other people want something, why don't they ask their MP instead of blaming MPs and parliament as a whole?

## Participant 3: Character Card A

You are a senior civil servant. During your career you have been responsible for ensuring that Rationaltopia has the expertise to develop and implement public policy. Everyone considers the bureaucracy to be insular, inefficient, and somewhat corrupt. No one seems to appreciate the fact that without it, all those short-termist members of parliament and presidents with delusions of grandeur would have run the country into the ground long ago.

When it is your turn to speak, introduce yourself as a civil servant. Remind everyone just how critical your work is. The civil service is not just there to create red tape; in fact, the civil service has kept Rationaltopia functioning every time the political system has gone into a tailspin.

### Participant 4: Character Card A

You are the head of a small nongovernmental organization (NGO) whose aim is to promote awareness about the exclusion of the poor across the country. However, apart from the fact that most politicians and policy makers are too busy to listen to you, you also face a challenge that people from the north and the south do not trust each other.

When it is your turn to speak, introduce yourself as a head of a poverty-focused NGO. Express your concern that, apart from the fact that politicians don't seem to care about the very poor (who generally do not vote), southerners and northerners are unwilling to come together to resolve common issues like poverty.

### Participant 5: Character Card A

You are the head of the Small Business National Chamber of Commerce. You are very worried that a growing number of existing businesses seem to be using their links to MPs or civil servants to obtain advantages over other firms. This skewed form of competition is not just unfair to new businesses but also to the public, who end up paying higher prices for poorer-quality goods and services.

When it is your turn to speak, introduce yourself as the head of the Chamber of Commerce. Let the other participants know that you see new businesses as an important engine of growth in Rationaltopia but that you are concerned about the increasingly unhealthy relationships among business executives, politicians, and bureaucrats.

### Group Work

Once all group members have introduced their characters, think about and discuss the following questions together. Record your answers below.

1. Which characters represent formal institutions?
2. Which character is policy seeking (wants to implement her policy no matter what)?
3. What factor seems to be driving the profits of some of the firms in the country?
4. Which character is election seeking (wants to keep her position no matter what)?
5. What role do cultural groups (even informal institutions, including bonds of trust) appear to have in the development of civil society?
6. Which character thinks a little that corruption is not such a bad thing?

# Exercise 2: The Budgetary Process in Rationaltopia

Group Briefing: *Read this information as a group. Then, individually, rank your budget priorities (on the Individual Instructions page) according to the character card assigned you in exercise 1. When you are finished, record the preferences of each character (on the Group Work grid) and discuss your findings.*

According to Rationaltopia's constitution and laws, the budget is developed by parliament (which must pass it by a simple majority). Once approved by the president, the budget is implemented by the civil service. The implementation is supposed to be overseen by parliament's Public Accounts Committee.

In practice, the budget is proposed by the president. Parliament usually does not add significant amounts of additional expenditure but, depending on who is in charge, does seem to divert a significant amount of money to projects favored by key supporters. In particular, the south of the country, which is more developed and has more people (and thus more votes), appears to do disproportionately well from allocations.

With respect to implementation, the Public Accounts Committee does not seem to be working very well. The committee convened only once last year (so that its members could receive their committee allowances). This means that the bureaucracy is not supervised in implementing the budget. The perception that some bureaucrats are developing "cozy" relationships with businesses is now considered a fact.

There are five main items in the budget and thus five possible alterations:

1. Defense and foreign affairs expenditure
2. Discretionary spending for miniprojects allocated by parliament
3. Money for the procurement and delivery of large domestic projects (administered by the relevant departments)
4. Money for welfare spending (for schools and health clinics), currently allocated so that, per capita, southerners obtain more funds)
5. Tax cuts and deductions for businesses.

## Individual Instructions

As your character (from the previous exercise), rank the budget options according to your perceived priorities. Give the item you would like to achieve the most a 1 and the item you care least about a 5.

| Budget item | Rank (1 = *most preferred*, 5 = *least preferred*) |
|---|---|
| Defense and foreign policy | |
| Parliamentary discretionary spending | |
| Large project procurement | |
| Money for welfare spending | |
| Tax cuts and deductions | |

## Group Work

Decide on a volunteer recorder. As a group, go around the table and discuss the preferences of the different characters. Record the preferences on the grid.

| Budget item | President | MP | Bureaucrat | NGO Head | Head of Chamber of Commerce |
|---|---|---|---|---|---|
| Defense and foreign policy | | | | | |
| Parliamentary discretionary spending | | | | | |
| Large project procurement | | | | | |
| Money for welfare spending | | | | | |
| Tax cuts and deductions | | | | | |

After this process is complete, discuss to what extent the characters agree over the budget priorities Rationaltopia should adopt. Then address the following questions:

1. Do you think that members of parliament who decide to sit on a committee have typical characteristics of an MP, or are they likely to be a self-selected type?
2. Does the behavior of Public Account Committee members in this case sound like a case of moral hazard or adverse selection?
3. Why would a parliament want to establish a committee to specialize in public financial oversight?

## Exercise 3: The Emergence of a Better Budget?

Group Briefing: *Read this information as a group. Then discuss the question that follows.*

Given the huge gulf between how the Rationaltopia budget should be implemented and how it is being implemented in practice, a group of concerned citizens and donors would like to organize a committee to generate ideas about how to improve budget formulation and implementation.

The group has two options for the composition of the committee's membership:

- A random but representative sample of citizens
- A group of civil society, public sector, and private sector leaders who are considered experts in the nature of public policy making.

Regardless of how it is composed, the committee will have access to a group of international experts who will help identify international best practice and the feasibility of different options of budget response.

As a group, discuss and make notes on the following question:

- What are the benefits and pitfalls of letting a representative sample of citizens make decisions rather than delegating to a group of experts?

## Exercise 4: The Committee Comes Up with a Proposal

Group Briefing: *Read this information as a group. Then read your new individual card for 2 minutes. (You should keep the same character as in the previous exercises.) Discuss the proposed reform as a group and take a final vote. After recording your vote results, talk about the final question and summarize your conclusions in the space provided.*

Having decided to adopt a hybrid model (including both a random set of citizens and a hand-selected group of policy-making leaders), the committee convened and has now come up with a set of recommendations for the budget process. These include a recommendation to introduce a participatory budgetary procedure; that is, to give ordinary citizens the right to be consulted and make authoritative decisions on the budget. This proposal is being widely reported in the media and is gaining traction as a viable solution for the budget situation.

After reading your character cards, discuss the proposal as needed, vote, and record your votes below.

|  | Yes | No | Conditional |
|---|---|---|---|
| The president |  |  |  |
| The MP |  |  |  |
| The bureaucrat |  |  |  |
| The head of the NGO |  |  |  |
| The head of the Chamber of Commerce |  |  |  |

Once you have voted, discuss whether the opposition of the different characters will keep the reform from passing. Summarize your conclusions below.

## Participant 1: Character Card B

As the president, you are indifferent to whether this proposal becomes law. After all, you have more important defense and foreign policy issues to deal with. If parliament ratifies the new law, you will not veto it—why agitate anyone?—but if parliament does not, this is of no concern to you anyway. You have a region to stabilize.

## Participant 2: Character Card B

As an MP, you are aghast at this proposal. How will you be able to target resources toward your loyal supporters if people who may not help your reelection can alter the budget? You must stop this silly proposal from ever becoming law.

## Participant 3: Character Card B

As a career civil servant, you know that having to deal with the "bright ideas" of even more uninformed people is the last thing you need.

## Participant 4: Character Card B

As the head of an NGO working with the marginalized, this reform is potentially great news. Finally, the politically marginalized, low-income citizens will have an opportunity to make their voices heard. Of course, it will be important to ensure that the north is provided with the same opportunities as the rest of the country. But despite these reservations, you are an avid supporter.

## Participant 5: Character Card B

As head of the Small Business Chamber of Commerce, you are concerned, on the one hand, that the uncertainty generated by a participatory budget procedure may adversely affect the business environment. On the other hand, if this makes it more difficult for politically privileged businesses and bureaucrats to collude and unfairly deprive new businesses of opportunities to grow, then maybe it's not such a bad thing. You are probably going to come out in favor.

## Exercise 5: A Tentative Coalition Emerges

Group Briefing: *Read this information as a group, discuss the questions, and record your answers.*

It has been a few months since the participatory budget proposal was first launched, and a few actors are trying to come together to support its realization. Many of the supporters of this process are pro-poor NGOs and small businesses. The most vigorous opposition is emanating from politically active citizens from across the political spectrum who have traditionally enjoyed privileged access to parliament and the bureaucracy.

As a group, discuss and record your answers to the following questions:

- How easy is it to build a coalition between actors with very different experiences (small profit-making businesses and NGOs)?
- What kind of coordination or collective action problems might such a coalition face?
- How might opponents of the reform try to split the coalition, especially given their additional financial resources? (Hint: Think about the definition of corruption.)

## Exercise 6: Building the Coalition

Group Briefing: *Again, read this information as a group, discuss the questions, and record your answers.*

Despite attempts by opponents to bribe some of its members, the coalition in favor of the participatory budget proposal is gaining traction. However, to secure passage in parliament, the coalition needs to communicate that it enjoys the support of a broad majority of citizens—unlike the opponents of the reform, who are a (very) vocal minority.

As a group, talk about how the following factors might help the nascent reform coalition achieve its objective or prevent it from reaching its goal. Record your discussion below.

• Currently, the coalition conducts its business through a council in which different stakeholders have the same power. How might developing a clear leadership structure affect the group's efficacy?

• Would the coalition benefit from using opinion polls and strategic communication techniques to dispel the appearance that the measure does not have broad appeal?

## Exercise 7: Coalition Case Study

Group Briefing: *As a group, compile the information from the previous exercises into a case study presentation. If your instructor indicates that Power-Point is available, consider creating slides; if not, think about other visualizations that might enhance your presentation.*

Use the following questions as a guide:

- Who are all the relevant actors?
- How does the institutional context affect the policy-making environment?
- What stakes do different actors have in the reform process?
- How can reform actors coordinate to develop a reform coalition?
- What kind of leadership structure or other activities can the coalition use to enhance its effectiveness?

The timing of reforms is also critical to success. Think about how the following events might affect the activities of the coalition. Then incorporate into your presentation how the coalition might deal with these events:

- Upcoming elections (in the next few months)
- Antireform actions (protests, communication campaigns, and the like) organized by powerful antireform groups
- The growing perception in the international epistemic community that participatory budgeting constitutes a sound reform that can enhance accountability
- Civil war in a neighboring country; the president commits Rationaltopia's army for peacekeeping, thus necessitating higher defense expenditures
- Economic crisis with global markets losing tolerance for opaque budgeting processes (demanding higher interest rates from countries that have poor budget practices).

Present your case study as a group during class, as scheduled by your instructor.

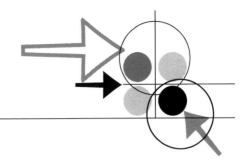

# INDEX

*Boxes, figures, notes, and tables are indicated by b, f, n, and t following page numbers.*

pro-development, 113
public goods and, 82–85, 88–91,
    249–54
    club goods vs., 83, 83*t*
    defined, 82–85
    electoral laws affecting, 126,
        127*b*
    incentives impact on, 82, 82*f*
    mobilization and production of,
        90–91, 249–54
    monitoring of, 221, 221*b*
    private goods vs., 83, 83*t*
    social dilemmas of delivering,
        88–91
    stakeholder dynamics and, 314–15*b*
    transparency and, 226–27
collective arrangements, 7
collective choice, 160
collective incentives, 82, 82*f*
Colombia, health care in, 119*b*
Committee on Rules (U.S. Congress), 159,
    167
common knowledge, 188
common-pool resources, 82, 83, 83*t*, 251,
    253–54, 255
communication. *See also* information
    asymmetries
    in collective action, 258–61, 265
    face-to-face, 259, 261
    institutional arrangements
        promoting, 253
    need to improve, 248
    political-economy analysis and, 315*b*
    problems in, 33
    stakeholder's resources, 311*b*
    strategic communication to garner
        support, 306
    strategic miscommunication, 290
communism, 31, 59, 117, 304
comparative statics, 289
complementarity of reform areas, 310
Condorcet winner, 162, 178*n*4
Congo, Democratic Republic of
    civil society organizations in, 254
    corruption in, 65, 65*b*
    leadership and trust in, 262*b*
    monitoring and sanctioning in, 256

Constituency Development Fund (CDF,
    Kenya), 35
constitutions and constitutional rights
    to health care, 119*b*
    lifespan of, 141*b*
    limits on power, 237–38
    to water, 119*b*
contracts in principal-agent
    relationships, 190
control schemes, 190. *See also* monitoring
    and sanctioning
corruption, 51–78. *See also* accountability
    administrative, 64
    in authoritarian regimes, 61
    blackmail, 131
    in budget systems, 26
    clientelism and, 66–69
    collection action-induced credible
        commitment and, 242
    conceptual map of, 52*f*
    cultural differences and, 63
    defined, 62–63
    economic development and, 70, 70*f*,
        74*n*10, 307, 323
    in education, 31
    grand, 63–64, 66
    in health care, 31
    incentive pay and, 216
    interventions to reduce, 72–73, 73*b*
    kleptocracy, 66
    large-scale, 71
    low-level, 63
    negative consequences of, 67–70
    nepotism, 64
    overview, 51–52, 62–63
    political-economy analyses and, 72
    positive consequences of, 70–72
    prebendal predation, 65, 65*b*
    prevalence of, 72
    in principal-agent relationships, 63
    public procurement and, 13, 22–23,
        324
    resource allocation and, 69–70, 194*b*
    small-scale, 70–71
    state capture, 64–65, 66
    systemic, 69
    types of, 63–67

financial management reform, 26–27

"fire alarm" oversight mechanisms, 190, 191*b*

fisheries and fishing, 89–90, 256

five percent rule of collective action, 93, 250

flooding, 219*b*, 220

formal agenda setting, 163, 167–68, 169, 170*b*

formal institutions, 118–26, 121*f*, 123–26*t*

France, credible commitment in, 240–41

free riding, 85, 90, 92–93

Friedman, Milton, 138*b*

game theory
    backward induction and, 188, 193–94, 195*f*
    collective action and, 94–98, 264–65
    concepts involved in, 317–20
    credible commitment and, 243–44
    election platforms and, 319–20
    institutions and, 144–45
    leadership and, 264–65
    Nash equilibria and, 95, 97, 194, 228*b*, 244, 321
    overview, 11–12
    payoffs and, 318, 319*t*
    principal-agent relationships and, 188, 193–94
    prisoner's dilemma and, 88–89, 95–98
    strategies, 265, 318, 320, 321
    trust and, 265

gender differences
    clientelism and, 67*b*
    demographic change and, 136

Germany, agenda setting in, 161

gerrymandering, 34

Ghana, public account committees in, 216, 217*b*

Gini coefficient, 207–8

global production and distribution, 137

Gonzalez, Neptali, II, 326, 327, 330

governance
    accountability and, 52
    systems of, 253–54

grand corruption, 63–64, 66

Greece
    financial crisis in, 211
    public account committees in, 216
    structural adjustment policies in, 308

grim trigger strategy, 265

guardian judiciaries, 238

Haiti, constitution in, 141*b*

Hayek, Friedrich, 213*b*

health care
    administrative constraints on, 31–33
    clientelism and, 33
    constitutional rights to, 119*b*
    corruption in, 31
    economic constraints on, 30–31
    HIV/AIDS policies, 38–39, 119*b*, 243*b*
    inequalities in, 30–31
    litigation, 291*b*
    political constraints on, 33, 34–35, 36–39
    public procurement of, 38
    public spending on, 28, 29*f*, 30–31
    stakeholder mapping and, 291*b*

heresthetics, 169

HIV/AIDS, 38–39, 119*b*, 243*b*

hometown associations, 22, 254

Honduras, elections in, 34

hostage mechanisms, 238

hybrid regimes, incentives for development and collective action, 123*t*

ideal points, 178*n*6

ideological shifts, 137–39

implementation capacity, 31

incentives
    for collective action, 122, 123–26*t*, 131, 132*t*, 241
    individual vs. collective, 82, 82*f*
    institutions and, 113–15, 122, 123–26*t*, 131, 132*t*, 313–14*b*
    outcome-based, 189
    in principal-agent relationships, 189
    public goods and, 82, 82*f*
    salary and, 216, 258
    selective, 216, 257–58

independent enforcement, 236–37

India
  collective action in, 247, 251
  development in, 259*b*
  electricity access in, 37, 90–91
  famine and flood relief in, 54*b*, 219*b*
  health care in, 119*b*
  labor relations in, 131, 133*b*
  manufacturing growth in, 133*b*
  media influence in, 218, 219*b*
  political competition in, 219*b*
  technology interventions in, 221*b*
  unions in, 251
  water conservation in, 89

indirect delegation, 185

individual incentives, 82, 82*f*

Indonesia, economic crisis in, 30

inductive approach, 284

inequalities in education and health care,
  30–31. *See also* poverty

infant mortality rates, 30, 38, 39

inferential political-economy analyses,
  289, 290

informal agenda setting, 168–69, 170–71,
  171*b*

informal economy, 143

informal institutions, 118–21, 121*f*, 127–31,
  132*t*

informal organizations, 128

information asymmetries, 207–32
  collective action and, 85, 87–88,
    224–29
  conceptual map of, 209*f*
  correctives for, 216, 218–21
  defined, 85, 87, 187, 207
  development and, 228*b*
  equilibria and, 217, 228*b*
  implications of, 217–18
  institutions and, 217–18
  media influence on, 216, 217*b*, 218
  monitoring and sanctioning of, 216
  overview, 207–10
  in political-economy analyses,
    210–12
  in principal-agent relationships, 187,
    216
  technology and, 221, 221*b*
  transparency and, 222–23, 223*f*

types of, 212–15
  adverse selection, 87–88, 215
  moral hazards, 87, 213–15
  self-selection, 212–13, 213*b*

inheritance rules, 134

initiative rules, 163

instability trap, 140

institutional enforcement, 141–44

Institutional Revolutionary Party (PRI,
  Mexico), 33

institutional veto players, 239*b*

institutions, 111–55
  changes in, 133–39
    demographic, 135–36
    global production and
      distribution, 137
    ideological shifts, 137–39
    political competition, 137
    power endowments, 134–35
    property rights, 136
    technological, 136
  collective action and, 8–11, 12*f*, 113–
    15, 114*f*, 253–54
  conceptual map of, 112*f*
  constraints and, 314*b*
  defined, 42, 115–16
  as equilibria, 116, 117
  failure of, 140–44
  formal, 118–26, 121*f*, 123–26*t*
  game theory and, 144–45
  incentives and, 113–15, 122, 123–26*t*,
    131, 132*t*, 313–14*b*
  informal, 118–21, 121*f*, 127–31, 130*b*,
    132*t*
  information asymmetries effect on,
    217–18
  intersection of, 121, 121*f*
  monitoring and sanctioning in,
    117–18
  as norms, 116, 118
  organizations distinguished from,
    116–17
  origins of, 131–33
  overview, 111–13
  path dependence and, 139
  public goods and, 253–54
  resilience of, 139, 140
  role of, 286–87